MARITIME SUPREMACY
&
THE OPENING OF THE
WESTERN MIND

MARITIME SUPREMACY

&

THE OPENING OF THE WESTERN MIND

Naval Campaigns that Shaped
the Modern World

PETER PADFIELD

THE OVERLOOK PRESS
WOODSTOCK & NEW YORK

For Jane

First published in the United States in 2000 by
The Overlook Press, Peter Mayer Publishers, Inc.
Lewis Hollow Road
Woodstock, NY 12498
www.overlookpress.com

Library of Congress Cataloging-in-Publication Data

Padfield, Peter.
Maritime supremacy and the opening of the western mind :
naval campaigns that shaped the modern world / Peter Padfield.
p. cm.
Includes bibliographical references and index.
1. Naval history, Modern. I. Title.
D215.P34 2000   359'.009'03—dc21   99-058999

Published by arrangement with John Murray Ltd.

Manufactured in the United States of America
ISBN 1-58567-002-2
1 3 5 7 9 8 6 4 2

Contents

Illustrations

The author and publishers would like to thank the following for permission to reproduce illustrations: Plates 1, 3, 5, 8, 10, 11, 17, 20, 21, 24 and 25, The Trustees of the National Maritime Museum, London; 2, Pepys Library, Magdalene College, Cambridge; 4, Woburn Abbey, Bedfordshire/Bridgeman Art Library, London and New York; 6, Science and Society Picture Library/Science Museum, London; 7, Wasa Museum, Sweden; 9 Rijksmuseum, Amsterdam; 12 and 14, AKG London; 13, Cheltenham Art Gallery & Museums/Bridgeman Art Library, London and New York; 15, 18, 19 and 22, National Portrait Gallery, London; 16, Louvre, Paris/Giraudon/Bridgeman Art Library, London and Paris; 23, Pennsylvania Academy of Fine Arts/Bridgeman Art Library, London and New York.

Maps and Diagrams

Acknowledgements

I SHOULD LIKE to thank Grant McIntyre of John Murray for his unfailing support and enthusiasm during my work on this book, and my son, Guy, who added immeasurably to the passages on philosophy; it would have been a poorer work without his insights, although responsibility for any conclusions drawn is mine alone. Bob Davenport edited the book with great sensitivity and provided good suggestions and advice, for which I am grateful. And I should like to thank Robin Jessup of Mullins, Dowse & Partners, Woodbridge, for the excellent maps and battle diagrams.

I am grateful to the editor of the *Mariner's Mirror*, the journal of the Society for Nautical Research, and to the authors of the following articles for permission to quote extracts: T. Glasgow Jr for 'Gorgas' Sea Fight'; R. Middleton for 'British Naval Strategy 1755–62: The Western Squadron'; Alan G. Jamieson for 'Two Scottish Marines in the American War'. And I thank the following authors and publishers for permission to reproduce quotations: R. Lonsdale, *The New Oxford Book of Eighteenth-Century Verse* and R. Mackay, *Admiral Hawke*, both Oxford University Press; P. Pierson, *Commander of the Armada: The Seventh Duke of Medina Sidonia*, Yale University Press; J. Dull, *The French Navy and American Independence*, Princeton University Press; J. T. Schliefer, *The Making of Tocqueville's Democracy*, University of North Carolina Press. If there is anyone I have overlooked, I apologize.

Introduction

MARITIME SUPREMACY is the key which unlocks most, if not all, large questions of modern history, certainly the puzzle of how and why we – the Western democracies – are as we are. We are the heirs of maritime supremacy. Our civilization (if we can lay so large a claim), our beliefs, our dominance are products not of superior minds or bravery, cunning, greed or ruthlessness – common attributes of mankind – still less of the Christian religion, the 'Protestant work ethic' or blind chance, but of the particular configuration of seas and land masses that has given the advantage to powers able to use and command the seas. It has been an evolutionary process. In the unrelenting struggle of peoples, those ascendant at sea have, at least in the modern era, proved consistently successful either singly or in alliance against those with a territorial power base;[1] hence it is the system of beliefs and of government associated with supreme maritime power that has prevailed.

Of course maritime supremacy offers no clue to the profounder questions of the spirit, pure philosophy or ethics, or to the directions in which we may be carried by venal science. It cannot explain our terrifying hubris as a species. It is, however, the key to simpler questions: our faith in democracy, personal freedoms and human 'rights', and the other comforting prescriptions of the humanist liberal credo, stem from the supremacy of maritime over territorial power. Pragmatists may deplore this as crude determinism, as another vain attempt to construct a general theory of history. They should reflect on the sort of political philosophy and structures we might now adhere to had the Habsburgs, Bourbons,

Bonaparte, Hitler, Stalin or his heirs prevailed in the titanic world struggles of the past four centuries.

Ultimately all failed. None found a formula for overcoming maritime supremacy. Their territorial empires and the great navies they built to challenge the maritime powers collapsed. It was not chance. There were potent causes. They were analysed towards the end of the nineteenth century by an American naval captain, A. T. Mahan, in a series of extraordinarily influential books describing the workings of what he termed 'sea power' and its influence on history.[2] That his chosen historical periods were practically confined to an era of British naval dominance under sail did not prevent him claiming that the principles adduced from his studies were 'of the unchangeable, or unchanging order of things, remaining the same, in cause and effect, from age to age', belonging 'as it were, to the Order of Nature'.[3] And it is true that, in the hundred years, two world wars and global stand-off since, amid bewildering changes in ships and weaponry, his principles and overall thesis have held good. The downfall of the Kaiser's Germany, Hitler's *Reich*, finally the Soviet empire in face of alliances led by powers commanding the seas appear to belong to his 'unchanging order of things . . . as it were, to the Order of Nature'.

Three centuries earlier, the Elizabethan adventurer and would-be colonizer of North America Sir Walter Ralegh expressed Mahan's central tenet: 'Hee that commaunds the sea, commaunds the trade, and hee that is Lord of the trade of the world is Lord of the wealth of the worlde.'[4] Mahan's explanation was rather fuller: traffic by water was and had always been easier and cheaper than by land – a principle that holds good for most commodities even after the development of railways, motorways and air transport – hence the use and control of the sea lanes was the central link in the chain of exchanges whereby wealth was accumulated. And wealth was, of course, the sinews of war.

The conditions Mahan held necessary for a state to control the sea were first geographical: a position on main trade routes, a coastline with deep-water harbours and, most importantly, no land borders requiring defence against powerful enemies or offering opportunities for aggrandizement, so allowing concentration on sea trade and naval power. His other conditions concerned the inhabitants, the size of population, the character of the people, and the type and disposition of the government.

It is these latter conditions that seem least persuasive today; indeed, the argument of this book is that the outlook and beliefs of peoples and their systems of government are results quite as much as determinants of their power base, whether maritime or territorial; that is to say, in those states which have enjoyed optimum geographical conditions for maritime supremacy in successive ages, the character of the people and the type of government have been moulded by the acquisition of sea power rather than the other way about. It is a natural process: seafaring and trade beget merchants; merchants accumulate wealth and bring the pressure of money to bear on hereditary monarchies and landowning aristocracies, usually poor by comparison; and sooner or later merchant values prevail in government. Chief of these are dispersed power and open, consultative rule, since concentrated power and the arbitrary rule of closed cabals are unresponsive to the needs of trade and fatal to sound finance.

The other distinguishing mark of merchant power is freedom, since both trade and consultative government require the widest dissemination of information and free expression of opinion; thus the basic freedoms of trade spread through all areas of life, tending to break down social hierarchies and the grip of received ideas, creating more open, mobile and enterprising cultures. Liberty has always been the pride and rallying cry of powers enjoying maritime supremacy.

Territorial empires provide a mirror image: having grown by land conquest or dynastic marriage and absorbed different cultures and ethnic groups, their most fundamental drives have been to preserve internal unity and to protect and extend the external borders. They have necessarily developed centralized, authoritarian governments – absolute monarchies, directorates, dictatorships – supported by landholding warrior elites and professional bureaucracies. These have exhibited total incomprehension and contempt for the needs of trade and sound finance. Central control of trade and industry has often led to spectacular gains in desired directions, but has been accompanied by a general, cumulative uncompetitiveness, the cost of which has been borne by the citizens. Meanwhile the ideals of the nobility of the sword, or latterly ideologues, and the necessity for internal control have produced static, hierarchical societies in which expression of ideas has been curbed by censorship, tortures and imprisonment. In place of freedom, the rallying call of territorial empires has been to patriotism and glory.

As systems, supreme maritime and territorial powers are each of a piece: holistic, self-sustaining, inevitably conditioning their peoples in different views of society and political philosophy. While all great powers in the modern era have contained elements hostile to their basic character – territorial power groupings within maritime states, and vice versa – all have conformed distinctly to one or other opposing system. It is the clash of the two systems, both within states and between states and alliances, which has provided the underlying structure of modern history, and the success of the maritime system which has resulted in the dominance of Western power and assumptions – in essence merchant power and merchant needs over warriors, bureaucrats and ideological compulsions.

It has been suggested that these profound differences – or, more specifically, the exceptional character of the maritime powers in an age of European absolutism – may be explained by the great financial and organizational demands that navies place on the state. While absolute territorial monarchs were capable of the relatively simple task of mobilizing huge armies, the complexities of creating a supreme navy – by far the greatest industrial-bureaucratic organizations of the time – required consensual government involving, in the words of one leading naval historian, 'maximum participation by those interest groups whose money and skills were indispensable to sea power . . . the shipowners and seafarers, the urban merchants and financiers, the industrial investors and managers . . . all the classes, in short, which absolutist government least represented and least favoured.'[5] This might be a description of merchant government; it is not an explanation for its development, since it is contradicted by the facts. The first results of the 'naval revolution', when ships grew larger and and mounted great guns on the broadside, were, like the contemporaneous 'military revolution' on land, to increase state bureaucracy and centralization under powerful monarchs.[6] Moreover, the fleets built under those archetypal absolute monarchs Louis XIV, XV and XVI of France were in general larger, better ship for ship, and more scientifically conceived and administered than those of their maritime rivals.

The reason territorial monarchs failed time after time against maritime powers was not that absolutist, non-consensual governments were incapable of building great fleets in peace – quite the reverse – but that they were unable to fund them in the crises of war. This was partly because they lacked the fiscal and financial institutions developed under the merchant governments of their maritime opponents (who could thereby raise more money more cheaply), but mainly because they were forced to divert resources from the fleet to their armies, to fight territorial rivals frequently financed by their maritime enemy from the profits of sea trade. By contrast, maritime powers in crisis invariably poured more funds into the navy to protect the commerce on which their very life depended.

Geography, then, appears to be the defining factor in the growth of both territorial and maritime power and their opposing systems of government. The primary concerns of Continental states like France, Austria and Brandenburg-Prussia were with land neighbours and the opportunities and threats they posed; maritime cities or states, on the other hand, enjoyed natural protection from their most powerful neighbours – usually in the form of sea or river moats – and were situated at the confluence of important trading routes. They lived or died by trade, and hence by the navy which protected their merchants' ships and interdicted those of their opponents. Inevitably merchants took power in government and attempted to achieve a monopoly of violence at sea. The events leading to this outcome were contingent and unpredictable, driven by character and chance, but the outcome itself, by whatever circuitous, aberrant routes it may have come about, was determined by geography and, of course, the powerful compulsions common to all human societies.

THIS BOOK DETAILS the struggles of the first supreme maritime powers of the modern age, the Dutch and the British, and ends with the emergence of their ultimate successor, the United States of America. By this this time the ground work had been done and the system had been established for the conquest of the world. Earlier maritime states had been supreme in particular seas, notably the Mediterranean. The greatest was the Venetian Republic, which engrossed the most valuable trades of the eastern Mediterranean and enjoyed a dazzling reputation for wealth, humanist thinkers, arts and a constitution based on tortuous checks to concentrated personal power. In the oceanic age which heralded Venice's decline, the Dutch were the first to employ the same trading and financial skills to dominate the most lucrative trades of the world, becoming in their turn famed for wealth, humanist thinkers, arts and a constitution exemplifying diffused power. In this sense there has been a direct transfer of market and capital expertise and associated political values from Venice and the city states of the Renaissance, and before them Athens and the thalassocracies of the ancient world, to the Dutch and their British and American successors. The final stages of the process, when the British maritime empire gave way to the American, and democracy and women's freedoms blossomed from the liberal ideal, require a further book.

Mahan's term 'sea power' has not been adopted here, since all great powers built navies and exerted a measure of power at sea; 'maritime supremacy' is used instead, to describe the mature system described above when trading, financial, industrial, in short merchant power prescribes the nature of government and permits (or dictates) the manifold expressions of a free society; when naval command is fundamental but just one manifestation of the whole.

In consequence, two distinct threads run through the book: on the one hand the ships, weapons, tactics, strategies and decisive sea battles with which the maritime powers overcame their territorial opponents – something rare in political or social histories; on the other hand a description of the effects wrought by trade and naval supremacy on government and society – something rare in naval histories. Yet neither thread is quite comprehensible without the other.

I

The Prehistory of
Modern Maritime Power

WEALTH FROM TRADE was the mainspring of Western material advance; the visible agents of change were great guns. These came of age in Europe in the fifteenth century. On land their potency in reducing castle walls favoured central over local power, since in general only monarchs could afford siege-trains; so nation states were consolidated and extended into great territorial empires.

At sea, guns transformed sailing ships into mobile castles virtually impregnable to opponents who lacked equally powerful ordnance. The oared warships known as galleys which had been the instruments of naval warfare for centuries were no match; they retained a role in expeditionary warfare in the Mediterranean and the Baltic, but they could not affect oceanic power. Apart from their lack of endurance at sea, it was not possible to increase their gunpower without drastically reducing oarpower, whereas a sailing ship could mount tiers of guns along along each side and in 'castles' at bow and stern without affecting the propulsion units stretched aloft. Hybrids known as galleasses were built in an attempt to incorporate the advantages of galleys and sailing warships in one hull, but generally proved inferior to both.

With the ocean-going gunned warship, western Europe began to extend around the globe. First, at the end of the fifteenth century, the two Iberian kingdoms reached out – Spain westward to Central America and the Carribean, Portugal eastward around the Cape of Good Hope into the Indian Ocean and the Indonesian archipelago. They had agreed to divide the world between them in this way after numerous sea fights during earlier voyages of trade and discovery down the West African coast. The Portuguese, who had made the running in the exploration of the south Atlantic and doubtless touched the coast of South America in the process, prevailed in having the demarcation line drawn over 1,000 miles west of the Azores, allowing them to claim the bulge of what is now Brazil. The Spanish claimed the rest of the subcontinent, the whole of Central and North America and, when it was revealed, the Pacific.

The voyages of discovery had been financed in the main with Genoese capital amassed from Mediterranean trade. Genoese merchants had been shut out from the Black Sea and the eastern Mediterranean by the advance of the Ottoman Turks, one of the territorial beneficiaries of the great gun revolution on land, who had breached the walls of Constantinople in 1453; in consequence, Genoa had turned turned westward for investment opportunities. A principal motive for both Spanish and Portuguese oceanic enterprise was to find sea routes to the East to outflank the traditional trade routes converging on Alexandria and other ports in the Levant lost to Genoa.[1]

In the event the Portuguese succeeded remarkably: imposing themselves on the traders of the Indian Ocean, whose vessels could not resist Western broadside artillery, they not only established trading bases (factories) and brought home spices and Eastern luxuries by the sea route around the Cape, making Lisbon a western mart for these high-value commodities, but also exercised control over the native traders and exacted taxes for protection. From the 1530s they also established sugar plantations along the coast of Brazil, supplying the colonists with slave workers from West Africa, where they built fortified trading and collecting stations in Sierra Leone, the Gold Coast (now Ghana) and Angola. There was nothing remarkable about the comparatively small beginnings of the transatlantic slave trade. Slavery was an established institution. A trans-Saharan slave trade had long supplied African workers for sugar plantations around the Mediterranean and for the islands colonized during Portuguese voyages in the south Atlantic. Peasants in central and eastern Europe had long been reduced to bondage, tied to the soil and the service of their lord. Nevertheless the oceanic transhipment now begun was to evolve with the growth of the New World economies into the greatest transfer of population and probably the most callous systematic reduction of human beings to commodities in recorded history.[2]

The Spanish, meanwhile, conquered much of Central and South America down the Pacific coast and the large islands of the Caribbean: Hispaniola and Cuba. Like the Portuguese, they began to cultivate sugar, and, since they decimated the native peoples by conquest and imported disease, they bought slaves from the Portuguese to work the plantations. The comparatively modest freights of sugar and agricultural products sent home were transformed from the 1540s by the discovery of huge deposits of silver ore in the viceroyalties of New Spain (Mexico) and Peru. Thereafter two silver streams – united at Havana, Cuba, and thence carried through the Florida Strait and north-easterly on the trade winds past the Azores to Seville – swelled the income of the king of Spain and provided him with almost boundless credit from merchant bankers, mightily augmenting his power. The treasure also proved an irresistible target for his enemies. Of greater importance, since this target proved elusive, silver primed the entire Western trading system.

Hitherto the system had centred on a cluster of north-Italian city states, principally Venice and Genoa. With the rapid growth of oceanic trading systems outside the middle sea, primacy passed to the Spanish Netherlands – an area comprising approximately modern Holland, Belgium and Luxembourg – which enjoyed a position between the Atlantic and the Baltic and across the mouth of the Rhine, with access to the inland markets served by that great trading river. Amsterdam and the ports of Holland had engrossed the bulk trades in grain, timber, masts, spars and naval stores from the Baltic and the herring fisheries of the North Sea; the Flanders port of Antwerp had become the entrepôt for high-value Eastern wares from the Portuguese and Spanish empires. Refining, finishing and manufacturing industries had grown up alongside warehouses, drawing in workers; farming methods in the surrounding countryside had been revolutionized to supply the growing populations. By the mid sixteenth century the coastal and river regions of the Low Countries, nourished by trade, had grown into the most advanced industrial area in Europe, with the highest urban density – some twenty-three walled cities of over 10,000 inhabitants, against just four in England at the time.[3] Antwerp, with a population of over 50,000, replaced the Italian city states as the commercial and financial capital of the Western world.

Part of this astonishing rise was due to the political affiliation of the Netherlands with Spain. Both were Habsburg possessions, acquired with a vast collection of other separated territories through the dynastic

HUDSON'S
BAY

R. St. Lawrence
Great
Lakes
Hudson
NEWFOUND-
LAND

R. Ohio
NOVA SCOTIA
Plymouth

Rio
Grande
Mississippi R.

Charleston

MEXICO
San Augustin
ATLANTIC OCEAN

Zacatecas
(silver mines)
GULF OF
MEXICO
Florida Strait
CANARY
ISLANDS
(Sp.)

Vera Cruz –
San Juan de
Ulloa
Havana
Cuba

Hispaniola
Puerto Rico

Acapulco
Jamaica
Leeward
Islands

VICEROYALTY OF
NEW SPAIN
CARIBBEAN SEA
Curaçao
Windward
Islands

Cartagena
Line of demarcation
between Spanish
and Portuguese
spheres

NEW GRANADA

Equator
Amazon R.

VICEROYALTY OF PERU
Pernam-
buco

PERU
BRAZIL
(P.)
Bahia

PACIFIC OCEAN

Potosi
(silver mines)

CHILE

Buenos
Aires

FALKLAND
ISLANDS

Strait of
Magellan
CAPE HORN

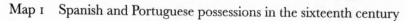

Map 1   Spanish and Portuguese possessions in the sixteenth century

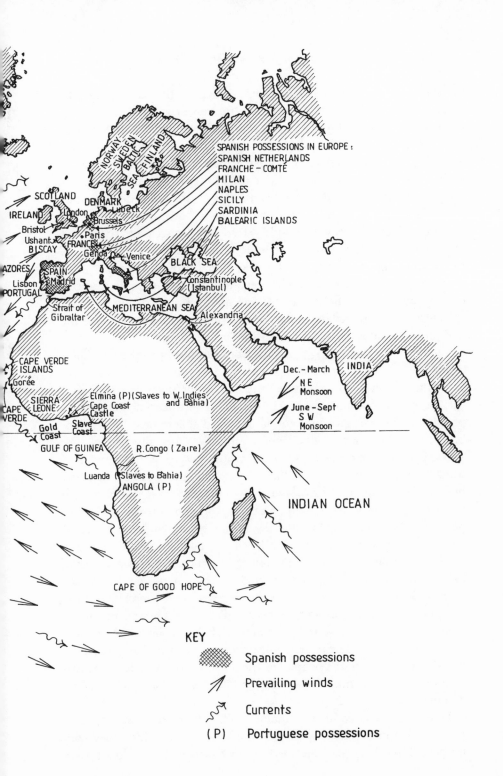

SPANISH POSSESSIONS IN EUROPE:
SPANISH NETHERLANDS
FRANCHE-COMTÉ
MILAN
NAPLES
SICILY
SARDINIA
BALEARIC ISLANDS

NORWAY
SWEDEN
BALTIC SEA
FINLAND
SCOTLAND
DENMARK
Lübeck
IRELAND
London
Brussels
Bristol
Paris
Ushant
FRANCE
BISCAY
Genoa
Venice
BLACK SEA
AZORES
SPAIN
Madrid
Constantinople (Istanbul)
Lisbon
PORTUGAL
Strait of Gibraltar
MEDITERRANEAN SEA
Alexandria
INDIA
CAPE VERDE ISLANDS
Dec.-March
NE Monsoon
Gorée
June-Sept
SW Monsoon
SIERRA LEONE
Elmina (P) (Slaves to W. Indies and Bahia)
Cape Coast Castle
CAPE VERDE
Gold Coast
Slave Coast
GULF OF GUINEA
R. Congo (Zaire)
Luanda (Slaves to Bahia)
ANGOLA (P)
INDIAN OCEAN
CAPE OF GOOD HOPE

KEY
Spanish possessions
Prevailing winds
Currents
(P) Portuguese possessions

marriages of the Austrian Habsburgs. Much of the silver mined in Spain's New World empire was drawn to Antwerp, whence it flowed through world trade. On the deficit side of the ledger, the Netherlands were embroiled in a Habsburg struggle for Continental hegemony against their territorial rivals: Ottoman Turkey in the east, Valois France in the west. In the early years of the century the struggle with France was fought out in northern Italy, but from the 1540s the land war shifted to the Netherlands, which became the strategic base of the Habsburg emperor, Charles V. Secure behind rivers, dykes, canals, walled cities and fortresses against the French border, he could provision and supply his forces from the most abundant markets in Europe, using the most efficient water transport, equip his siege-trains with the most advanced cast-bronze artillery from the districts about Antwerp and Malines (Mechelen) or freighted down the Rhine from Nuremberg or Frankfurt, and threaten Valois power at its heart in Paris.

Charles made increasing demands from this most prosperous region of his empire to finance his campaigns. The seventeen provinces of the Netherlands complied on a quota basis by levying taxes on wealth and excise duties on consumables and by selling interest-bearing bonds to the populace. The ever-growing economy seemed able to bear the burden, but beneath the surface disaffection spread – especially in Holland, Zeeland and the northern provinces, whose peoples were more than usually independent. Much of their low coastal and estuarial land had been wrested from salt or river marsh over the past three centuries with extensive systems of dykes, dams, drainage works and canals. Their fore-bears had been enticed to settle the reclaimed wetlands by grants of tenure for simple money rents with few if any feudal ties, and, since the growth of urban markets for agricultural produce, some 45 per cent of the land in the coastal provinces had come into possession of free peasant farmers.[4] Much of the rest belonged to town merchants, espe-cially brewers. Sailors, fishermen, river and coastal boatmen, and urban craftsmen and artisans were by the nature of their occupations equally free from vassalage. The landowning aristocracy retained its grip on the inland provinces, but the peoples of the thriving coastal belt, nourished by trade, served the market economy and ultimately the merchants who dominated it.

Despite prosperity, they remained, like their forebears, frontier peoples, bound together by danger from the waters which they con-fronted. They have been termed a 'flood society',[5] for floods were engraved in folk memory, and remained an ever-present threat. Traditionally, each community elected a local board of water guardians to oversee the maintenance or extension of the sea and river defences, and paid local taxes for this essential work. But Charles, regarding the multiplicity of authorities as wasteful, imposed regional dyke and drainage boards responsible to the central administration in Brussels, site of the viceregal court, where French, not Dutch, was spoken. He also imposed closer central supervision of the councils which administered the towns and cities. It seems to have been these attacks on local autonomy, together with the remoteness of the superior institutions and Habsburg officials, that provoked resentment as much as the extra duties levied for distant wars unrelated to the real concerns of the people.[6]

Bitterness at interference with ancient liberties was joined to and expressed through religious dissent. Christian humanism – stressing the importance of an individual's relationship to God and inner spiritual life, as against the outer rituals of formal religion – had developed in the northern Netherlands late in the fourteenth century; in the early sixteenth century it had spread to all provinces through the works of its most luminous scholar, Erasmus. The more rigid doctrines of Lutheranism had also been imported, in the main from the north-German trading cities, and then Calvinism, further undermining the established Roman Catholic Church. Charles had responded by setting up the Inquisition in Antwerp. The first two martyrs, friars of Luther's Augustinian order, had been burned in the great market square at Brussels in 1523.

Repression only drove the Protestant heresies underground, and Charles, who had learned through experience that heresy was synonymous with political rebellion, extended the Inquisition by setting up provincial tribunals on the Spanish model. The increased scale of executions by burning, beheading or, for women, burying alive deepened disillusion with the Established Church. Congregations decreased. Discontent with foreign rule intensified.

By 1555 Charles had been overwhelmed by the costs of his campaigns against France and the defence of his positions in south-eastern Europe, the Mediterranean and the Spanish Caribbean, which was infested with pirates and privateers from the ports of western France. Latterly he had been forced to pay almost 50 per cent, in some cases up to 75 per cent, interest on loans. He abdicated, leaving his Austro-Hungarian possessions and his claim to the Crown of the Holy Roman Empire to his brother, Ferdinand. The rest of his dominions – which included the Duchy of Milan, the south-Italian kingdom of Naples, Sicily, islands in the western Mediterranean, Franche-Comté, Burgundy, Luxembourg, the Netherlands and Spain, with its transatlantic and trans-Pacific possessions, were left to his son, who from the age of sixteen had represented him at Madrid and now became Philip II of Spain.

Magnificent as Philip's empire appeared, the centrepiece, Spain had been bankrupted by Charles's wars, and the most prosperous region, the Netherlands, seethed with resentment at religious and fiscal oppression.

Philip II was a man of high moral seriousness who regarded it as a sacred trust to preserve his inheritance in the True Faith – a task at which he was to labour diligently for the rest of his life. The idea of easing religious tensions with a policy of toleration would have been as personally inconceivable as it was politically unrealistic: people thought in religious terms; the Church was in consequence the most powerful instrument of social control and imperial cohesion.

In 1566 the underground resentment in the Netherlands boiled over in Calvinist demonstrations and the systematic stripping of images, paintings and furnishings from Catholic churches. Philip dispatched an army of 10,000 Spanish, Neapolitan and German troops under the Duke of Alva to restore order. The threat was sufficient to quell the risings, and many of the leaders of the revolt, including Philip's stadtholder, or governor-general, in Holland, Prince William of Orange, chose exile in Germany before Alva arrived. Despite this, the grim and zealous old warrior imposed a reign of terror designed to deter future risings; almost 9,000 people were examined for complicity in the rebellions – prompting a further exodus from the country – and over 1,000 were executed.[7] But the savage measures failed to root out dissent. 'Reformed' Protestant congregations continued to worship in secret throughout the land.

Alva also further violated the historic constitution of the Netherlands, whereby taxation was imposed with the consent of provincial assemblies, known as States, and the States General, composed of delegates from the States. On Philip's orders, he demanded another levy on wealth and a permanent 10 per cent sales tax. Once admitted, the principle of permanent taxation would remove the States' only tenuous influence over the Spanish administration. Moreover it was evident that, while it would be used primarily for Philip's wars against the Turks in the Mediterranean, the money would allow the maintenance of a standing army in the Netherlands, so suppressing the provinces with their own funds. The States delayed, but finally could not resist accepting the imposition. Only fear prevented insurrection breaking out again.

The rebels in exile – adopting the dismissive epithet *gueux* or 'beggars' bestowed on them by Philip's half-sister governing for him in Brussels – rallied under William of Orange and made incursions designed to provoke major uprisings, but without success. A rebel flotilla of heavily armed vessels adapted from the coasting and river traders known as hoys and operating from the river Ems on the northern border had greater effect. These 'Sea Beggars' preyed on Spanish and Portuguese shipping in the Channel and the approaches to the river Schelde and Antwerp, forming a loose alliance with French Protestant (Huguenot) privateers and with English privateers and pirates, and using French, English and southern Irish ports as convenient to provision and to dispose of booty.

Hitherto England had been in the Spanish orbit, sending her principal export of unfinished woollen cloth to Antwerp for finishing and marketing, and trading from Bristol, Plymouth and other western ports with the Spanish Canary Islands and Seville. France had then been the closer and more dangerous of the two great Continental powers. Now France, ruined by the wars with Spain, had collapsed in civil and religious conflict, and Philip, with his New World treasure and anti-Protestant crusade in the Netherlands, appeared the nearer and greater threat to England's independence.

English policy shifted accordingly. The Queen, Elizabeth I, and the Huguenot leader, the Bourbon Prince of Condé, whose power base was in the south-west and western coastal regions of France, signed a treaty whereby Elizabeth supplied the principal Huguenot port, La Rochelle, with arms, money and English sailors; and she encouraged English captains to join the Huguenot privateer assault in the Spanish Caribbean. From the galaxy of gallants and adventurers rekindling havoc in the New World, Francis Drake emerged as the most successful and feared, acquiring in the Spanish imagination a superhuman aura.

Meanwhile the Protestant onslaught on Catholic shipping in the Channel and its approaches sparked the decisive step in the Netherlands' revolt. The dislocation of trade and the counter-action against Protestant ships had rebounded on English merchants – particularly those from London exporting to Antwerp – and by 1572 their distress was such that Elizabeth felt obliged to reduced the mayhem. One measure she took was to ban the Sea Beggars from the English ports. A large detachment then in Dover was required to leave, and after cruising for some weeks the Beggars put in to the port of Brille below the Hook of Holland. There they found the garrison had been withdrawn by Alva to strengthen the southern borders against an expected rebel and Huguenot assault from France, and it was decided to hold the town for the revolt. This inspired the citizens of Flushing, whose citadel was not yet complete, to rise against their garrison and invite the Beggars in. With this important port commanding the mouth of the Schelde, the rebels were able to sever Antwerp completely from the sea.

Other ports in Zeeland followed Flushing's example, and were joined through that early summer of 1572 by many Dutch towns, with the notable exception of the great cities of Amsterdam, Rotterdam and Delft. Despite their absence, on 19 July a rebel States of Holland was convened in Dordrecht, and William of Orange was proclaimed stadt-holder and captain-general of the three provinces of Holland, Zeeland and Utrecht and Protector of the Netherlands as a whole. So began a war for control of the Netherlands which was to last with only brief remission for eighty years.

The Huguenot leaders on whom William counted for support were massacred on St Batholemew's day, 23 August, by the French Catholic faction. Nonetheless William went ahead with the invasion of the south Netherlands. The army he had gathered proved no match for Alva's veterans, but when Alva moved north to subdue Holland and the provinces above the Rhine and the Maas he found very different conditions. Whereas the firm, open ground of the south – roughly modern Belgium – suited his professional Spanish infantry, in the north the web of rivers, canals and low land which the rebels flooded served both as natural barriers to his advance and as supply and reinforcement networks for the Beggars who controlled the waterways. In May 1573 he wrote that he had never in his life found more difficulties waging war than in Holland, 'a province of dykes, ponds, and difficult passages'.[8] Moreover, with the sea route through the English Channel denied him by the Sea Beggars and other Protestant privateers, reinforcements had to make a long overland march to reach the rebel provinces.

It can be said, therefore, that at this turning point in the struggle between the Protestant fringes of western Europe and the great territorial power centres – in conventional historiography, between the Reformation and the Counter-Reformation – there was no true maritime power in the sense of a nation reliant on and driven by trade to possess a supreme navy. Indeed there had not been a true maritime power in this sense since the beginning of the century. Venice and the north-Italian city states had fulfilled such a role within the Mediterranean but had been outflanked by oceanic trade, and no power had yet arisen to control the global system.

Spain possessed a galley fleet for the Mediterranean but virtually no ocean-going sailing navy or naval establishment outside the galley service. Philip was persuaded to build and arm specialized war galleons for the defence of the Indies, but these were used as available to escort treasure fleets; they were never formed into battle squadrons.[9] Nor had Spain developed advanced industries or financial institutions; both these prerequisites for supreme maritime power had blossomed in the Netherlands, centred on Antwerp – within the Spanish empire but outside the territorial power base. Lack of substantial gun-founding capacity was a critical symptom of Spain's situation. Able to purchase all the high-quality guns she needed from her Netherlands or Italian possessions, she had failed to support the three home foundries of Medina del Campo, Málaga and Barcelona. Now the Netherlands had been cut off by sea, she was finding it increasingly difficult to procure guns.

Portugal was in a similar situation. She possessed fighting galleons, but these seem to have been employed chiefly to secure her dominion in the Eastern seas; they were managed by the same department of the royal administration that presided over Eastern cargo carriers.[10] Trade was run not as a merchant enterprise, but as a royal monopoly. Besides inherent corruption, prices were kept artificially high at Lisbon and Antwerp to meet the costs of the empire. And, by using Antwerp as her north-European market for spices and other high-value Eastern wares, Portugal had contributed to the phenomenal industrial and financial growth of this region outside her control.

As for the other states, France had had a considerable royal navy and Mediterranean galley fleet in the first half of the sixteenth century, but abandoned both during the civil wars at the beginning of the 1560s; by the early 1570s the only French forces at sea were Huguenot privateers.[11]

Across the Channel, England had retained the substantial royal navy built to counter the French navy of the first half of the century,[12] together with a highly efficient central administration and the priceless asset of cheap, good-quality cast-iron guns manufactured within the kingdom. However, the great ships which headed the fleet were high floating castles, more suitable for harbour defence or for fighting on calm days in the Channel than for oceanic warfare. Besides this, England entirely lacked the industrial or financial base required for supreme maritime power.

To the east, the two Scandinavian kingdoms of Denmark–Norway and Sweden both had substantial royal navies almost as large as England's – in Sweden's case possibly larger.[13] These resulted from a naval arms race between the two as they struggled to control the Baltic. They had defeated the north-German trading league, the Hansa, in the first half of the century and had imposed a dual control of the Baltic, rendering it probably the only area, certainly within the Western system, free from piracy or privateering. For this protection they exacted tolls and customs duties. Further, by ensuring that no merchant league, city state or territorial power on the southern or eastern coasts could monopolize Baltic trade – as the Hansa and the city of Lübeck once had – they gained the advantage of generally lower prices for imported goods and higher prices for their own exports. As a recent pioneering study of world naval building programmes puts it, 'the Scandinavian kings were selling protection to foreign shipping in exchange for customs duties and increased competition, beneficial for the trade of their own countries'.[14] In short they used their naval power monopoly to control the terms of trade. Neither, however, exerted any influence on the oceanic system outside the Baltic, and both were essentially undeveloped. Neither was therefore a true maritime power in the sense defined here.

The only region with the mercantile, industrial and financial strength to exert supreme power at sea was the Spanish Netherlands, yet it was not a sovereign state and possessed no navy. It had the largest merchant fleet anywhere in Europe – perhaps 1,800 seagoing vessels by the 1560s, of which some 500 were based at Amsterdam.[15] Those owned by merchants of Antwerp were conventional 'defensible' ships required in that era for most medium- or long-haul trades. The majority of vessels from Holland and the northern provinces, however, were more lightly built specialized carriers of bulk cargoes – in essence, seagoing barges, with flat bottoms, narrow hulls, the minimum running rigging and no armament. Built from cheaper timber cut to standard dimensions with saws powered by windmills, and manned with small crews, these were the vessels that had enabled the Dutch to undercut all rivals and take over the grain, timber, masts, spars, and naval stores trades of the Baltic, the bulk salt trade from western France and Portugal, and the fishing grounds of the North Sea, which they cruised in great fleets of specialized herring 'buses'. They could dispense with armament in the Baltic, because of the domination exercised by the Scandinavian kingdoms in their own interests; in the dangerous waters outside they might sail in convoys escorted by 'defensible' armed merchantmen. But apart from the rebel Sea Beggars' heavily armed 'cromsters' and 'flyboats', both of which were coastal or river craft and engaged chiefly in offensive war, neither the Dutch nor the wealthier merchants of Antwerp had a permanent naval force to protect their huge merchant fleets.

Moreover the country was split in civil war. Probably no contemporary observer could have predicted that from this embattled cockpit of religious and centrifugal struggle the smaller, humbler northern half, styling itself the United Provinces of the Netherlands – often called the Dutch Republic – would emerge as the first true maritime power of the modern age and progenitor of the Western democratic state.

2

The Spanish Armada, 1588

PHILIP'S MORE ABLE advisers told him that the key to the defence of the Caribbean was command of the English Channel, whence privateers sailed to attack his dominions; the key to the reconquest of the Netherlands was England itself. The Pope tried to persuade him to lead a Holy League invasion of England to return her to the True Faith. Yet up to the summer of 1588 Philip was resolved to reassert his authority in the Netherlands first, then perhaps deal with the 'heretic woman', Elizabeth I.

She, for her part, cautious by nature and necessity – her normal revenue being barely a tenth of Philip's – continued a flexible policy of aiding his enemies, the Huguenots and the Beggars, to keep them in the field while supporting joint royal–merchant ventures to attack his New World possessions, but never the Spanish homeland, taking care not to precipitate an irreparable breach.

From 1578 onwards, however, circumstances combined so favourably for Philip that she was pushed towards open hostilities. Outside the area, Ottoman Turkey had turned against Persia, relieving pressure on Spain in the Mediterranean and allowing Philip to concentrate resources against the rebel United Provinces. Appointing as his governor-general in Brussels Alessandro Farnese, Duke of Parma, the finest exponent of siege warfare of the age, he built up his Netherlands army to formidable size – some 61,000 troops by 1582. At the same time the quantities of silver from his New World mines increased dramatically, his 'royal fifth' of the annual shipments rising to 2 million ducats by 1580 – rather

over half a million pounds. While this did not cover the expenses of defending his worldwide dominions, it heartened the bankers on whom he relied for loans. Meanwhile the King of Portugal died without heir, allowing Philip to add that nation with its important West African, Brazilian and East Indian possessions, its shipping and fighting galleons, to his already vast empire. In the 1580s he bestrode the world.

In 1584 William of Orange was shot and mortally wounded by a fanatic inspired by Spanish propaganda. Leadership of the United Provinces devolved upon Holland, whose still flourishing Baltic trades and fisheries provided the major resources supporting the rebels. This leadership was expressed through Holland's dominating position in the States General at The Hague and a new executive council of state formed to take over William's responsibilities for the conduct of war and the armed forces. By this time the rebel position was precarious. Parma had reduced the southern provinces except for the major cities, which he had surrounded. In the north his ablest commander, Francisco Verdugo, had taken the inland areas and pushed the rebels back to the line of the river IJssel, practically confining the revolt to Zeeland, Holland and the provinces around the Zuider Zee west of the IJssel. In 1585 the southern cities surrendered. In desperation the States General at The Hague appealed to Henri III of France, offering him sovereignty in return for support. He refused, and they turned to Elizabeth of England.

Her most cautious chief minister, Lord Burghley, advised her the time had now come to throw in her lot openly with the Dutch, before Philip completed his conquests in the Netherlands:

> whereby he shall be so provoked with pride, solicited by the Pope and tempted by the Queen's own [Catholic] subjects, and shall be so strong by sea and so free from all other actions and quarrels, yea shall be so formidable to all the rest of Christendom, as that her Majesty shall in no wise be able with her own power, nor with the aid of any other, neither by sea nor land, to withstand his attempts.[1]

It is interesting to see such an early exposition of the Continental balance-of-power policy Great Britain was to pursue in her days as a great power. In fact English statesmen since the 1520s had been guided by the same concept of trying to prevent one power gaining hegemony in western Europe and control of the Channel coast.[2]

Elizabeth hesitated to accept the sovereignty offered by the rebels, since it would establish her as Philip's immutable enemy. Instead, she offered them a protectorate; she would provide a military leader to command in her name, two representatives to sit on the council of the state, an expeditionary force to aid their defence – later fixed as 6,000 foot and 1,000 horse – and £126,000 annually for their keep. As security, she asked to take over the ports of Brille and Flushing, which she promised to garrison with extra troops.[3]

Having committed herself, that September she unleashed the offensive by sea long advocated by a maritime group of courtiers and adventurers, Walter Ralegh and Francis Drake prominent among them. Drake, who had returned from an epic circumnavigation of the world via the Strait of Magellan five years earlier, was preparing to follow the same route to plunder Spanish Pacific-coast settlements and shipping. He was sent instead to the Caribbean, to strike at the heart of Philip's colonial empire and seize or interrupt the flow of bullion on which the Spanish finances rested. The expedition was a typical Elizabethan part-royal, part-merchant venture: the Queen contributed two of over twenty ships and a sixth of the capital; courtiers and London and West Country merchants and gentlemen, including Drake, made up the rest.

Drake sailed straight for the Spanish port of Vigo, to release English ships embargoed there. Occupying the harbour, he liberated jailed English sailors, seized the cathedral treasury, and forcibly completed his ships with provisions and water before following the trade-wind route to the Portuguese Cape Verde Islands, where he made more mischief. Thence he sailed across the Atlantic to Santo Domingo, Hispaniola (now the Dominican Republic), the arrival port for Spanish outward-bound fleets, and took the town in a surprise landing by night, burning it building by building to extort maximum ransom. He then sailed to Cartagena, principal port for the mainland viceroyalty of New Granada (now Colombia and Venezuela) and did the same, afterwards sacking San Augustin, a base the Spanish had established on the coast of Florida for the defence of the treasure route.

Philip, as shocked by Drake's depredations on his own coast as by Elizabeth's treaty with the rebels, reconsidered his strategy, and asked Parma in the Netherlands and his veteran Admiral of the Ocean Sea, the Marquis of Santa Cruz, to propose detailed plans for the invasion of England. In January 1586 he wrote to the Pope asking for a contribution

towards the huge expenses such an undertaking would involve. The Pope replied that Philip's real concerns were with grand strategy and revenge, not religion.

Santa Cruz's proposal listed an armada of 150 great ships, 6 galleasses, 50 galleys, 40 store ships, 320 small vessels and 200 landing barges to carry an invasion army of 55,000 infantry, 1,200 cavalry and 4,000 sappers, gunners and muleteers. He favoured landing in Ireland, thence crossing to England if Elizabeth would not come to terms. Parma, on the other hand, proposed massing a fleet of small craft along the Flemish coast, under pretence of preparing a raid on Zeeland; when the wind came into the east, these would be launched across the Channel, carrying 35,000 of his own troops, relying on secrecy and favourable winds to evade the enemy.[4]

Neither plan was sound, the former because of the huge cost and impracticability of gathering such an armada, the latter because it would be impossible to mass the number of invasion vessels necessary without alerting the enemy; once surprise was lost, the force would be exposed to defeat by the Sea Beggars and the English directly it put to sea. The two proposals were merged by Philip's principal adviser on foreign policy, Don Juan de Idiáquez, who became chief co-ordinator of the 'Enterprise of England'.

The compromise he arrived at called for a smaller armada – sufficient, however, to overcome the English fleet – carrying only 6,000 Spanish troops and their artillery. With this force, Santa Cruz was to fight his way up the English Channel, through the Strait of Dover and up the Kent coast to Margate on the north-eastern corner of that county, there to provide a shield for Parma's small craft carrying 30–40,000 of his troops from the southern Netherlands.[5]

While this appeared to combine the best aspects of both proposals, it took no account of navigational hazards or the chances of the wind; whether or not Idiáquez consulted pilots versed in English or Dutch waters, the well-known sandbanks off the east-Kent coast, the unpredictable shoals stretching out from the Thames estuary, and the shallows and tidal streams along the Flemish coast should have daunted any seaman in those days when sailing ships could at best make no more than ten degrees into the wind and were at the mercy of every shift and sudden squall. Moreover, anyone acquainted with the shallow-draft cromsters of the Sea Beggars and their mastery of the tidal estuaries and inshore waters off the Netherlands would have questioned how the deep galleons with which Santa Cruz was to force his way through the English fleet could possibly shield Parma's boats. Parma did question it. In reply to Philip's instructions to prepare to act in concert with the armada, he pointed out that he had no deep-water ports where a rendezvous could be effected. His protests were ignored.

In England, meanwhile, preparations to meet such an attempt were well advanced. The most important step, it appears in retrospect, had been the appointment in 1577 of John Hawkins as Treasurer of the Navy. Hawkins, the son of a prominent Plymouth merchant adventurer and connected by marriage to a senior member of the Queen's Navy Board, had led the first English expeditions to try to break into the slave trade to the Spanish colonies in the New World. He had practical experience both of the opportunities offered by Spain's weakness at sea and of the inadequacy of most of Elizabeth's warships for ocean warfare. He was a leader of the maritime-offensive school, and in 1577 neither he nor his patron, Burghley, was thinking of defence against invasion so much as of striking at the Spanish on their own coast and in the Indies. The ships he began to fashion for this purpose were to prove more than a match for the Spanish in all conditions.

There is debate about the origin of the type. They were described at the time as 'race-built' galleons. A recent theory suggests persuasively that they were evolved from galleasses built for Elizabeth's father, Henry VIII, in 1546.[6] These had a single bank of oars but in other respects appeared like long, low sailing ships, and were noted for 'exceeding nimbleness in sailing'. The terms 'galleasses' and 'galleon' both seem to derive from 'galley', and the chief feature distinguishing the galleon from other sailing-ships types was the construction of the bows, which had a projection (later known as the beakhead) resembling the vestigial ram of a galley, and a low forecastle set well back from the stem instead of overhanging it. The purpose of this arrangement, it is suggested, was to allow heavy 'chase-guns' to be mounted to fire forward in the same way as the battery of a galley.[7]

Sailing warships already carried heavy 'chase-pieces' firing from low, hinged ports either side of the rudder and rather lighter broadside pieces firing from similar gun ports along either side; now, with powerful chase-guns on the beakhead and firing from ports in the bows below, each side of the stem, a galleon could tackle an enemy on any bearing. More importantly, by hauling round, she could give the enemy her bow, broadside and stern guns in succession.

The English achievement was to combine the agility and speed of sailing of the earlier galleasses – derived from a higher length/breadth ratio and less superstructure than a conventional vessel of the same size – with the all-round firepower of the galleon. This technological leap forward was a response to England's weaker, interloping, position in the Spanish sphere. Like any corsairs, English captains needed to outsail potential prizes and to outsail and outmanoeuvre any escorts they might meet, to avoid being boarded and entered by more heavily armed vessels. That they also came to outgun them may have been due to England's lead in cast-iron guns. In any event, the first armament standard for Elizabeth's ships was laid down in 1569, after an expedition under John Hawkins had been surprised and overpowered by the annual Spanish fleet at San Juan de Ulloa in the Gulf of Mexico. It stipulated far more heavy long guns than were carried by the best of Philip's galleons.[8]

What is considered the prototype 'race-built' galleon, the *Dreadnought*, was launched in 1573, and it has recently been pointed out that the total weight of her guns amounted to 4.5 per cent of displacement – a hitherto unprecedented ratio.[9] This revolutionary trend in warship design, which marked the rejection of the traditional method of fighting by boarding and entering, was carried forward by Hawkins from 1577. He began by cutting down the lofty castles of the Queen's great and medium-sized ships and lengthening their hulls, not only improving stability, speed and manoeuvrability, but allowing them to carry a greater number of heavy guns below. The reduction of the tiers of decks and light guns in the castles also made for a smaller complement, which contributed to better health among the men.

Hawkins went on to construct new vessels to the same formula, and in 1585, as it seemed Spain would complete the reconquest of the Netherlands, when Spanish forces might be released for the overthrow of England, he was granted increased funds for an accelerated programme of new building and purchase. By 1588 he had provided a fleet of eighteen first-line warships, faster, more weatherly and better armed than any others in the world, with a ratio of gun weight to displacement in many places exceeding 6 per cent. Their advantages were enumerated by a gentleman volunteer in the armada campaign, Sir Arthur Gorgas, who witnessed these ships literally running rings around the taller, clumsier, more heavily manned but lightly armed Spanish galleons and great ships:

our swiftness in outsailing them, our nimbleness in getting into the weather of them, our little draft of water in comparison to theirs, our stout bearing up of our sides in all huge winds, when theirs must stoop to their great disadvantage many ways, our yawness in staying well [when tacking] and casting about twice for their once and so discharging our broadside of ordnance double for their single . . .[10]

Less obvious but equally important for England's survival were administrative initiatives begun in 1582, when hints of the Pope's efforts to persuade Philip to invade England were found hidden behind the looking glass of a Spanish agent. Burghley instructed the Lord Admiral to gather information with which to draw up defensive measures. The result was a list of all merchant ships in the kingdom and their tonnage, and the names of all masters and mariners in the maritime counties; a countrywide census provided further information on 16,255 men whose work was connected with the water. With this data, in 1584 Burghley drew up contingency plans for requisitioning ships and impressing men for service against a future Spanish invasion attempt, whose outlines he predicted with remarkable accuracy.[11] The problems of provisioning a fleet of the unprecedented size envisaged was tackled with the same vigour by a young officer of the Queen's household, James Quarles, who was appointed as Surveyor of Maritime Victuals.[12]

In 1586 reports from Lisbon and around Spain indicated preparations for a large expedition to sail against England. Early the following year Elizabeth yielded to Burghley's pressure to sign a warrant for the execution of her cousin, the Catholic Mary Stuart, exiled queen of Scotland and a focus for Philip's attempts to provoke insurrection by English Catholics. Mary's execution on 8 February 1587 signified a final break with Spain, and next month Elizabeth allowed herself to be persuaded to launch a pre-emptive strike against the armada which was gathering in Lisbon. Drake led the part-royal, part-merchant joint-stock expedition with instructions to 'impeach the joining together of the King of Spain's fleet out of their several ports, to keep victuals from them, to follow them in case they should come forward towards England or Ireland'.[13]

Off Portugal, Drake learned that Cadiz was full of ships with only galleys as protection. He headed there, arriving in the afternoon of 29 April and sailing straight into the bay without calling a council. Like Nelson later, he had an instant appreciation for a situation, and knew the prime importance of the initiative. He achieved complete surprise, scattered the galleys, and, falling upon a great gathering of merchantmen at anchor, plundered, captured or burned them at will. When he sailed out next morning the Cadiz division of Philip's armada, chiefly store ships, was no more.

Drake next made an unsuccessful attempt on the port of Lagos in southern Portugal, then took the nearby roadstead and castle at Sagres, Cape St Vincent. With this secure anchorage on the south-western corner of the peninsula, which all Mediterranean divisions and supply ships had to round to reach Philip's main fleet concentration in Lisbon, Drake had a stranglehold on the armada preparations. Had he been commanding a squadron fully committed to the state service he might have prevented the armada from ever sailing. However, in a part-state but chiefly merchant-privateering venture, profit, not blockade, was the driving force, and, after refitting and replenishing, he set off for the Azores to surprise the returning treasure fleet. Instead he found a large Portuguese ship returning laden from the East and took her home. The prize money she and her cargo fetched made the voyage, returning fortunes for Drake and Elizabeth and considerable profits for the other backers.

As it turned out, the strategic results of the expedition were equally satisfactory. Philip had ordered Santa Cruz to take a squadron from Lisbon to the Azores to shield the returning treasure fleet from Drake, and by the time the Spanish admiral returned in October the storm damage his ships had suffered and the bad weather to be expected in the winter months ahead prevented him sailing for England that year – so he insisted, against all Philip's pleas to refit and put to sea as soon as possible.

For Philip, after his latest humiliation from 'El Draque', it was a question of face and, intimately bound up with face, finance. In the first nine months of 1587 he had spent over 10 million ducats (£2.75 million) assembling and fitting out the armada. Each month that passed cost him a further 700,000 ducats,[14] besides losses from the disruption to trade caused by the requisitioning of so many ships.

In January 1588 he sent an emissary to Lisbon to report back on the state of the fleet and why Santa Cruz was still unprepared to sail. He learned that things were worse than could be imagined. Contractors, unpaid, were providing inferior victuals or none at all; sailors were dying of hunger; disease was sweeping their squalid quarters between leaking decks. Even Santa Cruz had caught typhus and lay dying.

Philip immediately cast about for a successor. Rather than an admiral or a general, he needed an able administrator who could pull the sickly and demoralized force together and take it to sea in the shortest time. The choice was not hard. The Duke of Medina-Sidonia had taken a leading part in the decisions and preparations for the armada from the start, and in 1586 those in the know had tipped him as the likely commander should the expedition sail against England. He was the first grandee of Seville, and his status ensured his authority over the naval and military officers. At thirty-eight years old, he was in the prime of life. And he was also probably the wealthiest noble in Spain – a vital, even perhaps the vital, consideration in that age when leaders were expected to oil the wheels of supply with their own funds, particularly so at this time when the unpaid bills on Philip's treasury were being exchanged at discounts of up to 30 per cent.[15]

As hereditary war leader in Andalusia, a major recruiting area for soldiers, Medina-Sidonia was better able than anyone to raise levies and harness the other vital resources of the region, most importantly grain and shipping. He also had personal qualities of diligence, trustworthiness and administrative ability. All he appeared to lack was seagoing experience; yet, with seasoned staff and divisional commanders, this was of less significance than his high position, wealth and name – especially if Philip's real purpose was to send the fleet into the Channel to threaten, overawe and bring Elizabeth to terms without a major invasion. Parma had already opened negotiations with her, and believed her so alarmed by her expenses that she desired peace.[16]

Philip's real expectations will never be known. All that is certain is that, having started the Enterprise of England and invested so much money and reputation, he had to push it forward with the utmost urgency. If he failed, Elizabeth would be emboldened, his coasts, colonies, treasure shipments and trade with the Netherlands would never be safe, and his credit with his bankers would dry up. Medina-Sidonia seemed the natural, probably the inevitable, choice for the task. Idiáquez wrote to inform him that the King had 'fixed his eyes upon him' to succeed Santa Cruz in command.

Medina-Sidonia attempted to decline, replying that he lacked experience of the sea or of war, 'for I have never seen war nor engaged in it', and claimed that he was without ability, health, strength or fortune for so important an enterprise.[17] Philip attributed this famous letter to modesty, but the Duke followed it with a second (as yet undiscovered) refusal so strong in self-doubt and misgivings about the outcome of the expedition that Idiáquez suppressed it, writing back that he had not dared give an account of it to Philip. He asked the Duke not to bother them with fears about the success of the armada:

> Because the appointment to which God and the King call your Lordship is so important, you ought to show more spirit. To preserve the reputation and opinion which today the world has of your valour and prudence, which would all be hazarded if it were known what you wrote (which we shall keep secret), it is important that you step forward with the determination expected of your Lordship.[18]

On the same day Philip replied to the first refusal: 'It is I who must judge of your capabilities and parts, and I am fully satisfied with these . . . prepare and steel yourself to the performance of this service.'[19] Medina-Sidonia dutifully complied, and on 27 February he left his estate at San Lúcar at the mouth of the Guadalquivir and took the road to Lisbon with a heavy heart, knowing he would have to dig deep in his purse to get the expedition under way, yet extremely doubtful of success and aware of his lack of experience in comparison to the veteran he was succeeding.

Whatever his personal misgivings, his activity once he reached Lisbon confirmed Philip's judgement. Besides the inadequate supplies of victuals and wine, he was confronted by a shortage of soldiers and sailors, due in large part to illness and desertion, and by insufficient heavy guns or ammunition. Gathering a small expert staff, he tackled each problem with energy and personally visited and inspected each ship – a sturdy, pale-faced figure of middling height, high forehead and thoughtful eyes, who impressed everyone with his energy and purpose. Soon a new order and confidence spread through the formerly dispirited expedition.

Despite his forceful direction, however, he was not able to procure as many experienced seamen as he required.[20] They were harshly treated in the Spanish service. Royal ships were commanded by military officers who may or may not have been to sea, and the numerous soldiery aboard regarded seamen as inferiors and treated them as such – like dogs, seamen complained. Royal seamen were also paid less than soldiers – when they were paid – and far less than in the merchant service.

Medina-Sidonia was also unable to remedy the equally serious shortage of heavy guns. Despite sending officers to scour the country for ordnance, and buying pieces from foreign ships in Lisbon, he could not make up for Spain's deficiency in gun foundries. He was eventually able to add 200 or so pieces, but they were a light and heterogenous collection. Of the 2,411 pieces detailed on his final muster list, it is probable that fewer than 120 were real ship-damaging weapons throwing balls of 15 lb or over.[21]

He was aware of this potentially fatal weakness. From intimate acquaintance with the Indies fleets that sailed from the Guadalquivir, he knew of the Protestant interloper tactics of standing off and battering with artillery instead of boarding; he had warned Philip the previous year that this was how the English would fight. His experienced officers were equally aware. One of the most senior told an emissary from the Pope that spring that the English had faster and more manoeuvrable ships and many more long guns, and would hold off and knock the armada to pieces out of range of effective reply. However, since the Spanish were fighting in God's cause, he was confident God would send a miracle allowing them to close, when Spanish superiority in numbers and quality of soldiers would give them the victory. They were sailing, he concluded, in the confident hope of a miracle.[22]

Towards the end of April, Medina-Sidonia felt his fleet was as ready as it could be: the guns had been distributed among the ships on a rational plan; shot had been increased to an average of fifty for each piece, and powder in proportion; sailing and fighting instructions, rendezvous and passwords had been issued to the captains; every detail of small arms and ammunition, provisions, pioneers' tools and wagons, the siege-train for use in England, mules to draw the great pieces, even rope-soled sandals for the muleteers had been attended to. On 25 April the voyage was dedicated and the royal standard was consecrated at Lisbon Cathedral; however, it was not until the second week in May that the first ships began dropping down to the mouth of the Tagus, and adverse winds prevented them from sailing until the end of the month.

For spectators ashore the departure was an unparalleled spectacle. It took two days for the 150 vessels, large and small, bright with paint and multicoloured pennants and ensigns bearing the devices of the squadrons to which they were attached, to work their way past the southern headland; the more sluggish were held off the shore only by tow ropes from small craft. Ballooning sails displayed the red cross of crusade. In his orders, Medina-Sidonia had stressed that the object of the enterprise was to regain countries oppressed by enemies of the True Faith, and he

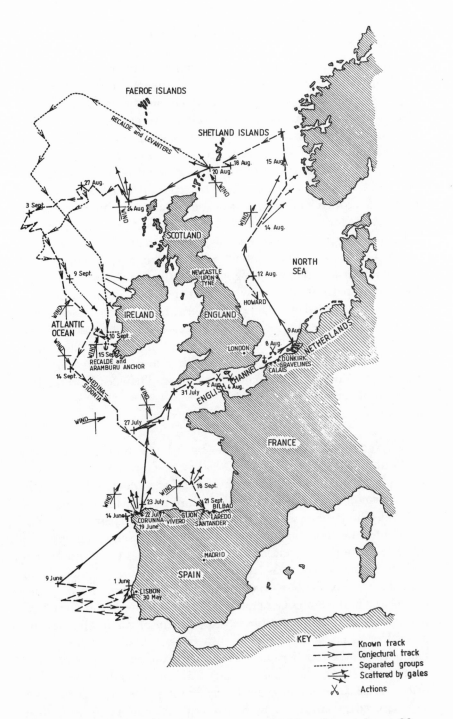

Map 2   Track chart of the Spanish armada, May–September 1588

had enjoined each man to be confessed and absolved before sailing, and to take special care on the voyage not 'to blaspheme or deny Our Lord, our Lady or the Saints, on pain of very severe punishment to be inflicted at our discretion'.[23] Nearly 200 friars sailed with the fleet.

Their early intercession did not augur well for the miracle anticipated in battle. The winds held in the north, and the mass of sluggish vessels was forced ever further south and west. Casked drinking water turned green; salt pork and fish rotted and stank so much they were thrown overboard. From 9 June a few days of south-westerly weather wafted the expedition as far north as Finisterre, then head winds set in again, and on the 19th Medina-Sidonia was forced by shortage of drinkable water and the rotting provisions to put in to Corunna. A large part of the fleet waiting to follow him in was caught by a southerly gale and scattered in Biscay. His pessimism, somewhat tempered in Lisbon by activity, returned, augmented by what he had seen of his fleet's often lamentable sailing performance. He wrote to Philip reiterating all his doubts, and advised 'making some honourable terms with the enemy' rather than continuing with the plan. Philip enjoined him to do his duty 'since you see that, pressed as I am by financial and other difficulties, I am resolute to overcome them with God's aid'.[24]

IN THE NETHERLANDS, meanwhile, the English intervention had proved a near disaster. Elizabeth's general, the Earl of Leicester, had become a willing focus for groups in the northern provinces who sought a monarchical form of government from the centre to curb the hegemony of Holland, whose ruling class of merchants (known as regents) had established a federal republic governed by and for themselves – thus in the interests of trade. The tensions between Leicester, a grand noble who disdained the regents as arriviste tradesmen, and Johan van Oldenbarneveldt, the 'Advocate' or principal spokesman for the States of Holland in the States General, were not conducive to the war effort, particularly as Holland contributed 64 per cent of the funding for the infant United Provinces.[25] The strains were exacerbated by the behaviour of the English soldiery. Confined in garrison duty, ill-fed and in too many cases unpaid, they took out their frustrations on the civilian populace and became as unpopular as the Spanish. The crowning calamities occured in January 1587, when Catholic officers Leicester had appointed to command two of the most important fortifications on the defensive line of the IJssel delivered them to the Spaniards. Dutch hatred of the English rose to new heights.

Parma was unable fully to exploit this, or the conditions of near civil war Leicester had fomented, because of the preparations Philip had ordered him to make for Medina-Sidonia's arrival in the English Channel. Instead of pressing in on the north, he had had to concentrate his forces, ammunition and supplies on the south and devote his energies to the construction and requisition of sufficient barges and small craft to transport some 30,000 troops, horses and guns to England. Since the Sea Beggars controlled the mouth of the Schelde, he had also had miles of canals excavated or enlarged to transfer vessels and supplies from Antwerp, Ghent and Bruges to the Flanders ports of Sluis, Nieuwpoort and Dunkirk.

His prodigious activity had not escaped notice. The Sea Beggars kept close inshore watch on these ports, and an English squadron under Lord Henry Seymour, composed of thirteen of Elizabeth's smaller warships and some twenty-three armed coasters, patrolled the narrows between Dover and Calais against a sudden invasion attempt. Leicester had returned home at the end of 1587, and Elizabeth, aware of the imminent approach of the armada, had instructed his successor to co-operate fully with the States of Holland and William of Orange's seventeen-year-old son, Mauritz, whom both Holland and Zeeland, attempting to curb Leicester, had elected as their stadtholder.

The main English fleet, under Elizabeth's Lord Admiral, Lord Howard of Effingham, lay at Plymouth. Like Medina-Sidonia, Howard had been appointed for political, administrative and personal reasons rather than for experience in sea fighting or command of fleets. A tall, athletic figure, who took pride in his prowess at sports and riding in the lists, he had a cautious, non-speculative and very practical intelligence and was completely reliable – as one contemporary put it, 'such a one as the Queen knew to be a fit instrument for her service'.[26]

Unlike Medina-Sidonia, he was enthusiastic about his command. After a minute inspection of every ship that spring of 1588, he had written to Burghley, 'I protest before God and as my soul shall answer for it, that I think there were never in any place in the world worthier ships that these are ... And as few as we are, if the King of Spain's forces be not hundreds, we will make sport with them.'[27] This was not by any means his first tribute to John Hawkins's navy. He described his flagship, *Ark Royal*, as 'the odd ship in the world for all conditions'; however far off they sighted a sail, 'we fetch them and speak with them'[28] – a comment that illustrates not only the speed and windward ability of the *Ark*, but also the almost complete absence of fleet signals at this time. About the officers and men of his fleet he was consistently warm: 'I think there was never a more willing company to venture their lives in Her Majesty's service than be here.'[29]

He had appointed Francis Drake as vice admiral. Drake, in the *Revenge*, had been at Plymouth with a small squadron since early spring, vainly importuning Elizabeth to allow him another pre-emptive strike at the Spanish on their own coast. When Howard arrived with the main body of the fleet in June, Drake, supported by all the senior command-ers – John Hawkins in the *Victory*, Martin Frobisher in the *Triumph*, and others – had given the same urgent advice that the best place to seek out and beat the enemy was on the Spanish coast. Howard was fully per-suaded, but had to wait for victualling ships to reach him from the Thames and could not sail until 15 July. Then he spread the fleet in three squadrons in the western approaches to the Channel, betweeen Ushant and the Scilly Isles off Cornwall, and as the wind went round to the north he led them down towards the Spanish coast. In Biscay another wind change forced him back; he returned to Plymouth.

By this time Medina-Sidonia had managed to gather and provision his scattered squadrons in Corunna. He had sailed from there on 22 July, and the same winds that prevented Howard from reaching him blew the armada north towards the planned landfall, Lizard Point, the southern-most cape of Cornwall. Sighting the cape from his flagship, *San Martin*, at four in the afternoon of the 28th, Medina-Sidonia had three guns fired and a banner flown at the masthead showing a crucifix flanked by Mary, mother of Christ, and Mary Magdalene; ordering the sails be taken in, he then lay to, to await stragglers.

He had no recent news from Parma, and at a council of war with his chief naval adviser and squadronal and army commanders aboard the flagship that evening or the following morning – no minutes have sur-vived – it was decided to deviate from Philip's instructions to sail straight up-Channel, and instead to anchor off the Isle of Wight until commu-nication with Parma could be established. He expressed the decision in a letter to Philip:

> As all along the coast of Flanders there is no harbour or shelter for our ships,
> if I were to go from the Isle of Wight thither with the Armada our vessels

might be driven on to the shoals, where they would certainly be lost. In order to avoid so obvious a peril I have decided to stay off the Isle of Wight until I learn what the Duke is doing.[30]

In the early-morning mists of 29 July one of Howard's scouts off the Scilly Isles sighted a detachment of the Spanish fleet he estimated as fifty ships. The wind was in the west, and he ran back to Plymouth under all sail, arriving some time that afternoon or early evening to find Drake playing bowls on the Hoe – the green overlooking Plymouth Sound – so legend has it. 'Time to finish the game and beat the Spaniards after!' Drake is said to have responded. In a symbolic sense it may be true: the line catches the swagger of this supremely confident, and by all accounts boastful, self-made fighting sailor. In a literal sense it is almost certainly untrue, for there is no contemporary record. Above all, there *wasn't* time. While many English ships were anchored in the Sound, others were in the sleeve known as the Catwater, with the wind blowing in; others were alongside taking in stores, others on the mud for scraping or repairs. All had to be made ready for sea and either towed or laboriously warped out by laying anchors ahead and heaving round on the capstans. For it had to be assumed that nothing would suit the Spaniards better than to find the English fleet bottled up inside, unable to manoeuvre or to dictate a stand-off battle.

While Howard and his captains worked feverishly to get to sea, beacons were lit along chains established on every hill and rise on the south coast and through the inland shires to London and northward, carrying warning of invasion. Church bells rang. Yeomen and farmers, servants and labourers forming the home-defence militias known as trained bands, who had spent evenings drilling with musket, harquebus, pike or bill, collected their arms and made for muster points in town squares or on village greens. It was a time of quickened rumour. Printed copies of Media-Sidonia's final fleet list in Lisbon, which showed the numbers of soldiers, sailors, guns and powder in each ship, had been circulating for some time, often with additional fictional inventories of instruments of torture carried in the holds. Leading English Catholics had been rounded up and confined. The hunt for spies and subversives had been intensified by offering informers half the property of those they denounced.

The English ships were still working out of the Sound the following morning, 30 July, while Medina-Sidonia, having collected his fleet – all but one great ship and four galleys attached for inshore work, which had been unable to weather Biscay – sailed slowly eastward through rain towards them. The leading English caught a glimpse of the Spanish sails through a brief break in the weather early that afternoon, but were not themselves sighted by the Spanish until dusk. That night Medina-Sidonia sent a dispatch vessel through the fleet with instructions to form battle order at dawn. He was roused at about two in the morning with a report that the enemy was in sight; a half-moon glinted through a break in the clouds, lighting groups of spectral sails far off in the south and south-west. The English had worked around them to seaward and gained the windward position, or 'weather gage', thus the ability to dictate when and where the action should begin and at what range. Unless the wind changed suddenly, there would be no chance for Medina-Sidonia to close them.

It is impossible to make more than an estimate of the strengths of the two fleets about to meet; armaments have to be extrapolated from incomplete lists, ship types and sizes from equally inconclusive evidence, buttressed by the findings from wrecks. The chief characteristics of both sides are, however, clear.

In specialized fighting ships, Medina-Sidonia had seven Portuguese royal galleons of from 750 to over 1,000 tons and two of 350 tons, seven Spanish galleons of 530 tons built to guard the Indies trade, two of 750 tons and one requisitioned galleon of 960 tons – thus nineteen warships, together with four galleasses of perhaps 500 tons carrying heavy guns. Against this Howard had five royal warships of some 800–1,000 tons, seven of 400–600 tons and three of 300–400 tons – fifteen in all, which mounted a useful broadside.

The chief disparity in the fleets was in armed merchantmen. Medina-Sidonia had sixty, many of great size, built up with castles at bow and stern and crowded with soldiers; Howard had perhaps four of any size and some twenty others no larger than the auxiliaries which brought the Spanish fleet strength up to 151 vessels of all descriptions.

The only advantages the English enjoyed – besides the nimbleness of their warships – were in long guns and expert gunners. It is probable that Howard's fleet mounted in the region of 330 of the long culverin type, against 172 in the Spanish fleet; in full culverins throwing a 16 lb ball or over the English advantage was of the order of 130 to 16, and in all types of heavy gun throwing balls of 15 lb or over about 185 to 120.[31] However, the quantities of powder itemized ship by ship in Medina-Sidonia's last muster list at Lisbon suggest that the Spanish heavy guns were distributed among forty-two warships and large merchantmen. Howard's effective pieces were mounted in fewer than twenty first-line ships. It is probable, therefore, that ship for ship that English had an advantage of over two to one in long guns and three to one in effective weight of shot.

As the commanders on both sides had long known, the opposing fleets were designed for quite different modes of fighting: the Spanish for a close-range mêlée in the galley-warfare tradition, grappling, boarding and a soldiers' battle aboard; the English for a stand-off artillery duel. But, while it is evident that if the English had allowed themselves to be drawn into a close encounter their fewer ships would have been overwhelmed by the soldiery massed on board every sizeable Spaniard, it is not evident how they could defeat or even halt the progress of the Spanish force. Given the inaccuracy and slow rate of fire of most guns, and the difficulty of laying them to achieve the correct range from a swaying, heeling deck, they would be fortunate to inflict serious damage on the enemy hulls.

The point was demonstrated at the first engagement on the morning of 31 July. The Spanish fleet drew up in what all contemporary descriptions and diagrams show to have been a crescent-moon formation with the horns towards the west, thus towards the English. It was an order taken directly from galley warfare, where fleets usually formed in three divisions, each in line abreast, the commander-in-chief in the centre of the centre division, the two wing divisions being either advanced in echelon – as here – or retarded to counter an enemy flank attack, in either case forming a crescent shape with support divisions behind to reinforce where required. From an order of battle sent to the Grand Duke of Tuscany by his ambassador in Lisbon, most accounts have assumed that Medina-Sidonia's divisions were each composed of two regional squadrons, with the main fighting strength – the squadrons of galleons of Portugal and Castile – forming the centre division.[32] A far more likely battle order has recently been unearthed, showing the regional squadrons – in which the fleet sailed – thoroughly mixed and the first-line fighting ships distributed among them, with particularly strong vessels at the ends of the wing divisions.[33]

This order provides for a centre division called the main battle (*batalla*) of thirty vessels (including sizeable store ships), with the fleet flagship, the 1,000-ton *San Martin*, in the centre, flanked by seven other first-line galleons and preceded by the four galleasses. These in turn are preceded by a 'vanguard' of four ships led by Alonso de Leyva in the 820-ton *Rata Santa Maria Coronada*. De Leyva was designated to command the 6,000 troops who would join Parma's army, and had been secretly nominated by Philip to succeed to the command of the armada should anything befall Medina-Sidonia. The right-hand division, or right horn (*cuerno*), was nineteen strong, including five rather small store ships, with the fleet vice admiral, Juan Martínez de Recalde, in the 1,000-ton Portuguese galleon *San Juan* at the outer end, supported by the 750-ton Portuguese galleon *San Mateo*, although it appears that she was exchanged for the great 1,160-ton converted merchantman *Gran Grin* from the centre division, at least for the first action. The left horn had twenty vessels (again including store ships), with the 790-ton Portuguese galleon *San Marcos* at the outer end, supported by a huge 1,300-ton Venetian armed merchantman, *Regazona*. These three divisions containing eighty ships spread in line abreast would have stretched at least eight miles and probably more; astern of each division was a 'relief' (*socorro*) of six to eight ships, together with dispatch vessels and other small craft.

The sheer mass of vessels and their good order inspired awe in the English. A contemporary chronicler wrote of the 'lofty, turret-like castles' of the enemy, who were 'sailing very slowly with full sails, the wind being as it were overrid with carrying them, and the ocean groaning under their weight'.[34] The wind was still in the west-south-west and light, the Spanish on the starboard tack, thus heading southerly towards mid-Channel; Howard was well to windward. He took some time gathering his fleet, then at about nine o'clock he led down towards the centre of the enemy crescent, where Philip's royal standard flew from the foretop of the *San Martin*, sending his pinnace, *Disdain*, ahead to give the Duke 'defiance'. After she had performed this duty by firing a small gun (accompanied by shouts of contempt and invocations to St George), Howard in the *Ark Royal* fired his bow guns, then hauled round, allowing his broadside gunners to fire as they came on target, finally luffing up to give the enemy his stern chasers. His seconds and the rest of his squadron following in rough line ahead repeated the performance after him, so keeping the Spanish centre under a continuous fire, but probably from no more than one or two ships at a time. How far distant they were when firing will never be known – perhaps 500 yards; perhaps much further, for an English volunteer with Howard described this first attack as 'more coldly done than became the value of our nation and the credit of the English navy'.[35] The Spanish

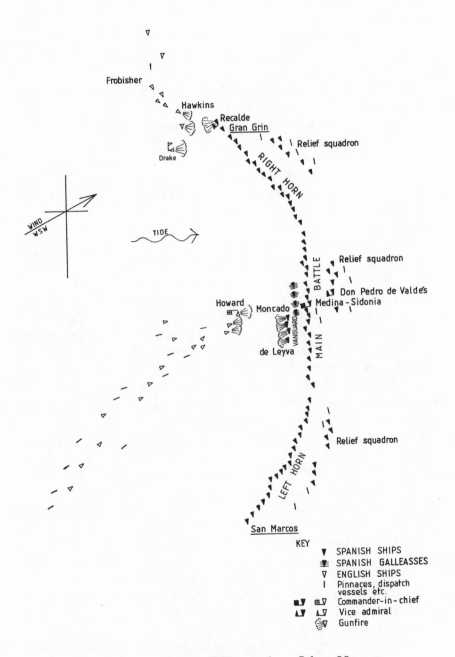

Frobisher

Hawkins

Recalde
Gran Grin

Drake

Relief squadron

RIGHT HORN

WIND
WSW

TIDE

BATTLE

Relief squadron

Don Pedro de Valdés
Medina-Sidonia

Howard

Moncado

VANGUARD

MAIN

de Leyva

Relief squadron

LEFT HORN

San Marcos

KEY

▼ SPANISH SHIPS
≢ SPANISH GALLEASSES
▽ ENGLISH SHIPS
| Pinnaces, dispatch
vessels etc.
Commander-in-chief
Vice admiral
Gunfire

Battle diagram 1 . Action off Plymouth, 31 July 1588, 9.30 a.m.

returned fire, but the distance was so great that little damage was done on either side.

Meanwhile Drake, Hawkins, Frobisher and ships attached to them bore down on the vice admiral, Recalde, in the *San Juan* at the extreme tip of the northern horn, again following one another into the attack, firing the bow pieces, rounding up to fire the broadside, then the stern chasers, filling away, and tacking to come in again with the other broadside after the others had done, so keeping up a continuous group fire, although each ship might not fire her guns more than once in an hour or so.[36] Recalde, being to leeward, could do little after discharging a broadside but listen to their shot whine through his rigging as his guns' crews went through the slow process of hauling in their pieces, swabbing the bores and worming out unburnt powder, recharging, hauling them out throught the ports, laying and aiming.

The *San Juan* was supported by the towering *Gran Grin*, but a gap opened up between these two and the rest of the division, who continued on the southerly course of the fleet without shortening sail. Seeing this, Medina-Sidonia put about and took the fleet northward to their support. By the time the centre reached him, about midday, Recalde's flagship had suffered fifteen dead and many more wounded from flying splinters, and was so cut up aloft she was crippled. Don Pedro de Valdés, leading the centre relief division in the 1,150-ton converted merchantman *Neustra Señora del Rosario*, attempted to take Recalde's place on the exposed wing, but the wind was freshening, the sea rising, and he fell aboard a consort, carrying away his bowsprit, spritsail and foreyard. Thus crippled, he drove down on another of his division and suffered further damage. Apprised of the multiple collisions, Medina-Sidonia took in his foresail and loosed his sheets as a signal to the fleet to lie to, so allowing the damaged vessels to drift down in its lee to make repairs.

The fight, which had started just to the west of Plymouth, outside the Eddystone Rocks, had been taken easterly by tide and wind, opening a view of the Sound and allowing the people of Plymouth, who were crowding the front and all vantage points, to witness an action unprecedented in English annals: sails stretched to the horizon; clouds of gun smoke rose from separated groups lit by the summer sun; gunfire reverberated like peals of distant thunder across the intervening white-flecked sea and into legend.

Spanish accounts stress the rapidity of the English fire and the speed and manoeuvrability of the English ships; Medina-Sidonia reported 'their ships being very nimble and of such good steerage, they did with them whatsoever they desired'.[37] The English were equally impressed by the strength of the Spanish and the order maintained. Howard wrote a hurried note to one of the Queen's ministers that evening: 'we made some of them bear room [retire downwind] to stop their leaks notwithstanding we durst not adventure to put in among them, their fleet being so strong'.[38] In view of the high castles of the Spanish ships, which caught the wind, the baggy shape of the flax sails and the fact that, like all large vessels of the time, they were steered not with a wheel but with purchases rove from the end of the tiller to the side timbers, or with a lever known as a whipstaff attached to the end of the tiller and extending up to the next deck, where the helmsman stood taking orders from an officer on the half-deck above, the seamanship displayed in preserving formation and avoiding collision was little short of miraculous.

In the afternoon, Medina-Sidonia attempted to work up towards Howard, to entice him to close action, but the more weatherly English ships easily held their advantage. At some time gunpowder in the stern of the *San Salvador* in the left wing division ignited, blowing off part of the vessel's aftercastle and killing or burning scores of soldiers massed there, setting off loaded guns, wrecking the rudder head and tiller, and starting fires about the decks. Apparently the master gunner – a German, like many gunners employed in the Spanish fleet – had been rebuked by the captain for poor shooting; this had so incensed him he had tossed a lighted match into a powder barrel.[39]

Medina-Sidonia put about to go to the aid of the crippled ship, followed by the rest of the fleet. As Pedro de Valdés conformed to the movement, his already weakened foremast broke near the deck and, in falling, carried away the main yard. Instructing a galleass to take the *San Salvador* in tow, Medina-Sidonia bore away with two other galleasses to the aid of Don Pedro's now unmanageable vessel. Wind and sea had by this time risen to such an extent that towing hawsers could not be put aboard, and as the evening closed in the Duke accepted the counsel of his chief naval adviser, Diego Flores de Valdés, that the whole expedition might be hazarded and perhaps lost if the flagship became encumbered with the *Rosario*, for the English were hovering to windward and their own ships were beginning to straggle downwind. He had a gun fired and bore away to gather his squadrons together, leaving a galleass and several other vessels to attend Don Pedro. As he led away up-Channel, the ships' companies gathered for evening prayers; with sunset, voices rose in the Ave Maria.

At a council held that afternoon aboard the *Ark Royal* it had been agreed that the only possible strategy against such a mighty force was to follow and harry to prevent the Spaniards anchoring, and if they attempted a landing to use the smaller ships to cut out the boats carrying the troops ashore: as Howard expressed it in a letter, 'We mean so to course the enemy as that they shall have no leisure to land.'[40] Drake was appointed to lead the fleet that night. Instead he followed the crippled *Rosario* trailing astern of the Spanish fleet, coming up with her at first light and demanding she yield: 'I am Francis Drake, and my matches are burning!' Don Pedro, raging at being abandoned by Medina-Sidonia, and honoured to submit to such a figure as Drake, soon agreed terms and, with his officers and gentlemen adventurers, came aboard the *Revenge* to proffer his sword.

The *San Salvador* was also trailing; later that morning Medina-Sidonia ordered the crew and attending vessels to abandon her. She too was taken and, like the *Rosario*, sent in to Weymouth with a prize crew.

Realizing the English intended following and harassing rather than risking a general engagement, Medina-Sidonia now formed his two wing divisions into a single rearguard, reinforced with three fighting galleons from his main battle and three of the four galleasses, and placed de Leyva in command – since the damage to Recalde's *San Juan* was not fully repaired. And, not satisfied with the conduct of some of his ships in the previous day's skirmishes, he sent regimental sergeant majors through the fleet with written orders empowering them to hang any captain who strayed from his new station. That afternoon he sent a dispatch vessel to Parma with a letter beseeching him for news of his preparations and asking for pilots for the Flanders coast. This was his second request for information since departing from Corunna; he still knew nothing of where or how Parma intended joining hands with him.

The winds of the previous day had dropped to the lightest of airs. The two fleets drifted slowly up the Channel, only some five miles separating them, and reached Portland Bill that night, where what breeze there was died completely. Next morning, 2 August, the wind sprang up from the north-east, giving Medina-Sidonia the weather gage for the first time. He bore down on the English, but Howard slipped away southward. One of the very few English ships retaining high castles, Martin Frobisher's great *Triumph*, which was holding the inshore station together with a sizeable merchantman and four smaller vessels, became separated astern and to windward of the English main body during this withdrawal, and Medina-Sidonia instructed his galleasses to use oars and sails to close the group, altering to starboard himself after them. The wind, which seems to have died away or veered, freshened from the south-east during this period in the late morning, then went round further to the south and south-westward, giving Howard back the weather gage. He led north to relieve Frobisher, whose broadsides had in the meantime smashed the galleasses' oars and forced them to keep their distance.

During this northerly run Howard sent a pinnace through the fleet with instructions to the captains 'to go within musket shot of the enemy before they should discharge any one piece of ordnance'.[41] This was a historic order: the first example of what was to become the standard in all English and British fighting instructions in the age of sail – to bear down until so close they could not miss their target.

The first ship to receive such closer attention was again Recalde's *San Juan* at the southern, now windward, end of whatever formation the Spanish had been able to maintain; again it appears to have been Drake and a group with him who led the attack. Medina-Sidonia went about and was steering to Recalde's relief as close to the wind as he could when Howard bore down towards him in the *Ark Royal*. The Duke lowered his topsails, inviting the English to close. Instead Howard, followed by seven consorts, including John Hawkins in the *Victory*, came to what was described by the English as 'half musket shot' – but was probably not inside 150 yards – fired, and filled away one after another to make room for the next. The *San Martin*, returning fire, withstood the concentrated fire for one and a half hours before supporting galleons could work upwind to her relief, during which time, by English account, 'the great ordnance came so thick that a man would have judged it to be a hot skirmish of small shot'.[42] Yet the damage was inconsiderable on both sides. The *San Martin*'s hull was holed and her mainstays were parted, but there was nothing the carpenters and crew could not make good, and her casualties were light. All the Spanish ships together lost only fifty killed that day. English casualties are not known but were almost certainly far fewer; all accounts agree that the English gunners were more expert and fired three times to the Spanish once.

Towards evening the English, exhausted and wishing to preserve their powder, hauled off. Medina-Sidonia re-formed his fleet and, leading

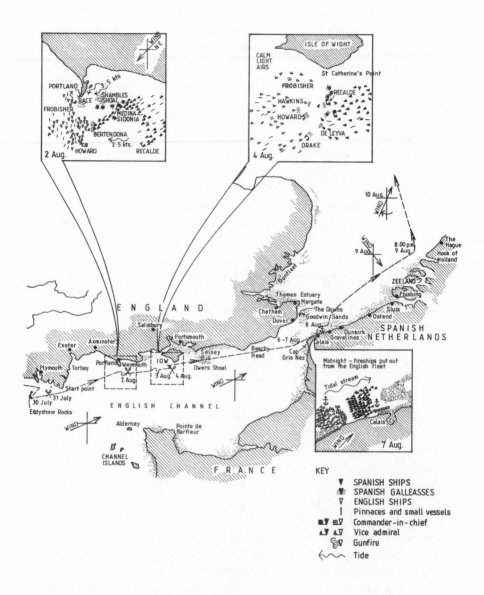

Battle diagram 2 The armada campaign, 30 July to 9 August 1588

away downwind, wrote to the chief of the squadron of galleasses, Hugo de Moncada, 'The important thing for us is to proceed on our voyage, for these people [English] do not mean fighting, but only to delay our progress.'[43] He would reinforce the rearguard with the best ships in the fleet, he went on, and would divide its command – one half under Recalde, the other under de Levya. He instructed Moncada to attach his own and two other galleasses to Recalde, and send one to him in the van. Whether he had given up his intention of anchoring off the Isle of Wight is not clear from the note, although it might be read into his words about the importance of proceeding with the voyage.

The wind continued from the west, and by dawn next day he was some distance south of the Isle of Wight. Recalde and his three galleasses at the northern tip and rearmost point of the rearguard skirmished with a group of English ships, then the wind died and both fleets lay rolling gently, sails flapping against the masts. Howard called another council aboard the *Ark Royal*, as a result of which the previous informal groupings were formalized into four squadrons under Howard, Drake, Hawkins and Frobisher. And, since it was feared the enemy might attempt a landing on the Isle of Wight, Howard instructed each to select six merchantmen to 'set upon the Spanish fleet in sundry places' that night, to keep them on edge and 'waking'.

This proved impossible because of the calm, but the following morning, 4 August, still south of the Isle of Wight, two large Spanish vessels were seen out of station astern of their main body. It has been suggested in several recent studies this was a bait offered the English to tempt them to close engagement. In the light airs stirring that early morning this would have been an unlikely and risky device. John Hawkins, Howard and his kinsman Lord Thomas Howard in the *Golden Lion*, and no doubt others, soon had longboats in the water towing their ships towards the stragglers. From the Spanish side Recalde and de Leyva had galleasses and boats tow them to the rescue and succeeded in preventing the English from capturing the vessels. Meanwhile the wind came up from the south, permitting another short action like that off Portland, during which the *San Martin* again took the force of Howard's squadron and on the northern wing Frobisher's *Triumph* again looked as if she would be trapped. Medina-Sidonia felt his moment had arrived at last; once they had boarded the great ship, the English must close to rescue her.[44] But the wind rose and Frobisher drew away safely. 'She got out so swiftly', one Spaniard wrote, 'that the galleon *San Juan* and another fast ship – the speediest vessels in the armada – seemed in comparison with her to be standing still.'[45]

Despite an enormous amount of shot thrown by both sides, again no serious damage resulted. The Spanish suffered fifty killed, seventy wounded, bringing their casualty lists to over 400. Nevertheless, it was probably an important action in denying Medina-Sidonia an anchorage to the east of the Isle of Wight or in Spithead, had he still intended it. Difficult enough at the best of times to work in with so large and heterogenous a fleet, it would have been fraught with hazard to attempt it under fire. As it was, when the English hauled off at about eleven, Medina-Sidonia fired a gun to collect his ships and continued up-Channel towards Flanders. That afternoon he sent another urgent letter to Parma by dispatch vessel:

> the enemy has resolutely avoided coming to close quarters with our ships although I have tried my hardest to make him do so. I have given him so many opportunities that sometimes some of our vessels have been in the very midst of the enemy's fleet to induce one of his ships to grapple and begin the fight; but all to no purpose as his ships are light, and mine are very heavy.[46]

He asked Parma to send him without delay gunpowder and shot of various sizes which he listed, and asked him to make ready to put out with his army at once to meet him – 'because, by God's grace, if the wind serves, I expect to be on the Flemish coast soon'.

While the Spaniards' morale must have been sapped by their inability to damage or close with the English, whose ships they described as 'responsive as well-trained horses', or to shake them from their tail, Howard was well pleased with his captains. The following forenoon, as the wind again died away, he called six of those who had been foremost in the actions to the *Ark Royal* and knighted them on the quarterdeck. Among those who knelt beneath the brailed canvas in sight of the enemy to be touched on the shoulder with his sword were Hawkins and Frobisher.

By contrast Medina-Sidonia, increasingly anxious about the lack of any reply from Parma, sent off yet another dispatch boat to Flanders, repeating his request for powder and shot and asking for forty 'flyboats' light and swift enough to catch the enemy and force them to fight.

That evening the wind got up from the south-west and he bore away easterly for the Strait of Dover. His English shadows followed in four squadrons. The wind freshened during the night, and next morning, 6 August, blew in with cloud and rain, through which the coast of France was sighted at about ten. Medina-Sidonia steered north and rounded Cap Gris Nez in the early afternoon. He and his naval and military advisers were anxious to continue to Flanders to join Parma, but his pilots persuaded him to anchor just short of Calais roads. Howard followed, dropping anchor some two miles west of his rearguard, 'within culverin shot'. There he was joined by Lord Henry Seymour with his light but fresh squadron from Dover.

Medina-Sidona sent another, yet more anxious, message to Parma:

to free myself from doubt as to whether any of my messengers have reached you safely, I am now dispatching this flyboat with the intelligence that I am now at anchor here, two leagues from Calais, with all the armada, the enemy's fleet on my flank, and able to bombard me, whilst I am not in a position to do him much harm. I . . . beseech you, if you cannot at once bring out all your fleet, to send me the 40 or 50 flyboats I asked for yesterday.[47]

Here was the insoluble dilemma at the heart of the plan for the Enterprise of England. For Parma could no more come out from the shallows of the Flemish coast than Medina-Sidonia could put in to join him. Parma's few light warships were blockaded in the Schelde by the Sea Beggars in Flushing; the hundreds of canal barges and small river and coastal craft he had assembled at Sluis, Nieuwpoort and Dunkirk for the transport of his army were under blockade from other Sea Beggar craft, usually lying over the horizon to entice him out, when, as he knew, they would fall upon and destroy him. Parma had warned Philip of this from the beginning, and had reiterated his anxiety as late as 22 June.[48] Philip had made a marginal note on this letter, 'God grant that no embarrassment may come from this', but he had not told Medina-Sidonia of Parma's apprehensions. Probably he expected his two chief commanders to liaise. They had attempted to, but Medina-Sidonia's first message after putting out from Corunna had not reached Parma until 2 August, and Parma's reply did not find him until 7 August, the day after he anchored off Calais.

Philip no doubt expected his armada to defeat the English fleet in the Channel. In traditional galley warfare it was numbers of soldiers that counted, and Medina-Sidonia had a decisive advantage there. Philip might indeed have expected to bring Elizabeth to terms without invasion, simply by the presence of his great fleet off her coast. This view could be supported by sealed instruction he gave Medina-Sidonia to be delivered to Parma when 'he has either landed in Britain, or exhibits uncertainty of being able to do so'.[49] These amounted to a reserve position if it did not appear the issue could be settled by force of arms. Parma was then to avail himself of the prestige of the armada and open negotiations with Elizabeth to gain three main points: freedom for English Catholics to worship and for Catholic exiles to return; the return of the Netherlands fortresses held by England, especially Flushing; and an indemnity for the injuries the English had caused Spanish subjects. But this last point was more in the nature of a lever to gain the other two.

Such an outcome may have been Philip's real aim. He could not have wanted to annex England militarily, since this would have opened another costly occupation struggle and brought France in against him. He might, however, neutralize Elizabeth – and, most importantly, be seen by his bankers to do so – by supporting her internal Catholic enemies, even provoking civil war. If such was his aim then the Enterprise of England was a huge deception and Parma's barges and troops were intended for Zeeland – as indeed he declared – not England. Many informed Englishmen believed so, including Lord Henry Seymour, who had been appointed to watch them. He was convinced Parma's real target was Walcheren Island at the mouth of the Schelde.[50] This is supported by Parma's response to messages from Medina-Sidonia and Philip apprising him of the armada's approach. Instead of going personally to the ports to supervise preparations for embarkation, as he surely would have done if serious about joining forces with Medina-Sidonia, he remained at his headquarters in Bruges, and the barges and other craft were not armed, provisioned or made ready to sail.[51]

Whatever Philip's and Parma's true aims, they had been frustrated by Howard's strategy of 'coursing' the armada up-Channel, allowing Medina-Sidonia neither the chance of victory nor even a breathing space to secure an anchorage. So he had been forced into this position off Calais where he could not remain long and Parma could never join him.

THE NEXT MORNING, 7 August, after a council aboard the *Ark Royal*, eight of the small vessels with the English fleet were chosen for use as fireships and were filled with combustible materials – old hemp, barrels of tar and pitch, fuel for the galley fires – and their guns were charged so that the heat of the flames would set them off. Medina-Sidonia's advisers suspected the English might try something of the sort; the captains were ordered to have boats manned and ready with grapnels to tow fireships away, and a pinnace was stationed to windward of the *San Martin* for the same purpose.

The moon had been full the night before; the tides were strong, and the wind had freshened from the west. Soon after midnight, when the tide was running at over two and a half knots towards the Spanish fleet, the eight small ships with fore and mainsails set began began their run in line abreast, each with one man aboard to steer, light the fires, and at a suitable time lash the helm, jump into a dinghy, and cast off to row back. The Spanish, seeing them bearing down burning noisily, leaped to the conclusion they were 'infernal machines' and Medina-Sidonia gave the order to slip cables. Tillers were hauled over to incline the bows to the port tack; seamen scurried up shrouds and along yards to loose the canvas; anchor cables were slipped or hacked through with axes. The tethered ranks of vessels dissolved amid shouting and confusion in a manoeuvring free-for-all in the darkness; yet only one serious accident was recorded: Hugo de Moncada's galleass, *San Lorenzo*, in trying to avoid collision with another galleass and de Leyva's flagship, fell across the cable of one of the Levant squadron which had not yet slipped and had her rudder torn off as she was pulled round by the tide. The other vessels got away without serious damage and headed north for the open sea as the fireships drove harmlessly by.

As soon as the fireships had passed, Medina-Sidonia fired a gun and tacked as a signal to the fleet to return, but only Recalde, two galleasses and a few others were with him when he dropped anchor somewhat further out and downwind of the former anchorage. He intended to work back in daylight with the change of tide to recover his previous position and anchors, which had been buoyed, but the dawn revealed his fleet so dispersed downwind that he weighed and stood out north-eastward to gather them. This was the first time the armada had lost its cohesion, and Howard weighed and sailed out with him at dawn on a freshening westerly wind.

Instead of leading the attack, however, Howard turned in towards Calais, where the rudderless flag galleass, *San Lorenzo*, had run aground while attempting to row into the harbour. He was followed by Seymour

and vessels from both their squadrons. It seems an astonishing abberra-
tion – less explicable even than Drake's diversion to capture the *Rosario*
while leading the fleet on the first night.

It was left to Drake to take the lead against the Spanish fleet. By the
time he caught up it was about seven o'clock. Medina-Sidonia had succeeded in collecting a large number of ships off Gravelines, some ten
miles up the coast from Calais, and had altered north to avoid shoals
stretching down from Dunkirk, re-forming in a defensive crescent with
the *San Martin* in the usual position in the centre, supported by the
Portuguese galleon *San Marcos*. Drake bore down on him, followed by
others of his squadron, closing to what Medina-Sidonia described as
'within musket shot, or even harquebus shot'[52] – which might have been
under 150 yards – before opening fire. After Drake's squadron, Hawkins
led his ships in against the *San Martin*, whose timbers were pierced time
and again by shot, spreading splinters, wounds and death.

Off Calais, meanwhile, the smaller vessels with Howard and Seymour
had succeeded in entering men and capturing the grounded galleass, but
the governer of the port, realizing they intended refloating and towing
the vessel away as a prize, enforced his jurisdiction by having the guns of
the citadel and sea walls open fire, driving the English off. They steered
away north-easterly towards the sounds of the main battle, with nothing
to show for the diversion but some small pilferage.

It was ten o'clock – some three hours after Drake had opened the
attack – when Howard and his fresh ships reached the scene and bore
down on the *San Martin*. Seymour led his squadron against the northern
wing, where it appears Recalde in the *San Juan* was at his former station.
The battle rose to a climax, 'the English discharging their cannons mar-
vellously well', according to one Spanish soldier.[53] Another wrote, 'the
combat was very terrible . . . Our ships were quite hidden from view by
the smoke.'[54] At the storm centre the *San Martin* was pierced again and
again; three of her guns were dismounted, her decks were spread with
dead and maimed and slippery with blood, her hull so holed low down
that two divers 'had as much as they could do to stop them up with tow
and lead plates'.[55]

Somewhere on the right wing the 800-ton Portuguese galleon *San
Felipe* apparently luffed up into the wind to challenge her tormentors to
come closer. Becoming separated from her consorts, she was soon surrounded by Seymour's squadron – seventeen vessels on both sides and
astern, according to one Spanish account – which 'approached so close

the muskets and harquebusses of the galleon were brought into service . . . They did not dare, however, to come to close quarters, but kept up a hot artillery fire from a distance, disabling the rudder, breaking the foremast and killing over 200 people.'[56]

The second in command of Seymour's squadron wrote, 'Great was the spoil and harm done unto them . . . and when I was furthest off in discharging any of the pieces, I was not out of shot of their harquebus, and most times within speech of one another.'[57] The Spanish raged, calling out to the English they were cowards and Lutheran hens, and, swaying out grappling irons, dared them to close. That some ships were now sailing contemptuously close is suggested by a story from the Portuguese galleon *San Mateo*, which bore up to the assistance of the *San Felipe* and also became separated: 'One of the enemy's ships came alongside the galleon and an Englishman jumped aboard, but our men cut him to bits instantly.'[58]

Recalde in the *San Juan* and another Portuguese galleon, the *San Luis*, worked up to the relief of the two separated galleons and were joined by four armed merchantmen. The English also concentrated here, quitting the *San Martin*, according to Medina-Sidonia's account. The merchantmen were forced to bear away downwind, so damaged or confused they fell aboard each other. Medina-Sidonia, who had climbed a mast to try to gain a view over the smoke, had directed his flagship to put about to support this embattled group, but by the time he and his close consorts managed to interpose themselves the *San Felipe*, the *San Mateo* and two of the merchantmen were wallowing wrecks, their sails and rigging shot through, masts splintered, hulls holed and taking in water; the worst afflicted, the *San Felipe*, had five of her starboard guns dismounted by shot, her pumps shattered, and her upper deck destroyed.[59]

It was afternoon. The English, exhausted by unremitting toil, their heads ringing with the crash of gunfire, were running as low in gunpowder and shot as the more heavily engaged Spanish ships, and Howard broke off the action and lay to, to repair damages. These were as light compared with those they had inflicted on the enemy as their casualties were low. The captain of the *Nonpareil* in Drake's squadron wrote some days later, 'God hath mightily protected Her Majesty's forces with the least losses that ever hath been heard of, being within the compass of so great volleys of shot, both small and great. I verily believe there is not three score of men lost in Her Majesty's forces.'[60] This must be an underestimate, since the English probably lost about fifty men in the fight for the galleass off Calais. Much later, after the English fleet returned, Spanish informants in London reported the English as stating 'their loss does not exceed 300'. The Spanish lost 600 killed and 800 wounded on that day alone, according to a report from the *San Martin*, which had taken 107 direct hits on her hull, masts and sails.[61]

Apart from the disparity in damage and casualties – the result of the English having heavier long guns, more skilful gunners and more weatherly ships using the advantage of the windward position[62] – the English had won decisively in strategic terms, having forced Medina-Sidonia into the North Sea beyond Dunkirk, where his pilots, for good reason, had not wished to go. The wind had risen, and while it remained in the west he could neither join Parma nor return to Calais roads or Margate, where Philip had instructed him to anchor. Drake wrote soon after the battle, 'God hath given us so good a day in forcing the enemy to leeward as I hope in God the Prince of Parma and the Duke of Sidonia shall not shake hands this few days.'[63]

Reports reaching Medina-Sidonia from his chief fighting galleons which had borne the heat of all the actions revealed they were very low in powder and shot and the *San Felipe* and *San Mateo* were close to foundering. He sent small craft to take off most of the survivors, leaving only the military commanders with skeleton crews aboard, and, gathering the fleet, stood north-easterly under very easy sail; he had no other option. Howard followed.

That night the wind veered into the north-west, driving the *San Felipe* and *San Mateo* downwind on to shoals between Nieuwpoort and Blankenburgh. They were found next morning by the Sea Beggars, who attempted salvage, but both were so holed and strained they sank before they could be towed to Flushing. That day at least one, possibly two, large merchantmen sank from damage received. For Medina-Sidonia it was the hardest day of the campaign. His remaining fighting ships were too low in ammunition to sustain another long action; his casked provisions were rotting and his water was foul; and, in addition to the wounded from the engagements, sickness had brought down hundreds in the cramped and unhealthy conditions between decks. Moreover, his pilots warned him that if the wind remained in the north-west none of the ships could weather the shoals off Zeeland. The *San Martin* sailed with an anchor hanging below the level of the keel and a man watching the trend of the cable so that if it touched bottom it could be let go to bring the ship up before she went aground. A leadsman stood in the chains casting the sounding line, intoning the depth. By mid-morning this had dropped to six fathoms, or thirty-six feet.[64]

The English, following closely, were unaware of Spanish anxieties, perhaps because there was no danger of their own more weatherly ships sagging into the shallows. There are no references to shoal water in any English account, and Howard did not attempt to drive Medina-Sidonia towards the coast by forcing action. He was more concerned with his own shortages and the possibility of the armada turning back towards the Strait. He wrote requesting powder and shot and victuals to be sent out with all possible speed, and added a postscript: 'Their force is wonderful great and strong; and yet we pluck their feathers by little and little. I pray to God that the forces on the land [in England] be strong enough to answer so present a force.'[65] It is evident from his letters and those of Drake, Hawkins and others that the English, deceived by the outward appearance of the great ships of the enemy and the good order they still preserved, had no idea they had won a historic victory.

The final stages of the campaign were decided by the weather. That evening, 9 August, when the two fleets had reached a position perhaps thirty miles off the Hook of Holland, the wind flew round into the north-east, allowing Medina-Sidonia to put about and steer away from the land. Next morning it veered into the west-south-west, forcing him northward, and he resolved to return to Spain northabout around Scotland. Surviving horses and mules were cast overboard to save fresh water; rations were reduced to eight ounces of bread (biscuit), half a pint of wine and half a pint of water per man per day; most of the salted provisions were inedible. And, when it appeared that the English might try to force another action and some vessels failed to obey orders to shorten sail, a court martial was convened to punish their commanders and others who were said to have quit their station during the previous engagements; twenty arrests were made, several offenders were reduced to the ranks, others were condemned to the oars in the galley service, and two received the death sentence. One of these was hanged from the yardarm of a dispatch vessel and exhibited through the fleet as a terrible warning; the other gained a reprieve and later wrote one of the most remarkable memoirs of the expedition.[66]

Howard continued to follow, but two days later, about the latitude of Newcastle, he parted on a change of wind and returned to the Thames, leaving two pinnaces to shadow the fleet he had attended so assiduously since its first arrival off the Lizard. He still appeared unaware of the magnitude of his victory.

On 14 August the armada was forced to run before a south-westerly gale towards Norway, where, according to oral tradition, at least one ship was wrecked. Scattered groups of ships were collected together again on the 19th and a westerly course was set which took the main body between the Shetlands and Fair Isle north of Scotland on the 20th. From there the course was set far to the west of the rock-bound Atlantic coast of Ireland, although a group of more damaged ships with Recalde were driven north-westerly into high latitudes.

The majority with Medina-Sidonia kept well together through mainly vile weather, storms and fog, until on the night of 12 September off the south-west corner of Ireland they were headed by a fierce southerly gale and scattered. By this date, almost eight weeks after departing Corunna, the surviving men – gaunt from hunger and unaccustomed to cold, constantly damp from leaking seams in the deck planking, breathing foul gases from the ballast and the stink of excrement and vomit from the sick, who relieved themselved where they lay packed together on the lower decks – must have exhibited that apathy which is one of the first signs of scurvy, that sailors' disease which claimed more lives and ships than all naval battles together. It took its toll now as vessels steered or were driven on to the Irish west coast and impaled themselves on rocks or dragged their anchors ashore.

On 21 September stragglers from Recalde's group astern were struck by a second great gale from the west and driven in helplessly before giant seas. A few by chance found their way into sheltered anchorages; more drove on to rocks or were pounded to pieces in the shallows. Thousands of men drowned, and more – too weak to do more than crawl ashore – were slaughtered by the English or their Irish mercenaries. The danger of a Spanish landing in force to overpower the isolated garrisons with which the country was held had seemed very real that month, and the order had gone out from the Lord Deputy in Dublin to apprehend and execute all Spaniards found 'of what quality soever'. That the Spaniards might be too weak or ill to mount a threat was not, of course, anticipated.

MEDINA-SIDONIA in the *San Martin* arrived off Santander on the northern coast of Spain on 21 September, with only eleven of his once great fleet in company. Over the next few days some thirty others straggled into various northern Spanish ports, damaged, several missing masts, the surviving crews so listless many could not even come to anchor but simply drifted aground. Medina-Sidonia wrote to Philip:

> The troubles and miseries we have suffered cannot be described to Your Majesty . . . on board some of the ships that have come in there was not one drop of water to drink for a fortnight. On the flagship 180 men died of sickness . . . and all the rest of the people on the ship are ill, many of typhus and other contagious maladies. All the men of my household, to the number of 60, have either died or fallen sick.[67]

Recalde arrived in Corunna on 7 October; he had managed to steer the *San Juan* into a safe anchorage in the Blasket islands off the southwest of Ireland before the great gale which caused the loss of so many of his group. However, he was so ill he died on 23 October.

By the end of that month 65 of the original 151 vessels had arrived home. Some 27 sizeable ships had been lost on the long northabout passage, including a second galleass wrecked in northern Ulster and the Portuguese galleon *San Marcos*, which had supported Medina-Sidonia's flagship throughout the battle off Gravelines. Added to the 8 or 9 important vessels lost as a result of the fighting up-Channel and off Gravelines, total losses of sizeable ships were at least 35; in addition, the official 'missing' list included 20 of the small auxiliaries, bringing the grand total to 55, or over a third of the original fleet. Since many of the vessels that did return must have been so strained or damaged as to be of little further use, it is possible that Philip lost over half the armada. A high proportion of the losses were in all likelihood caused by simple dietary deficiency – lack of fresh food, particularly citrus fruit – combined with the unsuitability of the comparatively lightly built Mediterranean merchantmen for Atlantic weather. Of ten great ships of the Levant squadron, eight were lost, chiefly on the Irish coast.[68]

The death toll was not reported; if all the returning ships suffered the same proportion of dead and dying as the *San Martin*, it could have amounted to 18,000 or more. The full count will never be known.

Medina-Sidonia was the chief scapegoat in the eyes of the populace, and has been for many historians since, but Philip never blamed him, preferring to ascribe the disaster to divine retribution for their sins. Of course Philip himself was the chief architect of defeat. Howard and the

English commanders who 'coursed' his mighty fleet up-Channel and the Sea Beggars who blockaded Parma merely ensured his major strategic error could not be retrieved. Medina-Sidonia was probably the wrong man to lead the expedition: inexperienced, unconfident and introspective leaders do not win great battles. But under a more audacious and imperious leader it is easier to imagine even greater disaster for the enterprise. Medina-Sidonia played an impossible hand as well as anyone might have; tried in the fiercest fire, he had not been found wanting, and but for the violent storms off Ireland he would probably have brought home most of the fleet, if not the men.

3

The Downs, 1639

THE DEFEAT OF the armada in 1588 and the legend of English gallants and sea dogs tormenting Philip II on every coast has overshadowed the real winners in this conflict: the rebel United Provinces. Parma had been deflected from his campaign to subdue them by Philip's orders to prepare his army to cross the Channel. Even if this was a gigantic deception and his true target was Zeeland, he had nonetheless spent three years on a project rendered abortive by English and Beggar control of the sea.

The following year, 1589, the last of the Valois kings, Henri III, was murdered in Paris and Philip again diverted Parma, this time to intervene in France to prevent the Protestant Henri of Navarre from succeeding to the throne. And, since Elizabeth's sailors continued to torment him, and her young favourite, the Earl of Essex, sailing with Howard, repeated Drake's sack of Cadiz, he launched two more powerful armadas against England. Both were scattered by gales and never reached their destination.[1]

The rebel provinces were thus allowed time to strengthen their defences, build up their army, reopen trade with the German interior via the great rivers, and tighten their naval grip on the coastline of the southern provinces, particularly the Schelde estuary. This finally ruined Antwerp and the other south-Netherlands cities. Since falling to Parma in 1585, they had suffered an exodus of merchants, money and skilled workers; by 1589 Antwerp's population had halved, from 84,000 to 42,000. The cities of the northern provinces gained most from this huge transfer of capital and skills, particularly Leiden (which became a new focus of textile industries) and Amsterdam.[2] Investment flowed into shipping, particularly for the 'rich trades' in the Eastern and New World commodities of Portugal and Spain that had formerly come to Antwerp.

Philip II tolerated this trade with the enemy because he had little option: Spain needed a northern outlet for colonial wares, and needed the Baltic grain and naval stores only the Dutch could supply. For their part, Dutch merchants never minded with whom they traded so long as they made profits. They even invested in privateers operating from Dunkirk against their own shipping in the Channel.[3]

The effect of grafting the 'rich trades' and associated finishing, refining and manufacturing processes on to the Dutch bulk-trade monopolies with the Baltic transformed the rebel provinces in remarkably short time into Europe's leading commercial-industrial power, and Amsterdam into the motor of world commerce. By 1594 the Dutch were ready to take the offensive on the oceans. The *Compagnie van Verre* – Long-Distance Company – was founded in Amsterdam, and over the following years increasingly large fleets penetrated the Portuguese monopolies in the Indonesian spice islands and on the West African slaving coast, reaping vast profits of up to 400 per cent of outlay. The Portuguese were unable to resist. Their galleons, like those that had sailed in the armada, were sluggish and unhandy by comparison with Dutch armed East-Indiamen. An Arab observer described the nimbleness of a 60-gun Dutchman fighting a lofty Portuguese galleon in the sort of terms so many Spaniards had used to describe Elizabeth's 'race-built' warships in 1588: 'when the guns of the first half [side] have been discharged, they [the Dutch] swing the galleon over so as to fire the other half, for they have the ability of manoeuvring it for the purpose of fighting just as a horseman can wheel his horse on dry land'.[4]

By the time Philip II died, in 1598, the prosperity of the rebel provinces had been translated into armed strength on the ground. William of Orange's young son and successor as stadtholder and captain-general, Mauritz of Nassau, had been able to place campaigning on a business footing, paying his mainly foreign troops regularly, supplying them with quantities of ordnance and engineering materials, and paying at generous rates for the labour and dangers involved in siege works – a remarkable and effective innovation in warfare.[5] Clearing Spanish garrisons from the inland provinces, driving the borders of the republic east and south, his army had become the most technically advanced in Europe.[6]

The same could not be said of the navy, which consisted almost exclusively of small vessels for river and coastal blockade and defence. Naval organization had been the subject of dispute for years, and was only resolved, unsatisfactorily, in 1597 with the establishment of five local admiralties – in Amsterdam, Rotterdam, the North Quarter (Hoorn and Enkhuizen), Zeeland and Friesland – each responsible for patrolling, exacting customs dues in its own waters, and providing escorts for merchantment trading with the enemy; charges for this last service, known as 'convoy and licence' money, provided their principal source of revenue.[7]

Since each admiralty maintained its own ships, shipyards, arsenals and recruiting organization, appointed its own officers, and was governed by the politics of its own region, the result was five distinct forces within the totality of the republic's navy, each with its own flag officers and ways of doing things. It was fortunate that this weakness was offset by the wealth of material filling the warehouses of the maritime cities: timber, masts, yards, cordage and canvas, ordnance, munitions and victuals of a quality and abundance unavailable – except through trade with the enemy – to Spain, which since the failure of the armada had built up an imposing fleet of great galleons.[8]

When Philip III succeeded to the Spanish throne, he attempted to strike at the wealth underlying the military strength of the United Provinces by reversing the policy of trade with the enemy and banning Dutch ships and merchants from Spanish and Portuguese ports. This spurred the States General into building larger warships to blockade the Iberian coast. But after one attempt in 1599 this forward policy reminiscent of Hawkins's and Drake's pleas to Elizabeth was abandoned in favour of building numbers of light, handy vessels for convoy duty.[9]

The other result of Philip III's embargo – apart from adding greatly to the difficulties of supplying the Spanish navy – was to provoke even heavier Dutch investment in direct trade with the East. This led to a glut of spices and oriental wares, forcing prices down. To stabilize the markets, in 1602 the rival Dutch companies were merged into the United East India Company – in abbreviation, the VOC. Like the navy, the VOC was actually a federation of distinct chambers. These were based in Amsterdam, Rotterdam, Delft, Hoorn, Enkhuizen and the chief ports of Zeeland, each having its own stock and commercial operations, but following guidelines set by a board of seventeen directors, on which Amsterdam, with eight of the so-called *Heeren XVII*, predominated.[10]

The charter granted by the States General gave the VOC monopoly rights in the East and the Pacific as well as virtually sovereign powers to raise troops, maintain warships, build forts, install governors, make alliances and conduct war. In effect this added another (federated) arm to the state's naval forces, and warships were transferred from time to time from the admiralties to the company.

By 1607 the VOC had so undermined the Portuguese hold in the spice islands that Philip III gathered a fleet headed by ten great galleons to drive it out. The States General learned of this in time to prepare a force of twenty-six armed merchantmen under the veteran Sea Beggar Jacob van Heemskerck, who found the Spaniards still at anchor in Gibraltar Bay. The more numerous Dutch, laying themselves along both sides of the fighting galleons, overwhelmed and destroyed every one.

Two years later, in 1609, bankrupted by war in France and threatened by the States General with the creation of a West Indies Company on the lines of the VOC, Philip III acceded to a truce to run for twelve years. With regained access to Iberian markets and the suspension of Spanish and Flemish privateering against their ships, the merchants of the United Provinces enjoyed another dramatic phase of trade expansion.

WAR WITH SPAIN was resumed at the end of the twelve-year truce, in 1621. While the VOC extended its empire in the spice islands, drove the Portuguese from Ceylon, and established bases in India, the West Indies Company (WIC) formed on similar lines and granted a monopoly from West Africa to America wrested the trade in African gold and ivory from the Portuguese, and later the African slave trade, invaded Portuguese Brazil, and engrossed the expanding sugar trade. Against the Spanish the WIC was less successful, although its assault in the Caribbean resulted in 1628 in a force under Piet Hein fulfilling the dreams of generations of privateers by surprising and capturing the annual fleet carrying treasure from New Spain and Peru. The haul of silver, jewels and other commodities amounted to perhaps 15 million Dutch florins – roughly £1.5 million – enabling the company to declare a dividend of 75 per cent.[11]

The WIC expended most effort in conquering Brazil, but also took small West Indian islands – most importantly Curaçao, with the finest natural harbour in the Caribbean – establishing an entrepôt for trade with the Spanish islands and mainland colonies. In North America it founded settlements on the Hudson river, notably Nieuw Amsterdam on Manhattan island near the entrance. Of more significance for the future, the WIC offensive so occupied Spanish defences that the English and French were able to establish colonies in the West Indies and up the eastern seaboard of North America. Similarly in the East under the shelter of the VOC's assault – although at times in alliance with the Portuguese – the English and French established trading bases in India.

In Europe, meanwhile, Spain was not only defending her southern Netherlands fortresses against Mauritz's successor as stadtholder and captain-general, Frederick Henry of Nassau, but was also embroiled with the ancient territorial enemy, France, in the anarchic conflict centred in Germany known as the Thirty Years War, and French troops crossing the Rhine had barred the Spanish overland route for reinforcements to the Netherlands. In this critical situation in 1639 Philip IV of Spain made a desperate throw reminiscent of his forebears, sending an armada north with orders to beat the Dutch and French fleets if encountered in Biscay or the Channel, and then to land troops and supplies in Flanders.

In supreme command of this last Spanish armada was Don Antonio Oquendo, son of one of Medina-Sidonia's divisional commanders. His fleet, headed by 1,000-ton, 60-gun purpose-built warships but including a squadron of light and handy Flemish privateers which normally operated from Dunkirk against Dutch shipping, represented the entire remaining strength of Spain's sailing navy built up since the end of the truce. Supplemented by hired and armed merchantmen, it numbered in all fifty fighting ships and twenty store ships – or approximately half the total size of Medina-Sidonia's armada.

The 10,000 'troops' embarked were untrained men seized by a commercial 'press' for twenty-one ducats a head. The almost constant warfare over generations had bled the country. In contrast to the maritime cities and towns of the United Provinces, which had grown prodigiously since the turn of the century,[12] large tracts of Spain had been depopulated. The scenes around Corunna, where the armada gathered that summer, beggared description; officers hid themselves to avoid involvement with miserable processions of chained men followed by their distraught womenfolk.[13]

The States General had news of the preparations. One division of their fleet under Maarten Tromp, lieutenant admiral of the United

Provinces, patrolled the narrows of the English Channel; a second, smaller, squadron blockaded Dunkirk; a third cruised the North Sea on fishery protection, for, despite her worldwide net of commerce, fishing remained one of the staples of Dutch trade.

The armada was sighted on 18 September between Selsey Bill and Beachy Head, some ninety miles short of the Strait of Dover. Tromp dispatched a small ship to summon the other squadrons to the flag, and worked up westerly into the wind towards the Spaniards. Next morning, with the wind still from the north-west, Oquendo dead to windward and the sails of the squadron from Dunkirk in sight beating up from the east, Tromp bore down to join them. Uniting off Beachy Head, he formed a single line close-hauled on the starboard tack, thus heading south-westerly, instructing the captains to keep their ships so close together the enemy could not force a way between them.[14]

These orders have an important place in tactical history, since they are held to be the first example of fleet line of battle, as opposed to group formations. They were in fact the typical and obvious formation for an inferior fleet – as Tromp's was – in the inferior position downwind of the enemy; probably the earliest example is provided by the Portuguese Vasco de Gama when fighting a numerically far superior fleet mustered by the Zamorin of Calicut off the Malabar coast of India in 1501.[15] Tromp was no theoretician. He was typical of the simple fighting sailors of Holland and Zeeland who literally grew up in ships; in contrast to the grandees who commanded Spanish warships, he was an unpretentious, paternal figure, known to his fleet as *Bestevaer*, 'Dear Father'; he was also fiercely independent, stubborn to the point of bloody-mindedness, and complete master of every aspect of navigating and fighting his ships. It is interesting, therefore, that he explained to his captains the importance of the whole line acting as one, so that each ship supported her consorts – precisely the argument used by the French master tactician Vicomte de Morogues when fleet line of battle reigned supreme in the eighteenth century.

The Spanish great galleons were larger and more heavily gunned than all except Tromp's flagship, *Amelia*, and in fighting vessels the Spaniards outnumbered the two Dutch divisions by about three to one – some fifty against sixteen. In consequence Oquendo, paying no attention to order, simply led down on Tromp for a boarding-and-entering contest – as Medina-Sidonia had intended and in one fleeting instance managed against Howard. Like the English then, Tromp stood to give

Oquendo his broadside, then bore away, leaving him astern, each ship following doing the same when the Spanish flagship reached it. Tromp then came up into the wind and again lay close-hauled to receive a second charge; this time Oquendo and the squadron of Dunkirkers had so far outstripped the rest of their consorts that, instead of bearing away after giving his broadside, Tromp tacked and fired his other side, followed by the rest of his line, taking care to ease the sheets and bear away if any Spaniard approached too close. So a running battle continued downwind, the nimble Dutch preserving their distance until, approaching the shoals off the mouth of the Somme, Oquendo lay to, to repair damage and allow the rest of his straggling force to catch up.

The fleets separated that night, but Tromp found the Spaniards next day and resumed the action after nightfall, all his ships carrying a light on the poop for recognition. The battle drifted easterly with the tide, and next day off Dover Oquendo shaped course for the Flemish coast. The wind had gone round to the south, giving the Dutch the weather gage, and Tromp harassed him exactly as Howard had harassed Medina-Sidonia and, with the advantage of the wind, employing the same tactics of group attack in succession: firing one broadside, tacking, and coming in with the other. He succeeded in so damaging Spanish masts and rigging that Oquendo could not hold his course close-hauled to the southerly wind, but had to bear away and return towards the English coast; he eventually dropped anchor off Dover at the southern end of the sheltered waters inside the Goodwin Sands known as The Downs.

Tromp sailed to Calais, replenished his ships with powder and shot from his French allies, and returned, at which the Spanish cut their cables and ran north into The Downs to anchor close by a small English squadron under Sir John Pennington. Tromp followed and anchored to the south of them. Pennington dispatched officers to warn both commanders not to fight in English waters, but it was apparent he lacked the force to prevent them. That night Oquendo sent his light Dunkirkers out through the difficult northern entrance to the anchorage with some 3,000 troops and silver to pay the Flanders army, but remained inside with the bulk of his fleet. Next day Tromp blocked off the northern entrance, and thereafter Oquendo could do nothing but watch as day by day fresh ships arrived from the Dutch admiralties to swell the force locking him in.

Tromp's instructions from the States General were to attack directly a favourable opportunity presented itself, without any consideration for territorial waters or any English ships which might attempt to hinder him. By mid-October he was ready. He had 103 warships and sixteen fireships, which he formed into four divisions; one, under Vice Admiral Witte de With, was to attend to the English if they should interfere, and two smaller squadrons were to guard the flanks. Gales caused him to postpone the attack until the morning of the 21st, when, weighing at sunrise, he steered for the Spanish under a light breeze. Oquendo was alert and already under sail, and Pennington also weighed and tried vainly to interpose himself between the fleets.

The first broadsides rent the quiet morning at about 8.30; within half an hour the gun smoke was so thick it was impossible to make out friend or foe. A disordered running battle ensued, erupting with bursts of fire when the smoke cleared. Dutch fireships were set ablaze, and in the confusion several Spanish vessels ran aground; others deliberately beached themselves. Oquendo, with a group of some twenty great galleons, escaped southward into the Channel and steered south-westerly, Tromp following. Pennington, after some token long-range fire at the Dutch, anchored, allowing de With to join Tromp in pursuit of the great galleons.

That afternoon, as the tide began flowing westerly, Tromp sent fireships down, two of which tangled with the flagship of Oquendo's Portuguese squadron and set her ablaze. When it became evident she could not be saved, Oquendo took off her remaining crew, set more sail, and continued westerly down-Channel. Tromp and de With followed, harrying and engaging again at dusk, but eventually lost the Spaniards in the dark.

So ended the Battle of The Downs. It was not the annihilation often claimed, for over the next days Oquendo and some seventeen great galleons with him succeeded in working back through the Strait of Dover and reaching Dunkirk. But it was decisive. Of the Spanish ships that had been locked up in the anchorage, some forty were lost – most wrecked on the Kent coast, one on the Goodwin Sands, three sunk, four captured, the Portuguese flagship destroyed by fire, and several of those that did escape so wounded they foundered on the Flemish shoals. Many of those that reached Dunkirk were in a shattered condition; the hull of Oquendo's flagship had taken 1,700 shot.

Only one Dutch ship was lost, and estimates of casualties show as great a disparity as that between the fleets in 1588: 7,000 Spaniards lost against about 100 Dutch. This supports other evidence suggesting that, while Spain undoubtedly built up a great sailing navy after the first armada campaign, and again after the end of the twelve-year truce with the United Provinces, and while her great galleons were soundly constructed of timbers so massy they could absorb the continuous punishment handed out by Tromp's ships at The Downs, her guns and gunnery remained backward and ineffective.

The moral effect of defeat was greater than the physical. Oquendo's was the last great northern armada ever dispatched from the Spanish empire. Oquendo himself was crushed, and died soon after returning home with the remnants of his fleet. Early the following year an amphibious expedition Philip had sent to Brazil at much the same time as the northern armada suffered a similar fate. Sailing in stormy weather from Bàhia (Salvador) towards the Dutch at Pernambuco (Recife), it was engaged by a Dutch force and suffered such damage from shot to masts and rigging that many ships drove helplessly ashore or broke up on rocks; after four days of sporadic engagements the beaten survivors straggled back to Bàhia.

These two maritime disasters signalled the end of the great days of imperial Spain. That same year, 1640, both Portugal and the province of Catalonia broke away from the Habsburg Crown, Portugal never to be reunited. The swift exchange in the fortunes of the empire whose treasure had lately dazzled the world and its diminutive rebel provinces is surely the most striking feature of the seventeenth century, and one of the most impressive examples of the potency of trading wealth. The simple fishermen, sailors, grain and timber merchants, and brewers of the northern Netherlands, utilizing capital and expertise transferred from Antwerp and the southern provinces, exploiting their three-way middleman position between the oceans, the Baltic and the heart of continental Europe, concentrating single-mindedly on shipping, commerce and control of markets and waging a remorseless war of attrition on the Iberian monopolies overseas, aided at first by English and Huguenot interlopers, latterly by the restructured territorial power of France, had played the major role in humbling Spain, certainly by sea. In the process they had become the leading commercial, industrial and financial power in Europe.

They were indeed the first true maritime power of the modern era – the first great power existing by and for trade, and governed accordingly by a merchant oligarchy through consultative assemblies. That they possessed first-class fighting services was as much a result as a cause of their market control and industrial supremacy; indeed their ocean-going navy had not been started until after they had become the leading trading nation, and had been built primarily to protect trade. It was this force of cruisers, armed merchantmen and Indiamen that had beaten the more imposing Spanish–Portuguese galleons off the seas.

The triumph had not been painless. The depredations of Spanish warships and privateers, especially those operating from Dunkirk, had resulted in steeply increased insurance and freight rates, eroding the competitive edge of Dutch shipping. Combined with the loss of Spanish commerce and commodities – only a partial loss, since the Dutch had continued their usual practice of trading with the enemy – this had allowed neutrals like the English into many of their southern European markets.[16] Above all, the cost of maintaining sufficient cruisers to protect merchant convoys and fishing fleets, of building barrier forts to defend the homeland, and of raising, arming and paying troops to garrison them and the outposts of the overseas empire, particularly in Brazil, had mounted alarmingly.

Taxes – especially excise duties on consumables – had been increased to levels far higher than the notorious impositions which had contributed to the revolt against Habsburg rule in the first place, yet the greater part of the extraordinary expenditure had been financed through public loans.[17] There was no central exchequer for receipts and payments; each province had virtual fiscal autonomy, but the scale of national indebtedness can be gauged from Holland, financial powerhouse of the confederacy, whose debt rose during the course of the war to some 150 million guilders (almost £15 million).[18] This was the price for the attainment of supreme maritime power: a permanent block of debt which could never be repudiated, since it was held by the citizens and constituted a guarantee of the financial probity of the merchant system. The rebel provinces had become, in today's terms, a 'fiscal-military state', dependent on taxation to service the public debt, bound to maintain military strength to preserve the position they had won in a Europe of competing powers, and thus locked into an ascending spiral of arms expenditure, loans and taxes. Already they were taxed more heavily than any other people in Europe; by the end of the century they would pay almost three times more per head than their French or English contemporaries.[19]

The system was fully able to bear it. In the East the VOC had won domination; in the West the WIC had seized the Portuguese sugar regions in Brazil. The trade of the Baltic and northern Europe remained in Dutch hands, and the capital and industrial base of Holland had expanded hugely from the development of the 'rich trades' in Eastern wares, sugar, tobacco, delftware, and fine linens, silks and cottons; the textile production of Leiden alone was worth almost half of the total overseas trade of England.[20]

In 1647 the rebels negotiated peace and resumed commerce with Spain; in the following year they gained formal recognition in the Treaty of Münster as an independent republic – the United Provinces. The most significant clause in the treaty stipulated the closure of the river Schelde to maritime traffic, ensuring that Antwerp could not re-emerge to challenge Amsterdam. With insurance and freight rates down to pre-war levels, vast capital stocks and a stable banking system providing incomparably low rates of interest on borrowing, the United Provinces ousted the English and others who had intruded into its Spanish, Mediterranean and Levant trades and took over much of the transatlantic commerce of Spanish America and the Caribbean, so achieving a dominant trading position around the world.[21]

4

The Dutch Golden Age

THE PROSPERITY OF the United Provinces in the mid seventeenth century was evident to all visitors. They marvelled as much at the freedoms its citizens took as their birthright. Descartes, acknowledged as the first modern philosopher, since he admitted the new principles of science into his system, wrote his seminal works in Holland, because of the unique intellectual and religious freedoms he found there; there was no other country in which one could enjoy such complete liberty, he declared.[1] The English ambassador at The Hague, Sir William Temple, who travelled incognito through Holland, afterwards expressed his admiration for the liberty 'the Dutch valued so much' – in particular, 'the strange freedom that all men took in boats and inns and all other common places, of talking openly whatever they thought upon all public affairs, both of their own state, and their neighbours'.[2]

Temple was equally struck by the religious freedoms. Calvinism was the official Protestant denomination, and no one could hold office in the republic without affirming membership of the Calvinist Reformed Church, yet a large Catholic minority and innumerable dissenting sects practised their own rites in their own places of worship and published their own sacred texts. Even Jews lived freely among the populace without being confined to ghettos; later they were permitted a synagogue in Amsterdam, which was opened in 1675. Such essentially pragmatic indulgence in an age of extreme religious intolerance so impressed the fourth Earl of Shaftesbury he recommended that England follow suit, in order likewise to attract and retain skilled workers.[3]

Continental observers in general took an opposite stance, viewing the republic as a 'seedbed of theological, intellectual and social promiscuity',[4] whose subversive ideas – broadcast through learned works, propaganda broadsheets, satirical prints and engravings – constituted a threat to ordered society everywhere. Holland was an international centre for typecasting, printing and publishing. In Amsterdam alone some forty presses turned out books, news-sheets and pamphlets in all European languages, which found their way to capital cities and commercial centres throughout the continent. Absolute monarchs and their ministers, who maintained strict control of information and censorship of unorthodox ideas, rightly perceived the republic and its presses as a menace to their authority.[5]

Of all the freedoms indulged by Dutch society, none surprised foreign visitors more than those assumed by women. Respectable women walked out and about unaccompanied; young women went unchaperoned, and worked and engaged freely in discussions, exchanged kisses in public on meeting or parting, held hands with men while promenading, and conducted themselves in mixed company with a relaxed informality that shocked many foreigners, particularly perhaps from France. Within marriage they enjoyed legal rights not generally found elsewhere; as to be expected in such a commercial society, these included the right to inherit and bequeath property, and even to apply to have a dowry returned if the husband appeared to be squandering money. Since they were also entitled to sign commercial contracts, and in the wealthier classes certainly would have learned mathematics alongside their brothers, they could and did conduct business, either as their husband's partner or on their own account. They did not enjoy equal status with men – they were not permitted to hold public office, and were generally excluded from the orgies of eating and drinking held to mark state or guild occasions – yet a few wielded great influence in some areas of public life, notably on the governing bodies of the many charitable institutions for the old, orphans, the unemployed and the sick.

A few also made their mark as individuals in cultivated society and the arts, as professional painters, printmakers, glass-engravers, designers, salon wits and writers: thus Anna Maria van Schurman of Utrecht, a woman of formidable learning and linguistic ability, published a Latin polemic entitled in its English translation (1659) *The Learned Maid, or Whether a Maid May Also Be a Scholar*, to demonstrate the natural right of women to use their intellect. The notion was evidently ahead of its time,

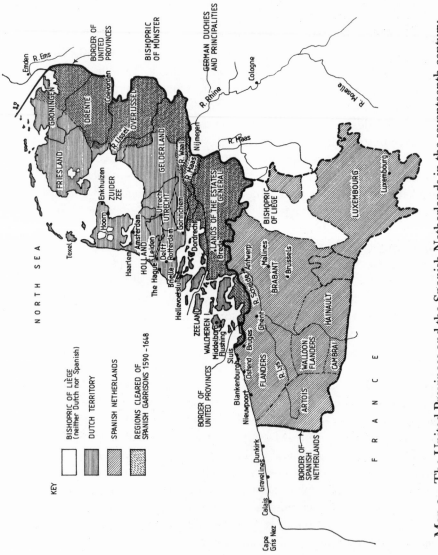

KEY

BISHOPRIC OF LIÈGE
(neither Dutch nor Spanish)

DUTCH TERRITORY

SPANISH NETHERLANDS

REGIONS CLEARED OF
SPANISH GARRISONS 1590–1648

NORTH SEA

FRANCE

R. Ems

Emden

BORDER OF
UNITED
PROVINCES

BISHOPRIC
OF MÜNSTER

GERMAN DUCHIES
AND PRINCIPALITIES

Cologne

R. Rhine

R. Moselle

GRONINGEN

DRENTE

Leeuwarden

FRIESLAND

OVERIJSSEL

R. IJssel

GELDERLAND

Texel

Enkhuizen

ZUIDER
ZEE

Hoorn

Amsterdam

HOLLAND

Haarlem

Leiden

Utrecht

UTRECHT

Gorinchem

R. Waal

R. Maas

Nijmegen

LANDS OF THE ESTATES
GENERAL

BISHOPRIC
OF LIÈGE

LUXEMBOURG

Luxembourg

The Hague

Delft

Rotterdam

Dordrecht

Brielle

Hellevoetsluis

Breda

Antwerp

Malines

BRABANT

Brussels

ZEELAND

WALCHEREN

Middelburg

Flushing

R. Schelde

Ghent

Bruges

R. Lys

FLANDERS

HAINAULT

WALLOON
FLANDERS

CAMBRAI

ARTOIS

Sluis

Blankenburg

Ostend

Nieuwpoort

BORDER OF
UNITED PROVINCES

BORDER OF
SPANISH
NETHERLANDS

Dunkirk

Gravelines

Calais

Cape
Gris Nez

Map 3   The United Provinces and the Spanish Netherlands in the seventeenth century

but Simon Schama is doubtless correct in asserting that 'only in the Republic could a work of such boldness have appeared in the 1650s'.[7] In 1655 the first woman appeared on the Amsterdam stage, several years before such a thing happened in London or elsewhere.

This relative emancipation extended through most levels of Dutch society, the female expression of an independent, anti-hierarchical spirit bred over centuries of struggle against the floods and latterly against Spain. The translation to great wealth and power had been too sudden to affect the traditions of communal solidarity and self-reliance, the attendant indifference to rank and style, or, as foreign visitors often saw it, the 'boorish bluntness of manner' of the people;[8] one English observer wrote of their lack of respect for 'person or apparel. A boor in his liquor'd slop shall have as much good use as a courtier in his bravery.'[9] Women's freedoms were the weft in the warp of this demotic society. They were also encouraged by the teachings of the Reformed Church. Calvin had rejected hierarchy as the basis of order both within each person – the assumption that the will and the emotions were governed by the intellect – and within communities, putting in its place a concept of practical utility. This challenged the conventional structure of society, including the subordination of women to men.

Calvinism had worked with the grain of dissent against a foreign ruling orthodoxy; whether it also inspired women to question their lot or men to question their authority over women, there is no doubt from foreign visitors' comments that wives showed their husbands less deference than in the feudal kingdoms surrounding the United Provinces. Servants – in the majority of households maidservants – also enjoyed better treatment than elsewhere, and frequently affection within the family, where in paintings of the time they often seem indistinguishable from the mistress or daughters of the house. Slapping servants was not tolerated, nor it seems was violence against women in the street or wife-beating at home – not, at least, among the urban populace.[10]

The combination of latitude and security that women enjoyed was guaranteed by the community rather than by authority. The neighbourhood watch and the local Church fellowship were the guardians of respectability; hence, while there was far less formal censorship than elsewhere in Europe, there was also less tolerance of deviation from the Calvinist-humanist ideal of modest behaviour, chastity before and within marriage, and the affectionate family as the basis of virtuous society. At a time when French and English female fashions flaunted bare bosom, Dutch necklines remained demurely high for wives and maids alike. Dutch actresses trod the stage, but never in such roistering bawdy as delighted English audiences. Prostitutes, who provided the safety valve for what has been termed in a recent study this 'powerful repression of the erotic',[11] plied their trade in inns and *musicos* where entertainment, dancing and gambling was provided, rather than openly in the streets – apart from the dockyard quarters of the seaport cities. Those judged irredeemable were flogged and branded. For other deviants from the model of burgher society – the workshy, vagrants, beggars, homosexuals – the prescribed punishments were savage: branding, mutilation and, for sodomites, execution by throttling, burning and drowning.[12]

If the freedoms of the United Provinces were confined within tight social limits, they were nonetheless exceptional. For the citizens themselves they formed a source of pride at the heart of a patriotic myth which sprang naturally and necessarily from the need for a national identity. They were seen as aspects of the 'True Freedom' which was both an inheritance from their ancient Batavian forbears and an expression of their merchant government. Hugo Grotius, the humanist scholar and jurist best known for his works on international law, particularly his defence of the freedom of the seas in *Mare Liberum* (1610), established the theoretical link in the early years of the century, showing with historical examples that liberty, order, virtue and prosperity were best preserved under a consultative government reserved to those with the wealth, education and leisure to devote themselves to public affairs – a description in fact of the close merchant oligarchies known as regents, who ruled the towns and cities and the republic itself.[13]

Liberty was a very practical ideal for the regents; as Grotius's son, Pieter de Groot, expressed it, 'What constitutes the wealth of the republic? The opulence of its trade. And what is the source of that trade? Good government. For nothing is more attractive for the whole world than freedom of conscience and security of possessions.'[14] It was impossible to guarantee either under a monarchy, he went on. This was the point, and it was demonstrated even in the internal politics of the republic, where the stadtholder represented the monarchical principle and the 'Orangist' party behind him provided a real counterweight to the power of the regents. The struggle between these forces was in truth a battle for the soul of the republic. The Orangists perceived the regents or 'States Party' as ready to compromise the principles, even the safety, of the state for base trading profit – a reproach echoed by most monarchs of Europe. The States Party feared the House of Orange might draw them into costly and unnecessary military or dynastic adventures, to the detriment of trade and the ruin of financial probity; on the ideological level, they represented the hereditary principle itself as contrary to their dearly bought freedoms, and were able to cite a wealth of historical examples in support.[15]

The regents had taken the crucial step in limiting the stadtholder's power early in the struggle against Spain in the aftermath of the Earl of Leicester's disastrous intervention: Johan van Oldenbarneveldt, Advocate of the States of Holland, had succeeded in transferring strategic and military decision-making from the Council of State formed to take over the responsibilities of William I after his assassination to the States General. Thereafter, throughout the life of the republic, the higher direction of the war remained under civilian control. William II of Orange, who became stadtholder in 1647 at a time of extreme tension between his adherents and the States General, then negotiating an end to the eighty years of war with Spain, the 'Antichrist', made a determined effort to restore his position. Gathering the army, zealots of the Reformed Church and a faction of Orangist regents under his banner, he attempted a coup against Amsterdam, citadel of merchant power. The plan miscarried and William died shortly afterwards, but the pamphlets of the time show how central to the merchant philosophy were the concepts of freedom and security of property: 'If my goods are stolen, my hands tied, my freedom taken from me, what matters it to me if he who does this is a Spaniard, a barbarian or a fellow countryman . . . Freedom is a noble and delicate thing which must not be touched by anyone.'[16]

One of those deeply affected by the abortive coup, since his father was imprisoned by William, was Johan de Witt, soon to be elected Grand Pensionary of Holland, the leading minister who represented the States of Holland in the States General. For de Witt, as for Grotius, the key to True Freedom was the consultation and compromise that resulted from sharing authority among those fitted by background, education and training to exercise it. Only thus could abuse of power be limited.[17]

Such in essence was the system evolved since the revolt against Spain. There was no written constitution. The founding document, the Union of Utrecht (1579), defined little more than a defensive alliance between seven provinces assuming the status of sovereign states, and retaining rights to raise their own taxes, appoint their own stadtholder and have a

say in the choice of overall captain-general of the alliance. A quota had
been drawn up for meeting common expenditure, but no provision had
been made for common institutions; the States General was supposed to
act only with the unanimous agreement of the other States. This implied
a wide consultation upwards, beginning in the town and city halls, where
the mainly regent councillors discussed issues drawn up by a permanent
committee of their States. Their recommendations were then debated
in the States, whence delegates represented the agreed policies at the
States General at The Hague. In practice, however, the States of
Holland, representing the largest concentration of wealth and contributing almost two-thirds of the revenue raised for the alliance,[18] dominated the lesser States – as Amsterdam dominated Holland – and nearly
all key resolutions were decided on Holland's interest and passed by
majority vote against the protests of one or more of the smaller States.
A recent historian of the republic has described it as 'a cross between
federal state and confederacy [i.e. sovereign states joined together in a
confederation], with more of the confederacy in form and theory, and
more of the federal state in substance and practice'.[19]

The balance of power between Orangists and regents – in effect
between the stadtholder and Amsterdam – shifted continually. It was at
its most unequal after William II's death in 1650. He left an infant as heir,
and the States of Holland, thoroughly alarmed and vengeful since the
attempted coup, took advantage of the situation to suspend the stadtholderate and take over all its remaining practical functions in the political
and military spheres. Their intention was to separate the post perman-
ently from the captain- and admiral-generalcy of the state, and for a
period of over twenty years after mid-century they succeeded in achieving a close approximation to the merchant ideal of government by and
for those engaged in trade and finance.

Such a part-traditional, part-contingent form of government was
completely at odds with the spirit of rational, centralized administration
informing the absolutist monarchies of the rest of Europe; what has
been termed the republic's 'institutional incoherence'[20] was quite as
exceptional as its freedoms. The republic's navy, with its five different
admiralties, was characterized by a similarly irrational and aberrant dis-
persion of control, as were the two great chartered companies wielding
sovereign powers overseas, the VOC and the WIC, with their regional
chambers. However, the majority of directors of these unique federated
joint-stock companies were regents, consequently the interests of over-

seas trade and empire were bound in closely with the realities of home politics. The army was the great difficulty for the States Party. Regular troops were needed to garrison the ring of superb modern fortresses built to defend the borders, yet history and most recently William II's attempted coup provided grim evidence of the danger armies posed for a republican government. After the peace with Spain, the States General reduced the strength of the army drastically, only partly for economic reasons, putting their faith in civilian volunteer militias which it was felt would support the republic from its internal enemies and in times of national emergency make up the garrisons.[21]

At bottom, regent power, and with it True Freedom, rested on prosperity; prosperity rested on control of markets. The Dutch were the ultimate middlemen: rings of merchants bought up whole crops or commodities when prices were low, whole forests before the trees had been felled, the wine of entire regions before the grapes had been harvested. The products were freighted in Dutch ships to Dutch ports, stored and held in order to keep prices up, then sold on a sellers' market – still undercutting local producers – and shipped out again in Dutch hulls. In this way not only the Baltic but western France had been made tributary to Amsterdam. Colonies of Dutch agents in the chief French Atlantic ports controlled the traditional wine and brandy trades through networks of merchants along the rivers of the vine-growing regions. They also controlled the import into France of Eastern spices, fine cloth, Baltic grain, Stockholm tar and other shipbuilding materials, and Caribbean sugar and tobacco. They had established sugar refineries at La Rochelle, and converted windmills in the Charente region to produce Dutch paper; they were indeed the masters of French commerce.[22]

The secret of their ability to corner markets was better credit and far lower rates of interest than other countries could provide. The crucial institution was the Exchange Bank of Amsterdam, founded in 1609, the first year of the brief truce with Spain. It is interesting that over half the major depositors were émigrés to the republic from the Spanish Netherlands.[23] The Bank existed purely as an instrument of deposit and exchange.[24] Attracting large capital deposits and the small savings of the populace alike, it provided a platform of financial stability guaranteed by its public character and the reputation of the regent magistracy which supervised its operations. It did not make loans to individuals or venture risk capital – functions discharged by lending banks established in Amsterdam and other commercial centres of the republic a few years afterwards – but it provided a pivotal conduit for trade worldwide as merchants made payments on bills of exchange drawn on its accounts. It was, in the words of one envious Englishman, 'the great sinews of trade, the credit thereof making paper go in trade equal with ready money, yea better in many parts of the world than money!'[25]

The metal deposits securing the Bank's bills were housed in the vaults of the city hall. Nearby was the bourse built in 1608 as a forum for regular trading in stocks and commodities. Modelled on the stock exchange in Antwerp, it comprised a cloister-like arcade with a roofed gallery above, where luxury goods were sold, running around the four sides of an open courtyard. Between noon and two o'clock each weekday, timed by a clock on a tower rising high above one end, the bourse became a raucous pit in which patterns of buying and selling between brokers, factors and speculators determined the prices of stocks, of the staples of world trade, and even of commodity futures. Deals were confirmed with ritualized double handshakes and, when the atmosphere grew more than usually frenzied, hand slaps amid 'shouting, insults, impudence, pushing and shoving'.[26] The Exchange Bank was the solid anchor of Dutch commerce, the bourse its extravagant antithesis whose transactions primed and regulated the capital flows, and in so doing set the price indices for all other European trading centres. This was indeed the hub of world commerce. In the bourse, the city hall and the taverns and coffee shops in the immediate vicinity could be found all the legal and technical skills connected with shipping, insurance, classification, commission agency and markets the world over. Those who congregated here for professional services and contacts or to glean the latest shipping and market intelligence or rumour formed a cosmopolitan community which knew no bounds of race or creed.[27]

Not half a mile away, warehouses stored with the products traded or gambled on the bourse lined the wharves of the river Ij, the northeastern boundary of the city, and fronted the canals intersecting the city itself. Amsterdam, as befitted the nerve centre of a state snatched from the waters, was built on a flood plain, the central island formed by a dam on the river Amstel where it joined the Ij, the quays and buildings beyond radiating to the city walls and the outer moat lapping the redoubts and towers, built on piles driven into estuarial mud and sand. Coastal and river craft plied the waterways between, providing an unrivalled system of low-cost bulk transport. Alongside the repositories exuding scents from around the world – Baltic pine, New World molasses, tobacco, Eastern cinnamon and other spices – innumerable refining, finishing, manufacturing and craft industries had grown up, each concentrated in its own quarter, each regulated by its own craft guild.[28]

The majority of workshops were small, but several industries were large-scale and employed wind power. Foreign visitors were astonished at the number of windmills in and about the city and by the variety of their uses: finishing and dressing cloth and leather, throwing silk, printing ribbons, extracting oil, preparing gunpowder, rolling copper plates, milling paper, and, above all, sawing wood.[29] The shipbuilding centre, Zaandam, just to the north of the city on the far side of the Ij, was thronged with windmills and has been described as Europe's first industrial zone.[30] Thus the demands of world trade and the use of wind power, long harnessed to drain and reclaim waterlogged land, together with the unmatched economy of water transport, had produced a revolution in industrial production. In turn, this had led in a virtuous circle to the capture of wider markets.

The effects were striking in every field. The most immediate impression was of wealth. The once plain frontages of the canal houses now boasted step- or bell-gables, their windows and other architectural features white stone trim. In the most fashionable quarter of the Herengracht, the innermost of the main canals which encircled the centre about the Dam, façades were extravagantly decorated with balustrades, crests, scrolls and scallops. Within, these town houses of the merchant princes resembled palaces 'many of them with splendid marble and alabaster columns, floors inlaid with gold, and the rooms hung with valuable tapestries or gold- and silver-stamped leather'.[31] Public buildings were similarly profuse in ornamentation, outside and in. Grandest of all was the new city hall overlooking the Dam square. The most powerful expression of Dutch Renaissance architecture when completed in the 1660s, it served as administrative centre and testament to the glory of the city and of the republic itself. Appropriately, this great building (now the Royal Palace) rested on piles – 13,569 of them, of an average forty feet in length.[32] Symbolically, the cupola rising high over the classical façade was topped by a monumental statue of the Maid of Peace holding in her right hand an olive branch, in her left the staff of Mercury, and by her side an overflowing cornucopia – the regents' essential trinity of peace, commerce, prosperity. One English visitor in the 1660s remarked that, though the city was commonly compared to Venice, 'For my part I believe Amsterdam to be much superior in riches.'[33]

The same observer noted that signs of prosperity and ease were not confined to the loftier strata, but extended throughout the population. The diet of all classes was rich and varied; Dutch control of Baltic grain and the North Sea fishing grounds, the plenitude of the market gardens serving the cities, and the efficiency and ubiquity of water transport meant that even the poorest ate well and seldom if ever suffered the desperate famines that afflicted peasants and workers in most of Europe after poor harvests. Wages were very much higher than in neighbouring countries; consequently, despite the high excise taxes, cheese, butter, fish and smoked meats – even fresh meat in season – were affordable by families through the social range. The chief differences between the tables of rich and poor appear to have lain in quality, not in substance or nutritional value.[34] The Dutch of all classes were notorious for prodigious feats of eating and drinking.

As with food, so with dress and accommodation: the differences between economic classes lay rather in quality than in content, each level emulating the one above so far as its purse allowed. Concern for cleanliness ran right through society. To the English it appeared obsessive. The gulf between the nations at this period is illustrated by the disturbing experiences of Sir William Temple at a state dinner at The Hague: every time he spat on the floor it was wiped up. When he complained, his host told him it was as well his wife was not present, for she would have kicked him out of the house. Any Dutch wife would have done the same: as another English visitor wrote, 'You must either go out to spit, or blush when you see the mop brought.'[35] Not only were most Dutch homes maintained spotlessly, but the doorsteps and paving before the house were washed daily; notwithstanding which, visitors were provided with slippers which they exchanged for their shoes when they entered.

For Dutch moralists the family was symbolic of the republic, the intimate community of the household a building block and microcosm of the neighbourhood, the city and the state.[36] While the United Provinces was far from a political democracy, it was in this sense socially democratic: its values were imposed, as already noted, not downwards from an aristocracy but outwards from the family and the tradition of self-reliance. Here the role of women was paramount. As the undoubted arbiters of domestic life, they were by extension guardians of the purity of the state. The Church, of course, exerted a major influence, and this too seemed to enhance the position of women, since Calvinism, and indeed humanism, sat uneasily with the riches and luxuries of which the Dutch now found themselves possessed. The home run by a chaste wife and helpmate provided a cleansed sanctuary where men could transmute their guilt at serving Mammon into love and pride in the family which depended upon them.[37]

At a practical level, social democracy was promoted by the advanced market economy which permitted the many to desire and purchase what in other countries was available only to the few. Besides enjoying higher material standards than elsewhere, Dutch urban society had created the first mass market in intellectual and artistic properties. Literacy was widespread. A French professor visiting Holland at the end of the previous century had been astonished to find even servant girls reading.[38] This has been attributed to the importance attached to Bible and catechism reading as the Reformed Church fought against Catholicism. For whatever reasons, the United Provinces had developed a literary-based culture quite unique in Europe, and Amsterdam publishers catered for the market with cheap editions of patriotic histories, theological works and, especially, journals of exploration and disaster at sea appealing to a popular craving for wonders and vicarious adventure. Similarly, engravings and oil paintings from the cheaper end of the art spectrum adorned the walls of the humblest homes.

Taken all in all, it appears the Dutch burghers of the seventeenth century had produced a prototype of late-twentieth-century Western civilization, without its licence. There was the same familiarity of manners and outspokenness on all subjects, the disregard for hereditary rank (combined with awe at great wealth), wide dissemination of information (and craving for sensation), the opportunities provided by literacy for intelligent or merely diligent men to climb the professional and even the social ladder, significant roles for women, although greatly restricted by their duties within the household, enjoyment of family life, and indulgence towards children and dogs, as affirmed in countless paintings and engravings and visitors' tales. As striking were love of flowers, concern for cleanliness, an abundance of material and intellectual goods, conspicuous consumption at every level up to the sumptuary splendour of the wealthiest regent family homes and villas in the countryside, and, at the other extreme, generous provision in charitable institutions for the poor, the elderly and the sick. Above all, the market reigned supreme, forging discipline, inducing desires.

There were, of course, differences from the late twentieth century.

Most obviously, the people could not vote for whom they wished to represent them; political power was in the hands of the self-perpetuating regent patriciates. Yet the form of government in which authority was decentralized in consultative chambers and the judiciary was independent of the 'eminent head', the stadtholder, embodied the more important features of twentieth-century democracies – argument, dissent and the rule of law – and undoubtedly had more effect on the type of society than the people's lack of a political vote. In fact the republican government was a source of great satisfaction to the Dutch of the coastal towns; they viewed themselves as an island of rational, freedom- and peace-loving statesmanship surrounded by vainglorious monarchs wont to sacrifice the real interests of their subjects to wars conducted for territorial or dynastic gain or mere vanity. Beyond this even, they created a patriotic myth in which they were the people chosen by God to reveal His design for the world.[39] For their part, the monarchs looked down on the ministers of the United Provinces as mean-spirited tradesmen concerned solely with commercial profit and loss.

The more important characteristic distinguishing seventeenth-century urban Dutch from late-twentieth-century Western society was the strict moral order imposed on the one hand by fear of God, on the other by the constraints of human biology unmediated by medical science. As the monarchies and their own churchmen and intellectuals feared, however, the seeds of a relative order of values had been sown in tolerance of free expression and dissident forms of worship; but, while this foreshadowed more extreme liberalism, it was a potential rather than an immediate threat to the social consensus.

In all other respects, the Dutch in the seventeenth century can be seen as harbingers of the modern West: they led the world in intellectual inquiry, the sciences and every significant technology. For shipbuilding, navigating instruments, charts, atlases, globes and the illustrated manuals of sailing directions known as Rutters, Amsterdam and the other ports of Holland were supreme. Similarly, on land the United Provinces was in the forefront of military engineering, ordnance, small-arms and ammunition production and the payment of troops. It was the same in all the advanced crafts and industries, from clockmaking, lens cutting and polishing, scientific instrument-making, typecasting, printing and publishing, diamond-cutting – one of the earlier imports from Antwerp – to dredging, draining, crop rotation, soil replacement, horticulture, and indeed invention of every kind. Foreigners were struck as much by the novelties and innovations as by the sense of abundance and freedom in Dutch cities. In 1669 the world's first public street lighting would be introduced in Amsterdam – some 2,000 glass and metal lamps, burning vegetable oil, fixed on high walls and posts along the thorough-fares.[40]

Perhaps the most spectacular result of merchant wealth, as before in Renaissance Italy, was the generation of great art. Here it was a visual expression of the Dutch humanist creed: mankind as the measure of all things. Human emotion, character and experience were delineated as never before by painters of genius working in several Dutch cities. The close bonds of affection between a married couple as portrayed by Frans Hals of Haarlem, the rapacity of a puckered whoremistress captured by Dirck van Baburen of Utrecht, more complex feelings of sadness and defeat delineated by the most profound artist of the early Utrecht school, Hendrick Terbruggen, were facets of a shift in artistic viewpoint as fundamental as the religious and political transformation of the country: heroic myth, spirituality and divine authority were replaced by the daily round and carnal reality. At the summit of this revolution stood Rembrandt van Rijn of Leiden and Amsterdam, surely one of the most penetrating interpreters of psychological truth on canvas of any age, and Jan Vermeer of Delft, whose explorations of the effects of light on substance transcend the limits of paint and time.

Besides the well-fed burghers, their modestly dressed wives and bonneted children, their maidservants and dogs, and the scrubbed interiors of their homes and well-stocked kitchens, the sea and ships were celebrated as they had not been by any former artists. *Jaghts* still lean to those breezes; sun brightens opaque, sand-stirred water; great ensigns with horizontal red, white and blue bands strain out stiffly above folds of backed topsails; warships and Indiamen, all solid timbers and easy curves from round beakhead to extravagantly carved and gilded poop, signify freedom and profit and the challenge of different cultures. A heroic age of maritime power is reflected in these animated canvasses from the golden age of Dutch art.

The United Provinces was not, of course, Utopia. Calvin viewed mankind as fallen and irretrievably lost, and in this at least the republic was no exception. In part the street lighting for Amsterdam – adopted soon afterwards in other Dutch cities – was in order to reduce night-time crime and the number of drunks falling into the canals and drowning. It was true that wages in the republic were much higher then elsewhere –

often double those in the southern Netherlands – yet the migrant workers drawn to the cities and the girls and older women hired from charitable institutions, particularly for work in the textile industries, were subject to all the abuses associated with an unregulated mass market in labour: long hours in harsh, often squalid, conditions, only to be thrown on the streets in periods of recession. And while the old-age, sick and poor relief were on a generous scale, each town competing in virtue, these benefits were used as a form of social control and were confined to natives of the town and long-term residents of good behaviour: 'undeserving' persons, the natives of other towns and foreigners fell outside the net and were expelled, and were flogged or branded if they found their way back.

The sailors on whom the whole system ultimately rested were a particularly brutalized class – although no more so than those of other nations. Many were foreigners, chiefly from the German states, who had come to the republic seeking work. Falling into the hands of 'crimps', nicknamed *Zielverkoopers* (soul-sellers), who promised board and lodging to be paid for later by deductions from wages after the men had been found a berth aboard ship, they were confined in insanitary cellars or attics and provided with a minimum diet until the next Indies fleet required men.[41] There were over 300 such crimping houses in Amsterdam alone. Aboard, savage punishments, undermanning, short rations and death from disease were too often the realities beneath the civilized abstractions of the republic's liberal thinkers.

The areas in which Dutch practice departed most flagrantly from libertarian ideals were slave trading and trade monopolies. Interestingly, trafficking in slaves had been renounced as immoral in the early years of the republic. A few individual merchants seem to have sent single ships to the African coast to attempt to break into what was still a jealously guarded Portuguese–Spanish monopoly, and after the formation of the WIC in 1621 some shareholders proposed that the company do the same. But the directors, after conferring with theologians, decided that trading in human beings was not morally justified.[42] The ruling was soon blurred by the exigencies of the renewed war with Spain. Slaves were found in captured Portuguese ships and sold in the Caribbean for profit or transported to new Dutch settlements in the Portuguese sphere in Brazil, Central America or the New Netherlands colony in North America. It was the expansion of the company's Brazilian sugar plantations, the consequent need for a more regular supply of labourers, that enticed it to enter the trade at source. In 1637 it seized the ancient Portuguese slaving fort at Elmina, and in the following years most of the other Portuguese forts and slave barracoons along the West African coast, taking over the commercial relationships forged with the local chiefs and slave merchants who controlled the supply. By the early 1640s the WIC was master of the transatlantic traffic.

It was no doubt inevitable that the trading arm of a merchant state driven by profit should compromise its moral and religious principles in this way: black African slaves were the essential power source for the plantation economies of the Caribbean and Central and South America, indeed for the entire Atlantic trading system which the company sought to dominate. However, the actions of the VOC in the East suggest that exploitation of weaker populations was not simply a reluctant response to perceived necessity, but was as fundamental to Dutch trade as to the earlier Portuguese and Spanish conquests. The Dutch in the Indonesian spice islands worked their plantations with native slave labour which they treated with as much brutality as their New World counterparts. By the 1620s they had either exterminated or deported the entire indigenous population of the Banda Islands to serve as slaves or soldiers; in 1651 a native rising provoked them into a series of punitive expeditions which resulted in the forcible transfer of some 12,000 persons from their native islands.[43]

As for Grotius's argument for the freedom of the seas, it appears disingenuous or wilfully blinkered. It was the natural position to take in European waters where Dutch ships were the universal carriers; in the former Portuguese stronghold on the West African coast, however, in eastern seas and off Brazil, the WIC and VOC protected their monopoly spheres as forcibly as the Portuguese or Spanish ever had. And one of their most conspicuous violations of *Mare Liberum* was on their own border, where in order to preserve the primacy of Amsterdam they had forced the closure of the river Schelde to trade.

From a universal perspective, the area in which Dutch society most closely resembled Calvin's metaphor of mankind lost in a labyrinth from which there was no escape was in its attitude to the natural world. The Dutch were not, of course, unique in believing in the primacy of humankind. Catholicism no less than humanism placed man at the pinnacle of the natural order, and savages no less than the civilized people of Europe exercised unthinking dominion over the other species with whom they shared the earth. Calvin's repudiation of hierarchy and the role of the intellect should, perhaps, have caused the Reformed Church to moderate its teachings on man's superiority to 'lower animals'. The conceits of humanism are more apparent. In parallel with their exploitation of more weakly armed native peoples encountered around the world, the Dutch had reduced all creatures to commodities for the purposes of trade or consumption, sport, scientific inquiry or classification. In this they were no different from other Europeans: having far greater capital resources, they were simply more successful over a wider range.

They had long made the North Sea fishing grounds their own; by mid-century their whaling ships were predominant in northern waters, and whale-rendering yards and train-oil reservoirs occupied a large section of north-western Amsterdam. On land, selective breeding had produced fine meat and dairy herds; poultry, geese and game birds were plentiful, as paintings and etchings of Dutch kitchens stuffed to the beams with carcasses testify. As noted, the people enjoyed a variety and abundance of diet that could not be found elsewhere and, despite the humanist precept to find the golden mean between frugality and over-indulgence, gorged on a scale that astonished visitors. Normal as this undoubtedly was, it still seems remarkable that in this sanctum of free thought and free expression no one of influence appears to have raised a voice against the assumptions underlying such wholesale massacre, deeply embedded though they were in Old Testament and Christian doctrine that all creatures were provided by God for man's use, enjoyment and consumption. Surprisingly, in view of the ecclesiastical censorship in France, the first Christian intellectual to have challenged the dogma had been the Catholic essayist Michel de Montaigne of Bordeaux, late in the sixteenth century:

> Let him [who holds all other life to be brought into being for man's sole use and pleasure] show me, by the most skilful argument, upon what foundation he has built these excessive prerogatives which he supposes himself to have over all other existencies . . . Is it possible to imagine anything so ridiculous as that this pitiful creature, who is not even master of himself . . . should call itself master and lord of the universe?[44]

Another Catholic, the Provençal scientist and philosopher Pierre Gassendi, voiced the same concerns in the first half of the seventeenth century.[45] However, it was a third Frenchman, René Descartes, working, as noted, in the United Provinces because of the unique intellectual freedoms there, who had overwhelmingly the greater influence, and it was in the contrary direction. Justifiably celebrated as the father of modern philosophy, he had endeavoured to replace subjective opinion and belief with knowledge founded on logic and theological certainty. Stripping away all sensory perceptions as open to doubt, he had arrived famously at what he supposed the irreducible core of knowledge: 'I think, therefore I am.' On this he proceeded to construct a new body of knowledge by pure reason. So he asserted; so perhaps he believed. Yet the core of his new structure was Christian dogma, and the logic was entirely circular: his own thought, therefore his existence, was predicated on the existence of God, which was in turn a construct of his own thought.

Descartes was undoubtedly a giant founding intellect of what came to be known as the Enlightenment, but, by relying on reason and denying the validity of experience, observation, emotions or the more practical tenets of religion, he provides an example of the level of idiocy achievable by pure intellect – and never more so than in his proof of the uniqueness of mankind.

Maintaining that the bodies of men and animals were mere machines governed by the laws of physics, he explained human consciousness in Christian dogmatic terms as emanating from a soul implanted by God, the primary cause of both the material universe and the laws which governed it. He located the soul in the pineal gland in the forehead. This led him to the remarkable deduction that, since, in Christian doctrine, animals lacked immortal souls, they also lacked consciousness, and hence feelings. They were automata. By implication, mankind had free reign to harvest, use and abuse them in any way. Vivisection was already widely practised – especially in France and the United Provinces, which led the world in anatomical discovery – and would undoubtedly have continued without Descartes's philosophy. But for him and his followers who nailed conscious dogs and other animals to tables by their paws – for there were no anaesthetics – and cut them open to explore or remove their vital organs it was reassuring to imagine that the victims' frenzied moans and whimpers were merely the triggered responses of machines. As one appalled eyewitness reported, 'They said the animals were clocks; that the cries they emitted when struck were only the noise of a little spring that had been touched, but that the whole body was without feeling.'[46]

The United Provinces of the mid seventeenth century was a great power, leading exploration and invention and the funding of new industries in every quarter. The citizens were justifiably proud of their success and the exceptional freedoms they enjoyed and the form of republican government that guaranteed them. Beyond this, however, they were consumed by a sense of moral superiority which in retrospect appears without foundation. At bottom their wealth was built on the subjugation of materially weaker peoples and the exploitation of every defenceless species encountered in every quarter of the globe. They were merely human: as Montaigne wrote, 'Presumption is our [human] natural and original disease.'[47] Just as the civilization they had built was the herald of modern Western society, so too was their humanist presumption. They left many touching prints and paintings showing the fondness of urban housewives and families for their pets; the anguish of countless other animals offered as living sacrifices on the tables of medical science, instruction and cruel curiosity is less visible and seldom noticed in works on art or the history of European civilization.

5

Sole Bay, 1672

THE CENTRAL PROBLEM confronting the merchant system of the United Provinces was that the more successful it became, the more danger it attracted. If reason could have resolved the quandary, Johan de Witt, most luminous of Holland's Grand Pensionaries during the golden age, might have done so. His policies rested on three principles: the security of the state, its independence and the furtherance of trade. In pursuing the first two, he strove to keep the republic out of wars. In pursuing the third, he could not avoid arousing hostility, for the tighter the Dutch grip on world markets, the more ubiquitous Dutch ships on the trade routes, the greater the envy and resentment provoked in neighbours – particularly France and England. And the more complex the network of shipping bringing in raw materials and food for the urban population and carrying away exports of finished or manufactured products, the more vulnerable the whole structure. Not only the prosperity, but the very existence of the United Provinces had come to depend on the uninterrupted passage of ships to the ports of Holland and Zeeland. Both France and England lay on the flanks of these routes.

First to strike, in 1652, was England. She had just emerged from civil wars in which parliamentary forces based in the more prosperous south and east of the country, and financed by the merchants of the City of London and duties on trade, had deposed and executed the Stuart king, Charles I.

Charles's navy, taken over by Parliament, had been the crucial element in the civil war. Strategically, it had given parliamentary forces the mobility to outflank the royalists; financially, it had given Parliament control of the customs revenues from overseas trade, which had fuelled the war effort.[1] The fleet Parliament acquired included the most impos-ing warships of the day: the *Sovereign of the Seas*, of three gun-decks, and *Prince Royal* – renamed *Resolution* – which would not have been out of place in a line of battle a century later, together with sixteen other war-ships larger and more powerful than the largest Dutch flagships. In addi-tion, Parliament had built an unprecedented number of smaller cruisers to protect the commerce on which it relied for finance, and had contin-ued building at a prodigious rate after the war.[2] A committee dominated by City merchants, the lord mayor of London prominent among them, had remodelled naval administration, rebuilt the seagoing officer corps with military officers and merchant captains of reliable republican atti-tude, and laid down the first 'Laws and Ordinances Martial' to govern discipline, so taking the first step in establishing a professional navy which would act for the state rather than primarily for booty and prize money – although this inducement was to remain for centuries.

The naval build-up had begun in response to the need to protect trade against royalist privateers, to transport and supply the army and to counter any foreign intervention in favour of the Stuarts; that the Dutch stadtholder William II of Orange, who had married Charles I's daugh-ter, had wanted such intervention had been a principal ground of his dispute with the regents. Increasingly after the defeat of the royalist forces in England, Parliament's motive for building warships was to force a more favourable division of trade from the United Provinces. Frictions caused by what was perceived as England's economic subservience to the Dutch had been growing for decades.[3] Wherever the English looked, Dutch shipping dominated. The greater part of the vital shipbuilding materials from the Baltic came to England in Dutch *fluyts* – the ultimate expression of the long, box-like, minimally manned seagoing cargo car-riers developed through the sixteenth century; Dutch fishing fleets virtu-ally monopolized the North Sea; Dutch merchants still controlled the finishing and marketing of England's woollen exports; and, since the end of their war with Spain, the Dutch had taken over so much formerly English trade with Spain and Portugal that many English firms faced ruin. Dutch traders from the New Netherlands on the Hudson river were even penetrating the English North American colonies, while in the East the English had been squeezed out of the spice islands by the VOC and had neither forgotten nor forgiven an execution of ten English

Map 4   Western Europe and the Mediterranean in the seventeenth
century

merchants by VOC authorities in the Molucca islands in 1623. The episode had entered legend as 'the massacre of Amboina'.[4]

The first English move to redress the imbalance came in 1650, after the death of William II; it was a proposal for a political and military union between England and the United Provinces, to be governed by a great Common Council sitting in London. The regents rejected such an obvious attempt to subordinate them and prise open their hard-won trading monopolies.[5] The following year Parliament passed a Navigation Act restricting the carriage of imports to English ships or ships of the country of origin of the merchandise, restricting imports of fish or fish products to those caught by English fishermen, and banning foreign vessels from the English coastal trades. Aimed at Dutch shipping and middlemen, it was also designed to boost English shipping, commerce and trade with the colonies. The regents reacted by sending a delegation from the States General to England to negotiate a repeal.

Events at sea moved too fast for them. French privateer interests had seized the opportunity to plunder English merchantmen by declaring for the English royalist cause. English privateers, issued in return with 'Letters of Reprisal' against the French, were seizing Dutch ships which might be carrying French goods or supplies for royalists overseas, torturing crew members for information about the cargo, and holding Dutch skippers in solitary confinement while their vessels awaited jurisdiction in English admiralty courts.[6] During 1651 some 126 Dutch ships were captured in the Channel, the Irish Sea, the Atlantic or the Caribbean and brought to English ports.[7]

English warships, meanwhile, enforced 'sovereignty' in the Channel and home waters by having foreign ships dip ensigns and topsails to them in salute. New life had been breathed into this traditional claim by an English jurist, John Selden, in *Mare Clausum*, published in 1631. Against Grotius's arguments for the freedom of the seas in *Mare Liberum*, Selden upheld the ancient concept of territorial waters – of unspecified extent – and sought to prove the legality of the salute claimed by English men-of-war in home waters. Also, besides considerably extending the definition of contraband of war from armaments to anything that might help an enemy prolong the fight, he rejected arguments put forward by Grotius that neutrals were entitled to trade with anyone, maintaining the opposite: goods were *not* covered by the flag of the ship carrying them, and thus could be seized by a belligerent from neutrals or even from allies.

Selden's assertions were as appropriate to an aspiring predator poised over a main artery of trade as Grotius's were to the universal trader whose ships were at risk. But, at the level where history was made, what moved minds and provoked violence was the emotional nationalism of pamphleteers inspired by the English mercantile interest and disseminating stories of atrocities committed by Dutch privateers with royalist commissions and of the 'massacre of Amboina'. By the end of 1651 this had brought the two countries to the edge of an open breach.

In the first month of 1652 the English seized another thirty Dutch ships and the States General began preparing for war. They had left it too late. Since the end of the war with Spain, the admiralties had sold ships and run down their forces to a peace establishment. They had scarcely over sixty warships between them, virtually all single-gun-deck cruisers mounting main batteries of 12-pounders, with perhaps a few larger-calibre guns as bow and stern chasers.[8] They were no match for the English two-deckers mounting main batteries of 18- or 32-pounders, and in overall fleet size they were at a disadvantage of three to five – under 30,000 tons total displacement to almost 50,000 tons. The Dutch sought to remedy this by converting 150 merchantmen to warships, but it was difficult to find this number and they could never be as effective as purpose-built fighting ships. The Dutch commander-in-chief, Maarten Tromp, was to write from experience at the end of that year, 'undoubtedly we shall accomplish more with sixty ships properly built for war than with 100 such as we have now'.[9]

The war was sparked in May by the English claim to sovereignty in the Channel. One of the escorts of a Dutch convoy sailing home from the Mediterranean refused to strike her flag to an English warship in the western Channel until compelled by gunfire, after which the convoy was detained by an English squadron and boarding parties were sent to search the ships. The Dutch fleet was at sea, and directly Tromp learned of this latest outrage he steered down to release the merchantmen, by chance falling in with a detachment of the English fleet under one of the joint commanders-in-chief, General at Sea Robert Blake. There was another dispute over 'the honour of the flag', this time leading to a general action in which the numerically superior but lighter Dutch force came off worse and retired, leaving two disabled vessels for the English to take.

This pattern was repeated with only few exceptions in the war that followed. The smaller, more lightly gunned Dutch warships were battered in a series of confused running battles in the Channel and the North Sea and were driven home; hundreds of Dutch merchantmen were captured; convoys were held up while the English fleet was at sea, and trade was paralysed for long periods. It was said that grass began to grow on the streets of Amsterdam. Riots broke out in the major sea ports, directed against the regents and for the Orangists.

Outside home waters, though, the Dutch remained the masters. With the aid of their ally Denmark, they closed the Baltic completely to English shipping, and thus to the timber, masts, spars and naval stores vital both to the navy and to merchant shipowners. They also closed the Mediterranean, while in eastern waters the VOC continued to reign supreme. In the west the WIC lost its grip on Brazil to the Portuguese as a direct result of the English assault, but this was of little comfort to English merchants who were suffering both from the shutdown of their trades and from the activities of Dutch and French privateers against those merchantmen still moving. Lacking the financial resources of the United Provinces, many were ready for peace before the end of 1653.

By this time Parliament had been dissolved by Oliver Cromwell, who had established himself as a dictator, Lord Protector of England; and in Holland Johan de Witt had been appointed Grand Pensionary. Cromwell dreamed of a union between the two Protestant republics against Spain. He told a peace delegation from the United Provinces that the interests of both nations lay in commerce, and the world was wide enough for them both. De Witt made it clear, however, that the United Provinces was determined to preserve freedom of action. It would fit out a powerful fleet, augment it with the fleet of its ally Denmark, and construct alliances with France and Poland – the latter to contain Sweden in the Baltic.[10] Cromwell then moderated his demands, and the final peace terms, signed at Westminster in April 1654, were considered extraordinarily mild in view of the devastating naval defeats the Dutch had suffered in home waters.

Cromwell was concerned by the political dangers had the war continued – particularly the prospect of the Orangists gaining the upper hand over the regents and attempting to restore the Stuarts to the English throne, probably in alliance with France. In this respect he and de Witt had a common interest, and the peace treaty stipulated that neither side should shelter or help the enemies of the other, while a secret clause committed Holland to bar for ever any member of the Orange–Nassau house from the stadtholderate or captain-generalcy of the province. On the vital issues which had caused the war the treaty was mostly silent. The Dutch gained no amelioration of the Navigation Act; the English did not move the Dutch from adherence to the freedom of neutrals to trade wherever and with whomever they wished. For this reason the peace could only be temporary.

Thwarted in his vision of England and the United Provinces carving the trade of the world between them, Cromwell launched his magnificent fleet against the Spanish Caribbean and Central American colonies. This allowed the Dutch to take over what remained of English trades with Spain; they also advanced their eastern position, taking Ceylon and the chief ports of southern India at the expense of the Portuguese, and enjoyed another burst of expansion based on the 'rich trades', reinforcing their dominating position and widening the gap with England, so naturally increasing the frustration and envy of English merchants and hastening the next trial of arms.

That Cromwell died and Charles II was restored to the English throne in 1660 made no difference: the fundamental policy of any English government was to increase wealth by increasing trade – looking to the Dutch as the prime example. New Navigation Acts were passed, designed to channel key imports and exports into English ships and to bind English colonies completely to the mother country by requiring them to buy from England all the European goods they needed. Overseas, an offensive policy of reprisal was pursued for 'wrongs, dishonours and indignities' suffered at the hands of the Dutch. A Company of Royal Adventurers into Africa, founded soon after the Restoration, headed by Charles's brother James, Duke of York, and incorporating leading courtiers, London merchants and a group of ambitious politicians riding the prevailing anti-Dutch attitudes of the City of London, sent a fleet to the West African coast to break the Dutch slaving monopoly. Dutch forts and ships from Gorée Island just south of Cape Verde to Cape Coast Castle in the Gulf of Guinea were surprised and taken. Meanwhile another expedition was sent to North America to deal with the colonists of the New Netherlands on the Hudson river, who were trading with their neighbouring English colonies in defiance of the Navigation Acts. The capital and chief port, Nieuw Amsterdam, was taken in August 1664 and renamed New York in honour of the King's brother.

De Witt's response was to raise a loan of a million florins (some £100,000) at 3 per cent on the capital market and to attempt to persuade the inland States to contribute to a war chest for the trial of strength obviously coming. Meanwhile he expressed secret orders to the commander of the Dutch fleet in the Mediterranean, Michiel de Ruyter, to sail to Africa and retake the forts. De Ruyter accomplished this in short time, and took a haul of 'reprisal' goods from English ships he found.

In London, Samuel Pepys, Clerk of the Acts to the Navy Board, one of the principal officers in the naval administration, listened to merchants bewailing 'the news of our being beaten to dirt at Guinny by De Ruyter with his fleete . . . it being most wholly to the utter ruin of our Royall Company, and reproach and shame to the whole nation'.[11] The following day he noted in his diary rumours of the Dutch preparing reinforcements for the Mediterranean 'where without doubt they will master our fleete. This put to that of Guinny makes me fear them mightily'.[12] And on the last day of December that year, 1664, he noted, 'Public matters are all in a hurry about a Dutch warr. Our preparations great. Our provocations against them great; and after all our presumption, we are now afeared as much of them as we lately contemned them.'[13]

War broke out formally early in 1665. This time the United Provinces was far better prepared; in particular, the admiralties had taken in hand a naval construction programme of larger ships designed for fleet action rather than trade protection. The heaviest of these, classed as first rates, mounted up to eighty-four guns with a main battery of 24-pounders on the lower deck able to inflict serious ship damage. They were substantially beamier than English ships of their size, chiefly because the shoal approaches to Dutch harbours forced them to build broad rather than deep, and were in consequence more stable than the notoriously overgunned English warships and better able to use their lower tier of heavy guns in any weather. Nevertheless the Dutch fleet remained inferior in total tonnage and average broadside weight to the ships Charles had inherited from Cromwell, and completely lacked the great three-deckers mounting main batteries of 32-pounders which headed the English navy.[14] As Pepys noted from conversations with naval officers after the first fleet battle, these were 'the ships that do the business'.[15]

In keeping with their more heavily gunned vessels, the English had adopted fleet line in battle. As discussed in relation to Tromp's use of fleet line in 1639,[16] this was the obvious formation for broadside-armed sailing vessels; it enabled them to develop their full firepower without endangering consorts, and to support their next ahead or astern in distress. It had been used from the earliest days of gunned sailing warships, particularly as a defensive tactic when in inferior numbers. English fleet line was also in a sense defensive, as it had emerged formally in 'Instructions for the Better Ordering of the Fleet in Fighting' after a battle in the first Dutch war when one division of the English fleet, separated upwind, had been overwhelmed by massed Dutch before the other divisions had been able to work up in support.[17] In another sense fleet line was a military response by Cromwell's generals at sea to the problems of controlling vast numbers of sailing vessels and attempting to ensure their power was focused, not dissipated in separated mêlées. Above all, it reflected a decision to decide naval battles by stand-off great gunnery – where the English had the overwhelming advantage in weight of shot – rather than by boarding and entering men. As such it was both offensive and very effective, as the subsequent battles of the first Dutch war had proved.[18]

By contrast, Dutch admirals, knowing they lacked the weight of gunpower to prevail in an artillery duel, favoured the somewhat anachronistic tactics of group attack to overwhelm and separate sections of the English line and capture ships by boarding and entering.[19]

Had England's naval advantages in home waters and her favourable position and deep-water harbours flanking Dutch trade routes been the sole determinants of the war, the United Provinces must have been overcome in short time. But, as in the first war, the Dutch retained their command overseas – particularly in the East, where the VOC captured several English bases, along the West African coast, where James's Royal Adventurers' company was ruined, and in the Baltic, where again English ships were completely excluded by the Danes. The other important European trading centres on the Atlantic coast and the Mediterranean also remained in the Dutch orbit – except Lisbon. Moreover, the English fleet lacked the sea endurance to blockade the Dutch coast for any length of time: sickness, lack of provisions, storm or battle damage always forced it home in a matter of weeks. Even English victories in the dour series of fleet battles seem in retrospect to have been counter-productive, as they reinforced French fears about the dominant position England might attain if allowed to defeat the Dutch, and so helped to bring Louis XIV of France into the war on the Dutch side.

The key decider, however, was financial. The utter poverty of the English Crown, its lack of solid securities such as mineral rights with which to guarantee loans, and the want of any institutional apparatus such as the Dutch had for long-term borrowing against the state meant that Charles was forced into short-term loans at high rates of interest. These were judged as an index of overspending rather than as tools of state policy, and Members of Parliament had come to distrust him and the uses to which he had put the millions they had voted most eagerly for the war; they now allowed him scarcely more than sufficient to clear his debts.[20] This further undermined his credit in the financial markets, as the money men perceived that his indebtedness had become a major constitutional issue.[21] The result was a collapse of the naval administration, by far the largest charge on the royal purse. Unpaid crews rioted; unpaid workers left the dockyards, which were in any case short of vital materials; unpaid contractors refused to deliver materials. For the campaigning season of 1667, Charles was forced to lay up the battle fleet and merely fit out cruisers to prey on Dutch trade.

This led to probably the blackest day in English naval history, 12 June 1667: de Ruyter, the Dutch commander-in-chief, having led his fleet into the Thames itself, sent a light squadron up the river Medway towards the premier fleet base at Chatham, where they burned a first rate and two second rates, cut out the great fleet flagship, *Royal Charles*, and towed her home on the tide. This brilliant feat owed rather more to Johan de Witt's brother, Cornelius, sailing aboard de Ruyter's flagship, than to the admiral himself: using his authority as plenipotentiary of the States General, Cornelius de Witt forced the decision to attack Chatham against the opposition of de Ruyter and all flag officers in council.

The presence of the Dutch fleet in the mouth of the Thames aroused such panic in London that Pepys put his wife and father into a coach for the country, with a bag of gold which they were to hide, and afterwards 'continued in frights and fear' all night long for the rest of his money.[22] It is an instructive vignette, an illustration of England's unreadiness to take her place as a maritime power in the sense in which that term is used here. Had she been one, Pepys's gold would have been invested, together with all the other hoards under mattresses, and the state would have been able to borrow at low rates of interest against the security.

One of the most potent strokes in naval history, the Medway raid had the most immediate and measurable effects on the subsequent peace treaty of Breda.[23] England conceded the principle that freight – except specified contraband of war – was covered by the flag of the vessel carrying it, and agreed to amend the Navigation Acts to allow Dutch vessels to bring to England the produce of German states defined as the United Provinces' natural hinterland. Most territory conquered was retained, but the English returned two small West Indian islands, one of which, Nieuw Zeeland (St Eustatius), was to become a centre of Dutch trade in the region, particularly in slaves. Of greater significance in the long run, England kept the New Netherlands (New York and New Jersey), completing a chain of possessions up the eastern seaboard of North America.

WITHIN FIVE YEARS of the Peace of Breda, England made a third attempt to overcome the Dutch merchants by force. This time trade was not the primary motive – indeed the merchant interest and Parliament were strongly opposed to war, and had earlier called for an alliance with the United Provinces to curb the growing power of France.[24] Charles II and a cabal of courtiers planned the assault in secret, as a means of restoring absolute power to the Crown and removing what they saw as humiliating dependence on Parliament for money. Their patron and model was the 'Sun King', Louis XIV of France.

Louis was the ultimate territorial monarch. Having seen his country ruined by internal factions, he had concentrated all power in his own hands and, appointing a new breed of administrators from among the wealthy merchant class – a 'nobility of the robe' – to reduce his dependence on the traditional nobility of the sword, had succeeded in restoring his populous country to greatness.

His chief instrument was Jean-Baptiste Colbert – now Marquis de Seignelay – an administrator of genius. Taking his cue from the Dutch, whom he regarded as mortal enemies for having engrossed such a vast proportion of French trade,[25] Colbert had set about rebuilding French commerce and industry on the three pillars of overseas colonies – as sources of raw materials and captive markets for finished and manufactured goods – merchant shipping and a royal navy to protect the shipping. This had led him inevitably to the imposition of high protective tariffs to keep the Dutch out, and to the creation of three joint-stock companies for the East Indies, the West Indies and the Levant. Unlike the great Dutch chartered companies on which these were supposedly modelled – even to nominal decentralization with local boards of directors – these were not in the main merchant-driven. The King and government officials were their chief shareholders; they were kept going by government support and were in practice directed by their Paris boards, guided by Colbert himself. As to be expected in such a highly centralized state, they were virtually arms of government set up and controlled to achieve government aims overseas.

Colbert, who despised the merchant class as self-centred, narrow-minded, unpatriotic profit-seekers, was always on guard against their advice and continually overrode it, sure that he knew better than they where their best interests lay. Criticizing the directors of the West Indies Company for thinking 'only of their own interests and not of the general welfare of the state', he wrote, 'But we should raise ourselves above our private interests to seek the general good.'[26] Trying to mimic the Dutch, he had thus missed the key to their success: that it hung on the success of merchants pursuing their own interests unfettered by the state, still less by patriotism. They had never made any secret of it. From the beginning they had extolled True Freedom as the absence of concentrated political power and the absence of central direction. Colbert used self-interest at the individual level, enticing foreign entrepreneurs and skilled workers with subsidies, tax advantages, pensions, even freedom of worship and patents of nobility; yet, like his centralizing predecessors and successors, he was too rational and too much of an idealist to imagine self-interest could play any part in his national aims.

Attempting to create a thriving commerce by central direction was inherently contradictory; eventually the market distortions created were bound to lead to general uncompetitiveness, which the people would have to bear. Above all, Colbert needed peace for success, but was bound to provoke foreign enmity and war when the government funds keeping the system turning would inevitably be directed towards the military. In the short term, however, while the central finances were healthy, he achieved astonishing results in certain desired directions.

He raised France in very short time into the foremost naval power – at least on paper – with 120 warships, four as large as the great English three-deckers and mounting an even heavier main battery of 36-pounders (equivalent to 40 English pounds). Altogether, by the early 1670s his fleet displaced some 115,000 tons, against an English fleet (run down because of debt from the Dutch war) totalling about 84,000 tons and a Dutch fleet of 102,000 tons. The Dutch still lacked three-deckers, but had many more cruisers than either of the other two.[27]

These were the three leading navies. Spain was exhausted after attempting unsuccessfully to regain Portugal and her colonies, and both Iberian powers had slipped into the third rank behind the navies of Denmark–Norway and Sweden, which disposed of little more than

30,000 tons (displacement) each.[28] It had become a triangular contest for predominance at sea, and from the English point of view France was now the more dangerous rival. Besides a first-class navy, Louis had built up the greatest army in Europe, and his plain ambition was to take the southern Netherlands, which Spain had become too weak to defend, on his way to the subjugation of the United Provinces. Colbert's ambition was to take over the Dutch monopolies. The prohibitive tariffs he had raised against the import of a range of Dutch specialities had already started a trade war; he had also established a Company of the North to trade directly with the Baltic, cutting out Dutch middlemen and shipping, and was challenging the VOC and WIC with expeditions to their spheres in the East and West Indies. In the West his ultimate ambition was to supplant the Dutch completely on the coast of Africa and in the Caribbean, and so take control of the slave trade and acquire the valuable stake the WIC had taken in the contract (*asiento de negros*) for supplying slaves to the Spanish colonies.[29]

The danger to England if Louis and Colbert should achieve their aims, thereby raising Louis to the hegemony of Europe by land and of the world by sea, was evident to English parliamentary and public opinion generally. It was as plain to Charles II. Yet the compulsions of debt and his desire to dispense with Parliament and rule, like Louis, as an absolute monarch proved more powerful than his misgivings. In 1669 he began secret negotiations with Louis for an offensive and defensive alliance directed against the Dutch – in effect, from his point of view, a continuation of the last war at sea with the aid of French subsidies and a French naval contingent, while the French army invaded the enemy homeland. To guard against Louis gathering all the fruits from the anticipated disembowelling of the republic, Charles asked Louis for sufficient money to fit out a commanding fleet and for bases on the Dutch coast as his share of the spoils; he also sought guarantees to prevent France from absorbing the Spanish Netherlands.

Louis finally agreed to pay some £200,000 annually for Charles's naval expenses – a quarter of Colbert's annual peacetime naval budget – and to provide a squadron of thirty warships to act with the English battle fleet. In addition he agreed to pay over £100,000 for Charles to convert to Catholicism. Whether Charles really intended to become a Catholic as well as an absolute monarch or whether this was a convenient device for extracting more money from the French king is uncertain; in the event he did not convert, although his brother, James, did. He was promised ports in Zeeland and Flanders as bases from which he might control the Dutch trading centres. The terms were signed in secret at Dover on 22 May 1670, the two kings agreeing to fall on their prey simultaneously.

This shameful conspiracy illustrates the extraordinarily divergent fortunes of the United Provinces and England in the hundred years since the Dutch revolt against Spain and the glories of Elizabeth's reign: both had sought and fought for overseas trade, but while one had become undisputed financial-commercial mistress of the world, the other had declined into a penurious supplicant to the King of France. It is a telling demonstration of the difference between true maritime power and the mere possession of a first-class navy.

Louis followed his pact with Charles by making similar alliances with the Elector of Cologne and the Prince Bishop of Münster on the inland borders of the United Provinces, each to be rewarded with territory when the republic was dismembered.

De Witt was aware of Louis's intentions but could not believe that Charles would act against the strong opinion in England opposed to war; he thought Charles would simply abstain. His first intimation of the truth came in 1671, when the English ambassador at The Hague, Sir William Temple, a good friend of the republic and of de Witt personally, was called home. Confirmation was provided by the appointment of his successor, George Downing, an accomplished troublemaker. Downing's instructions were to blow up a deliberately contrived quarrel about England's sovereignty at sea into justification for war. The dispute concerned a small royal yacht sent to fetch Lady Temple from The Hague; its captain had been instructed to sail through the Dutch fleet and exact 'the honour of the flag'. He had attempted to do so by firing shotted guns, but the Dutch had not struck ensigns or topsails. Downing demanded the punishment of the Dutch admiral and recognition of England's sovereignty in all waters, to be signified by Dutch fleets dipping to any English man-of-war of whatever size or class.

By this time Charles was in deeper financial trouble. Louis's small subsidy and £800,000 he had wrung from Parliament the previous year were quite inadequate to meet the naval debt, still less the expense of fitting out a battle fleet to beat the Dutch. Knowing he would not be able to extract any money from Parliament in its present mood, on 2 January 1672 he suspended payments to his creditors, converting the debts of over £1 million into interest-bearing loans. The shock this created undermined any remaining trust in his financial management; and, as the first open sign of divergence between his policy and the merchant interest, it may be seen in retrospect as marking the beginning of the end of the Stuart monarchy.

His hope was that he would soon replenish his treasury from Dutch prizes – in particular from a rich convoy from the Levant expected home in the spring with freight said to be worth £75,000. The convoy was intercepted off the Isle of Wight on 23 March by a squadron prepared for the purpose in Portsmouth, but the escorts made such stout resistance that only three merchantmen were taken. After this humiliating failure, on 27 March, Charles declared war on the United Provinces. Louis followed suit on 6 April, and the Prince Bishop of Münster and the Elector of Cologne the following month.

De Witt, meanwhile, once persuaded of the real threat from Charles, had concentrated his attention and resources on fitting out a fleet sufficient to deter him, but had rather neglected the threat on land. The regular army had been run down to a peace establishment of little over 30,000 men. Apparently placing his trust in the volunteer militias, certainly thwarted by lack of co-operation from the inland States, de Witt had left it too long before attempting to raise an additional 50,000 regulars and concluding treaties with Spain and the Elector of Brandenburg.[30] The latter promised 20,000 men in return for subsidies, but the men would take time to mobilize and were in any case a small force to set against the hostile alliance. Louis alone mustered 140,000 troops. Had the barrier fortresses on the Rhine been in good repair Louis would have needed his ratio of superiority, but they had not been properly maintained.

Within the United Provinces, alarm at the French threat had caused a surge of Orangist fervour. De Witt had attempted to neutralize it by granting William II's son a seat in the supreme Council of State, dominated by Holland, which directed strategic and military affairs. But as the true nature of the Anglo-French alliance and the unpreparedness of their own defences became apparent in early 1672 de Witt was forced to concede the appointment of the twenty-one-year-old Prince of Orange as captain-general, to become in addition admiral-general on completion of his twenty-second year.

The admiralties had succeeded in outbuilding England in two-decked battleships during the previous decade, and in all probability the fleet was also superior to the heavier but comparatively inexperienced fleet

Colbert had constructed for Louis.[31] De Witt had urged a pre-emptive descent on the Île d'Oléron, off La Rochelle, to use as a base for blockading the French west coast and, later, an attack on the French squadron fitting out in Brest to join the English; but more cautious counsels had prevailed. Now the task was to get the fleet to sea before the French united with the English fleet. The winning combination of Admiral de Ruyter as commander-in-chief and Cornelius de Witt as plenipotentiary of the States General was chosen again. They were instructed to sail to the Thames, enter the river, and attack and destroy whatever ships they met. Delayed by the late sailing of the Zeeland division, they did not reach the Thames before the English fleet under Charles's younger brother, the Duke of York, had left the river.

The French squadron under the Comte d'Estrées had sailed from Brest a few days earlier and awaited the Duke of York in Spithead, between Portsmouth and the Isle of Wight. Besides d'Estrées's 78-gun flagship, *St Philippe*, it comprised seven 70-gun two-deckers, a further sixteen mounting between 50 and 68 guns and three single-deckers of 45–46 guns, altogether twenty-seven fit by the standards of the day to fight in the line, together with three frigates, six fireships and various smaller vessels.[32] The 70-gun two-deckers particularly impressed English observers. Like Dutch warships, they were broader and carried their lower gun ports considerably higher out of the water than comparably armed English ships. The lines of one, the *Superbe*, were taken, and the English chief designer, Sir Anthony Deane, built a copy which was to prove so successful it was followed with a class of nine more.

The Duke of York, flying his flag in the 100-gun three-decker *Royal Prince*, arrived off the Isle of Wight on 7 May, whereupon d'Estrées weighed and joined him with much noise from saluting guns and ships' companies calling out hollas. That evening it was learned that the Dutch fleet was in the Strait of Dover, but a strong north-easterly prevented the combined fleet sailing. De Ruyter and de Witt for their part decided that, now their enemies had joined, it would be imprudent to bear down and engage them in the Channel between two hostile shores; instead, following renewed instructions from Johan de Witt for offensive action in the Thames, they stood back to the estuary and sent a light squadron in to attempt a repeat of the Medway action. The forts at the entrance had been strengthened, however, and they were unable to get past.

During this time the Duke of York, 'very earnest to get up with the Dutch fleet',[33] beat up-Channel, passing Dover on the 16th, and steering northward. De Ruyter's sails were sighted in the morning of the 19th, whereupon the Duke hoisted the Union flag at the mizzen peak – the signal to form line of battle. His 'Instructions for the Better Ordering of the Fleet in Battle', virtually unchanged from instructions he had issued in the previous war,[34] had been copied to d'Estrées and his captains. They prescribed a strict order of squadrons and of ships within squadrons. The fleet vice admiral's squadron – in this case d'Estrées's – flying white ensigns was to lead; the Duke's own squadron flying red ensigns was to form the centre and the fleet rear admiral's squadron, flying blue ensigns, the rear. A similar pattern was followed within each squadron, with the squadronal admiral commanding the centre division, his vice the leading division and his junior admiral the rear.

All emphasis was on keeping a strict line, each ship following her next ahead at half a cable's distance – a mere 100 yards – in 'reasonable weather', and maintaining the line so long as the enemy retained his formation; thus ships were not to 'pursue any small number of the enemy before the main [body] of the enemy fleet shall be disabled or shall run'.[35] The ideal aimed at was to gain the windward position and form a line extending the whole length of the enemy formation and parallel to it, before bearing down to engage from very close range on the same tack as the enemy, tacking with him if he went about and so retaining the weather gage. With the heterogenous collection of ships of all sizes and sailing qualities forming the line, all still steered by whipstaff to instructions called down from the quarterdeck, the ideal was impossible in practice. Nonetheless there is ample testimony from all sides that the English had preserved formidable order during the 'line' battles of the previous war.

The Dutch, too, had adopted a line formation in three squadrons, to prevent the confusion that had marred many of their actions. Their aim, however, remained to close and board, so taking advantage of 'the special aptitude and enthusiasm which our sailors have in jumping aboard and entering enemy ships'.[36]

It took most of the day for the combined fleet to stretch into its order of battle and close within three miles, the French van opposite the Dutch van. The allies outnumbered the Dutch by 103 sail to 85, including smaller vessels and fireships in both cases; in ships of 40 guns and upwards the superiority was 75 to 62, and in guns 4,810 to 3,846. In weight of shot and concentrated firepower the disparity was greater, since the flagships of the six divisions forming the two English squadrons were three-decker first rates of 96 or 100 guns.[37] Since the combined fleet also had the advantage of the wind, de Ruyter wisely retired south-easterly towards the shoals off the Flanders coast. The Duke of York followed, but sent small craft ahead to sound the depth; when these began firing guns to signify less than five fathoms (thirty feet) he signalled the fleet to put about, then stood westerly under easy sail. De Ruyter conformed, keeping in touch with the allies through the night. The wind strengthened next day, raising high seas which made it impossible for the English heavy ships to open their lower gun ports. The Duke of York nonetheless formed line again, and de Ruyter again retired towards his own coast. During the night the two fleets became separated, and next morning, with no sign of the Dutch, the Duke steered northward for Sole Bay on the Suffolk coast to water and provision.

He dropped anchor on 23 May some two miles off Southwold – the church tower bearing west-north-west – the rest of his squadron anchoring about him, the lighter ships closer inshore. The Blue squadron, commanded by Pepys's patron, Edward Montagu, first Earl of Sandwich, in the 100-gun *Royal James*, anchored some distance to the north of him, and d'Estrées some miles to the south between Dunwich and Aldeburgh. Over the following days, as boats plied between ships and shore ferrying fresh water in casks, animals for the table, bread, fresh vegetables and other victuals, scouts were sent out to reconnoitre seaward. The Duke expected that, if the wind changed into a favourable quarter for the Dutch, de Ruyter would sail across and attempt to surprise him at anchor. On the 27th the wind did go round into the east; yet, apparently lulled by an earlier sighting of the Dutch at anchor off their own coast, the Duke took no further precautions and even permitted preparations for heeling his flagship to scrub her bottom next morning.

It was during this evolution before sunrise next day, 28 May, that the fleet was startled by guns to seaward fired by one of d'Estrées's scouts, which could be seen standing in with her t'gallants flying free – the signal for the enemy in sight – and beyond her the upper sails of the Dutch fleet silhouetted against the eastern sky.

It was a stunning moment. The fleet flagship was heeled, parties from ships were ashore, boats were fetching stores, gun-decks were cluttered. Had the wind not been light, it might have been a prelude to disaster. As it was, the combined fleet was allowed some three and half hours to recall all hands, make sail, weigh, and clear decks for action. Even so the surprise de Ruyter achieved affected the engagement, for the line was never properly formed and the Duke of York, whose written instructions attempted to provide for almost every eventuality, failed to communicate his intention to his squadron commanders.

The tide was flooding, running southward along the coast, the ships riding with heads to the north; the wind was from east-south-east, the Dutch fleet in the north-east quarter. The Duke resolved to sail off in the direction the ships were heading, to meet the enemy on a northerly course, with Sandwich rather than d'Estrées leading, thus with the normal order of the line inverted. This was not explained to the officer whom d'Estrées sent to the *Royal Prince* for instructions; he was merely told to keep as close to the wind as possible.[38] Having weighed, therefore, d'Estrées went about and steered close-hauled southward, no doubt expecting the Duke to tack and follow him in the prescribed order. He did not do so. A huge gap opened between the French and the two English squadrons sailing northward.

The English experienced great difficulty forming line, especially those lighter ships which had been anchored closer inshore; these had to work up into the light breeze towards the divisional flagships, which by reason of their size dared not ease off the wind to help them for fear of being boxed into shoal water. Sandwich's flagship, *Royal James*, was furthest from the shore of all the Blue squadron, and her captain, Richard Haddock, did ease off the wind for a while to assist his division, all but two of whom managed to claw up into line with him; he still remained to windward of both his leading division, commanded by Vice Admiral Sir Joseph Jordan in the 100-gun *Royal Sovereign*, and his rear division, under Rear Admiral Sir John Kempthorne in the 96-gun *St Andrew*. Astern of them came Rear Admiral Sir John Harman, leading the Duke of York's Red squadron in the 96-gun *Royal Charles*; his instructions were to 'keep next the Blue' squadron. While he endeavoured to comply, only three of his six battle ships managed to close him. The Duke's centre division was in even worse order: of ten ships which should have been in line with the *Royal Prince*, which was further from the shore even than Sandwich's *Royal James*, only the 82-gun *Victory*, commanded by the Earl of Ossory, was in position astern, and the 90-gun *St Michael*, under Sir Robert Holmes, almost in position off the larboard – lee – bow. Two of his fireships also contrived to reach their stations close in the flagship's wake, ahead of the *Victory*, but the other eight battle ships straggled to leeward. Last in the English order and well to leeward was the van division of the Red under Vice Admiral Sir Edward Spragge in the 96-gun *London*.

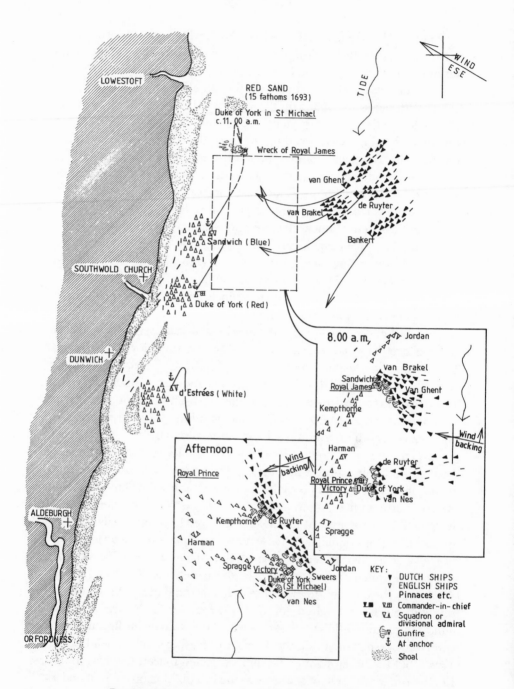

LOWESTOFT

RED SAND
(15 fathoms 1693)

Duke of York in St Michael
c.11.00 a.m.

Wreck of Royal James

van Ghent

van Brakel   de Ruyter

Bankert

TIDE

WIND
ESE

SOUTHWOLD CHURCH

Sandwich (Blue)

Duke of York (Red)

DUNWICH

d'Estrées (White)

8.00 a.m.   Jordan

van Brakel

Sandwich
Royal James   Van Ghent

Kempthorne

Harman   de Ruyter

Wind
backing

Royal Prince
Victory   Duke of York
van Nes

Afternoon

Royal Prince

Wind
backing

Kempthorne   de Ruyter

Harman

Spragge   Victory
Duke of York Sweers
(St Michael)

van Nes

Spragge

Jordan

ALDEBURGH

OR FORDNESS

KEY:
▼ DUTCH SHIPS
▽ ENGLISH SHIPS
ı Pinnaces etc.
▼▣ ▽▣ Commander-in-chief
▼▲ ▽▲ Squadron or
          divisional admiral
▽ Gunfire
⚓ At anchor
Shoal

Battle diagram 3   Battle of Sole Bay, 28 May 1672

The Dutch tactics of mass attack to overwhelm sections of the enemy fleet and overpower individual ships by boarding were particularly suited to exploit this disarray in the English formation. The squadrons were organized for attack in small groups of two or usually three ships led by a flag officer, each flag officer adhering to his squadron admiral. In this instance de Ruyter had taken vessels from each squadron to form an additional advanced squadron of eighteen ships and eighteen fire-ships to create confusion before the main bodies came to action. This was commanded by Captain Jan van Brakel, a fiery officer who had led the decisive assault up the Medway in the previous war.

In the van of the main fleet, thus at the southern end as they bore down south-westerly, was the predominantly Zeeland squadron led by Lieutenant Admiral Adriaan Bankert flying his flag in the 70-gun *Walcheren.* Under him were two vice admirals – from Zeeland and Friesland – and two rear admirals, termed scouts by night. De Ruyter led the centre squadron with his flag in the 80-gun *Zeven Provincien*, supported by Lieutenant Admiral Aert van Nes in the 76-gun *Eendracht*, a vice admiral and a scout by night, all of the Maas (Rotterdam) admiralty. The rear was led by Lieutenant Admiral van Ghent of Amsterdam in the 82-gun *Dolfijn*, supported by Vice Admirals Sweers (Amsterdam) and Schram (North Quarter) and two scouts by night.

Seeing the French squadron sailing off southward, Bankert led the Zeeland squadron south-westerly to contain them while de Ruyter, van Ghent and van Brakel of the advanced squadron put their helms down and wore round to a north-westerly course converging on the two English squadrons stemming north-easterly against the tide. With the wind behind them, the Dutch admirals were perfectly poised to bring overwhelming concentrations to bear on whichever ragged English divisions they chose. There was nothing the Duke of York could do to prevent it. Moreover, with Bankert's squadron reduced to fifteen – since the withdrawal of ships for the advanced squadron – taking on twenty-seven French, the odds against the English had narrowed almost to equality: forty-seven to forty-eight, although the English still had more and heavier guns.

De Ruyter had no difficulty picking out the royal standard flying at the main of the *Royal Prince*, and pointed her out to his sailing master: 'There's our man!'[39] De Ruyter appeared and sounded like the plain sailor he was. Born in 1607, fifth son of a poor family in Zeeland, he had gone to sea as a boy of eleven, studied navigation in his twenties, and by thirty was commanding a privateer. Despite the renown he had since won leading numerous Dutch fleets, he remained unaffected – a simple, God-fearing man, hating drunkenness or excess, who at home read the Bible to his wife in a broad Zeeland accent or sang psalms with her.

Nearby, on the flagship's quarterdeck, Cornelius de Witt, suffering from gout, sat on a velvet upholstered chair by the companion skylights, surrounded by a guard of twelve halberdiers uniformed in the red and yellow of Holland. The two could hardly have been more different in background, education, experience or indeed appearance. They provide an apt vignette, representative of the two classes, sailors and regents, on which the power of the United Provinces was founded.

Some time soon after seven, as the *Zeven Provincien* and her two seconds and fireships, and to larboard van Nes in the *Eendracht* with his two seconds, wafted slowly in the light breeze on a converging course towards the *Royal Prince*, still to windward of all her squadron save the *Victory* and two fireships astern, van Brakel's advanced squadron began exchanging fire at comparatively long range with Sandwich's centre division, and van Ghent adjusted his course towards Sandwich's great flagship, *Royal James*. Within half an hour the spearheads of all Dutch groups had closed inside a quarter of a mile and rounded up to open their broadsides: van Brakel, van Ghent, Sweers and their consorts against the *Royal James* and the ships with her; to the south, de Ruyter and van Nes against the *Royal Prince*. The English gunners responded.

Gun smoke rose in the clear air of a perfect summer morning, reflected in a sea scarcely rippled by a dying wind; the *Royal Prince*'s senior lieutenant, John Narborough, described the water as 'smooth as a milk bowl'.[40] Accompanying the thunder of the great pieces, shot rushed with sounds like tearing canvas or thudded through timber, sending shivers of wood like darts across the crowded gun-decks. The first wounded were carried to the ladders and down to surgeons' teams on the orlop deck; the remains of those killed outright were eased through the ports and dropped into the sea.

The English divisions ahead and astern of both the *Royal James* and the *Royal Prince* were scarcely engaged, and were soon cut off from all sight of their embattled centre divisions by the drifts of smoke. In the van, Jordan, by his subsequent account, clawed up close to the breeze, attempting to stretch ahead far enough to weather the Dutch and then tack down on them from to windward; astern and some way to leeward of the fighting around Sandwich, Kempthorne was only lightly engaged. Astern of him Harman, leading the Duke of York's squadron with the three of his own ships that had been able to form up with him, found himself unable to see anything of the ships he was attempting to follow. In the extreme rear Spragge was also left out of the fight; in the light airs he could not work his way up to the storm about the Duke of York, and soon lost all but the most general idea of the whereabouts of his commander-in-chief in the smoke.

In tactical terms, de Ruyter had achieved all he could have hoped. He was prevented from decisive victory at the two key points in the English formation only by the massive strength and firepower of the three-decker flagships there.

By eight o'clock he, van Nes and their seconds and fireships were within 'musket shot' of the *Royal Prince*. This may have meant as little as 150 yards, but in view of the numbers of vessels engaged must surely have been over 200 yards. John Narborough counted seven of them about the flagship: de Ruyter off the bow, van Nes on the quarter, and other large two-deckers between them on the broadside, all 'firing at us very briskly'.[41] The *Victory* was astern, but to Narborough it appeared they were fighting alone; 'none of our squadron could get up with us for their lives, they being so becalmed'.[42] The Duke of York went the length of the ship encouraging the guns' crews at their warm work and when aft called continually to the quartermaster to luff up closer to the enemy; in Narborough's words, he was 'General, Soldier, Pilot, Master, Seaman; to say all, he is everything that man can be, and most pleasant when the great shot are thundering about his ears'.[43]

Shortly after eight two fireships emerged from the smoke under tow, one rowing herself with sweeps. The flagship's helm was hauled up to turn away and bring the heavy stern chasers to bear. As the Duke and his flag captain, Sir John Cox, watched from the poop, a ball killed Sir John; command of the flagship passed to Narborough. The fireships, as they neared, were hit repeatedly by shot and so holed that one sank; the other veered off course and was lost to sight.

In the mêlée to the north, van Brakel, with the recklessness he had shown at the Medway, bore down from the smoke in his 62-gun two-decker *Groot Hollandia*, across the course of Sandwich's flagship. The flag captain, Haddock, ordered the helm up and the mizzen brailed to try to swing the bows clear and take her on the broadside, but there was insufficient wind to turn her more than two or three points before the Dutchman, urged by the tide athwart her keel, fell aboard. Hurled grappling hooks caught in the flagship's rigging; sharpshooters from the tops fired at the defenders summoned to the forecastle as the ships jarred together, the *Groot Hollandia* caught across the *Royal James*'s bows, her larboard guns able to sweep diagonally down the English decks.

With the flagship unmanageable and pressed by fresh enemy ships, Sandwich asked Haddock whether it would not be best to send a party aboard the Dutchman against the bow, to take her by force. Haddock replied that this would take men from the guns. He estimated they had already lost over 250 men, and must expect to lose another 100 in a fight to capture her. Even then they would be unable to cast her loose, as the tide was binding her fast athwart their hawse. Moreover, if they reduced the guns' crews, another enemy might board them. Sandwich accepted his arguments.[44]

The two ships, locked together, drifted slowly southward with the tide. Almost all the *Royal James*'s upper-deck guns on the engaged side were by now dismounted by shot and their crews dead or wounded. The heavy pieces in the lower tiers remained in action, however, and, when van Ghent ranged up within 'musket shot' to starboard, his broadside fire and volleys from small arms were more than repaid. Van Ghent himself was mortally wounded; command of his squadron passed to Sweers.

Kempthorne, coming up from astern of the mêlée, was still so far to leeward and the smoke was so thick he could not make out what vessel was lying against the flagship's weather bow. Judging she must be English, he sent a pinnace to find out what had happened, and stood on past. Way ahead in the van, Jordan's division had managed to stretch past a Dutch group which had engaged them in an attempt to prevent them gaining the wind. Jordan now tacked and led southerly, forcing the few Dutch ships to go about as well and fall back on their consorts engaging the *Royal James*. Earlier, Jordan had received a message from Sandwich by boat requiring him to tack and bear down to his relief. But the smoke of the action was too thick for him to make out the desperate predicament the flagship was in, and, instead of bearing down in support, he concentrated on keeping his windward advantage. Haddock saw his ships and wrote in his subsequent account, 'Sir Joseph Jordan passed us by to windward very unkindly, with how many followers of his division I remember not, and took no notice at all of us.'[45]

In the action to the south, the *Royal Prince* remained virtually alone against de Ruyter's concentration. Among many dead were several gallants from the Duke of York's retinue. The rigging was cut to pieces by shot, but no one could go aloft to repair it, such was the volume of fire. At about ten o'clock a ball shattered the main topmast, which fell to the deck, smothering the mainsail and many upper-deck guns and making it impossible to work the ship. The Duke of York decided to shift his flag to Holmes's *St Michael*, still off his lee bow, and, instructing Narborough to bear away downwind to repair damages as soon as he saw the royal standard hoisted in that ship, he and a few of his surviving aides and his pilot left by boat. It took some time for de Ruyter and van Nes to perceive the new flagship through the smoke, but Narborough managed to have the *Royal Prince*'s head towed round to sail her downwind, after which the Dutch became aware of the transfer and turned their attention to the *St Michael*.

The breeze had backed during the morning and was now rather to the north of east, so the fighting groups continued on a northerly course which took the Duke of York, de Ruyter and van Nes up past and inshore of the mêlée about Sandwich towards the shoals stretching out below Lowestoft. Some time after eleven the Duke's pilot came to him and reported the soundings down to twelve fathoms (seventy-two feet); it was time to tack, or they risked going aground on the Red Sand shoal off Lowestoft. No sooner had he uttered the words than he and another standing by him were killed by the same round shot.

Sir Robert Holmes's pilot agreed with the advice – particularly as the flood tide had ended and the ebb set in, pushing them northward – and the ship was tacked. The smoke of action and burning fireships concealed this manoeuvre from de Ruyter and the Duke's own division, and, as the breeze was too light to blow the royal standard out, the Duke had another period of respite. Steadying on a south-easterly course, he sent a pinnace to acquaint his ships of his whereabouts. Van Nes closed one of these which had become isolated, the 82-gun *Royal Katherine*, and poured in such a withering fire that two of his smaller ships were able to board and take her.

In the *Royal James*, meanwhile, Haddock was struck in the foot by a musket ball fired from one of the Dutch tops. His shoe filled with blood, forcing him to go below to have the wound tended. In the orlop with the maimed and wounded, he remembered that the ebb would have begun, and sent word up to Sandwich advising him to drop a stern anchor. This was done, and, as the great ship brought up to it, the *Groot Hollandia* was carried by the northerly set away from the bow. Sandwich sent a party over the head and bowsprit to board her and cut away grappling lines and rigging still snaring her; she drifted free, some 200 of her 300 men dead or wounded.[46] The English scrambled back aboard the *Royal James* as she went. Haddock then sent up another message, advising cutting the anchor cable and setting the mainsail. Sandwich again complied and sent down to thank Haddock for his good advice 'and withal to be of good cheer, for he doubted not that we should save our ship'.[47] It was not to be. They were beginning to get under way when Sweers closed to attack and a blazing fireship commanded by Captain van de Ryn, another of the heroes from the Medway, succeeded in getting alongside.

Flames licked up the *Royal James's* paintwork and gilded carvings, igniting hanging rigging and tarred shrouds, curling in through open gun ports and the holes pierced and splintered by shot, forcing the men at their quarters to retreat. Sandwich's own fireships, which should have towed the burning vessel clear, had not been able to work out to the flagship; the one that had been in company had borne away downwind after her captain had been killed by a shot. So the fire took hold and spread across the decks and up the masts. As it became evident the ship was lost, Sandwich took boat to transfer his flag. But by this time men were leaping into the sea to save themselves and some of these, clutching at the sides of his boat and trying to scramble in, overturned it. Sandwich and his aides were drowned.

Sweers's division meanwhile transferred their attention to the flagship's principal second, the 82-gun *Henry*, which they surrounded, boarded and took. Thus far the concentration de Ruyter and his admirals had achieved had brought spectacular results: the crippling of the fleet flagship, the destruction of the Blue flagship and the capture of two important 82-gun second rates, besides inflicting heavy damage on many others alow and aloft. However, with the light breeze still in the east, neither of the prizes could be sailed into the safety of the Dutch fleet, and both were later to be retaken, the *Royal Katherine* by her own crew.

The south-easterly course the *St Michael* was now steering took her straight towards the blazing hulk of the *Royal James*, and, as it seemed she might not weather her, the helm was hauled up to pass to leeward. Seeing survivors clinging to spars and timbers in the water, the Duke hailed the captain of a frigate from Spragge's division that had come up under his lee and told him to save as many as he could. Sailing on, followed still by the *Victory* and three others of the centre division who had

found the flag, the *St Michael* steered between Sweers's squadron to windward and van Nes and others to leeward, and was heavily engaged by
both 'at musket shot'. Spragge, so far scarcely in action, had caught sight
of the royal standard and was trying to get up with the *St Michael* with
four of his division and a frigate, as was Harman. To windward and
astern, Kempthorne, with some of his ships and some of Sandwich's,
was engaged with de Ruyter and his seconds; and to windward of everyone was Jordan, with six or seven in his line.

So the fighting continued in smoke-clouded groups south-eastward,
followed to leeward by those English ships which had not been able to
work up into their divisional lines and by Narborough in the *Royal Prince*,
with the wreckage now cleared from the upper deck, the rigging spliced
and a spiritsail rigged on a spar serving as main topsail.

The hulk of the *Royal James* was still burning when Narborough
passed her some time after three o'clock, and several boats were rescu-
ing men from the water. A little later he saw the first English successes:
the 48-gun *Stavoren* of the Amsterdam squadron disabled and taken, and
the 54-gun *Josua* from de Ruyter's group sunk by broadsides from the 72-
gun *Edgar* of Sandwich's division following astern of Kempthorne.
Against these two comparatively light losses, Sweers's group succeeded
in crippling two heavy ships, the *Cambridge* and the *Resolution*, both of
seventy guns, forcing them out of the Duke of York's line. The *St Michael*
herself was by then heavily damaged aloft and taking in so much water
through holes low in the hull that Spragge in the *London* and some of his
division were able to pass her to leeward and take the lead; indeed, after
four o'clock it became evident the *St Michael* would have to fall off downwind to refit and stop her leaks. The Duke again transferred his flag, this
time to the *London*, although Spragge had stretched so far ahead it took
his boat three-quarters of an hour to reach her. Meanwhile the *Victory*,
which had stood by the Duke's successive flagships from the start of the
action in the early morning, was also forced to bear away out of the fight
to make repairs.

An officer from the *Royal James* who had been taken aboard de
Ruyter's flagship afterwards described the Dutch commander-in-chief
during these close engagements of the afternoon in words strikingly
similar to those used by Narborough of the Duke of York: 'Is that an
admiral? That is an admiral, a captain, a master, a seaman and a soldier.
This man, this hero, is everything at once.'[48]

Shortly after the Duke of York hoisted the royal standard in the

London, the van of Bankert's Zeeland squadron was sighted in the south-west returning northward, the French van to leeward. In containing d'Estrées's numerically stronger squadron, Bankert had not engaged in close-mêlée tactics like de Ruyter and van Ghent, but had wrought considerable damage by stand-off gunnery and had inflicted some 450 casualties against under 350 sustained in his own ships.

When de Ruyter made out the Zeelanders' sails from his position in the centre of the Dutch lines, about three miles astern and to windward of the Duke of York, he hoisted a blue flag at his fore-topmast head, the signal for the divisions to form on him, and lasked down some two points off the wind – now in the north-east – to join the groups to leeward; all then bore down towards Bankert, who tacked and stood south-easterly to meet them. D'Estrées also tacked, while the Duke of York backed his sails until joined by Jordan and Kempthorne's divisions, then bore away after the Dutch, now for the first time that day all to leeward of him. De Ruyter, when he had collected his fleet together, set his foresail and top-sails and continued south-easterly. The Duke and the comparatively few ships with him followed just out of gunshot through the evening and the rest of that night.

It was effectively the end of the Battle of Sole Bay. Although the Duke managed to draw most of the English and the French squadron into line of battle with the advantage of the wind the following afternoon, fog followed by heavy weather prevented them closing the Dutch. Eventually both sides retired to their own harbours to refit. For those who had borne the brunt of the day, it had been the most harrowing, bloody encounter. De Ruyter, sixty-five years old, said he had never before taken part in so desperate and prolonged a battle.[49] The bodies of well over 1,200 slain drifted in the tides or fetched up on the East Anglian coast, among them three out of the twelve halberdiers who had surrounded Cornelius de Witt in his armchair on the quarterdeck of the *Zeven Provincien*; three other halberdiers had been wounded. Total casualties were well over 2,000 on each side.

Tactical honours had undoubtedly gone to de Ruyter. In material terms too the complete destruction of the 100-gun *Royal James*, which burned to the water's edge, although without blowing up – apparently because the powder in her magazines was damp – was worth more than the two lighter Dutch ships and another lost the following day to accidental fire; while if the Dutch had managed to carry off their two 82-gun prizes, and some other English heavy ships crippled and forced out of the line had not been able to retire so easily into the Thames, the material advantage would have been much greater.

More important was the strategic result. The English claimed they had forced the Dutch back to their own coast. Yet they were in no condition to keep them there. De Ruyter and de Witt had wrought such damage that the principal English ships were forced back to port to refit. This was the crucial outcome of the battle. The English had for the time being been rendered incapable of blockading the Dutch coast, intercepting the returning Dutch Indies fleet or supporting a planned seaborne invasion of Zeeland. In this sense the battle was decisive, for the other arm of the Anglo-French assault, the land invasion, had met no obstacles. Louis's armies had advanced along both banks of the Maas, bypassing the key Dutch fortress of Maastricht, crossed the Rhine below the junction with the river IJssel, and stood poised behind the main lines of defence to march upon Holland itself. Meanwhile the troops of Münster had invaded the inland province of Overijssel. Had the English been able to establish themselves in strength on the Zeeland coast, so winning command of the sea approaches, the survival of the United Provinces would have been doubtful in the extreme.

As it was, the sluices were opened and the dykes cut to flood the low farmland and gardens of southern Holland to form a barrier of water and marsh from the Maas to the Zuider Zee. The water rose only slowly, because of dry summer weather, but Louis missed his opportunity: instead of advancing directly on Holland, he set about reducing the IJssel barrier fortresses and garrisoning the inland provinces. The situation remained so dangerous, however, that the States General opened peace negotiations, and the populace, already disillusioned by the rotten state of the country's defences, and suspecting treachery, rose in fury against the regents and for the Orangists. Such pressure was generated that in early June the States of both Zeeland and Holland elected the young Prince of Orange as their stadtholder, William III, and a few days later the States General proclaimed him captain- and admiral-general of the Provinces for life.

The popular fear and resentment of the regent government was not stilled. Demonstrations continued, orchestrated by the Orangists for their own power purposes. In August, Cornelius de Witt was arrested on the word of a convicted perjurer for conspiracy to murder William. When William refused to intercede and the judge proceeded to torture to extract a confession, Johan de Witt resigned his office as Grand

Pensionary of Holland. He had already been wounded in the shoulder in an assassination attempt. Later that month, while visiting his brother in prison, a mob trapped them both. A company of the Hague militia supported by regular cavalry was responsible for maintaining civil order, but the cavalry were called away to a fictitious uprising elsewhere, whereupon the militia – in this case notoriously Orangist in sympathy – stood aside and incited the mob to violence.[50] The brothers were clubbed, stabbed, shot, hung by the feet from a scaffold, and subjected to a frenzy of mutilation during which their internal organs were cut out, roasted and eaten. As an example of the primal savagery festering beneath the brilliant surface of the wealthiest, most civilized nation in Europe, it is an instructive episode. Sir William Temple commented that his good friend Johan de Witt had 'deserved a better fate, and a better return from his country after eighteen years spent in their ministry, without any care for his entertainment or ease, and little of his fortune'.[51]

After these contrived murders, William purged the States of Holland and Zeeland of those who had been sympathetic to de Witt, replacing them with his own supporters and gaining greater real power than any previous stadtholder. Meanwhile de Ruyter had escorted the Indies fleet safely home from the Ems, which it had reached northabout around Scotland. The water had risen in the inundated areas, obstructing all Louis's routes to the heart of the Dutch state, and troops provided by the treaties de Witt had concluded with Spain and the Elector of Brandenburg reached Cologne and drew off French forces south-eastward. The danger was not over, but the crisis had passed. Louis and Charles had missed their most favourable opportunity.

For the campaigning season of 1673 a French squadron under d'Estrées again joined the English fleet, now under the command of Prince Rupert, a cavalry officer who had served Charles I brilliantly in the English Civil War. De Ruyter was again outnumbered and heavily outgunned, but fought a series of defensive actions in the shoal waters off Zeeland and finally off the Texel which denied the allies any opportunity to launch a seaborne invasion or even to paralyse commercial traffic. Meanwhile, as in the previous wars, English ships were denied entry to the Baltic and were preyed on by privateers from the Channel to the Mediterranean and the Caribbean. The merchants' dislike of the war had turned to despair and deeper distrust of Charles's government. They perceived France now as a far greater naval-commercial threat than the United Provinces. Moreover, William had agents of subversion within the country who exploited the internal dangers of Charles's French policy so well there was scarcely a member of either House of Parliament who did not equate the alliance with Louis with popery and absolutism in England; and no doubt they were correct.

In the supply debate in the Commons that October 1673, the feeling was almost unanimous against providing money to continue the war. Among the many who addressed the vital strategic issues was Sir William Coventry: 'The interest of the King of England is to keep France from being too great on the Continent, and the French interest is to keep us from being masters of the sea'[52] – a concise policy summary that was to be repeated in the House and government in many forms down the centuries.

As for the Dutch, Sir William said, 'since the Act of Navigation, we have grown upon them, not they upon us; they have only gained upon the nutmeg trade since the Amboina business, but in all other parts of trade we grow upon them'.[53]

Charles was refused money to set out the fleet the following year, and had no option but to drop out of his alliance with Louis and conclude peace with the United Provinces.[54] It was the third time the English had been forced to back down; and once again nothing had been gained from all the blood and treasure expended. Charles had succeeded only in building a formidable opposition within the country.

With England out of the way and the water line holding, William III and his German and Spanish allies were able to take the offensive against France. Louis was held to a long struggle which turned inevitably on economic strength. And, since war had ruined the foundations of Colbert's mercantile policy by forcing the diversion of state support from his commercial projects and exposing French colonial and Baltic trade to the superior power of the Dutch overseas, it was the merchants of Amsterdam who prevailed. In the peace Louis was forced into signing at Nijmegen in 1678, the high tariffs with which Colbert had begun the trade war against the Dutch were cut drastically.

In other respects the war ended in stalemate, both principals exhausted with debt. Yet for a very small nation with a population of no more than two and a half million set upon by Europe's greatest army and greatest navy in combination for the purpose of robbery, a favourable draw was an outstanding success, indicative of the supremacy of commercial-naval strength – or true maritime power – against great territorial odds. The decisive battles had been won early on by de Ruyter, first against the Duke of York at Sole Bay, subsequently by the masterly campaign against Prince Rupert – assisted by the inexperience and lack of total commitment of the French. These defensive triumphs had allowed the United Provinces to survive the first terrific onslaught of territorial power and granted the republic time to harness allies for a long war.

De Ruyter died of wounds to his left foot and right leg sustained in action against the French in the Mediterranean in 1676. In truth he had been depleted by years of continuous high command. In the roll call of great admirals, he stands second to none. His career spanned the three Anglo-Dutch wars and some of the most prolonged, grimmest naval battles ever fought. The fate of the United Provinces had rested upon his shoulders, and he had borne it triumphantly. If at times he displayed more caution than some celebrated British admirals of the late eighteenth and early nineteenth centuries, it was because he generally commanded numerically inferior fleets and lighter, more lightly gunned ships. His body was embalmed and brought home in his flagship to Amsterdam, where, after lying in state, larger crowds than had ever been drawn to the city followed his funeral cortège to the Nieuwekeerk on the Dam square. Unlike his predecessor, Maarten Tromp, who had been an ardent Orangist, de Ruyter was always a States Party republican.

6

The 'Glorious Revolution', and Beachy Head, 1690

A HUNDRED YEARS after Philip II of Spain first attempted the invasion of England from the Netherlands – if that was indeed his aim – William III of Orange accomplished it. Seen in isolation, William's enterprise was bold to the point of recklessness, his success a miracle depending on a succession of crucial wind changes, the result a major shift in the direction of world history. From the maritime perspective, though, it was little more than a realization of existing trends; and, however achieved, the result – a union between England and the United Provinces against France – seems to have been ordained by the growing power of Louis XIV.

Such a union of the two 'maritime powers' had been advocated for decades in England. The Dutch merchant community had naturally resisted, but the young Prince of Orange prepared himself for his destiny. He had inherited Stuart blood from his mother, the daughter of Charles I, and in 1677 he had married his cousin, Mary, daughter of the Duke of York, subsequently James II of England. Long before this, his Anglophilia had been noted by the English ambassador Sir William Temple, who reported on him in 1669 as 'a most extreme hopeful Prince . . . a young man of more parts than ordinary, & of the better sort; that is not lying in that kind of wit which is neither of use to one's self nor to anybody else, but in good, plain sense, with show of application . . . and that with extreme, good, agreeable humour and dispositions'. Temple had concluded the glowing testimonial with 'and never anybody raved so much after England, as well the language as all else that belonged to it'.[1]

William's master motive, however, was the containment of Louis XIV. The creation of a grand European alliance to prevent France gaining Continental hegemony had been his goal from the first, and was to remain the single guiding principle of his foreign policy; as the Marquis of Halifax was to put it, 'he hath such a mind to invade France that it would incline one to think he took England only in his way'.[2]

The English had long distrusted French aims. Debates in the English parliament from before the third Anglo-Dutch war make it clear that the growth of Louis's fleet had focused attention on the French king as the real enemy. It was suggested as early as 1675 that 'those we were so tender of before, our friends the French, are now become the object of our fears' and 'the nation can never be beaten at sea by the Dutch, but may be by the French'.[3] Lord Shaftesbury had said, 'The French king is the most potent of us all at sea . . . shall a Prince so wise, so intent upon his affairs, be thought to make all these preparations to sail overland and fall on the back of Hungary, or batter the walls of Kamnitz?'[4]

William had been constrained from acting on this natural convergence of views by the Holland regents; it was they who had insisted on calling a halt to the last war after Louis had offered a reduction in Colbert's prohibitive import duties. Since then, Dutch overseas trade, shipping and commerce had enjoyed a resurgence and France had again become a principal outlet for the manufactures and re-exports of the United Provinces. Another war with the republic's great neighbour appeared to be against every merchant, hence every national, interest; the regents worked to consolidate friendship with Louis, not to confront him, and once again in peace they cut back on their army and navy. Yet, just as Colbert's protective tariffs had provoked the last trade war, so Dutch post-war penetration of French markets, depressing French commerce and industry – to a greater extent perhaps in perception than in reality – was bound to provoke another round of trade war.

It began in August 1687: Louis banned Dutch herring from France – unless preserved in French salt. In September he reneged on the peace terms of Nijmegen by reintroducing prohibitive import duties, increasing the tariffs in the following months until by the end of the year it had become impossible to sell Dutch cloth in France.[5] Regent opinion swung towards William's belief in the need to contain Louis with a grand alliance by land and sea. The latter was particularly pressing since the fleet built by Colbert, who had died in 1683, was now, under his son, the Marquis de Seignelay, the strongest in the world, exceeding even the fleet of James II of England and twice the size of the United Provinces' own run-down service: approximately 140,000 against 68,000 tons displacement, headed by magnificent 110-gun three-decker first rates *extraordinaires* almost twice the size and gun weight of the republic's largest warships.[6] Moreover there was the fear, assiduously fostered by William, that Louis would conclude an alliance with James II as he had with Charles, so bringing the two premier navies against the republic again.

In this critical situation an alliance was born between the regents, or States Party, and William of Orange which would have been unthinkable even the previous year, and selected Amsterdam regents were initiated into a secret strategy for a pre-emptive invasion of England and the overthrow of James II. It was a plan of high audacity which, if it failed, would precipitate precisely what it was designed to prevent: an alliance of the two largest navies and the largest army in Europe against the United Provinces.

Extraordinary preparations were required. Apart from the mobilization of an army and siege-train strong enough to provide a credible focus for English rebellion against James, transports had to be requisitioned and concentrated to carry the troops and horses, draught animals, equipment and provisions; a strong war fleet had to be fitted out to escort the transports, and sailors had to be hired to man both. Home-coming convoys had to be diverted northabout around Scotland; agreements had to be struck with Brandenburg and other German states to provide garrisons for the defence of the homeland in the absence of the pick of the regular army; and in England a clandestine opposition network had to be established and supported for the dual purposes of intelligence and subversion.

The English end of the operation was crucial. William could not hope to invade with a sufficient force to defeat James's standing army of some 40,000 men unless a large number of English officers and troops were to defect and join him after the landing. The key figure here was Henry Sidney, a former army officer and diplomat with connections at Court, who used his many personal links with the army to initiate like-thinking officers into William's aims, cloaking his activities beneath a well-known fondness for pleasure.[7] In the fleet, the leaders of rebellion were Edward Russell, one of the few aristocrats to enter the navy as a profession, and Arthur Herbert, a licentious but able, if brutal, admiral. Both had personal as well as political reasons for disaffection. Russell's cousin Lord William Russell had plotted to exclude James, as a Roman Catholic, from succeeding to the throne, and had subsequently been executed for allegedly conspiring to murder both Charles II and James; Herbert had been dismissed the service when, as a Member of Parliament, he had opposed the repeal of the Test Acts, whereby only members of the Church of England were permitted to hold public office. James's purpose in attempting the repeal of the Acts appears to have been to allow Catholics religious and political freedom; in the eyes of the Opposition it was part of his ultimate goal to introduce 'popery' and absolute monarchy to the country on the lines of his patron, Louis XIV.

The targeting of officers and men of James's armed forces, and leading figures who would instigate uprisings in the provinces, proceeded alongside a propaganda drive to convince the population at large that James aimed to subvert their liberties and overthrow their Protestant religion. Pamphlets were devised and printed in Holland in tens of thousands, smuggled into England in bulk cargoes, and distributed by agents through booksellers, taverns and coffee houses; refutations published by James's court were sent to The Hague for rebuttal in further pamphlets.[8] Meanwhile William was supplied with a constant stream of intelligence on the state of opinion in the armed forces, the country and the court, and James was served disinformation on William's true intention. From autumn 1687, when it appears the first serious steps were taken to build the English underground, through to summer 1688, James was deceived into believing that Louis XIV was the object of the extraordinary financial and warlike preparations in Holland. It was not until mid-August that he heeded Louis's warnings that he himself was the target. This suggests dangerous deficiencies in James's intelligence system, yet it is not too much to say that the project so successfully concealed by William's agents was scarcely credible. In the words of a recent study, 'James can hardly be blamed for finding it difficult to believe that his kingdom would be invaded by his son-in-law, with his daughter's approval',[9] or that the States General would allow William to carry away the best part of their army for an invasion attempt while the English fleet was undefeated and Louis was mobilizing a great army.

The subversive and material preparations for the many-layered operation proceeded with a speed and efficiency that was probably beyond any other state of the day, with the possible exception of France. It showed the United Provinces at the height of its potency, and it is an extraordinary coincidence that it was literally at the apogee of its trading strength and political influence; for, while it was to remain in relative terms the greatest mercantile power until well into the first half of the eighteenth century, in absolute terms it started a period of continuous decline from about 1687–8, displayed by contraction in the urban population where before there had been expansion.[10] It is interesting that this coincided with a departure from ancient Dutch simplicities in dress and manners in favour of more conspicuously extravagant consumption and overt parading of wealth.[11]

England, by contrast, was experiencing a strong increase in trade. Despite successive failures to seize Dutch monopolies by force, shipping and commerce had been boosted enormously by the growth of English North American and West Indian colonies and the channelling of their trade through the mother country by the Navigation Acts, together with England's role as the only neutral trader among the northern nations during the latter stages of the last war, after Charles II had been forced from the conflict. The merchant fleet had grown by at least 50 per cent over the past three decades, chiefly in large ships for the Atlantic and Baltic; warehouse accommodation along the Thames and Medway had expanded by over 300 feet a year.[12] In the process, many exotic and colonial products, notably tobacco and sugar, had been transformed from luxuries into ordinary necessities for large sections of the population. William could hardly have been aware of it at the time, but in retrospect it is clear that he was stepping from a maritime power whose golden age was past to a rival in the ascendant whose prime lay all before it.

By late September 1688 an armada of over 50 warships and 400 transports had gathered in the wide arm of the Maas off Helvoetsluis, south of Rotterdam, where the army of 14,350 Dutch, 5,000 English, Scots and Huguenot volunteers, 5,000 horses and 50 siege-guns was embarked. In command of the fleet was Arthur Herbert. He and Russell had returned to England that summer on William's commission to obtain definite promises of support from the chief opposition figures. Herbert had returned in July, disguised as a seaman, carrying a letter to William signed by seven of the leading conspirators, including Sidney and Russell, who pledged themselves to carry out their allotted tasks after William landed, and asserted that many army officers and men and nineteen in twenty of the population were dissatisfied with James and sought a change. This was more in the nature of an assurance than the 'invitation' usually represented.[13]

On 29 September William revealed his plans to the States of Holland in secret session. He argued that war with France was inevitable, because of the damage inflicted by Louis on their commerce, shipping and fisheries. Rather than stand on the defensive, when they would probably be overwhelmed by France and England in alliance – as had almost happened in 1672 – they should invade England while the country was divided by the considerable opposition to the King's party, break James's 'absolute power', and establish in its place an anti-French, anti-Catholic parliamentary monarchy limited by the constitution, so bringing England into the scales against France. The States approved.

James, meanwhile, had begun to take precautions. In mid-August, before he was certain of William's intention, he had stationed the peacetime 'summer guard' of twenty-seven sail off the approaches to the Thames, concentrating detached vessels on it over the following weeks, and had ordered the fitting out and mobilization of a further twenty-one warships 'as for life and death'. On 23 September he had authorized 'pressing' to man the additional ships, and on the 24th he had appointed Lord Dartmouth as commander-in-chief with orders to meet 'a great and sudden invasion from Holland'.[14] Towards the end of October Dartmouth had over sixty sail riding at anchor in the Gunfleet in the Thames estuary off the Essex coast.

Winds and bad weather held William in the Maas through that month until the 29th, when he attempted to put out but was driven back by a gale. Some of his advisers now urged caution, suggesting the fleet should carry out a sweep towards the English coast before the transports ventured out. William held firm. He was a believer in predestination, and had been inured to perilous decisions from an early age in 1672 when confronted by Louis's invasion. As then, he knew that if it were God's will, he would succeed. And it was more than ever urgent that he should, since a son born to James's wife that June made it unlikely that his own wife, Mary, would in the normal course of events inherit the English throne; moreover, he had firm reports that James, on Louis's prompting, intended purging his army that winter and remodelling it with a greater proportion of Irish and Scots Catholics. He had to act now or the chance might be lost for ever.

Directly the wind abated and went round into the east, he ordered Herbert to put out again with the whole invasion force; by 2 November they had cleared the river. His intention was to make an unopposed landing far from James's army concentrated in south-east England, and he led northward for the Yorkshire coast. Next day the wind went round to the north-east, heading him and forcing him to reverse course; at the same time it prevented Dartmouth from leaving the Gunfleet. William swept down past him to the Strait of Dover and altered westerly, holding the same fortunate wind all next day to fetch the coast of Devon on the 5th. The wind then veered into the south-west for a while, enabling him to run in to Torbay and anchor; afterwards it died away almost completely, leaving an unseasonal calm in which he landed the troops on the 6th. That evening a south-westerly gale blew up and Dartmouth, who had at last worked out around the Kent coast and started down-Channel, was headed and forced back to The Downs for shelter. William was able to complete disembarkation without opposition.

He entered Exeter on 9 November, received with wild delight, and was joined over the next few days by so many leading defectors, West Country gentry, officers from James's army and recruits to his flag, whom he armed with weapons brought across for the purpose, that by the end of a week he felt confident of success. On the 21st he began the long march towards London. Dartmouth, meanwhile, had sailed from The Downs down-Channel only to be headed once again by fierce south-westerlies, which had scattered his fleet and forced him to run for Spithead to shelter. He remained there in a state of indecision as reports came in of risings around the country in support of William.

James was unnerved by the scale of hostility shown by his subjects and the jumpy state of his officers after the defections. Formerly a fearless leader, he was now paralysed by doubts and suspicions. He had concentrated his army at Salisbury, on the road between Exeter and London, but could not decide whether to advance against William or retreat to cover the capital. Finally, after a council of war on the 23rd at which he received conflicting advice, he ordered retreat. That night the most accomplished of his officers and courtiers, John Churchill, deserted him, taking his whole brigade to join William, then at Axminster. Churchill was one of the key figures who had assured William of his support during Sidney's preliminary soundings. His equally brilliant wife, Sarah, fled London the next night, taking with her James's second daughter, Anne, nominally her mistress but utterly dependent on her.[15] This completed James's moral disintegration. On 11 December, while William was still advancing on London, he fled the capital. The next day Dartmouth surrendered the fleet.

It remained only for William to enter London, facilitate James's escape to France – his first attempt having failed – and negotiate a settlement with his new subjects. The issues were complex, and the debate

was sharpened by ferocious divisions between the main political groupings of 'Whigs' and 'Tories'; nonetheless, an agreement was hammered
out in remarkably short time by a new Parliament that William called,
as he had promised, and on 13 February 1689 he and his wife, Mary, were
jointly offered the Crown in 'An Act Declaring the Rights and Liberties
of the Subject and Settling the Succession of the Crown', passed the previous day by both Houses, Lords and Commons. The 'Bill of Rights'
which William and Mary accepted, with the Crown, encapsulated the
aims of the opposition to James, and indeed his predecessors, by subor-
dinating the royal prerogative to Parliament in most important areas and
determining a Protestant succession.

The ways in which James 'by the assistance of divers evil counsellors,
judges and ministers' had endeavoured 'to subvert and extirpate the
Protestant religion and the laws and liberties of this kingdom' were
listed, after which it was declared illegal for the Crown to suspend or
execute laws, levy money or raise or keep a standing army within the
kingdom in time of peace without the consent of Parliament. It was
further asserted that Parliaments ought to be held frequently, that elec-
tions to them should be free, and that excessive bail – 'to elude the benefit
of the laws made for the liberty of the subjects' – ought not to be
required, 'nor excessive fines imposed, nor cruel and unusual punishments inflicted'.[16] Finally, the succession was given to Mary's sister,
Anne, if there were no children from William's marriage, and was thereafter determined as irrevocably Protestant.

By confining the monarch's competence and powers of coercion
within defined legal limits, the Bill of Rights signalled a fundamental
break with the past and the practice of the absolutist monarchs of
Europe, and brought to England a truly consultative form of government similar to that with which William was familiar at home, although
less dispersed. Despite the speed with which it had been forged, it was to
prove an enduring pillar of the British constitution and, as in the Dutch
system, the foundation of boasted liberties over centuries.

There had been nothing inevitable about William's success, styled by
the Whigs, who benefited most, the 'Glorious Revolution'. Had James's
fleet not been windbound in the Gunfleet, then twice prevented by head
winds and gales from getting up with the invasion force in Torbay, had
it been William's fleet scattered by gales, the outcome might have been
very different. Whether, if Dartmouth had managed to bring on an
action, all his captains would have fought wholeheartedly is another

question. Russell and Herbert had worked to undermine loyalty, and their canvassers were confident they had won over most of the senior captains;[17] yet English naval officers had been raised on hostility to the Dutch. William was evidently not convinced they would hold off, since in his instructions to Herbert he had laid emphasis on avoiding action. This would have been comparatively simple for such an experienced commander had it not been for the unwieldy collection of transports he had to protect. The questions must always remain open. In the event it was the aptly named 'Protestant wind' that assured the success of the invasion. Beyond that, in conception, organization, prior intelligence, propaganda and deception, William's coup ranks alongside the 1944 Normandy landings as one of the great decisive strokes of maritime power in history.

While William's initial takeover was practically bloodless, conquest was not to be completed without bloody battles against James's supporters – 'Jacobites' – in Scotland and Ireland. Meanwhile, even before arriving in London, William had instructed Herbert to fly the English flag if attacking French vessels, and had ordered home Louis's ambassador in London. Louis, for his part, fulfilled an earlier threat to the States General that he would declare war on the United Provinces if the invasion of England went ahead;[18] he also ordered the seizure of English ships. William, after his coronation in April 1689, formalized hostilities by declaring war on France from his English throne. He thus fulfilled his prime aim of joining the two Protestant maritime powers in a Grand Alliance whose major Continental allies – the Austrian emperor, Spain and Brandenburg – had already been drawn into a ring around France.

The numbers of warships to be supplied by each of the maritime powers for joint operations had already been agreed in the ratio of five English to three from the United Provinces, the English providing the commander-in-chief. This accurately reflected the strengths of the two fleets, and followed proposals put forward by a mission from the United Provinces in January; yet the formalization of England as senior naval partner caused disquiet in the republic. The Dutch were required to provide the greater proportion of land forces – half to defend the revolution in England, Scotland and Ireland; half to man the barrier fortresses in the southern Netherlands. Locked into a junior partnership at sea and a defensive posture on the Continent, the regents had every cause for concern.

While the English fleet appeared strong on paper, it was burdened with debt from James's administration. William was able to secure a sizeable loan from the City of London to tide him over before Parliament convened[19] – an indication of the powerful merchant interest behind the revolution – but he was unable to take the initiative at sea. The chief difficulty lay in manning the ships: pay was in arrears, volunteers were not coming forward, and an expedient of turning men over from one ship to another without paying them off had raised a dangerously mutinous spirit. In these circumstances the seas were left open for Louis to dispatch James to Ireland, where the Earl of Tyrconnel had promised support for the overthrow of the Protestant elite who ruled in the English interest over the Catholic majority. From northern Ireland it was but a step to Scotland and Highland clansmen who were eager to rally to the Stuart banner.

Arthur Herbert got to sea with a small and ill-manned English squadron in time to deflect a second and larger French force carrying volunteers, arms, provisions and money for James; instead of putting in to Kinsale, the French ran westerly and entered Bantry Bay on the southwest corner of Ireland. There Herbert found them on 1 May landing men and supplies. The French weighed to meet him, but, despite the advantage of the wind and a slightly heavier force, they were unwilling or too unpractised to close, and after a running encounter up and down the bay, exchanging cannonades at comparatively long range, the two sides separated – the French to return to their transports, Herbert to lie to and repair the considerable damage to spars and rigging from the high-angled shot.

Strategically Bantry Bay was an undoubted victory for the French squadron, which had protected its transports and went on to complete its mission, if at some distance from the intended disembarkation port. It also inflicted more casualties – some 350, to under 150 in the French ships.[20] But William, who needed a success to bolster his new regime, claimed it as an English victory, in honour of which he made Herbert Earl of Torrington, knighted two of his leading captains, and ordered a bounty of ten shillings to be paid to every man in the squadron.

Louis failed to follow up his advantage. Although annoyed that his squadron returned to Brest after landing men and supplies, instead of maintaining itself in Irish waters to support James and prevent reinforcements reaching his opponents, he made no attempt subsequently to establish command in Irish waters. With his main fleet at Brest, to windward of the English Channel and the Irish Sea, and with English main fleet bases in the east of the country, facing the Dutch, he was well placed to command the approaches to Ireland. Instead he took an entirely defensive posture, instructing Seignelay to keep the fleet in port, yet always looking as if it were about to sail. In this way the allies would be forced to hold their fleet in readiness and would not attempt an attack on his coasts. Seignelay protested, but failed to move him.

So the initiative passed, and later that summer William dispatched an expeditionary force to Ireland unmolested. The Anglo-Dutch fleet, meanwhile, held the seas off Ushant to watch Brest; but scurvy took hold of the men, and by late summer, when the fleet put back to Torbay, over 500 were dead, more than 2,500 sick. The losses – matching those to be expected in a fleet action – were the price for the lack of western bases to suit England's new strategic posture, and for inadequate organization to supply the fleet at sea with fresh victuals.

The following year, 1690, Louis again struck first, reinforcing James in Ireland with 6,000 fresh troops in early March. Seignelay, who had persuaded the King to reverse his former negative strategy, bent all efforts to fitting out and manning the fleet so that he could send it into the Channel before the Dutch contingent joined the English. In this he was to be disappointed, partly due to the late return of the warships from the Irish expedition and sickness in their crews. Meanwhile William assembled an army of mixed Dutch and Continental troops under his personal command, and on 11 June made an uncontested crossing to northern Ireland. He left Mary in charge of the government with a council of nine members drawn from both Whigs and Tories to guide her.

The combined French fleet was ready by this time. It sailed two days later in full strength under the Comte de Tourville, a completely professional naval officer of great experience, a master of fleet handling and tactics. His orders directed him to enter the Channel and seek out and attack the allied fleet, which had now joined together. Light airs delayed his progress, and it was not until 23 June that he reached the Isle of Wight, where the English and Dutch were riding at anchor off St Helens.

The allies, commanded by Arthur Herbert, Lord Torrington, were not up to strength. In particular, two substantial squadrons were on detached duties: one, under Sir Clowdisley Shovell, had covered William's crossing to Ireland; the other, under Sir Henry Killigrew, was escorting merchantmen returning from the Mediterranean. Both had orders to join the fleet. Torrington was very conscious of his weakness by comparison with the French, whose presence in strength off the English coast had been reported by his scouts. He put on a bold front nonetheless, and on the 25th, after manoeuvring to gain the wind, formed line and bore down towards the enemy. Tourville bore away, declining action.

Afterwards Torrington wrote to Mary's chief naval adviser on the council, the Earl of Nottingham, describing his attempted attack as a 'rashness', for which his best excuse was that, while he had known the enemy were stronger, he had not known by how much. Now he had 'had a pretty good view of them' and estimated there were 'near if not quite 80 men of Warr, fitt to lye in a line and thirty fireships'.[21] This was an accurate assessment. Tourville had seventy ships in his line and five others of forty to fifty guns – thus fit for the line – as a reserve division to lie on the disengaged side under the privateer commander Jean Bart. Torrington had only fifty-seven in his line; as he wrote to Nottingham, he 'very heartily gave thanks to God they [the French] declined the battle yesterday, and indeed I shall not think myself very unhappy if I can gett rid of them without fighting'.[22] He went on to say his council of war had agreed unanimously 'that we are to shun fighting if they have the wind of us, and retire if we cannot otherwise avoid it, to the Gunfleet, the only place where we could make our party good with them'.

Nottingham and Mary's other naval adviser, Admiral Edward Russell, and the other members of her council were shocked at the possibility of the fleet withdrawing to the Thames, leaving the enemy in command of the Channel and free to overwhelm the two detached squadrons making their way from the west to join Torrington, together with the Mediterranean trade under convoy. Moreover, their intelligence from France indicated positively there were no more than sixty enemy ships of the line and they were poorly manned.[23] Consequently, believing Torrington's attitude excessively cautious, Nottingham and Russell composed a 'pretty sharp letter' instructing him to attack. Toned down by Mary, it was expressed to him on the 29th:

> we apprehend the consequences of your retiring to the Gunfleet to be so fatall that we choose rather that you should upon any advantage of the wind give battle to the enemy . . . But in case you find it necessary to goe to the Westward of the French fleet in order to the better joining with you of Our ships . . . from the Westward, we leave it to your Discretion so that you by no meanes ever loose sight of the French fleet whereby they may have opportunities of making attempts upon the shoar or rivers of Medway or Thames or gett away without fighting.[24]

Such were the orders that precipitated one of the most controversial battles ever fought by a British main fleet. The council, having overruled the assessment of odds that Torrington had made from personal observation over several days, had ordered an attack. It was conditional on having the wind, yet unless he had the wind he could not attack in any case: a fleet to leeward could never force an action on a fleet to windward.

Much has been made of the fact that both Nottingham and Russell hated Torrington, and that Russell was his arch-rival.[25] Yet personal feelings cannot explain the misjudgment that resulted in such muddled orders. False intelligence was a factor; another was genuine anxiety about leaving the Channel open to the French; yet another was the need for a success for the regime. And probably Nottingham, who had been sending William over-optimistic reports about the strength of the allied fleet, was much influenced by calls for action from the non-naval members of the council.

Torrington certainly had many enemies. He was a libertine in the highest Restoration tradition who drank to excess, whored immoderately, expressed himself in relentlessly foul language, and, according to Pepys, was cruel, lazy, vain and bellicose. 'Of all the worst men living,' Pepys wrote, 'Herbert is the only man that I do not know to have any one virtue to compound for all his vices.'[26] This was too extreme. Herbert had shown great personal courage during his career. He was also, like his opponent, Tourville, a master of his profession. He had fought in the Dutch war, commanded a ship at Sole Bay, and lost an eye fighting Algerian corsairs in the Mediterranean; and it appears he had a following of officers who were loyal and loved him as much as others hated him. These were to save him from the consequences of his new instructions.

On 29 June, when he received Mary's orders, the allied fleet was at anchor some ten miles south-east of Beachy Head, halfway between St Helens and the Strait of Dover, with the French fleet hull down over the horizon eighteen miles distant in the south-south-west. Torrington called his flag officers to a council of war aboard his flagship, the 100-gun *Sovereign*, which lasted several hours. Details were not recorded, only the outcome: the Queen's order to fight had to be obeyed '*nemine contradicente*', as a Dutch flag officer put it afterwards, 'yet with this consideration, to keep as much as was possible to windward, that the succour which we expected from Sir C. Shovell and Vice Admiral Killigrew might come into us'.[27] This obviously meant attempting to work round the French fleet to the westward, whence the two detached squadrons were expected and the prevailing winds blew. It was in accordance with the second part of Mary's order; it was also what Lord Howard and Drake had done against the Spanish armada in 1588.

Had the wind been in the south-west the following morning, 30 June, favouring the French, it would no doubt have given Torrington the opportunity to emulate his great predecessors. Instead it was from the north-north-east, blowing down directly from him towards the French fleet. His orders left him no choice. Weighing at first light, he put out the signal to form line of battle, and as the ships drew out into their order – the Dutch van (White) squadron under Cornelius Evertsen northern-most, next his own centre (Red) squadron, with the rear (Blue) under Sir Ralph Delavall to the south of him – he bore down towards the French, who were forming line on the starboard tack, heading north-westerly. A weakening ebb tide bore both fleets west down-Channel towards Beachy Head as they closed.

By eight o'clock the allies were within three miles of the French – somewhat closer at the head of the line, since Tourville's centre (White) squadron was somewhat to leeward of the French van (White and Blue) under Lieutenant General (Vice Admiral) the Comte de Château-Renault – and Torrington broke out the signal to engage, the red or 'bloody' flag at the *Sovereign*'s fore-topmast head. Tourville laid his head-sails aback to await him; the French line conformed.

According to the conventions of battle, Torrington should now have borne down on Tourville's flagship, the magnificent 104-gun *Soleil Royal*. However, he counted some forty ships in the line astern of her – thirty-six were actually in the line – while he had only twenty-three ships astern of him. His rear squadron under Delavall was particularly short, con-sisting of only thirteen ships against the French rear (Blue) of twenty-three ships under the Comte d'Estrées. Assuming, no doubt correctly, that Tourville intended 'doubling' him from the rear – that is, having the overlapping ships work up to windward of his rear to take it between two fires – he ordered his helm up and altered south-westerly to prevent it. His divisional vice and rear admirals, Sir John Ashby and George Rooke, conformed, as did Delavall with his rear squadron; the Dutch continued westerly towards the French van. Consequently a gap opened between the Dutch rear division under van der Putte and Torrington's van division under Ashby. As it widened, Ashby altered north-westerly

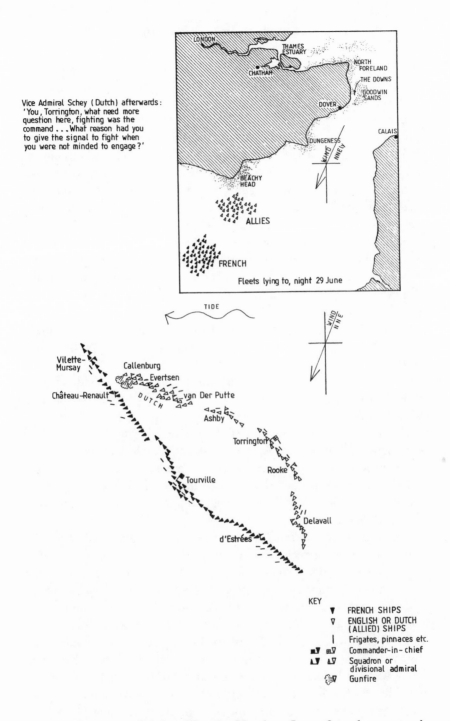

Vice Admiral Schey (Dutch) afterwards:
'You, Torrington, what need more
question here, fighting was the
command . . . What reason had you
to give the signal to fight when
you were not minded to engage?'

LONDON

THAMES
ESTUARY

NORTH
FORELAND

CHATHAM

THE DOWNS

GOODWIN
SANDS

DOVER

CALAIS

DUNGENESS

WIND
NNE'ly

BEACHY
HEAD

ALLIES

FRENCH

Fleets lying to, night 29 June

TIDE

WIND
NNE

Vilette-
Mursay

Callenburg

Evertsen

Château-Renault

DUTCH

van Der Putte

Ashby

Torrington

Rooke

Tourville

Delavall

d'Estrées

KEY

▼ FRENCH SHIPS
▽ ENGLISH OR DUTCH
(ALLIED) SHIPS
| Frigates, pinnaces etc.
Commander-in-chief
Squadron or
divisional admiral
Gunfire

Battle diagram 4   Battle of Beachy Head, 30 June 1690, the approach to close it, and set more sail, while the Dutch backed topsails to await him.

The gap closed, but another opened between Ashby and Torrington's own centre division of the Red. Torrington luffed up and briefly lay to, no doubt to assess the situation, then continued edging down towards the enemy under topsails. Since Ashby had his foresails and topsails set, an elbow developed in the allied line below the widening gap in the centre. Tourville's line was sagging somewhat in the opposite direction downwind in a bow; thus the opposing centres were much further from each other than the opposing van and rear squadrons.

Half an hour later, at about nine o'clock, the Dutch reached within long gunshot of the French van (well outside half a mile), put their helms down to parallel the enemy, and opened fire before bearing down again. Tourville, meanwhile, filled his topsails and stood on north-westerly two or three points off the wind; and Château-Renault, commanding the van, signalled his leading division under the Marquis de Vilette -Mursay to stretch ahead of the Dutch, gain the wind, and double on them – as Jordan had done at Sole Bay. Torrington's 'Sailing and Fighting Instructions', issued to all captains, appear to have been identical to those issued by James when Duke of York in the aftermath of Sole Bay. The eighth article stipulated that, when to windward, the leading squadron was 'to steer for the headmost of the enemy's ships'. This Evertsen conspicuously failed to do. As the twenty-two Dutch ships converged on Château-Renault, also twenty-two strong, the leader, the 64-gun *Wapen van Utrecht*, closed the ninth ship from the head of the French line, leaving Vilette-Mursay's leading division free rein to crowd sail and claw up to windward ahead.

This was obscured from Torrington by clouds of gun smoke from the action now raging fiercely about Château-Renault's centre and rear divisions as the Dutch, alternately backing and filling their topsails to keep a line, closed the range inside 200 yards, or 'musket shot'. Ashby, following them, admired the way they bore down 'like men of undaunted courage'.[28] Château-Renault eased further from the wind, no doubt to assist Vilette-Mursay in his task of working upwind of the Dutch, and Tourville pushed his centre ahead to engage the Dutch rear division.[29] Thus, with the French a whole division ahead of their equivalents in the allied line, Ashby found himself engaging Torrington's rightful opponent, the magnificent *Soleil Royal*, and three powerful three-decker 80-gun seconds.

Torrington, still more than a mile from the French line and now separated from Ashby by almost the same distance, again lay to. His motives
have been questioned ever since. The most probable explanation is that
he was aware from the advanced relative positions of the French divisions that the danger now was of being 'doubled' from ahead; hence he
kept up to windward to meet the threat. It is unlikely he was holding off
deliberately to fight a defensive action at long range, as at the council of
war the previous evening he had given instructions that there was to be
'no firing till we come near the enemy'.[30] More surprising, perhaps, than
his caution were the actions of his subordinates: Evertsen, as mentioned,
failed to lead his squadron to the head of the enemy line; Ashby, after
first keeping in line with Torrington, had altered course and pressed sail
to get into line with Evertsen; now Delavall bore down to engage
the French rear, pressing in to 'musket shot' inside 200 yards. Of all
his squadronal and divisional commanders, only the rear admiral of his
own Red squadron, Rooke, kept in line with him. The others appear to
have acted on their own initiative, disregarding both the fighting instructions and alignment with their commander-in-chief.

By ten o'clock all allied squadrons were engaged, the van and rear
closely, Torrington at extreme range and, because of the gap between
him and Ashby, firing at the last ship of the French centre and the
leading two of d'Estrées's rear squadron, small vessels of forty-four to
fifty-eight guns.

The French were still sailing several points off the wind. Rooke stated
afterwards, 'We sailed all the day two points and sometimes four from
the wind and as we bore down upon the enemy they lasked away from
us.'[31] His impression was that the allies were having the better of the
battle; but in the van the lighter Dutch ships were suffering, and the firepower concentrated in the three-deckers about the *Soleil Royal* was beginning to cripple Ashby's division. By noon the Dutch rear had lost
cohesion and two of Ashby's ships had been disabled and forced out of
the line. Tourville and the Marquis de Nesmond, commanding his
leading division, pressed their advantage, sailing up close-hauled into
the spaces created; while way ahead of the fighting Vilette-Mursay, now
to windward of the Dutch van, signalled his division to tack. They came
about in succession and bore down on the disengaged side of the Dutch.

This was seen from the *Sovereign*, whose captain, John Neville, asked
Torrington 'whether he would suffer them [Vilette-Mursay's division] to
weather him also'. The reply was, 'Not if I could help it',[32] whereupon

Neville luffed the flagship into the wind, further distancing the centre from the French.

The critical point in the battle was reached soon afterwards, at about one o'clock, when Ashby's flagship was crippled by the loss of her fore-topmast and fell out of the line. This enabled Tourville to complete his movement through the gap into the Dutch rear, just as Vilette-Mursay came down from ahead on their weather side. Grouped three deep in places, in complete confusion and under fire from all sides, the Dutch began taking fearful punishment. Torrington directed Neville to bear down to their relief, but the wind, which had been dying since the late morning, now fell away completely. In the calm, boats were lowered and ships were towed towards the encircled Dutch. There was at least a mile for the ships with Torrington to pull, and the Dutch ordeal continued until some time after three, when Torrington, realizing the ebb had started, signalled Evertsen to anchor. Obeying the order immediately, without taking in sail, the Dutch ships brought up to their cables while the French, surprised, were carried away out of gunshot.

One Dutch vessel, the 68-gun *Friesland*, was so shattered and her company so reduced they were unable to let go an anchor in time; she drifted alone into the French formation and struck her colours. French officers who went aboard found dead and dying heaped promiscuously where they had fallen and scarcely any undamaged area. They took off 120 men, all that were left of her original 350, then scuttled her. Torrington, meanwhile, used the ebb to drift and tow down between the Dutch and the enemy, where he anchored.

That concluded the fighting. When the tide turned that evening, Torrington weighed and the fleet was borne up-Channel on the flood. Next morning at a council of war it was decided to continue the retreat eastward, sacrificing any ships that could not keep up rather than risk another engagement. In the event, when the wind rose, allowing Tourville to pursue, a further four disabled Dutch ships of the line – including the *Wapen van Utrecht*, which had led the attack, and one English 70-gun ship – together with several smaller vessels were set alight by their own companies and abandoned.[33] Tourville might, perhaps, have inflicted greater losses had he allowed his less damaged and swifter ships to chase ahead and harry the laggards; instead, he kept his squadrons together, allowing the remainder of the allied fleet to reach the Thames without further fighting.

The battle of Beachy Head – known in France as Beveziers, a corruption of Pevensey, a coastal village just to the east of Beachy Head – was one of the most humiliating defeats ever suffered by an English fleet. In Paris, reports hailed a victory, putting an end to the long-held English pretensions to superiority at sea. While the Dutch had fought *'avec beau-coup de courage'*, it was said, the English, apart from the Vice Admiral of the Red (Ashby), had distinguished themselves by the little valour they had shown in combat.

From the Dutch came furious recriminations that Torrington had sacrificed their squadron. His distance from the action throughout and the disparity in ship damage and casualties – some 2,000 Dutch against only 350 English[34] – appeared to prove it. Gilles Schey, commanding one of the leading Dutch divisions, wrote, 'You, Torrington, what need of more questions here? Fighting was the command . . . what reason had you to give the signal to fight when you were not minded to engage?'[35]

Even English captains found it difficult to understand their commander-in-chief's behaviour, and thought that if he and Rooke had pressed the enemy as closely as the other divisions the outcome might have been very different; as it was put at his subsequent court martial, 'many of the officers of those two divisions wished they might have been nearer the enemy'.[36]

Nottingham, who was chiefly responsible for the defeat by overruling his admiral's appreciation on the spot, wrote to William, 'by all that yet appears, my Lord Torrington deserted the Dutch so shamefully that the whole [Dutch] squadron had been lost if some of our ships had not rescued them'.[37] Queen Mary wrote to the States General apologizing for the disaster, accepting blame, offering to refit all the Dutch ships at English expense, and contributing 10,000 guilders for the widows of those killed – a message which has been described as the most abject ever sent by a government to an ally. Torrington, meanwhile, was arrested and taken to the Tower pending trial for 'High Crimes and Misdemeanours'.

It was necessary for William and Mary's government and the alliance that Torrington should be made scapegoat for the disaster. But, removed from the political tensions of the time, it is clear that the Dutch contributed to their own undoing by failing to stretch up to the head of the French line; this failure, moreover, led directly to Ashby having to face the superior concentrated power of the *Soleil Royal* and her formidable seconds. It is equally clear that Torrington was right to veer southward to prevent Delavall from being doubled by d'Estrées's far more numerous squadron. Nor can he be faulted for holding up to windward: to have allowed such a superior fleet as Tourville's to gain the weather gage would have invited greater disasters. As it was, he was prevented from coming down to Evertsen's aid only by the untimely calm, and his order to anchor after the tide turned had been a master stroke.

His court martial in December was packed with his supporters and resulted in acquittal – surely a just verdict. Indeed, he seems to have been one of the few who kept their head during this anxious time when a French invasion was feared, coining a phrase later immortalized in naval historical writing: 'I said that whilst we had a fleet in being, they would not dare to make an attempt.'[38] This has been held up as the first statement of the deterrent effect of 'a fleet in being'. In fact it was far from even the first English statement of the idea, which was current among Elizabeth's captains, while the laurels for its practical application surely belong to de Ruyter for his epic defensive campaign in the third Anglo-Dutch war.

In Ireland on the day after Beachy Head, William decisively defeated James's Catholic army by the river Boyne. One of William's confidants wrote that what he feared most from the French triumph was that Tourville would send some frigates into the Irish Sea to cut William's communications with England.[39] Tourville did dispatch a small squadron of five of the line to Ireland, but they did not affect William. Tourville took the main body to Le Havre to refit and reprovision, afterwards finding nothing better to do than beat back down-Channel, enter Torbay, and send the small force of troops with the fleet to raid the fishing port of Teignmouth ten miles up the coast. By this time 2,000 of his men, 8 per cent of his total complement, were down with sickness. He put back to Brest, arriving on 7 August.[40]

Louis and Seignelay were furious at his failure to exploit victory, and he was relieved of his command – like Torrington, a scapegoat for political strategic failure. Seignelay's intention had been to crush the allied fleet as a preliminary to taking control of Irish waters and so assisting James to secure Ireland. Yet Louis, with his armies fully committed to Flanders, on the Rhine, in Italy and Spain, had not provided sufficient troops or specialist equipment to affect the campaign, let alone mount a major invasion anywhere. In addition the fleet had been too late in getting to sea; Tourville's victory had come too late, and lack of pilots for the North Sea together with serious action damage had prevented him following it up. The English and Dutch ships were quickly repaired in port,[41] the detached squadrons returned, and by August command of the Channel had passed by weight of numbers back to the allies. These were the realities of naval warfare at the end of the seventeenth century: the disease inevitable during prolonged sea-keeping and the rapidity with which timber warships could be repaired rendered even such a victory as Beachy Head transient.

In September, John Churchill, whom William had created Earl of Marlborough, exploited allied superiority in home waters by crossing to southern Ireland with a small expeditionary force and seizing the key ports of Cork and Kinsale from the Catholics. It was the final demonstration of the futility of Seignelay's efforts that year.

This was not lost on Louis's advisers. Military leaders resenting the rival power base Colbert had created and ministers responsible for the vast sums to maintain the war against most of the other powers of Europe openly criticized the great expense and uselessness of the fleet. Considering its prime purpose to be protection of French coasts – so little had Colbert's mercantile dreams penetrated this territorial court – they put forward a proposal to dissolve the navy and defend the coasts at a fraction of the cost with cavalry militias stationed at key points.

Seignelay died in October. His successor, the Comte de Pontchartrain, a courtier who knew nothing of naval affairs, prepared to adopt the cavalry-militia proposal, but Louis turned for a second opinion to the chief of naval administration, the Intendant-General, Bonrepaus, who wrote a corrective that might have been dictated by Colbert himself: stressing the importance of the fleet for protecting French sea trade and troop transports and for reducing the trade on which their enemies relied, besides carrying the renown of His Majesty's name to the far corners of the globe, he provided historical examples illustrating the perils of weakness at sea.[42] Louis accepted his arguments; the fleet was saved, although there was a shift in emphasis away from the apparently failed strategy of seeking battle with the enemy main fleet towards attacking enemy trade – the so-called *guerre de course*.

The reaction in England and the United Provinces was the reverse. The damage to trade and the position in Ireland which might have resulted from Tourville's triumph in the Channel if the campaign had been properly prepared provoked calls for increases in the fleet. Parliament voted over half a million pounds for new ships, raising new or higher taxes on a range of consumables and luxury goods to fund the expenditure. In addition, construction was begun on a dockyard and naval base in south-west England at Plymouth to command the approaches to the Channel, and improvements were sought in the victualling services to enable the fleet to keep the sea for longer periods.[43] It was the natural response of a powerful merchant interest.

7

Barfleur/La Hougue, 1692

IN 1691 THE English and Dutch allies had numerically the stronger fleet, although the French were convinced, not without reason, that class for class their ships were better. Edward Russell, succeeding the disgraced Torrington, got to sea in early June with orders to destroy the enemy inside Brest. He was delayed by head winds, and Tourville, reinstated in command, sailed before he could make this improbable attempt. Tourville's orders were to cruise in the mouth of the Channel to keep open communications with Ireland and deter an allied assault on the French coast – without, however, engaging a superior fleet – meanwhile attacking allied trade, in particular a returning Mediterranean convoy. His subsequent evasive manoeuvring from the Scilly Isles to Biscay, termed the *campaign du large*, was a masterly demonstration of the effects of a 'fleet in being'. By absorbing all Russell's attention and drawing him out of the Channel, he prevented an allied descent on the French mainland and allowed privateer squadrons from Dunkirk and Saint-Malo to prey on allied trade; and, while he missed the Mediterranean ships, he caught a West Indian convoy.

The negative aspect was more apparent at Louis's court: French supply ships had got through to Ireland, but so had William's; the Catholic rebellion had collapsed, and James had fled back to France. Moreover, the spectacle of a powerful French fleet deliberately avoiding battle had not impressed a nobility dedicated to martial glory. Pontchartrain, Tourville and the navy were subjected to further bitter attacks. Similarly in England and the United Provinces Russell was impugned for failing to bring the French to action or to protect trade.

FOR THE 1692 campaign Louis again changed his strategy. Convinced by reports from English Jacobites that, if James were to land in England with sufficient force, many who were disenchanted with William and Mary's government would join him, he determined to launch an invasion. His plans called for some twenty regiments of Irish and French infantry to assemble with transport shipping at the fishing port of Saint-Vaast-la-Hougue on the north-east corner of the Cherbourg peninsula, cavalry at Le Havre, while the Toulon, Rochefort and Brest divisions of the fleet combined early, entered the Channel, and escorted the troop transports across from La Hougue before a Dutch contingent could join the English fleet. The key to success would be speed, for, once the Dutch did join, the allied fleet would be so much stronger that the project would be doomed.

The timetable was impossibly tight and more suited to military than naval affairs. Adverse winds and storms delayed the Toulon squadron under d'Estrées as it attempted to beat out through the Strait of Gibraltar; two ships were lost and much damage was suffered by the rest, while at Brest and Rochefort it proved impossible to draft enough men for all the ships.

At the same time, William was planning an invasion of Normandy. With the forces released from Ireland, he hoped to strike behind Louis's armies on the frontiers to break a stalemate that had developed on land from the Netherlands to Spain. He, too, urged the fleet forward, in order to make the landing before the French fleet could combine and dispute the passage. In April, however, captured documents and prisoners' testimony revealed the extent of Louis's plans and he swung to the defensive: leading Jacobites were arrested, Catholics were ordered to move ten miles from London, soldiers were deployed above Portsmouth, trained bands and militia were alerted, and the efforts to get English and Dutch warships to sea early were driven forward with even greater urgency; the need now was to unite before the French fleet could combine to cover James's invasion.

In the race to get to sea first, it became clear to Louis that he could not win if Tourville waited until his whole fleet was concentrated and manned. He therefore ordered him to sail with as many ships as he had

– even if the enemy were reported outside in superior force – proceed to La Hougue, escort the invasion force across to Torbay, then return to attach the remaining divisions to his flag off Brest. The orders were desperate enough, depending as they did on an unlikely chain of favourable wind changes; they were rendered as potentially disastrous as the instructions Mary had sent Torrington before Beachy Head by a later instruction that, if Tourville should meet the enemy on his way to La Houge, he was to engage whatever their strength and fight them hard. The reasoning was that, even if he were defeated, the allied fleet would be so damaged it would be unable to dispute the passage of the invasion transports. In reality, if both main fleets were forced to retire to repair damages, the lightest allied squadron would be able to prevent a landing. Below Pontchartrain's signature, Louis wrote, 'I add this word in my own hand to this instruction in order to tell you that what it contains is my will and I wish it to be exactly followed.'[1]

It was also made clear to Tourville that if he postponed his departure or failed in any way to follow the King's instructions he would be replaced. Summoning his flag officers, he told them they already stood accused of prudence; they must not lay themselves open to charges of cowardice.[2] Like so many of his successors, he was betrayed by a military caste with little understanding of the unpredictability of sea fighting.

He sailed on 29 April with only thirty-seven ships of the line, leaving Château-Renault behind to complete the manning of another twenty. Delayed by easterlies, it was 15 May before he had worked up-Channel as far as Plymouth, where he was joined by part of the Rochefort squadron under Vilette-Mursay. This brought his total to forty-four of the line – little over half his potential strength. D'Estrées with the Toulon squadron was still far to the south.

Meanwhile the winds which had headed him had allowed the Dutch squadron to cross the North Sea and anchor in The Downs. Russell in the 100-gun *Britannia* had passed them under full sail, leading the main body of the English fleet down from the Gull stream, the narrow northern passage inside the Goodwin Sands; it was a risky short-cut with three-deckers, justified only by the urgency of his orders and his faith in his experienced chief pilot and navigator, termed 'master of the fleet', John Benbow. As the *Britannia* ran by to depart from the southern entrance and bear away through the Strait of Dover into the Channel, the Dutch, under Lieutenant Admiral Philips Almonde, weighed and followed. By 12 May, while Tourville was still beating up past the Lizard, Russell had reached the Isle of Wight and added two detached English divisions to his flag, bringing his strength up to at least eighty-two of the line (the sources differ on exact numbers).[3] He waited until 18 May, when his scouting frigates brought him firm intelligence of the enemy off Portland, then sailed southward, finding the French fleet early the following morning north of Pointe de Barfleur at the north-eastern corner of the Cherbourg peninsula.

Tourville was running before a light south-westerly in a cruising formation of six columns when Russell's sails were sighted over the horizon to leeward through an early mist. He made the signal for line of battle on the starboard tack, to head southward in the same direction as the allies, and called a council of war, lying to to receive his flag officers. By the time they had seated themselves in gilded chairs around the table in the *Soleil Royal's* exquisitely furnished and hung great cabin the mist had dispersed to reveal the whole allied fleet stretching into the distance and twice their own strength.

No tactical skill could hope to overcome such odds. They had the weather gage, and thus the choice of whether or not to fight, and at what range. All believed they should avoid action. But Tourville, like Torrington in the similar but less hopeless situation on the eve of Beachy Head, showed them his instructions and the King's handwritten injunction to obey them to the letter. It left him no choice; besides, all knew that their courage had been questioned at Court. No doubt Tourville told them to stretch the length of the enemy line by leaving gaps between the divisions as they bore down, and warned commanders of the van and rear to hold up to the wind to avoid being doubled. As they departed, he shook each by the hand.[4] No sooner were they back aboard their own ships than he put out the signal for battle and steered down for the centre of the allied formation.

Russell was lying to as Tourville began his approach. The allied line was not quite formed: in particular, the rear squadron under Sir John Ashby straggled downwind, the result of a signal to him to tack which Russell had made when the French were first sighted in the early morning, heading north-westerly. He had boats in the water to tow the great ships upwind. Now, as the enemy bore down, Russell signalled the Dutch van squadron to stretch ahead of the French van and tack to gain the wind. But the leading French division, under the Marquis de Nesmond, lasked southerly with all sails set to foil the manoeuvre. Long gaps opened between the French divisions as he did so, for the van squadron numbered only fourteen in the line against twenty-six Dutch.

The opposing centres were as unequal: sixteen French ships mounting 1,150 guns against twenty-seven or more English mounting in excess of 2,000 guns. Despite this, Tourville closed resolutely under topsails as if determined to leave no question of any kind about his courage, holding his fire until within close range, as did the English lines. By eleven o'clock he had pressed in to 'musket shot' – 200 yards or less perhaps. As at Beachy Head, he had three three-deckers grouped about the *Soleil Royal.* He brought this powerful phalanx against Russell, the *Soleil Royal* rounding up on the *Britannia*'s windward quarter, the 84-gun *Conquérant* on the quarter of her next ahead, the 96-gun *St Andrew*, commanded by Marlborough's younger brother, George Churchill, while astern of the French flagship the 84-gun *St Philippe* and 90-gun *Admirable* opposed the 96-gun *London*. With the sea barely ruffled by dying breezes, all three tiers of gun-port lids were up; the great guns beneath erupted in smoke and darts of flame; round shot flew in pairs between the floating fortresses, ploughing through the massy oak sides, launching showers of splinters across the decks, smashing flesh and bone, gouging masts, snapping rigging, tearing holes in canvas.

This was the thunderous epicentre of battle. Elsewhere in the centre, as in the van, the line was broken by long gaps as Vilette-Mursay commanding the leading division and the Marquis de Langeron in the rear sought to extend their few ships the length of the enemy squadrons and hold up into the wind. In the rear the English still trailed somewhat to leeward so that only the leading divisions were engaged.

By noon an English fourth rate of fifty guns ahead of Churchill's *St Andrew* had been crippled and forced to drop down to leeward, and Tourville's flagship was so damaged aloft she had boats down to tow her out of the line to repair damages. Soon afterwards the light airs of the morning gave way to a steadier breeze which veered into the north-west. It was the turning point: the change in wind direction gave the allies opportunity to put their helms down and steer through the large gaps between the French divisions. Clowdisley Shovell led the rear division of the centre through to gain the wind of the French centre, separating Tourville from his rear squadron under Louis Gabaret, while the leading division of the English rear under Richard Carter led through to windward of Gabaret, cutting him off from his rearmost division under Panetié, who had fallen some way astern in his efforts to extend the line.

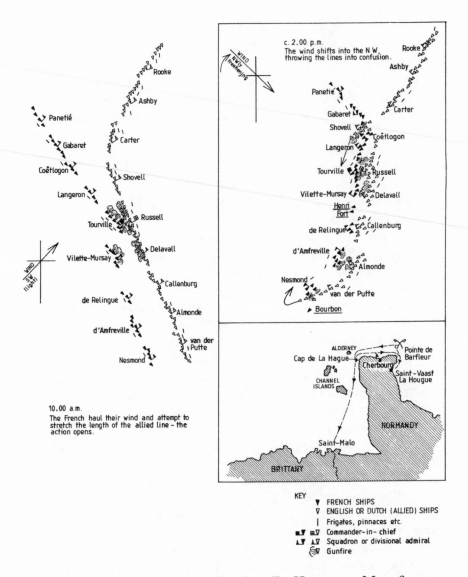

c. 2.00 p.m.
The wind shifts into the N.W.
throwing the lines into confusion.

WIND
N'ly freshening

Rooke

Ashby

Panetié

Carter

Gabaret

Shovell

Coëtlogon

Langeron

Tourville

Russell

Vilette-Mursay

Delavall

Henri Fort

Callenburg

de Relingue

d'Amfreville

Almonde

Nesmond

van der Putte

Bourbon

Rooke

Ashby

Panetié

Gabaret

Carter

Coëtlogon

Langeron

Shovell

Tourville

Russell

Vilette-Mursay

Delavall

Callenburg

de Relingue

Almonde

d'Amfreville

van der Putte

Nesmond

WIND
S.W.
(light)

10.00 a.m.
The French haul their wind and attempt to
stretch the length of the allied line - the
action opens.

ALDERNEY
Cap de La Hague
CHANNEL ISLANDS
Cherbourg
Pointe de Barfleur
Saint-Vaast La Hougue

NORMANDY

Saint-Malo

BRITTANY

KEY
▼ FRENCH SHIPS
▽ ENGLISH OR DUTCH (ALLIED) SHIPS
| Frigates, pinnaces etc.
◼▼ ◼▽ Commander-in-chief
▲▼ ▲▽ Squadron or divisional admiral
🌀 Gunfire

Battle diagram 5   Battle of Barfleur/La Hougue, 19 May 1692

In the van, the Dutch forced the French up into the wind and cut off the leader, the 68-gun *Bourbon*. The French van then tacked back to the support of their embattled and now doubled centre, allowing the leading Dutch under van der Putte to gain their wind and tack on them.

Tourville was now in a desperate situation, his line utterly broken into divisional groupings everywhere caught between fire from both sides, and often raked from ahead or astern, surrounded by overwhelmingly superior numbers, his once magnificent flagship pierced and shattered alow and aloft, her decks strewn with wrack and torn bodies and stained with blood, her hold filling from holes about the waterline. His seconds, particularly the *Admirable*, were in a similar state, as were several of their opponents; but more of the allied ships were scarcely damaged, and the two English rear divisions had not yet been in action. At this point, as so often during great fleet battles, the wind began to die. By four o'clock it had fallen to a flat calm and a thick mist had risen, cutting off ship from ship. Tourville started to tow northward. Russell, anxious he might be cheated of what seemed certain victory, wrote a brief instruction to 'Use all possible means to tow your ship into the line of battle during this calm',[5] and sent it by boat to all commanders; in the thick mist it is doubtful if it reached any but the nearest.

At about five a breeze sprang up from the east, dispersing the mist. The French set all the sail they could to escape northward, and Russell ordered a general chase. Shovell and Carter, both now to leeward of the main body of the French about Tourville and blocking their route down-wind, renewed the action, but as Tourville tried to force his way through them the breeze died and mist rolled up again. Tourville now sent boats north and south among his ships, instructing them to anchor. He was apparently reminded of this device of Torrington's in a note from Vilette-Mursay.[6] It was not so successful on this occasion. The tide had begun to flood and, as the French brought up to their cables with all sails set, Shovell's and Carter's divisions which had been to leeward should have drifted easterly through and past them. However, Shovell managed to get an instruction to his ships in time for all except one to let go an anchor before passing into the enemy; the one ship that failed to do so was raked by broadside after broadside and severely mauled before she drifted clear, as were several of Carter's ships. Carter himself was mortally wounded.

Through the evening, sporadic breezes sprang up from the east, shifting the curtains of mist and allowing the two so far unengaged divisions of the English rear under Sir John Ashby and George Rooke to sail and tow into action against the French main body. Shovell also sent fireships down on the tide, causing the *Soleil Royal* and several of her consorts to cut their cables. They anchored again when the danger was past.

Later the undamaged French rear divisions moved down against Shovell. Fearing he would be overwhelmed when the tide turned, allowing the whole French fleet to fall upon his few ships, Shovell ordered his captains to cut their cables. They drifted through the French grouping, some almost touching yards as they passed, suffering severely from the enemy fire, but causing equal damage with their own broadsides before passing clear into the allied lines. This marked the last series of engagements as the evening closed in with impenetrable fog.

Tourville weighed soon after one that night, directly the ebb began, and attempted escape down-Channel, aided in the early hours by light breezes from the east. By the time the fog had dispersed sufficiently for the allies to sight his sails, he was hull down over the horizon. Russell had the signal for general chase flying and pursued for the rest of that day, the 20th, the Dutch in the lead, both sides anchoring when the tide turned against them.

A few of the French had taken their own escape route – five of the van division under Nesmond and one other south to the invasion anchorage at La Hougue; Gabaret and three consorts north across the Channel – but thirty-four were grouped around Tourville, with the Dutch following closely and the English stretched out astern. This French main body was slowed by the more damaged ships, in particular the *Soleil Royal*, which had taken in so much water from holes and leaks she was barely manageable; in case it became necessary to sacrifice her, Tourville shifted his flag after dark to Vilette-Mursay's *Ambitieux*. Among the English, Shovell shifted his flag to one of his seconds, the 70-gun *Kent*.

The chase continued westward with the ebb in the early hours of the next morning, the 21st, the French rounding Cap de la Hague at the north-west corner of the Cherbourg peninsula before being forced to anchor by the onset of the flood and winds from the west. Tourville was determined to elude his pursuers by steering through the notoriously dangerous race between the cape and the island of Alderney – judging that Russell would not dare to follow with his great ships – but his new flagship, *Ambitieux*, was one of a group of thirteen, including the *Soleil Royal* and other more damaged larger ships, which dragged their anchors and were forced to cut cables and run. They were carried eastward so rapidly by wind and tide that they passed the Dutch and some of the English before these could react. Russell ordered his squadron to pursue, and was joined by several from the Blue squadron; others from the Blue, including the admiral, Ashby, remained to support the Dutch against the twenty-one French vessels still at anchor ahead.

Of those running eastward, three put about as they reached the open roadstead of Cherbourg: the *Soleil Royal*, her almost equally crippled second, *Admirable*, and one of Gabaret's seconds, the 76-gun *Triomphant*. It seemed as if they would attempt to beat back against the wind, but the pursuit was too close and all three ran themselves ashore. The following morning they were burned by a force commanded by Russell's vice admiral, Sir Ralph Delavall.

Tourville continued eastward with the other ten, rounding Pointe de Barfleur and steering down to the invasion port, La Hougue, where he joined two of the ships which had made straight there after the battle; the other four, under Nesmond, had since run eastward to attempt an escape up-Channel and northabout around Scotland into the Atlantic. The twelve ships with Tourville now moored in two groups of six, each close under a fort commanding the anchorage, while their pursuers came to anchor in the offing.

Next day Russell deputed Shovell to take command of the smaller ships of the line, frigates and fireships, and sail in to a position from where he could launch an attack on the moored enemy. After completing the necessary preparations and orders, Shovell, who had been wounded by a splinter during the battle, became too ill to continue. His place was taken by Rooke, vice admiral of the Blue squadron. After a preliminary bombardment in the morning of the 23rd, Rooke sent in armed boats under cover of a fireship against the northern group of ships lying under the lesser of the forts. Initial resistance collapsed as the boats reached the ships and sailors started scrambling up the sides and starting fires. Before the end of the day all six had been set ablaze.

Next morning Rooke launched a similar assault on the southern group. Troops from James's invasion force lining the spur enclosing the harbour and behind the parapets of the fort at its end fired fusilades as the flotilla approached, but from too great a range to halt the advance. James himself was watching from a vantage point above, and as the boats reached the moored ships he is said to have exclaimed to his companions, 'Ah, none but my brave English could do so brave an action!'[7] As before, all six of the enemy were put to the torch, together with a smaller warship with them. Afterwards Rooke, directing operations from his barge flying his vice admiral's flag at the bow, re-formed the boats together with two unexpended fireships and led them inside the harbour, where the invasion transports lay. These were also burned – all but a few at the inner end, which had dried out and could not be reached by boat.

Such was the blazing, exploding epilogue to Barfleur. It was the greatest English naval victory to date. Together with those burned at Cherbourg, fifteen French ships of the line had been destroyed, including the fleet flagship and most of the other flagships and seconds. Apart from fireships, no allied vessels had been lost, and English casualties in the final phases at Cherbourg and La Hougue had been minimal.

For the rest, the twenty-one ships anchored off Cap de la Hague on the 21st had escaped the Dutch and Ashby by navigating through the Alderney race, guided by a Breton sailor who had been pressed into naval service; thence they had found safety in the rock-bound harbour of Saint-Malo. These were generally the smaller vessels, although Panetié's flagship and another second rate were among them. Gabaret's flagship, another second rate and two third rates which had fled north with him from Barfleur reached Brest down-Channel; Nesmond's first-rate flagship and one consort eventually reached Brest northabout around Scotland; the other two were left at Le Havre; one of these grounded and broke her back, bringing total French losses to sixteen of the line.

It was the end of any prospect of invasion, and for James, broken with remorse at the losses Louis had sustained on his behalf, the end of his attempts to regain the Crown. Yet Louis, true father of the defeat, took such pride in the glorious way his ships had borne down on the enemy and fought against impossible odds he rewarded Tourville with the baton of a marshal of France.

The allies, after the euphoria of victory, made no better use of their command of the Channel than had the French after Beachy Head. The troops and transports for the invasion of Normandy had been dispersed; when an expeditionary force was gathered and dispatched with the fleet to Saint-Malo to destroy the French warships sheltering there, disagreements between the naval and military commanders prevented an attempt. Then William, leading the allied army in the Netherlands, called for an attack on Dunkirk from the sea to aid his campaign, but the port proved too strong and little was gained.

Meanwhile Pontchartrain, unable to pursue a battle-fleet strategy, turned to the *guerre de course*, sending out small squadrons of fast warships to prey on allied shipping and leasing frigates to private syndicates known as *armateurs*, who fitted out privateers as a business enterprise. Almost twice as many privately armed corsairs sailed from Saint-Malo that summer as in previous years, and they claimed 200 prizes – a figure never achieved before or subsequently.[8] Dunkirk and Ostend reaped similarly rich harvests as Jean Bart, Claude de Forbin and other heroes of French legend preyed in groups on lightly protected convoys or lone merchant ships in the Channel and the North Sea.

It was not the end of Louis's battle-fleet hopes. Eleven new first rates, six second rates and six third rates slipped down French ways over the course of that year and the next, more than replacing the losses of Barfleur/La Hougue and bringing theoretical fleet strength up to ninety of the line. Moreover, Louis still planned in terms of battle-fleet victory. In the event the campaign the following year, 1693, hinged on a vast allied convoy for the Mediterranean. Intelligence from English Jacobites revealed that the allied fleet would cover the convoy only as far as Ushant. Tourville was consequently ordered to sail early from Brest and lie in wait to the south. By this means he captured or sank over ninety mainly Dutch and German vessels with cargoes worth more than a million pounds, leaving others blockaded in Iberian ports and continuing his pursuit into the Mediterranean, where he remained. Since the allied main fleet stayed off Brest until forced back to Torbay by the inevitable spread of sickness, there was no fleet action that year. Yet again, perversely, allied fleet command in the Channel and western approaches failed to protect trade from serious losses and disruption; Dunkirk squadrons enjoyed a record haul, capturing as many prizes as in all previous campaigns of the war together.[9]

THE END OF the campaigning season of 1693 saw the turning point in the naval war, and indeed of the war as a whole, since William and Louis began secret peace soundings. These decisive shifts were the result of financial exhaustion. Having spent prodigiously over six years of conflict across the continent and surrounding seas, both monarchs were not only deep in debt, but faced difficulties in raising more money.

For Louis, this problem derived chiefly from his previous extraordinarily costly wars against the United Provinces and Spain, when he had cleared his debts by the sale of titles and offices – many hereditary

– carrying salaries or annuities and exempt from taxation. This had locked him into permanent payments absorbing a large proportion of his revenue. More insidiously, with such large classes of nobles, *officiers* and the clergy exempt from direct taxation, the tax burden fell heavily on the rest of the populace, engaged in trade, industry and agriculture, so tending to depress and discourage investment in the wealth-making sectors Colbert had been at pains to encourage.

Louis had continued his system in the present war; those who had made money in commerce or industry were only too eager to buy office and the social cachet it conferred. So successful financiers, merchants and entrepreneurs were constantly seduced from productive to administrative or judicial work, not only depriving the wealth-making sectors of leaders but also creating additional layers of officialdom whose regulations hampered active business.[10] Moreover, tax collection was complicated by regional immunities and revenue boundaries which encouraged large-scale internal smuggling, and the collectors were not royal officials but employees of private syndicates of financiers – known as tax farmers – whose methods were arbitrary rather than fair or efficient. Besides being weighed down by what amounted to the permanent debt of his previous wars, Louis was thus denied by a chaotic and manifestly unjust tax system the revenue he might have raised from his populous country.

The position had been exacerbated by dislocation of trade caused by allied naval squadrons and English, Zeeland, Spanish and Barbary privateers; even trade within the country was affected, since poor communications meant that many goods were sent by sea around the coast. In addition, bad harvests in 1691 and 1692 were followed in 1693 by a worse failure, threatening famine. The allies attempted to stop grain entering the country with a twin policy of maritime blockade and the purchase of Baltic supplies. They were not entirely successful, but prices rose to such an extent that French peasants and urban workers, always close to a subsistence level, were left with no purchasing money after they had bought bread; so recession deepened and unemployment and bankruptcies spread, further lowering tax yields.[11]

In this critical situation, Louis was forced to cut expenditure drastically. The navy was an obvious target. For years the battle fleet had been criticized for its vast expense and uselessness; recently France's most distinguished military engineer, Sébastien de Vauban, who had Louis's ear, had proposed moving to a single-minded concentration on the *guerre de course*. His plan involved reducing the battle fleet to half its present strength and dispersing it in three squadrons at Dunkirk, Brest and Toulon to support the private war against trade, meanwhile encouraging *armateurs* by various incentives including the relaxation of duties on the sale of captured enemy goods. Vauban argued that it was the wealth England and Holland derived from their sea trade that kept the armies of the Grand Alliance in the field against France; consequently the destruction of that trade was the surest, indeed the only, way to destroy the alliance and force a satisfactory peace.

The strategy was shot through with the flaws that had bedevilled Elizabethan attempts at state–private ventures and reduced Charles II's navy to impotence against the Dutch. Moreover, it failed to address the problem of preserving or building up France's own wealth by sea trade: it was simply predatory. The naval intendant at Brest penned a memorandum in favour of grand fleet strategy in the spirit of Colbert and Bonrepaus, but feeling at Court was too deeply hostile to the navy, too indifferent to the needs of trade and industry, and the financial crisis was too pressing for such arguments to be heard. Over the next two years expenditure on the fleet – excluding the galley service – was almost halved, from 29 million livres (£1.7 million) in 1693 to 14.6 million (£860,000) in 1695;[12] fleet strength fell in a similar proportion. The army, meanwhile, was maintained at full strength.

William's financial problems were of a different kind. The English Channel and the inability of English monarchs to borrow on any scale had saved the country from prolonged engagement in the wars that had ravaged continental Europe and forced Louis into his cycle of future obligations and diminishing tax base. There were fewer salaried Crown servants in the whole of England than in the single province of Normandy, and taxation per head was a quarter to a third of that in France;[13] as importantly, it fell on all classes and was seen to do so. Apart from William's immediate need for money to pay off James's naval debt – soon forthcoming from his supporters in the London financial community – he had begun his mission to curb the French king with a virtually clean fiscal slate.[14]

His difficulties stemmed chiefly from Parliament. James had lost his Crown because he had been suspected of manoeuvring towards an absolute monarchy in the style of Louis. William had been welcomed as guarantor of English – parliamentary – liberties. Members of Parliament, perceiving they had contributed to their impotence under James by granting him a permanent income from various tax and customs yields, were resolved not to repeat the mistake: William was made to apply to Parliament even for his ordinary revenue. This not only kept him in financial dependence but ensured the regular convening of Parliament, which gave opportunity for scrutiny of his every transaction and future intention.

Parliament also sought to prevent the growth of permanent taxation and the state apparatus necessary for its collection and distribution; consequently the sums granted William were raised by taxes or duties for limited periods only – usually three years. Land tax was preferred to indirect (excise) taxes on commodities, since it affected the Members' own pockets and would consequently be reduced or repealed at the first opportunity; moreover, it was collected locally by the gentry, not by Crown tax collectors. The determination to limit and control William extended to underfunding his war expenditure deliberately, forcing him to borrow to make up the difference, so increasing his dependence by saddling him with interest payments from his ordinary revenue.[15] These heroic efforts to prevent what would now be called big government and deficit financing in the Dutch style – referred to disparagingly by the landed interest as 'running the country head over ears in debt' – were quite incompatible with the conduct of a great European war, and resulted in 1693 and 1694 in major financial crises.

The solution – plain in retrospect, and plain to William's Dutch advisers and many others then – was to spread the extraordinary expenditure of war over a longer term. The first tentative step in this direction was taken in January 1693, with the sale of life annuities at rates of interest up to 14 per cent, the payments being guaranteed by Parliament on the yields of additional duties on beer, vinegar and imported drink. It was not a success, and was followed in March 1694 by the sale of 100,000 ten-pound lottery tickets, the winners receiving annual sums for a period of sixteen years, again guaranteed by Parliament on specific additional duties and taxes.[16]

However, the crucial move towards long-term borrowing was taken that summer, 1694, when subscribers to a loan of £1,200,000 were incorporated as the Bank of England. Attempts to form such a bank on the model of the Bank of Amsterdam had failed under Charles II and James II because sound finance was impossible under arbitrary rule by royal prerogative. The difference now was that William was observing constitutional constraints and loans were guaranteed not by the Crown but by Parliament, so forming not a royal but a 'national' debt.[17]

The critical importance of the political changes was appreciated by the English moneyed interest and foreign observers alike: the leading Dutch political writer Ericus Walten suggested that since the 'Glorious Revolution' there was no great gap between the political systems of England and the United Provinces, both being under an 'eminent head' who scrupulously observed the constitutional limits of his authority, which was the essence of stable and responsible government.[18]

The foundation of the Bank was a logical development, particularly under the extreme pressures of war. Naturally it met bitter opposition in a Parliament dedicated to preventing the growth of government. The landed classes particularly saw the Bank as a mechanism for harnessing the financial community which stood to gain from war to an administration intent on waging war, and feared the inevitable escalation of public debt and taxes to service the debt. Their apprehensions were to be justified beyond their worst fears. It is a measure of the strength of the merchant/financial interest that the fierce opposition failed. It is an indication also of the dilemma facing all traditionalists: William was the guarantor of their liberties and religion, yet in protecting them he had to increase borrowing, hence the power of the financial interest. Or, as it is put in recent study of this turning point in English history, the cost of defence against Louis was the creation of a state which threatened the traditional vision of English society and politics, and 'one of the major political concerns of the period was how to steer a safe course between preserving the regime and avoiding its excesses'.[19]

The influence of the merchant interest can be seen as clearly in parliamentary debates about the losses caused by the French war against trade, particularly after the destruction of the Mediterranean convoy. Attempts were made to interfere in the detailed organization of convoys. These failed, but many more warships of the fourth and fifth rates suitable as escorts were laid down in succeeding years,[20] and continuing parliamentary agitation led in 1696 to the formation of the Board of Trade to liaise between merchants and the Admiralty on the sailing and protection of convoys. That year the sum voted for the navy rose to over two and a half million pounds – more than double French naval expenditure.[21]

So the two principal naval protagonists veered in opposite directions. Louis in financial crisis had little choice but to sacrifice his fleet; William was moved by the concern for trade protection to increase his and develop alongside the battle fleet stronger, more professional escort and patrol/blockade forces amounting virtually to a second fleet.[22] The merchant/financial interest which provided the means was calling the tune, as it had in the great days of the United Provinces, Venice and other historic maritime powers. Indeed, England was on the way to becoming, if she had not already become, a true maritime power.

As if to mark the transformation, in the same summer as the foundation of the Bank of England, 1694, and using the funds thus made available by the subscribers, Russell led the allied fleet, headed by eight three-deckers, into the Mediterranean, shutting up the reduced French combined fleet in Toulon. By wintering at Cadiz instead of returning home, Russell continued to command the middle sea throughout the campaigning season of 1695, freeing allied trade, cutting French trade to a trickle, and stopping supplies reaching French forces advancing on Barcelona – so symbolizing for allies, neutrals and enemies the might of the maritime powers.

It was the first time an English main fleet had entered the Mediterranean, the first time the great ships had not been laid up for the winter. The effort and expense of sending out naval stores, supplies, dockyard officials and workers to Cadiz indicated a new level of financial and administrative competence. Russell's cruises on the southern European flank attested a new scale of military and diplomatic leverage. The beginnings of Dutch financial methods had enabled England to take up her much heralded, hitherto disappointed, role as a major European power. Meanwhile the former supreme maritime power, the United Provinces, confined to a junior naval partnership, was being bled on land by continuous defensive campaigns on its southern-Netherlands frontier.

The peace negotiations which had begun towards the end of 1693 were concluded and signed at Ryswick near The Hague in September 1697. Louis restored all the territory his armies had won, renounced claims to the Spanish Netherlands, allowed the United Provinces to garrison the border fortresses, and recognized William as king of England, Scotland and Ireland and his heirs as successors; he also cancelled the ruinous import duties that had persuaded the Dutch regents to support William's plans for a grand alliance against him. Satisfactory as it appeared, the treaty was no more than a truce of exhaustion. None of the questions concerning French territorial or colonial ambitions and the conflicting economic compulsions of the maritime powers had been settled. They were to be fought out through the next century.

8

Málaga, 1704

THE SECOND ROUND of hostilities between France and the maritime powers began in 1702. It was sparked by a chance of inheritance that brought a Bourbon, Louis XIV's grandson, Philip of Anjou, to the Spanish throne. The underlying causes though, unchanged from the last war, were trade rivalry and Louis's drive for European hegemony.

Louis had reneged on his promise to the Dutch to cancel the prohibitive import duties on manufactured goods barely three months after the Treaty of Ryswick. Since his grandson's accession to the Spanish throne, the two had concerted trade policies which resulted in the virtual exclusion of Dutch and English merchants from Spanish ports;[1] and the *asiento de negros*, the contract for supplying African slaves to Spanish American colonies, earlier held by a Portuguese consortium with links to the Dutch West Indies Company, had been granted to the French Guinea Company. Defence policies had been similarly co-ordinated. French troops had marched into the Spanish Netherlands and forced the Dutch to withdraw from the barrier fortresses, not only removing the buffer between France and the United Provinces, but threatening the merchants of Amsterdam with the abolition of their vital restrictions on trade up the Schelde to Antwerp.

None of the powers wanted to fight, for none had recovered financially from the previous bout – least of all France. The regents of the United Provinces had particular cause for not wishing to repeat the experiences of the last war, when English naval and merchant power had expanded so rapidly. Yet Louis's responses to his kinsman's accession left them no option. Nor could William III stand by while Louis again threatened to dominate Europe and indeed world trade. He and the Grand Pensionary of Holland, Anthonie Heinsius, set about forging another grand coalition to check the French king, drawing in as their principal territorial allies the Habsburg emperor of Austria – whose son was a claimant to the Spanish throne – and Friedrich I of Brandenburg-Prussia.

Louis, as soon as he realized war was inevitable, should by the rules of the territorial power game have struck before the alliance was ready and while his real and easily reached target, the United Provinces, was still on a peace footing. He did not do so – a failure which has been ascribed to an uncharacteristic loss of nerve.[2] No doubt his desperate financial situation was the major inhibiting factor: his finance minister wrote to a colleague before the outbreak of hostilities, 'I have the misfortune of serving as Controller General at the beginning of a new war following another which has exhausted all the reserves necessary to sustain it.'[3] Other ministers took equally pessimistic views, considering they would be fortunate if they managed to defend Spain and their West Indian possessions.[4]

While Louis advanced fatalistically towards a great war made inevitable by his own policies, but which he could not expect to win, and the Amsterdam regents feared England would be the chief beneficiary of any trade or colonies wrung from him, the English merchant interest behind William supported the war as a business venture. The Earl of Marlborough, entrusted by William with the detailed negotiation of alliances, was instructed to pay particular regard in the treaties he made 'to the security and improvements of the trade of our kingdoms'.[5]

William died in early 1702, before the outbreak of war. Mary had died eight years earlier, and the Crown passed to her sister, Anne. William's role as director of the new Grand Alliance against France and leader of the allied army passed to Marlborough, whom he had groomed for the task and who was to prove his equal in diplomacy and superior in generalship. The considerable funds needed to support Marlborough's campaigns were raised with the aid of the merchant community of London by his long-time ally at Court, now Lord Treasurer, Sidney Godolphin. These three – Queen Anne, Marlborough and Godolphin – were to achieve a near-perfect strategy for maritime power, blending naval and Continental land operations and the payment and supply of mercenary armies to encircle, bleed, blockade and finally stifle and bankrupt the Continental monarchies.

The allied fleet was the vital element. Louis's navy, although strong on paper, was ageing and poorly maintained, and his dockyards were ill-supplied at the start, while the Spanish fleet was practically non-existent. Above all, as in the previous war, but rather sooner this time, financial crisis obliged Louis to cut expenditure on the great ships and turn to Vauban's strategy of the *guerre de course*.

Before this happened, there was one fleet action. In August 1704 the Brest and Toulon divisions succeeded in combining in the Mediterranean under the Comte de Toulouse. The allied fleet under Sir George Rooke had recently seized the rock spur of Gibraltar as a base from which to command the Mediterranean and the trade passing through the Strait, and Toulouse interposed his fleet off Málaga between the allies and the rock. Rooke, with the advantage of the wind, bore down to engage him on the morning of 13 August – by uncanny coincidence, just as Marlborough, after an astonishing march to the upper Danube to join his Austrian ally, Prince Eugène, below the village of Blenheim, was flouting the rules of war by attacking a numerically superior enemy established in a strong defensive position on rising ground bordered by swamps and streams.

To examine Marlborough's and Rooke's attacks that day is to apprehend the tactical gulf between land and sea warfare. Marlborough had used feints on his march and feints in his preparations for assault, to strike when and where his enemy least expected it; he was holding back reserves, and would use cover and the configuration of ground to deliver a decisive concentration of force and unleash his cavalry at the opportune moment. Rooke and Toulouse had only the flat open sea on which to deploy their cumbersome timber fortresses, the fickle wind to provide motion. Neither could achieve surprise nor make a feint that could not be parried by an alert opponent. Their fleets were numerically almost equal; to detach a division to double and bring a concentration to bear on the opponent's van or rear was to invite being doubled in return – or perhaps a wind change might leave the detached ships isolated and open to defeat by the massed enemy. All they could do was form up in full sight of each other in equally extended, more or less parallel lines and exchange broadsides as the windward fleet closed within effective range.

The formal line of battle and the 'Sailing and Fighting Instructions' in which it was enshrined in both English and French navies have received regular criticism from naval historians. Rooke's instructions, which were taken over verbatim from Russell's and which were to last virtually unchanged through most of the eighteenth century, have been disparaged as producing 'a constricting effect on tactics, tending not only to encourage defensive methods, but defensive thinking as well'.[6] And it has been usual to blame the line for the inconclusive results of most fleet actions of the period.

The line, however, had evolved through half a century of continual sea fighting during which experience had shown the difficulties of bringing a fleet into action as a cohesive force, the impossibility of controlling it once battle was joined, and the equalizing effects of damage aloft, which could cripple those ships having the better of the action as severely as those they were beating. In these circumstances, decisive results were the exception; as the veteran admiral Clowdisley Shovell put it two years before the Battle of Málaga, 'when men are equally inured and disciplined in war, 'tis without a miracle numbers that gain the victory. For both in fleets, squadrons and single ships of nearly equal force by the time one is beaten and ready to retreat, the other is also beaten and glad the enemy has left him.'[7]

Fleet line of battle was the natural outcome of the development of the specialized sailing warship as a floating fortress deploying tiers of great guns with narrow arcs of fire limited to the broadside. Only the single line could ensure that all guns would bear on the enemy; in the smoke and confusion of battle, only the line could ensure cohesion and mutual support. Of particular significance in this respect was Rooke's Article XXI: 'None of the Ships in the Fleet shall pursue any small Number of the Enemies Ships until the main Body be disabled or run.'[8] It was not until the latter decades of the century, when the French service suffered internal disruption and fell below its former professional standards, that British admirals felt able to experiment with more flexible tactics, as will appear.

The Battle of Málaga, in which Shovell commanded the van division, confirmed all his experience. Action was joined at about ten in the morning and lasted into the evening, when groups of battered ships, many crippled aloft, drifted apart to repair damages, each side glad to be rid of the other. No ships were lost or captured, but casualties were heavy – some 2,700 in the allied divisions, rather fewer in the French, although precise figures are not known. The only tactical novelty was the deployment of two English 'bomb ketches' fitted with high-angle mortars, probably the only instance of such vessels taking part in a fleet action in the open sea. They succeeded in lobbing explosive shells into the flagship of the French van and a consort, detonating cartridges in the latter which blew off part of her stern. Málaga may also be noteworthy as the first fleet action in which some of the ships on the English side were steered by a primitive wheel placed abaft the mizzen-mast, since this feature began to appear on Navy Board models from 1703; but the wheel's evolution is impossible to date precisely. Certainly French warships continued to steer by whipstaff through most of the first half of the century.[9]

The stalemate off Málaga contrasts with the outcome at Blenheim, where broken remnants of Louis's army were in full flight as night fell, leaving 38,000 of their number behind dead, wounded or captured. They had been making for Vienna to accomplish Louis's aim of knocking Austria from the Grand Alliance. That danger had been decisively countered. As Marlborough wrote to his wife next morning, it was 'as great a victory as has ever been known'.[10]

Yet Málaga, despite being tactically indecisive, was to prove as decisive as Blenheim in strategic terms, and of even greater consequence for the future. For, although the wind swung round to favour the French next morning, the majority of Toulouse's flag officers had been convinced by the pounding and damages received that they could never force a decision, and Rooke was allowed to take his perhaps even more damaged fleet back to Gibraltar unmolested. It was a misjudgement with epic consequences. Although Rooke had seized the rock and anchorage with an Anglo-Dutch force, ostensibly on behalf of the Austrian pretender to the Spanish throne, it was to remain in British hands thereafter, the impregnable hinge of British Mediterranean and world strategy.

For the French fleet, which returned to Toulon, it was the final sortie of the war. Already in financial extremity, Louis was again forced to sacrifice his navy. The great ships were laid up and new construction was abandoned; as in the previous war, lesser rates were sent out in joint royal–private cruises against allied trade. The principal squadrons operated from Dunkirk and Brest under leaders whose names joined the legend of French privateer commanders: the Chevalier de Saint-Pol-Hécourt, Claude de Forbin and, from Saint-Malo, René Duguay-Trouin, one of the most outstanding of all French naval officers. His force of usually four royal warships, the largest of fifty or sixty guns, was fitted out and maintained by private *armateurs*; the smaller warships operating from Dunkirk were maintained from navy funds. Privateers attached themselves to each squadron; if a convoy were intercepted, these would cut out vessels while the escorts were drawn off or engaged by the warships, although the greater number of prizes came from stragglers or from ships sailing independently.

In England, their depredations resulted in the usual outbursts from the merchant interest against the Admiralty, and in 1708 Parliament passed a Convoys and Cruisers Act which obliged the Admiralty to reserve forty-three warships of specified ratings for the protection of trade in home waters.[11] It is doubtful if the Act had more than a moral effect, for by this time co-operation between the Admiralty and the principal merchants was close, many warships had already been drawn from the battle fleet for trade protection – following the total collapse of the French fleet – and the system of convoys combined with patrols off enemy bases had been refined. It serves as an illustration of the power Parliament had won to scrutinize and bridle the administration, and of the dominating position within Parliament of those instrumental in funding the war. There is no doubt that shipping losses were contained: English trade, after suffering severely in the years immediately after Málaga, was to rise by the end of the war to a greater volume than at the start in 1702.[12]

The United Provinces was hit harder by the disruption. Its industries and great port cities were so dependent on trade with France, Spain and Spanish America and its expenses in setting out the largest army it had ever deployed to resist the French in the southern Netherlands were so great that it very soon resumed its old custom of trading with the enemy. This caused anger in England, but the English were not above resuming trade with Spain.[13] This indeed was their principal war aim. If Marlborough's purpose was to curb the power of France, the English merchant interest was intent on obtaining a dominating trading influence in Spain and her colonial dependencies and acquiring the *asiento* to supply them with African slaves.[14] A treaty had already been concluded with Portugal, which provided a valuable market for English exports, a source of gold from mines opened in Portuguese Brazil in 1695 and a wintering base for the Mediterranean fleet in Lisbon, which also served as a supply base for Gibraltar.[15]

Knowing that English trading ambitions caused apprehension in the United Provinces, Marlborough sought to appease the States General by holding out the prospect of their control of the southern Netherlands. He wrote to Heinsius, 'England can like no peace but such as puts king Charles [the Habsburg pretender] in the possession of the monarche of

Spain, and as for yourselves I think you ought to have garrisons in Antwerp, Namur and Luxembourg.'[16] In May 1706 he decisively defeated a French army at Ramillies, thirteen miles north of Namur, enabling the States General to fulfil these ambitions and gain economic dominion over the southern Netherlands. It was some compensation for their lost trades and industrial contraction, but could not resolve the anxieties over England's increasing maritime ascendancy. As in the last war, they were pledged to provide three warships for every five English, but could not manage even this ratio and were frequently late in fitting out those ships they did contribute.[17]

Of the three great trading rivals, however, it was once again France that suffered most. It was the inevitable result of her naval collapse. The increase in French privateering was itself a symptom of the difficulties of conducting normal trade through seas where enemy squadrons – and privateers – roved at will from the Mediterranean to the Channel. By 1708 French industry had been decimated by the effects of enemy action on shipping bringing in raw materials and exporting manufactured goods. Markets in the Middle East had been completely cut off.[18] Only those industries supplying war materials or clothing for the troops flourished.

The situation was aggravated by Louis's desperate attempts to raise money. What was needed was a radical reform of the entire tax-farming system and the exemptions enjoyed by nobles and clergy. It was not to be expected in the middle of a great war: the vested interests were too strong; Louis's reliance on advances from the tax farmers was too great. The usual solutions were adopted: new or increased excise duties on commodities, which had the effect of restricting production; supplements to the *taille*, or property tax, discouraging investment on the land and in industry and cutting the purchasing power of the middle classes, further depressing trade; forced levies on individuals and organizations; and the sale of offices, diverting the capital of more successful men of business from productive investment.

In addition, Louis amplified the trials of business by frequent arbitrary changes in the value of the *livre* and by issuing paper money and interest-bearing notes which circulated, and depreciated, as money. The result was a complete loss of confidence in the currency, leading to flights of capital abroad, hoarding of specie at home, and exorbitant rates of interest when Louis borrowed.

Thus the combined effects of the exigencies of war against the two leading maritime powers and their Continental allies, the venality and inefficiency of tax collection, the chaos of internal boundaries and tolls, and the impulses of arbitrary power resulted in fiscal reactions to ever-increasing war debt which might have been designed to ruin trade and industry, and in large measure did so.[19]

The contrast with financial management in the two maritime powers could not have been greater. Credit was the lifeblood of the trading system, and neither the States General nor Parliament could consider compromising it. England (or, after the union with Scotland in 1707, Great Britain) financed the war exclusively by higher taxes and voluntary loans to bridge the gap between tax revenue and expenditure; the United Provinces did so chiefly by loans, with little extra taxation.[20] There was no manipulation of currency or coinage, no sale of tax-exempt office or honours, no forced loans nor reneging on interest payments.

The British Lord Treasurer, Godolphin, developed the Dutch methods of long-term borrowing tentatively begun against much opposition in the last war. As then, each loan raised at the rather lower rate of 6½ per cent interest, falling after Ramillies to 6¼ per cent, had specific excise or customs duties earmarked to guarantee interest payments; there was a consequent inexorable shift towards ever-higher indirect taxation, much of it incurred simply to service the growing debt. Soon the British, who had started the first war against Louis as the most lightly burdened of the three major powers, had become the most highly taxed, paying twice as much per head as the French.[21] Yet, because the imposts were passed by Parliament and levied on all classes, they did not bear down so heavily on trade or agriculture nor cause the distress and resentment induced by the tax farmers in France.

The fair and open system of tax collection was one of the two key factors enabling Great Britain to sustain this most expensive of all the wars she had ever fought: it not only tapped a greater proportion of the country's wealth than the French system, but provided the certainty that underlay public confidence in the war loans. Paradoxically, its efficiency stemmed from the efforts of Charles and James Stuart in the previous century to break free from all parliamentary constraints by replacing private tax farmers with their own salaried officials. From these beginnings a highly professional corps of excise and customs collectors had evolved whose nationwide networks, answerable to the centre in London, were not constrained as in France and the United Provinces by regional jurisdictions and exemptions, and were marked by such modern features as entrance by examination or training scheme, performance monitoring, a graded salary structure culminating in a pension, and an ethos of public duty and pride in the integrity of the service.[22]

The other key factor underlying British financial strength was, of course, trade. It was ultimately upon these two, trading profits and efficient collection of taxes and duties, that the edifice of British power was built: the dominating battle fleets in the Mediterranean and the Channel and the immense organization of dockyards and supplies that maintained them; Marlborough's army and the payment of Dutch contractors to provision him on the march; and the greater share of the subsidies paid by the two maritime powers to the Continental troops of the Grand Alliance.

The pressure these resources exerted by land and sea brought France to the edge of disintegration. By early 1709 Marlborough and Prince Eugène had destroyed Louis's Flanders army;[23] the French people faced famine; banditry and civil and religious disorder were widespread, and the court was infected with defeatism. Louis was prepared to sign almost any terms. But the British government, in the hands of the Whig partnership of great landowners and the moneyed interest, in triumph overplayed its hand, demanding not only a secure position in Spanish–American trade, but the removal of Philip V and his replacement on the Spanish throne by the Austrian claimant. It would have been an intolerable humiliation for Louis to banish his own grandson. He held out. Dutch financiers aided him with loans; Dutch merchants averted the threatened famine by shipping in Baltic grain, evading British blockading patrols.

In the long run, Louis was saved by two other factors. The first was the international balancing mechanism: he had been cut down, but Great Britain was beginning to replace him as the threat to European equilibrium, and the other members of the Grand Alliance were less willing to conform to British strategy. On the Mediterranean flank, the Austrian emperor pursued his own interests in Italy instead of maintaining pressure on Louis through Spain. Meanwhile the strain on British finances from maintaining the largest navy in the world, subsidizing the Continental allies and servicing the huge debt accumulated by Godolphin led to a monetary crisis precipitating the downfall of the government.[24] The Whigs were replaced by the Tories, representing the squirearchy, who detested money men, high taxes and deficit financing, and were thoroughly tired of the war. Louis was able to detach them from the Dutch and agree peace terms.

These were signed at Utrecht in 1713. The Dutch were furious at British perfidy, the Whigs almost equally furious that the Tories had failed to obtain fortified British trading posts in Spanish America as the price for peace. Nonetheless, the terms formalized Louis's utter defeat and Great Britain's emergence as the dominant naval and colonial power. In the Mediterranean she retained two fleet bases taken by the allies, Gibraltar and Port Mahón, Minorca, and in Northern America the northern territories of Acadia, Newfoundland, Nova Scotia and the Hudson's Bay area; in Spanish America she acquired the coveted *asiento* to ship African slaves to the colonies, and the right to send one ship a year to Spanish America with trade goods. In the Channel, Louis agreed to the destruction of the privateer port of Dunkirk. And while Philip V retained his Spanish Crown and possessions, his European territories were ceded to Austria. Thus the strategically and economically valuable southern Netherlands passed to a non-maritime power whose weight in the territorial scale traditionally balanced that of France. In this respect the treaty was thoroughly 'Whiggish': in peace as in war, the main territorial power was to be checked by a rival, allowing the Royal Navy to tip the maritime and colonial balance in favour of the island kingdom.

The United Provinces gained as the Netherlands reverted to a buffer between Louis and itself. And it was able to secure Austria's agreement to abide by the former prohibitions on trade up the Schelde,[25] confirming the commercial dominance of Amsterdam, although the British blocked its attempt to control the canal network linking Ostend, Bruges and Ghent, the principal access for British manufactures to the area.[26]

Yet for the republic the most significant result of this culmination of the struggle with Louis XIV was loss of naval supremacy. As its resources and men had been poured into defence against French armies on land, the trident had passed irretrievably to Great Britain. Loss of military power was to follow rapidly. The policy of paying for the war with loans rather than increased taxation had led to a huge increase in the national debt, whose interest payments now absorbed over 70 per cent of ordinary tax revenue,[27] and the regents of the States Party, who had seized back all power after William's death, were forced into drastic cuts in the army. By 1715 the republic had been reduced from a first-class to a middle-ranking military power. It was never again to play the leading role in Europe.

It remained for a while the strongest commercial nation, with the largest merchant fleet, and Amsterdam remained financial centre of the world, its banking, exchange and investment services indispensable for international trade.[28] Yet even these vestiges of the golden age were eroding: the decline of the urban population, which had started around the time William seized the English Crown and marked the beginning of a contraction of the republic's industries, was about to accelerate, for with loss of armed might the republic lost leverage in most of the 'rich trades' from which its industrial dominance had sprung.

The situation of the great territorial neighbour that had bled it was far worse. Louis XIV was bankrupt, his revenue entirely swallowed by interest payments on his debts, which were two years in arrears. Other debts had been laid on cities, provinces, craft guilds and religious and other bodies by forced loans.[29] Large sections of industry were ruined, cities had declined, and the overall population had fallen by perhaps 2 million, probably more;[30] roads and waterways had fallen into disrepair. In 1716 the Deputies of Trade recorded their opinion that two factors had been responsible for the great changes in the pattern of trade in France. The first had been the flight of the Huguenots – persecuted by the Catholic Church and in 1685 denied freedom to worship by royal edict[31] – who had transported French industry to foreign soil, 'and the second is the war of 1702, which we fought with the two leading maritime powers. These two events absolutely changed the entire complexion of our trade.'[32]

The unqualified victor in the three-cornered struggle for trade was Great Britain. The acquisition of Mediterranean bases and her treaty with Portugal had given her the ability to exercise maritime command right around the coasts of western Europe. Her navy was now more than equal to the combined fleets of France, the United Provinces and Spain,[33] and the only theoretical limits to her control were the short time fleets could keep the sea before ships' companies went down with scurvy, the number of ports to be covered, and the chances of weather. Her trade had increased during the latter years of the war, although not spectacularly,[34] and she had penetrated the Spanish–American system. Above all, her own North American and West Indian colonies, tied to her commercially by the Navigation Acts, were the most rapidly developing trading areas. The Dutch had lost their foothold in North

America, and the French position on the extreme northern and southern flanks, the St Lawrence and the Mississippi, was vulnerable and lacked cohesion.

Great Britain's arrival as the dominating sea power can be ascribed to many causes. Politically it might be said that England had been taken over by William III on behalf of the United Provinces to resist Louis XIV. It is certainly true that the constitutional settlement whereby Parliament rather than William or his successors controlled the public purse and raised and spent money on behalf of the nation was the key factor in securing the credit on which the war was won, for those with capital were quick to appreciate the difference between a king's word and a national commitment as security for investment.[35] It was this fundamental change that allowed the establishment of the Bank of England and the Dutch methods of long-term loans, without which neither war could have been sustained for longer than two or three years.

In strategic terms it was the combination of maritime and Continental pressure that ruined Louis. Naval dominance had stifled French trade, wooed allies, and made possible amphibious operations or 'descents' around the coastal peripheries of Bourbon territory, but it was the great military campaigns in Flanders and the heart of the Continent that drained the French king financially and forced him to abandon all pretence of a battle-fleet policy.[36] In the sixteenth century, Elizabeth I and Burghley had understood the fine balances to be struck between naval and Continental operations and subsidizing allied armies; it was the immensely greater resources William III, Queen Anne, Marlborough and Godolphin deployed that enabled Great Britain not merely to retain independence from the dominant territorial state, but to break its power.

The question remains how and why such a favourable conjunction of political, strategic and financial factors occurred at this time in England – and, conversely, why they were not duplicated in Louis XIV's vastly more populous nation, which was also richer in natural resources and had at least as favourable a geographical position, flanking both Atlantic and Mediterranean trade routes. One answer is the burden of debt and vested interests carried over from previous wars which made it impossible to reform France's chaotic tax system. The more profound answers lie in the compulsions of the military caste which dominated Louis's court. Merchants and financiers were despised as they had been at the court of Philip II; their needs were not understood. Here lies the clue to

England's winning constitution: merchants who provided the money were calling the tune. Although William had taken over the country, the financial constraints placed on him through Parliament actually harnessed him and his successors to the merchant interest.

The system had transformed the nation in short time into the most heavily taxed state in western Europe, built up a permanent debt amounting by 1713 to over £40 million, costing 50–60 per cent of normal state revenue to service,[37] and led to the development of the most highly centralized and efficient fiscal bureaucracy of the age. The worst fears of the traditional landed interest had been realized. Their unencumbered England of limited government and light taxes had, like the United Provinces earlier, become a fiscal-military state dependent on high levels of taxation to service debt and pay for the large naval and military establishments required to sustain the great power position achieved. Above all, government and the moneyed interest had become inextricably linked, and the country locked by the nature of the armed rivalry between nations and the dominant role she had won at sea into an irreversible cycle of war, mounting expenditure, increasing debt and an expanding and more intrusive civil administration. This last was not, however, so intrusive as French officialdom; nor were the military ever allowed to threaten civil liberties.

Louis XIV has been assigned some responsibility for this remarkable change, since it was the defence of the English state and the Protestant religion, and indeed the balance of Europe, against his ambitions that had led to the unwanted growth.[38] Yet the ambitions of English merchants had been plain from before the Anglo-Dutch wars, and their drive for trade had played as large a part as the need to defeat Louis – a larger part towards the end, or peace might have been concluded much earlier. And it was their commercial drive which was to shape the rest of the century.

9

Rule, Britannia

IN THE PEACE after the great wars of Louis XIV, all governments involved strove to reduce the unprecedented debt they had accumulated. The British government was able to take advantage of a market in stocks which had developed in London since 1688 to convert its short-term debts into long-term securities at rates of interest falling to 5 per cent.[1] There could have been no better indication of the confidence now placed in the financial institutions of the City and the stability of the government; indeed, the two were mutually dependent. It will be recalled that the first essays in long-term borrowing in the early years of the revolution had been at up to 14 per cent interest.

In 1717 Robert Walpole, most able of the younger generation of Whigs, now serving as First Lord of the Treasury and Chancellor of the Exchequer, made the first effort to reduce the amount of the national debt by creating a 'sinking fund' from revenue surpluses; as debt was paid off from the fund, additional surpluses would accrue from the lower interest payments on the debt, so creating a benevolent reducing cycle.

Queen Anne had died in 1714; she had been succeeded, under the terms of the settlement with William and Mary, not by the absolutist and Catholic Stuart heir, but by the Protestant Elector of the small German territory of Hanover, a descendant on his mother's side of James I of England. He was crowned as George I of Great Britain.

The following year Louis XIV had died, leaving his five-year-old great-grandson to succeed. Louis's nephew, the Duc d'Orléans, took power as regent during the infant's minority, and attempted radical changes designed to restore the traditional nobility in government in place of Louis's more recently ennobled ministerial class. This was to end in failure and a return to the former system. Meanwhile he made the more costly mistake of entrusting French finances and the reduction of the debt – the single most vital problem bequeathed by Louis – to a Scottish self-publicist named John Law.

Law had studied commerce and political economy in London – perceived as a model of financial expertise – and assured Orléans he would not only rid the government of debt but reform the entire financial and taxation system, and in addition so regenerate trade and industry that France would be able to 'give the law to all Europe'. At the core of Law's assurance lay the conviction that money was a dynamic force. He had seen it at work in Amsterdam, London and the British provincial capital markets, and he believed that by increasing the quantity in circulation he could stimulate the growth of trade and industry. Consequently his first step, in 1716, was to establish a Banque Générale in Paris, with authority to print paper money.

Next he set up a company in place of the old French West Indies Company with monopoly rights in all westward trade and the particular aim of developing the vast tracts of French Louisiana along the Mississippi valley in North America. This was perceived as the French El Dorado, and Law's prospectus for the shares of the new Compagnie d'Occident reflected this. The price rocketed immediately, and in 1719 he merged the company with the Banque Générale and all other overseas monopoly companies such as that of Senegal (with exclusive rights in the African slave trade, which had been ruined by the late war and loss of the *asiento*) and the East Indies and China companies. Shares in the new corporation, which he named the Nouvelle Compagnie des Indes, were issued as state securities – *billets d'état*. His intention was that their sale or exchange for holdings of government debt would discharge the entire national debt.

A frenzy of buying ensued, in keeping with the scale of the enterprise and the easy fortunes anticipated from establishing new plantations in America. The wild speculation spread from Paris to the exchanges in London, Amsterdam and other trading cities, driving the price up from the original 500 to 10,000 *livres* (approaching £500) – an enormous sum. The Banque contributed to the fever by printing notes to facilitate purchase as the price rose, adding monetary inflation in France to soaring overvaluation of the stock. The following year, inevitably, the bubble burst, bankrupting many investors and leaving the company itself with huge debts. Law fled the country. The government, as guarantor of the *billets*, consolidated the debt and raised taxes to fund their repayment. However, so important was West Indian sugar, the most dynamic single sector of the economy, and the African slave labour that worked the plantations, that the company was retained and was promised a bounty from the Crown of 143 *livres* (over £6) for every slave landed in the islands.[2]

More serious than this disaster, which was due not so much to Law's theory of paper money as to inexperience and gross overambition, was his failure to reform the tax system. The great Colbert and others had failed before him; many more able ministers were to fail after him. None was able to break the opposition of the Paris and local *parlements* – controlled by the tax-exempt nobility, equally jealous of their provincial rights – and their supporters at Court and in the Church.

Before Law's project collapsed, it had provoked alarm in London lest France obtain relief from her debt first and so gain the advantage in the next round of the colonial trading struggle. The system of competing national monopolies made it inevitable it would be a trial of arms, and the nation that restored its economy before the other would be in the best position to finance its forces; this was the assumption. The British government hastily organized a scheme similar to Law's

The vehicle was the South Sea Company. It had been founded in 1711 by incorporating holders of government short-term debt, granting the company so formed a monopoly of the trading rights in Spanish America, particularly the slaving *asiento* anticipated from the peace treaty. The slaving monopoly on the African coast, which had been held in turn by James's Royal Adventurers and a new Royal African Company (RAC), had long been penetrated by slavers from British ports other than London, and the interlopers' rights as 'separate traders' on the coast had been formally recognized in 1698. However, the forts and trading stations on the coast were still maintained by the RAC, and it was from them that the South Sea Company bought slaves to fulfil the terms of the *asiento*. These stipulated 4,800 slaves annually; for the privilege, the company paid 200,000 pesos (over £60,000) as an advance on 33$^{1}/_{2}$ pesos (£10) due to the king of Spain for each healthy slave landed in Spanish colonial markets.[3]

Now, in 1720, holders of government annuities, which formed a substantial portion of the national debt – £12.5 million of over £40 million – were offered the chance to exchange them for a new issue of shares in the South Sea Company. The government would owe the company the total value of the annuities exchanged, paying interest at 5, reducing to 4, per cent – considerably less than the rates paid to annuitants, which in some of the earlier issues were as high as 14 per cent. As important, the government would be able to pay off portions of the debt when it wished. It could not do this with many of the annuities, which were unredeemable. For the annuitants, the very tempting bait was capital appreciation in the rising market for the company's shares.

By the time the first annuities were exchanged, in May 1720, doubts about Law's scheme were diverting speculative buying from Paris to London and into South Sea shares, which had risen threefold, from 128 in January to 380. In June, foreign, especially Dutch, buyers flooded the market, driving the price up to almost 1,000. Thereafter it fell back; by September, panic selling heralded a collapse which left many ruined, dragged down government stock, and triggered similar market crashes in Amsterdam and Paris.

The immediate cause of both the South Sea and the Mississippi 'bubbles' was speculative hysteria; underlying it, though, was the desire of both rival powers to rid themselves of excessive war debt. And it is an indication of the prime importance of the colonial trades of the West Indies and Central America, and the slaves who powered them, that both countries turned in this direction for their financial salvation.

Walpole had been ousted as Chancellor before the South Sea scheme. He had invested in it, but had been saved from ruin by his banker. Now, untainted by the scandal, he was returned as First Lord of the Treasury to manage the crisis. He succeeded, commanding the respect of Parliament and the money men of the City of London, and continued as principal minister – in retrospect the first prime minister – for the following two decades, during which he achieved a steady reduction in the size of the national debt and the rate of interest paid. This was the more remarkable since the Royal Navy was maintained at almost war strength throughout the period – equal on paper, probably more than equal in action, to the combined fleets of the next three naval powers, France, Spain and the United Provinces.[4] It was used, like the navy of the United Provinces in the republic's great days, to control the power balances and protect trading interests in the Baltic and the Mediterranean.

While using the fleet as the lever of foreign policy – and the defender of merchant interests – Walpole's overriding concern was to keep the country out of another European war. He hated war for its cost in blood and treasure, and he believed a long period of peace essential to restore the economy and promote growth – again recalling the great days of the United Provinces and Johan de Witt's primary aims of peace, security and the furtherance of trade.

Echoes of de Witt's Amsterdam were abundant in London. All the financial, legal, technical and information services connected with trade which in Amsterdam were concentrated around the bourse could be found in the City within a web of coffee houses and taverns in very short walking distance of the Bank of England in Prince's Street. Each establishment had its niche. Garraway's and Jonathan's coffee houses in Exchange Alley between Cornhill and Lombard Street were the gathering places for stock jobbers and brokers. The intense drama and numerous private tragedies of the South Sea Bubble had been played out in their crowded, smoke-hazed rooms. The Jerusalem and the Jamaica in Cornhill were patronized by West Indies, India and Levant merchants, Lloyd's coffee house in Lombard Street by marine insurers, or underwriters, shipowners, merchants and factors of every nationality. Since 1696 the proprietor, Edward Lloyd, had provided listings of ship arrivals and departures, marine casualties and other maritime information in a paper titled *Lloyd's News*, changed in 1734 to *Lloyd's List*. By this date the informal association of London underwriters had eclipsed its counterpart in Amsterdam as the centre of marine insurance.[5]

Credit, contacts, the latest information and rumour were the vital elements in this hub of the trading nation, as they were in all the scores of coffee houses throughout London devoted to different professional, political, scientific, literary, artistic or social clienteles. A foreign visitor in 1726, after describing the 'chocolate, tea or coffee and all sorts of liquors served hot' which could be had, noted that 'What attracts enormously in these coffee houses are the gazettes and other public papers.'[6]

London now outdid Amsterdam in news-sheets and periodicals; the first English daily newspaper had been started in 1702, by which time twenty-five other journals of various kinds were in circulation, and the number rose year by year. One of the more illustrious in the early days was the *Spectator*, run by Richard Steele and the essayist, poet and Whig politician Joseph Addison, whose ambition, as he put it in the first number in 1711, was to have it said he had 'brought Philosophy out of Closets and Libraries, Schools and Colleges, to dwell in Clubs and Assemblies, at Tea-Tables and in Coffee-Houses'.[7]

That spirit of free inquiry which had distinguished the United

Provinces from the other powers of Europe now animated intellectual London. It will be recalled that Sir William Temple, travelling through Holland as recently as 1667, had expressed equal surprise and admiration at 'the strange freedom that all men took in boats and inns and all other common places, of talking openly whatever they thought'.[8] Two of the most celebrated French writers of the age, Voltaire and Montesquieu, expressed much the same wonder at the freedoms now enjoyed by Englishmen. In France, orthodoxy was preserved by royal and religious censorship and there was no concept of freedom of expression or indeed of individual rights: the king had the power to order imprisonment without trial for indefinite duration.

Voltaire suffered this fate in 1717 for lampooning the regency, and in 1726 he was forced into exile in England. His *Lettres sur les Anglais* (1733) describe the surprising society he found, in which men were free to say or publish what they liked, there was no torture or arbitrary imprisonment, and religious sects of all kinds flourished. Moreover 'A nobleman or a priest is not exempt from paying certain taxes. The peasant eats white bread and is well clothed.'[9]

Montesquieu, who came to England in 1729, reported on it as 'the freest country in the world. I make exception of no republic. And I call it free because the sovereign, whose person is controlled and limited, is unable to inflict any imaginable harm on anyone.'[10]

It is clear that the flame of True Freedom had passed with naval supremacy and constitutional, consultative government from the United Provinces to Great Britain, where it was regarded with quite as much national pride. As early as 1704 Addison, writing from Italy, which he saw as suffering under 'Proud Oppression and Tyranny', was able to equate the triumphs of British arms with preservation of freedom:

> 'Tis Liberty that crowns Britannia's isle,
> And makes her barren rocks and her bleak mountains smile . . .
> 'Tis Britain's care to watch o'er Europe's fate,
> And hold in balance each contending state,
> To threaten bold presumptuous kings with war,
> And answer her afflicted neighbours' prayer . . .
> Soon as her fleets appear their terrors cease . . .[11]

Sir James Thornhill, the first and probably the finest English artist in the Italian baroque style, adorned the interior of Greenwich Naval

Hospital (later to become the Royal Naval College) with the same message. The hospital had been the gift of William III's wife, Queen Mary, in memory of the sailors killed and wounded ensuring the country's independence at the battles of Barfleur/La Hougue. When she herself died shortly after providing the land in the grounds of Greenwich Palace by the Thames, William, in his grief, ordered construction to go ahead in her memory to designs drawn up by his chief architect, Sir Christopher Wren. On the ceiling of the great hall, known now as the Painted Hall, Thornhill painted a grand allegory of the triumph of Peace over Tyranny: William and Mary, seated in the heavens, oversee the cap of liberty being handed to the French.

It would be an overstatement to suggest that all scientific and liberal or humanitarian thought in Britain began with the liberties ushered in by constitutional government: the Royal Society, dedicated to experimental research, was founded in London in 1660, and in 1665 began publishing *Philosophical Transactions*, one of the earliest periodicals. Sir Isaac Newton, whose formulation of the laws of mechanics fundamentally changed perceptions of the physical universe, made his major discoveries before 1688; he had been preceded by Francis Bacon, while the forerunner of experimental science, Roger Bacon, lived 300 years earlier. Nonetheless, the scientific, humanitarian revolution that had begun with the burgher ascendancy in the United Provinces was carried forward apace in Britain, and more especially London, after the political system had been adapted to conform so closely to that of the republic.

The novel was an important vehicle. Its development had been foreshadowed even before William's revolution by the poet and popular playwright Aphra Behn, the first woman in England to earn her living by the pen. Her *Oroonoko, or the History of the Royal Slave* (1688) told the story of a Negro of noble descent whom she had known while living in Suriname (now Dutch Guiana). Besides lighting the way for the future novel, *Oroonoko*, which was adapted for the theatre and played successfully for many years, was an important influence for change in the generally uncomprehending attitudes towards Negroes and the institution of European slavery.[12]

Daniel Defoe took the imaginative embellishment of real persons and events a stage further in *The Life and Surprising Adventures of Robinson Crusoe* (1719), often regarded as the first English novel. The son of a prosperous small businessman and religious Dissenter of Cripplegate, London, Defoe was also a living example of how trade had bred a clamorous and articulate middle class. His own attempts to set up as a merchant failed spectacularly, ending in the Fleet prison for bankrupts, and obliging him, like Aphra Behn, to earn his living from writing. Nonetheless, he remained a prolific publicist for trade, which he called his 'beloved subject'. He had previously taken part in the rebellion against James in the cause of both trade and religious dissent, and had written a verse eulogy of William of Orange as *The True-Born Englishman* – an illustration of the depth of the historical tide William had ridden, which must surely have brought about revolutionary change very soon with or without the 'Protestant wind' down-Channel.

Defoe's most famous protagonist, Crusoe, had made two slaving voyages to Africa before setting himself up as a planter in Brazil; there he told his Portuguese neighbours how easy it was on the coast of Guinea to buy Negroes 'for trifles – such as beads, toys, knives, scissors, hatchets, bits of glass and the like',[13] as a result of which they persuaded him to guide an expedition to Africa and bring back slaves for them. On the way, he was shipwrecked and cast ashore on a deserted island; perhaps Defoe intended a moral. Basing Crusoe's subsequent experiences loosely on those of a real castaway, Alexander Selkirk, Defoe entered his mind so powerfully and portrayed his lonely struggle in such straightforward prose the book entered popular mythology and enjoyed immediate and lasting success at home and in continental Europe. Encouraged, he wrote a second novel, taking his readers into the mind of a girl, Moll Flanders, coping with even less promising circumstances in a debtors jail.

The next original genius of the English novel, Samuel Richardson, also came from the middle classes. He was a printer who had married well and established one of the best presses in London. In *Pamela, or Virtue Rewarded* (1740), he used the device of letters written by his characters to tell the story of a maid resisting extreme attempts at seduction from her former employer's son, until eventually the young man marries her; whereupon she embarks on a second, equally successful, struggle to disarm those who disapprove of the misalliance. This very moral and sentimental story and the novel method of its telling won extraordinary acclamation, and Richardson followed it in similar epistolary style with *Clarissa: or the History of a Young Lady*. Here the heroine's family attempts to force her into marriage for money; in her refusal and subsequent adventures, Clarissa exhibits more sublime moral virtues even than Pamela.

Meanwhile Richardson had provoked Henry Fielding, most accomplished and witty of the pioneers of the novel, into the genre. Fielding came from the gentry, but while studying at Leiden University his allowance had been stopped and like Defoe he had turned to his pen to earn a living, principally as a satirical playwright. In 1737 he lampooned Walpole so savagely that the Prime Minister retaliated by steering through an Act of Parliament requiring all new plays to be licensed by the Lord Chamberlain before being produced. It was a small dent in British liberties – plays could still be printed and published – but put an end to Fielding's career in the theatre. He studied law to become a barrister. When Richardson published *Pamela*, however, Fielding was evidently so struck by what he regarded as its sentimentality and prim morality – although, like *Robinson Crusoe*, the novel was based on a true story – he produced two parodies of the type. The second, *Joseph Andrews*, in which the protagonist, a footman, resists all attempts of a well-born lady to seduce him, was a masterpiece of observation and irony which took on its own life; together with two later novels by Fielding, *Tom Jones* (1749) and *Amelia* (1751), it established a pattern in plotting, characterization and authentic contemporary setting that was to dominate English fiction thereafter, and indeed spread across continental Europe.

These trailblazing books were written by middle-class or professional men, and won a huge middle-class readership which identified with the realistic characters and social settings depicted. The prominence accorded women is striking. Apart from *Robinson Crusoe*, the extraordinarily popular novels mentioned all had strong, admirable women as the central character or in a major role: a beautiful, high-mettled girl, Sophia Western, inspired Tom Jones's odyssey; like Amelia in Fielding's subsequent book, she was based upon the novelist's own beloved wife. This was an accurate reflection of the strong position women enjoyed in society,[14] despite their unequal legal status, and another echo of the United Provinces of the previous century, where, as noted, women of all classes moved and expressed themselves freely as individuals, enjoying a far greater measure of independence than anywhere else in Europe at that time.

The novels, plays and journals were products of a free, trading society – their success or failure depending upon volume of sales – and also agents of change, undermining, often none too subtly, aristocratic or dogmatic assumptions, replacing them with more bourgeois attitudes. In the same way, other branches of art were metamorphosed into new, more popular and subversive forms as they emerged from patronage into the market place.

In opera in 1728 the Italian imports favoured by the aristocracy were seriously wounded by the huge success of *The Beggar's Opera*, written by the poet John Gay, with simple ballads arranged by a German orchestral player who had settled in London, Johann Christoph Pepusch. Introduced by a beggar in rags, the piece parodied fashionable opera and, in the guise of a story of thieves, highwaymen and whores, mounted a savage satire on corruption in society and politics. Walpole moved to have the sequel, *Polly*, banned. Gay nevertheless earned a very considerable sum from publication of the libretto.

The Beggar's Opera sparked a host of imitation. By the end of the following year no less than fifteen so-called 'ballad operas' had played in London, and in 1733 a total of twenty-two were produced.[15] Handel complained they had pelted Italian opera off the stage with Lumps of Pudding – the title of the final air in *The Beggar's Opera*. The type was not to survive past mid-century – with the exception of *The Beggar's Opera* itself – but was succeeded by a similar form employing spoken (English) dialogue within a specially composed musical setting.

What Gay and Fielding accomplished in the theatre and the novel, William Hogarth did for the visual arts. His first dated painting was of a scene of low life from Gay's opera. Later, in 1732, he inaugurated a new form of narrative print or painting in series, portraying ordinary men and women trapped in the vices and follies of contemporary society. Like the satirical engravings produced by the Dutch in the previous century, and no doubt influenced by them to some degree, since Hogarth was a keen student of his craft, he showed the bare human realities beneath the pretensions of everyday life, and indeed fashionable art. His angry irreverence made him many enemies among the great Whig families and connoisseurs but, again like his Dutch predecessors, gained him wide popularity: *A Harlot's Progress*, *The Rake's Progress* and *Marriage à la Mode* sold so well they established his financial independence, besides inspiring a host of imitators at home and in continental Europe.

Of all the talents that graced or, in the eyes of the powerful and more conservative, disgraced this renaissance in British art and letters, none was more truly liberating than the wit and prolific satirist Jonathan Swift, now chiefly remembered for the fantastical adventures bowdlerized for children as *Gulliver's Travels* (1726). Swift's scorn was directed not merely at the political jobbery, ostentation, louche morals, loose think- ing and vice in society, but at the nature of mankind. He wrote to his friend the poet Alexander Pope shortly before publication of *Gulliver's Travels*, 'I have ever hated all nations, professions and communities, and all my love is toward individuals . . . principally I hate and detest that animal called man, although I heartily love John, Peter, Thomas and so forth.'[16] The Latin epitaph he composed for himself concludes, in English translation, 'He is gone where fierce indignation can lacerate his heart no more. Go, traveller, and imitate, if you can, one who strove with all his strength to champion liberty.' Professor Maurice Johnson has remarked that the liberty Swift had in mind was not so much political as a freeing of the human mind from error and of the human spirit from baseness.[17]

Confronted with such variety of unconstrained self-expression in Britain, French authors became more aware of the shackles that bound them. As Montesquieu's friend Lord Chesterfield put it, 'No wonder, say they [the French], that England produces so many great geniuses; people there may think as they please, and publish what they think.'[18] Chesterfield, the model of a liberal aristocrat guided by reason and decorum, was not sympathetic to their complaints: if authors thought 'in a manner destructive of all religion, morality or good manners, or to the disturbance of the State, an absolute government will certainly more effectually prohibit them from, or punish them for publishing such thoughts, than a free one could'. But how, he asked, did that cramp genius?[19]

The question of how the political, social or moral order could survive the free dissemination of extreme or threatening ideas had preoccupied de Witt, Grotius and most political thinkers in the great days of the United Provinces; in their defence of True Freedom they had supported freedom of conscience and toleration of different religious persuasions, but within the context of a powerful state Church imposing political and social as much as spiritual control.[20] So it was in Great Britain: the estab- lished Protestant Church of England provided the social and moral cement.

Nowhere is the link between freedom of expression as enjoyed in the maritime trading powers and the development of liberal thought more marked than in philosophy – especially political philosophy. Descartes, as already mentioned, lived and published his sceptical works in Holland

1. John Hawkins, who transformed the English fleet in the decade before the Spanish armada

2. A design for one of Hawkins's 'race-built' galleons. Note the low forecastle set back from the stem and the 'beakhead' reminiscent of a galley's ram

3. *(left)* Philip II of Spain

4. *(above)* The 'Armada Portrait' of Elizabeth I of England

5. A contemporary diagram of the Spanish armada, in crescent formation, as it was 'coursed' up-Channel by the English fleet

6. *(left above)* Charles I's magnificent *Sovereign of the Seas* (1637), the first true three-gun-deck warship

7. *(left below)* An original cannon from the Swedish *Wasa* (1628) on a reconstruction mounting

8. *(right)* Admiral Maarten Tromp, hero of 'The Downs' (1639)

9. *(below)* Admiral Michiel de Ruyter's flagship, *Zeven Provincien*, by van de Velde the Elder

10. *(left)* Admiral de Ruyter

11. *(below)* One of de Ruyter's many triumphs, the burning of the *Royal James* at the Battle of Sole Bay (1672)

12. *(right above)* Grand Pensionary Johan de Witt, 'the wisdom of Holland'

13. *(right below) The Fat Kitchen*, by Jan Steen, illustrates a weighty aspect of Dutch humanism

14. William III of Orange, who seized the English throne to direct a maritime alliance against Louis XIV of France

15. *(below)* Caught between William's and Louis' ambitions, the brothers Johan and Cornelius de Witt were lynched and disembowelled by an Orangist mob at The Hague

16. Louis XIV, the archetypal territorial monarch

17. *(above)* Jean-Baptiste Colbert, the consummate French centralist bureaucrat, who created Louis XIV's magnificent fleet

18. *(left)* Colbert's antithesis, the empiricist philosopher John Locke, whose views perfectly suited the British merchant interest

19. *(opposite)* William Pitt (the Elder), strategist of Britain's victorious Seven Years War, who set the standard for 'the British (maritime) way in warfare'

20. The climactic naval action of the Seven Years War, fought in squalls and high seas inside the rocks and shoals of Quiberon Bay; *(left centre)* Admiral Hawke lays the *Royal George* alongside the French flagship, *Soleil Royal*. Painting by Nicholas Pocock

21. *(above)* Admiral Sir Edward Hawke, victor of Quiberon Bay

22. Adam Smith, founder of liberal economic theory

23. Benjamin Franklin, American polymath and diplomat, one of the key figures in separating the American colonies from Britain

24. Rear Admiral Thomas Graves, the man who, in naval legend, lost the American colonies at the Battle of Chesapeake Bay (1781)

25. *(below)* Admiral Sir George Rodney, victor at the Saints (1782), the deciding battle of the real colonial war against France

in the previous century. His English contemporary Thomas Hobbes, exiled in Paris during the Civil Wars, had his books published in Holland. The next influential rationalist philosopher, Benedict de Spinoza, was a Dutch Jew whose parents had fled the Spanish Inquisition and settled in Amsterdam. His English contemporary John Locke, whose influence on eighteenth-century thought can hardly be exaggerated, was forced to take refuge in Holland in 1683 and returned to England only after William III had seized the Crown.

The celebrated Dutch freedoms were, of course, never absolute. As noted, they did not extend to perceived intellectual threats to the state or Church; Spinoza, indeed, reached the limits. The only work he published in his lifetime, *Tractatus Theologico-Politicus* (1670), was brought out anonymously in Latin. Significantly in such a self-consciously tolerant society, it was a plea for tolerance. Profoundly critical of the authority of the Church, he reasoned that freedom to philosophize was not only compatible with piety and public order but essential for the preservation of both. In politics, the same theme led him to assert 'democracy is of all forms of government the most natural and most consonant with individual liberty'[21] – an idea that had upset the regent oligarchies as much as his criticisms of the Church, and the book was widely denounced as conceived in hell. Since his major work, *Ethica*, was to introduce even more fundamental heresies, Spinoza decided against its publication.

His experience may be compared with that of his German contemporary Gottfried Leibniz, who worked in Hanover and relied for a living on the patronage of successive Electors. Like Spinoza in *Ethica*, but from an opposite premiss, Leibniz denied free will, and hence the Christian doctrines of sin and individual immortality. However, in order to please his patrons, he omitted these heresies from his published works, which were left, in Bertrand Russell's words, 'optimistic, orthodox, fantastic and shallow';[22] Voltaire caricatured him as the philosophical optimist Dr Pangloss. The private papers and essays revealing his profound, logical and philosophically important system were not published until nearly 200 years after his death.[23]

Locke had no such problems after his return to England. His philosophy was as rigorously logical as that of his great contemporaries, but directed to observed effects rather than to the inner nature of reality. Regarding knowledge as derived only from experience, he was practical, empirical, commonsensical and contemptuous of the metaphysics that had led Spinoza and Leibniz to their heretical conclusions. Above all, his political thinking was so precisely attuned to the practice of merchant power that he might have been commissioned by the moneyed interest calling the tune in England at the time of his return in 1689.

His first *Treatise on Government*, completed that year, demolished the theology of the divine right of kings; his second, published shortly afterwards, established in its place a doctrine of government for and by consent of men of property. He based his arguments on the theory of the social contract, propounded by Hobbes, whereby people living 'in a state of nature' had come together voluntarily to choose a sovereign or governing body. For Locke, the chief purposes of this governing body were to protect individual rights – in particular 'the regulating and preserving of property'[24] – and to protect the community from foreign enemies.

The emphasis Locke placed on property can best be understood in the light of his first *Treatise*, since monarchs exercising God-given rights were notorious for seizing property, imposing levies and taxes (which had the same effect), and arbitrarily imprisoning or suppressing those who displeased them. Locke, by contrast, stood for the minimum government necessary to ensure individual rights, and espoused the principle of checks on personal and government power by separating the legislature – by which he meant Parliament – from the executive – the king – so balancing the power of each. By inference and in practice, this also came to mean a separate and independent judiciary; from 1700 judges held office while 'of good behaviour', and could not be dismissed on purely political grounds. Locke's other great principle was the accountability of the legislature to those governed, and hence the right of the governed to depose the legislators. It is apparent that his premiss of an original 'social contract' was probably as fanciful as the proposition he was denying, that all kings were descended from Adam; it is equally clear that his proposed system of checks and balances bore all the hallmarks of government by and for merchant trading oligarchies, Venice and the United Provinces being the latest outstanding examples.[25]

Besides political treatises, Locke published in 1690 *An Essay Concerning Human Understanding*, a defining work of empiricism which has been judged 'the first comprehensive statement of the liberal philosophy'.[26] He also published between 1689 and 1692 three *Letters on Toleration*, which argued, like Spinoza, for freedom of thought and religious belief: 'the business of laws is not to provide for the truth of opinions but for the safety and security of the commonwealth and of every particular man's goods and services'.[27] From this he reached the logical, astonishingly modern, conclusion that freedom of worship and assembly and all civil rights should be granted Dissenters and even Jews, Mahommedans or pagans. Since the view accorded with the practice of a cosmopolitan trading community it was accepted almost as a commonplace, and, while France and continental Europe remained locked in civil and religious oppression, Great Britain, notwithstanding perceived dangers of Jacobitism from Catholic families, became more tolerant of different faiths even than the United Provinces.[28]

Meanwhile Locke's pure empirical philosophy was carried forward between 1709 and 1713 by an Irishman, George Berkeley, and taken to its ultimate conclusion by a Scot, David Hume, whose master work, *A Treatise of Human Nature*, was published in London in 1739–40. Hume explained his object as the scientific examination of the mind of man: 'And tho' we must endeavour to render all our principles as universal as possible . . . 'tis still certain we cannot go beyond experience; and any hypothesis, that pretends to discover the ultimate original qualities of human nature, ought at first to be rejected as presumptuous and chimerical.'[29] The results of this sceptical system were not, perhaps, as Hume expected. He found it impossible to discern the substance behind perceptions of the world, impossible to gain any notion of the mind 'distinct from the particular perceptions' flitting rapidly across it,[30] and was forced to deny the validity of reason itself, which he described as 'the slave of the passions'.[31] The scientific method of philosophy thus reached its paradoxical dead end. Hume was perhaps the greatest British philosopher, but it was of course Locke's theories of government and toleration, so perfectly reflecting merchant ideals, that produced the practical effect on men's minds.

The flowering of British science, letters and arts was matched in industrial invention and technology, in which Britain was far ahead of France. Recognizing this, John Law had initiated a systematic drive to acquire the secrets of British technology and lure skilled craftsmen from Britain, especially in the clock- and watch-making, metal, glass, textile and shipbuilding industries.[32] The reverberatory furnace, in which ore to be smelted did not come into contact with the fuel; the use of coke instead of charcoal to smelt copper and iron; the first primitive steam engines, designed for draining deep copper mines and coal pits, had been developed in Britain in the very early years of the century. The advances had been provoked by the demand for metal for armaments and shipbuilding in the great wars. In turn the new, cheaper methods of production had widened markets for domestic metal goods at home and abroad – most notably in copper and brass, later in iron wares.[33] Textile production was similarly transformed from 1733 by John Kay's invention of 'a New Engine or Machine for Opening and Dressing Wool', which incorporated a 'flying shuttle' enabling one operator to weave fabrics of any width more rapidly than two traditional weavers.

These early harbingers of an industrial revolution to be centred on coal power and iron, steel and textile production were, like the United Provinces' earlier wind-power manufacturing revolution, symptoms of a trading nation; the changes were provoked not simply by the stimulations provided by maritime war and colonial commerce, but by the capital and credit available, and they were embraced because of the open, mobile society – in particular the respectibility accorded trade – in which the largest landowners were linked through investment or marriage. They were accompanied by the rapid growth of ports and new manufacturing towns and by the beginnings of an agricultural revolution to feed the increasing urban population.[34] This too was commercially driven, and followed or adapted Dutch cash-crop farming methods.[35]

The intellectual, artistic and technological achievements flowed, as they had in the golden age of the United Provinces, from the freedoms necessarily accompanying merchant power. Liberty, tolerance and wealth unlocked natural genius. But, as in the Dutch example, the freedoms did not extend overseas, or even in many cases to the poor and uneducated within the country. A commoner was equal in law to a peer and was protected from arbitrary imprisonment by *habeas corpus*, but there was little practical difference between the expectations of an English villager before his local Justice of the Peace and those of a French peasant farmer subject to the feudal laws of seigneurial justice.[36]

Seamen, on whom the whole edifice of freedom ultimately rested, were peculiarly exploited and liable to lose their own liberty. In war there were never enough of them to man the expanded Royal Navy, privateers, and merchant and fishing fleets; they were seized from homecoming merchantmen or rounded up ashore by the Impress Service to complete the companies of men-of-war, and at the end of a cruise they were frequently 'turned over' to another of HM ships, so saving the cost of paying them off and the inconvenience of pressing them again. As described by Admiral Edward Vernon:

Our fleets are first manned by violence and cruelty. When our ships are to be fitted an impress is sent into the streets to bring those who shall fall in the way by force into the vessels. From that time they are in effect condemned to death, since they are never allowed to set foot again on shore, but turned over from ship to ship.[37]

The death referred to was too often from scurvy or tropical fevers. The most persuasive authority on the Royal Navy of this period asserts that, although pressing was highly distasteful to all, it 'was accepted by everyone who had any experience of the subject as an unavoidable necessity';[38] and he cites an articulate sailor who wrote that pressing was 'a hardship which nothing but absolute necessity can reconcile to our boasted freedom'.[39] Another view is that the manning difficulties were due to resistance to any increase in naval seamen's pay by landowners and merchants in Parliament: the former to avoid further rises in land tax, the latter to prevent merchant seamen being attracted to the navy.[40] Undoubtedly the problem was exacerbated by low pay, but, with the huge fleets needed in war and the numbers of men lost to disease, no expedient could have produced enough prime seamen.

Of all the paradoxes of British freedom, as of Dutch True Freedom before it, none was more conspicuous than the commerce in and carriage of Negro slaves and the colonial slave labour on which the increase in trade and prosperity of the country was believed to depend, and in consequence did so. Those whose consciences pricked could argue that slavery was an institution of ancient lineage; that black Africans were pagans and, it was said, not on the same level of humanity as Europeans; that it was an act of beneficence to bring them under civilizing and Christian influence.

Daniel Defoe dismissed the humbug:

> In vain they talk to them [slaves] of shades below:
> They fear no hell, but where such Christians go.[41]

Other literary figures expressed similar sentiments: James Thomson, Scottish forerunner of the Romantic poets, wrote of 'that cruel trade, which spoils unhappy Guinea of her sons'[42] in his verse masterpiece *The Seasons* (1726–30), the first extended nature poem in English. Thomson's later ode to Britain's maritime dominance, 'Rule, Britannia' (1740), more widely remembered in its musical setting, echoed Addison's vision of other nations suffering under tyrants while Britain flourished 'great and free', their dread and envy and a refuge for the Muses:

> Thy cities shall with commerce shine;
> All thine shall be the subject main,
> And every shore it circles thine![43]

The first book to portray the reality as distinct from the abstract notion of suffering in the slave trade was written by a naval surgeon named John Atkins, who had been sickened by barbarities he witnessed during service on the Guinea coast and in the Caribbean in the 1720s. His *Voyage to Guinea, Brasil, and the West Indies* (1735) detailed the appalling cruelty with which Negroes were transported and driven to work; significantly, his denunciation included all Britons as accessories to their countrymen who treated slaves like cattle.[44]

However, the few individuals roused to condemnation were powerless in the face of the huge and vital interests involved – notably the rapidly expanding consumer industries, sugar and tobacco, which together made up three-quarters of all British imports from the New World, and both of which relied on slave labour,[45] but also the gunmakers and metal and textile manufacturers who supplied the goods demanded by African chiefs and slave merchants. Moreover, every western-European nation was engaged in the transatlantic slave trade and used slaves in its colonies. It is estimated that during the decade of the 1720s British ships, chiefly from London and the main interloping port of Bristol, carried over 100,000 Africans to the West Indies or America;[46] French ships carried over 80,000, Portuguese ships nearly 150,000 to Brazil,[47] responding in this case to a huge demand from gold mines opened towards the end of the previous century, while the Dutch still carried large numbers to their Caribbean-island entrepôts; and the British North American colonies, the Austrian Netherlands, Denmark and other northern Europeans had also entered the trade.

Since trade in colonial products was the fastest-growing, most profitable branch of international commerce, inextricably interlinked with all other branches, and sugar was particularly competitive, with only the most ruthlessly cost-conscious planters able to survive,[48] it would have been impossible for a seafaring nation to abstain on moral principle without virtually retiring from the mercantile colonial race – not, at least, until that nation had achieved total commercial dominance. In any case, there was no question of it: English merchants and adventurers had been among the first to attempt to break into the Iberian monopolies in the New World; their more prosperous successors were determined to continue, and slaving was the key.

In the light of modern research,[49] it is clear that Africans, who practised slavery themselves, regulated the market: they sent expeditions to seize men, women and children from agricultural tribes, determined which in terms of age and gender should be supplied for the transatlantic trade, and strove to ensure that no single European trader gained a monopoly in any source of slaves or on any route. They were as culpable as the Europeans. They did not, however, boast of freedom or Christianity.

Great Britain, like the United Provinces and every other western-European nation, was locked into the commerce in lives by the system of colonial trading rivalry. The chief purpose of British governments was to fund and administer the armed forces which maintained the struggle: up to 85 per cent of annual expenditure went on the upkeep of the supreme navy and the army, or on servicing the debt incurred by both from previous wars.[50] The armed forces owed allegiance to the Crown, but at bottom they were the striking arm of the merchant landowning oligarchy that ran government and Parliament. It was therefore inevitable that the country would be drawn into further wars and that the national debt would rise, drawing taxes up with it. There was no way out of the ascending military-fiscal cycle, as there was no way out of an ascending slaving cycle, which would see during the course of the eighteenth century the greatest ever continental transfer of labour – over 6 million Negroes from Africa to the New World.[51] The great Whig landowners, money men and merchants did not desire escape from either cycle; nor did the commercial middle classes, who thrived on increased trade and consumed its products; nor did naval officers, for whom war was the grand lottery, promising glory, honours and fortunes from prize money. War was as central to the merchant system as to the territorial or dynastic system; it was both natural and acceptable.

Finisterre, 1747

WORLD TRADE INCREASED steadily in two and a half decades of peace after the end of Louis XIV's wars. It was driven chiefly by growth in the plantation produce of America and the West Indies, in particular sugar, and was primed by precious metals mined in the New World – silver from the Spanish colonies of New Spain and Peru, gold from Minas Gerais in Portuguese Brazil; production of both probably reached levels at least double those achieved during Spain's sixteenth-century peak.[1] Of the three major trading rivals, France had access to silver through trading links with Spain and Spanish America via Cadiz; Great Britain had access to gold through links with Portugal and her trade with Brazil, and to silver by virtue of the slaving and commercial contract with Spain and the opportunities this allowed for illicit trade with Spanish colonists.[2] The Dutch also had access to precious metals, as Amsterdam remained the intermediary between France and Baltic and northern-European markets and suppliers.

The Dutch, however, entirely lost their trading dominance. Dutch industries were hit by a growth of manufacturing in the southern (Austrian) Netherlands and through northern Europe and Scandinavia, accompanied by protectionist policies to nurture the infant industries. Great Britain and France were able to absorb the loss of these markets through the general growth in trade to colonial America and the re-export of produce from their own colonies. The Dutch had neither sufficiently populous colonies nor, since the drastic rundown of the army and navy due to the debt from Louis XIV's wars, the power leverage to win compensation elsewhere. The result was a progressive collapse in manufacturing and finishing, shipping and shipbuilding, and a drastic contraction of the urban economy and population. The money men, seeing few attractive opportunities at home, increasingly invested abroad – especially, but not exclusively, in London – contributing both to the cycle of Dutch decline and to the expansion of the republic's rivals.

By contrast, France enjoyed a trading and industrial resurgence. After recovering from the financial disasters associated with John Law, her traditional industries regained markets in Spain, Italy and the Levant, while the rapidly expanding sugar production in her West Indian islands, Martinique, Guadeloupe and Saint-Domingue, provided a commercial momentum which gave her a faster rate of growth even than Great Britain.[3] Between 1730 and 1740 her seaborne trade increased by 86 per cent, until it was equalling or even surpassing the value of British overseas trade.[4]

In 1735 the French East Indies Company overtook both the Dutch VOC and the British East India Company in value of sales. This growth was intimately linked with the driving force of the economy in the West Indies, since three-quarters of cargoes from the East were Indian textiles, a large proportion of which were then shipped to West Africa to barter for slaves for the sugar plantations.[5] African demand for brilliantly coloured Indian textiles was such that the French west-coast port of Nantes, centre for Indian-textile imports, dominated the French slave trade, as in England the corresponding centre for Indian textiles, Liverpool, was beginning to rival Bristol as the leading slaving port.[6]

So France, still the territorial threat to the balance of European power, emerged also as Great Britain's most dangerous colonial and trading rival. At the same time, throughout the 1730s British merchants became increasingly bellicose. The South Sea Company had not reaped the rewards expected in Spanish America from the commercial and slaving treaty. France, linked to Spain by the Bourbon royal dynasty, had become chief official – as opposed to contraband – supplier of manufactured goods to Spain and, through Spanish merchants, her colonial empire. Moreover, Philip V of Spain had begun to rebuild and reform his navy on French lines, and to tighten control of trade with Spanish America to keep out all foreign vessels – particularly those of the British South Sea Company, which was engaged in massive smuggling under cover of its legal contract.[7] This had led to a succession of incidents with

British ships attempting to smuggle in trade goods, most notoriously the case of Robert Jenkins, captain of the *Rebecca*, whose ear had been hacked off by a Spanish coastguard 'making use at the same time of the most insulting expression towards the person of our king, an expression no British subject can decently repeat'.[8] The British merchant community exploited these violent clashes to whip up a clamour for war. At bottom their aims were no different from those of Cromwell or the Elizabethan adventurers before him: to seize the silver and take over the lucrative trade of the Spanish colonists. Underlying the predatory ambitions was unease at the way peace in Europe appeared to be working to the advantage of their French trade rivals.

Walpole attempted by every means to avert war and cool tempers. In early 1739 he appealed to the reason of Members of Parliament: admitting there was something 'peculiarly bewitching to an Englishman' in the history of wars against Spain, he pointed out that the days when the king of Spain was the dread of Europe were past:

> At present, if I may advance a paradox, his greatest security lies in his visible weakness . . . at present there is scarce any nation in Europe who has not a larger property in her [Spain's] plate ships and galleons than she herself has. It is true all that treasure is brought home in Spanish names . . . but Spain herself is no more than the canal through which all these treasures are conveyed all over the rest of Europe. Should therefore we or any other people pretend to seize these treasures, we could not fail to meet with a powerful opposition.[9]

France, he went on, would not remain neutral, and, 'however great an opinion gentlemen may entertain of the power of this nation, we are not invincible'. As to their late allies, the Dutch, 'every gentleman here is sufficiently sensible of the present low circumstances of that Republic'. Their fleet lay in harbour in a very bad condition requiring more money than they could furnish to fit it out. Moreover,

> The French have a fine army on foot which they can almost with no expense or danger march down into Holland. Thus we might in short time . . . [see] these Provinces again in danger of falling into the hands of France . . . Formerly the French in case they made any attack upon Holland were sure of drawing the Emperor [Austria] upon their backs . . . But now, sir, the Emperor is no longer in a condition to give any diversion that way. His

own army and finances are in the utmost disorder by his late unsuccessful campaign against the Turks.[10]

He went on to consider the disastrous consequences of war to the valuable British trade with European Spain and the damage that might spread to British trade with Portugal and the Indies, and asked whether it were not true that 'a trading people ought by all manner of means to avoid war; that nothing is so destructive of their interests, and that any peace is preferable to a successful war' – sentiments that might have been coined by Johan de Witt in the previous century.

Lord Portland carried Walpole's theme to the House of Lords, making the point that Britain's differences with Spain were 'not founded on her aspiring to the universal monarchy as in the days of Queen Elizabeth . . . our differences are founded entirely on affairs of commerce, to which nothing can be more fatal, nothing more destructive than a war'. Moreover, going to war would sound 'an alarm to all Europe that Great Britain was resolved to obtain, by the terror of her guns, what she had no right to expect from the sense of her treaties'. There might then be seen as powerful a combination against Great Britain as had been formed not many years since against the ambitions of France.[11]

Reason made as little impact as might have been predicted by David Hume, the first volume of whose *Treatise* was published that year: the arguments that forced Walpole's administration to armed hostilities were prompted by national pride and expectation of plunder. Preparations to attack Spanish trade were put in hand early that summer, 1739, as in the Anglo-Dutch wars of the previous century, months before an official declaration: the Mediterranean fleet received orders to cruise off Cadiz, seizing Spanish merchantmen, warships and privateers and committing 'all sorts of hostilities' against Spain in reprisal for seizures by her coastguards in the West Indies, and a squadron was fitted out to cross the Atlantic and carry the war to Spanish America. A smaller squadron was prepared to attack Spanish trade and possessions on the Pacific coast, but this took so long to fit out and man that it did not sail until September the following year.

Early results were disappointing. France was naturally determined that Britain should not overpower Spain and engross her colonial trade. She remained formally neutral, but fitted out her Brest fleet, so ensuring that the British main fleet would remain in home waters, and neutralized other British squadrons by sending detachments to threaten action in concert with the Spanish. Meanwhile British trade suffered the usual disruptions from privateers.

These failures were used to force Walpole's resignation. Before his downfall, he was considering how to form a grand coalition as in previous wars to deflect France's energies to the land. The question was resolved for his successors by Louis XV himself. The Austrian emperor died in October 1740 without male heir, precipitating a scramble for Austrian territory known as the War of the Austrian Succession. Louis, persuaded by the dominant military group at Court that the chance to seize the Austrian Netherlands and Luxembourg and bring the United Provinces under French control was too good to forgo, joined the anti-Austrian coalition. It was a fateful decision: the United Provinces and Great Britain were bound to join Austria in defence of the Netherlands, so creating the hostile combination that had fought the wars of Louis XIV.

So it turned out, and the outcome was remarkably similar. French resources were drained in campaigns in Flanders, Germany and Italy, and the French fleet, after joining the Spanish fleet and engaging in one indecisive line battle with the British Mediterranean fleet off Toulon (1744), was laid up for want of money; after which there was no option but to repeat Vauban's strategy of the *guerre de course* with light squadrons and privateers. This allowed British fleets undisputed sway in the Mediterranean and off the Atlantic ports. French trade with Italy and the Levant was again crippled, and the vital communications with her American and West Indian possessions were seriously dislocated – as will appear. Industry declined; hunger and civil unrest spread. At the same time, Britain's trade increased substantially and her stock of merchant shipping rose by over 20 per cent, largely from captures.[12]

On land, however, the pattern was not repeated. This was due, as Walpole had warned, to the weakness of Britain's principal allies, Austria and the United Provinces. Despite heavy British involvement in Flanders, the Austrian Netherlands and barrier fortresses fell to the French, who advanced to the borders of the republic. Elsewhere, substantial British subsidies to Austria, Hanover and German mercenaries, together with British Mediterranean-fleet support for Austria's Italian campaigns, failed to bring the prospect of victory for the anti-French coalition. Meanwhile the extraordinary expenses of the war by land and sea raised the British national debt by over 50 per cent, to £70 million. French finances were in a more desperate condition, for all the old reasons, and in 1748 a compromise peace of exhaustion was signed at Aix-la-Chapelle whereby all conquests were returned to the former owners; so the southern Netherlands reverted to Austria.

The great days of the United Provinces were definitively over. During the war it had seldom been able to meet a much reduced quota of only twenty warships for the allied fleet; its army had been poorly commanded, the troops disaffected; now its populace rose in revolt. Dispirited by industrial decline, which had halved the populations of some of the principal cities – Leiden, Haarlem, Delft and the shipbuilding centre of Zaandam[13] – humiliated by military collapse, the people swept out the regents in favour of William IV of Orange as stadtholder. Much of the intellectual argument for change was based on John Locke's treatises on government; and the state which emerged from the revolution was a constitutional monarchy in all but name.[14]

OF THE TWO leading trading rivals, the portents for France were dire, despite the apparent stalemate in which the war had ended. The British merchant government had launched a blatant assault for the Spanish colonial system which it was in France's interest to defend. Yet once again she had allowed herself to be seduced by the temptations of geography and the compulsions of her military into a major Continental war; as a result, she had again been forced to lay up her battle fleet and had had to resort to a form of trade warfare which had proved harassing but strategically ineffective every time it had been tried. Once again her own trade and industries had suffered while British trade had expanded; again revenue from the corrupt tax system had failed to sustain her treasury, and Louis had been forced to borrow at extravagant rates of interest. Significantly, the British government had borrowed at half the rates incurred in Marlborough's war – 3 per cent at the beginning, rising to only 4 per cent in the final three years, when over £14 million had been added to the permanent debt[15] – a measure of the maturity of British financial and fiscal institutions and the trust in which they were held. A significant portion of the permanent debt – some £10 million of the total £70 million – was held by foreigners, chiefly Dutch.[16]

Equally ominous for France was the message carried by a successful British blockade of the Atlantic ports in the final year of the war. The strategy of keeping a powerful fleet cruising to the west of the main naval base at Brest had been proposed by Sidney Godolphin during

William III's war. He seems to have been the first to draw strategic conclusions from the fact that Brest's exits faced the Atlantic and a large fleet could leave the port only with easterly winds. While these would also blow a blockading fleet from the coast, the emerging French fleet would still be contained, since it could enter the English Channel only when the wind went round to the west, and it would hardly dare do so with an English fleet to the west, both to windward and able to interpose between the fleet and its base.

The strategy was probably ahead of its time. It was proposed again in 1745 by the commander of the home fleet, Admiral Edward Vernon. Louis was preparing an invasion force to support the 'Young Pretender' to the British throne, Charles Stuart, grandson of James II, who had landed in Scotland. To counter the threat, Vernon advocated 'a western squadron formed as strong as we can make it' to watch the French in Brest and so 'cover both Great Britain and Ireland and be in a condition to pursue them wherever they went, and to be at hand to secure the safe return of our homeward bound trade from the East and West Indies'.[17]

The formation of the 'western squadron' and the destruction of a French coastal convoy of troop transports was sufficient to deter Louis from his planned support for Charles Stuart; without reinforcements, the Jacobite cause was snuffed out by an English army recalled from the Netherlands.

The following year George Anson succeeded Vernon. Anson had commanded the small squadron sent out around Cape Horn in 1740 to prey on Spanish trade and possessions in the Pacific. He had returned in 1744 by way of the Cape of Good Hope after an epic of endurance, seamanship and resolution which had brought him fame and enormous wealth from the capture of a treasure galleon. Requesting a larger force, he ranged with seventeen of the line from Ushant to Cape St Vincent, covering all French and Spanish Atlantic ports, and in May 1747, some distance off the north-west corner of Spain, he surprised an outward-bound convoy from La Rochelle and overpowered the weak escort of five of the line in what is known as the first Battle of Finisterre. Many of the merchantmen were taken; most of the rest turned back for France.

Next month a detachment of five of the line sent out to relieve those of his ships in need of repair surprised a homeward-bound convoy from the French West Indies and captured forty-eight merchantmen loaded with sugar, coffee and indigo valued at over a quarter of a million pounds. As with the former haul, the greatest share of the prize money went to Anson as commander-in-chief, but captains received £8,000 each – a small fortune – lieutenants £1,000 and sailors £26, a substantial sum when compared with their normal pay. Although the Royal Navy was by this date a disciplined fighting arm of the state, it retained features of the predatory force from which it had sprung and the reward system of the merchant state it served.

The squadron's grip on the Atlantic coast was maintained through the summer and into the autumn, bringing French West Indies trade to a standstill. In October a vast convoy of over 250 merchantmen which had assembled at La Rochelle put to sea under escort of eight of the line, virtually all the warships that could be fitted out from Brest, under *chef d'escadre* the Marquis de L'Etanduère. It was a desperate compromise between trying to evade the British blockade and fighting the convoy through it.

The western squadron now comprised fourteen of the line. Command had passed to Rear Admiral Edward Hawke, who had distinguished himself as a captain at the Battle of Toulon. He had ample intelligence of the French preparations and attempted to lure the French out by showing himself off Spain, afterwards cruising far out to sea in the track he anticipated the convoy must take and spreading in line of search some 140 miles west of Ushant. His judgement proved precise. The French sails were sighted to the south-west in the morning of 14 October, and he hoisted the signal to chase.

De L'Etanduère formed a line, while his merchantmen crowded sail to the north-west before the wind. Hawke replaced the signal for chase with that for the line, then, seeing the French warships bear away in succession and run south-westerly to draw him from the convoy, he again hoisted general chase, hauling down the line signal. The leading British ships arrived up with the rearmost French warships shortly before noon, engaged, and pressed on to the ships ahead; those following did the same as they came up, most passing to leeward but others working up to windward so that the French were doubled as the fighting spread forward. Individually the British ships were lighter and more lightly gunned, but the French rear, which bore the concentrated fire of succeeding fresh ships coming into action, was soon isolated and beaten; afterwards the leading French were subjected to a similar overwhelming concentration, although two managed to escape into the gloom as the October light faded.

Of the six French warships captured at this second Battle of

Finisterre, two had only foremasts standing; the rest were swept clean of masts. 'No ships behaved better than the enemy's', one British captain wrote of the courage they had displayed in defence, 'or sold their liberties dearer.'[18]

De L'Etanduère's squadron had indeed written one of the most glorious chapters in French naval history, inflicting so much damage on Hawke's ships that they were unable to pursue the convoy. Nevertheless Hawke sent a sloop to alert the British commander in the West Indies, as a result of which forty of the merchantmen were taken as they approached the islands. The other immediate result of Hawke's victory was that over 100 French merchantmen which had gathered at Martinique were deprived of escorts home. Many had been waiting for over a year.[19] The western squadron had not only destroyed the greater part of the French Atlantic fleet in commission, it had in effect severed mainland France from her most economically valuable colonies.

Among the French warships captured at first and second Finisterre were three 74-gun two-deckers which were larger, sailed better and carried heavier batteries higher from the water than British 80-gun three-deckers[20] – or, indeed, than the 70-gun two-deckers based on the design of the earlier French model, the *Superbe*. A new Board of Admiralty which included Anson had been trying hard since 1744 to introduce a similar class of large 74-gun ship into the British service against the obstruction of the long-serving official responsible for warship design. The power and handling qualities of the French prizes provided added stimulus for the Admiralty. Nevertheless it was to take many stratagems before the first comparable British 74s were laid down in 1755, just in time for the next encounter with France. They and their successors which mounted twenty-eight 32-pounders on the lower gundeck married the destructive power of a first rate's main battery to the speed and handling qualities of a frigate.[21] They were to play a prominent role in the decisive battles of the next round of Anglo-French struggle, and became the backbone of the British battle line for the rest of the century.

Quiberon Bay, 1759

THE LESSONS OF the three great Anglo-French encounters were not lost on Louis's ministers, but a solution was not apparent. No one doubted the next war would soon erupt; skirmishes continued in North America and India. Advice to Louis swung between opposite poles: to reject Continental war in order to concentrate on the navy and protect the North American colonies and trade in the western approaches to the English Channel; or, alternatively, to mount a swift Continental campaign to seize territorial bargaining counters to exchange at the subsequent peace treaty for colonies which had been lost. The first strategy played into Great Britain's long suit; the second carried all the pernicious implications for French trade and industry realized in past wars. In the meantime, Louis embarked on an ambitious fleet-building programme in the expectation that a similar Spanish effort would ensure a combined Bourbon fleet at least equal to the British. Over the next eight years France launched forty-four ships of the line, more than half of them two-decked 74s, Spain launched thirty-six, mainly large two-decked 70s, together succeeding in attaining approximate equality with Great Britain.[1]

Unfortunately for Louis, when hostilities erupted, Ferdinand VI of Spain would not join him. The war was triggered by fighting in North America. The British colonies were by now thriving merchant communities with a territorial and trading dynamic that was taking them west into the interior. There they came up against the French from Canada who were building a chain of forts from Lake Erie to the Ohio river to establish a line of communications from the St Lawrence in the north via the Ohio and Mississippi rivers to French Louisiana in the south, encircling the thirteen British colonies along the eastern seaboard. In early 1755 the British government sent out two regiments to support their colonists attempting to break through this line. France responded by preparing an expeditionary force of six regiments for Canada at Brest; whereupon the British sent a squadron across the Atlantic to cruise off the mouth of the St Lawrence to capture or destroy them when they appeared, meanwhile reactivating the western squadron with sixteen of the line. By early August the orders to these and other British squadrons and cruisers in the Mediterranean, the Channel, the North Sea, the West Indies, and off Newfoundland, Carolina and Virginia had been extended to the capture of French merchantmen and privateers. So informal hostilities began, as in previous wars, with a great haul of prizes.[2]

On the Continent, meanwhile, the traditional power balances had been upset by an increase in the strength of Russia and Prussia. Austria had turned to her former enemy, France, for support against the territorial ambitions of Frederick II of Prussia, whose formidably disciplined army was now third largest in Europe, and during the alliance bargaining Prussia had swung into the British camp; whereupon Russia joined the Franco-Austrian alliance. Ferdinand VI of Spain, having no desire to side with Austria, Spain's rival in Italy, or to receive another naval drubbing from Great Britain, this time on behalf of France, remained neutral, as did the United Provinces.

The pattern of coalitions thus changed dramatically, but the situation of the two major colonial rivals remained much as before. Lacking Spanish naval support, France had little option but to strike at the British king's German domains as hostages for the return of colonies she expected to lose in America, thus embroiling herself once again in a major Continental war. Great Britain, for her part, relied on Prussian, Hanoverian and mercenary German troops to keep France fully occupied on land and to defend the king's possessions while she herself stifled French trade and seized French colonies. In another sense the situation had entirely changed: in earlier wars the maritime powers had led Continental coalitions to curb France's ambitions for hegemony in Europe; now France was attempting to curb the predominant maritime power, Great Britain, whose ambitions appeared to extend to colonial and trade hegemony.

The resulting conflict, known as the Seven Years War, began badly for Great Britain, despite her pre-emptive moves. The bulk of the French expeditionary force for the St Lawrence arrived safely, somehow evading the waiting squadron, and early the following year, 1756, it overpowered the British and colonial force preparing to march into Canada. In the East, four trading posts and the Bengal headquarters of the British East India Company were lost to the rival French company; and in the Mediterranean a force from Toulon seized the British fleet base at Port Mahón, Minorca. Vice Admiral John Byng, whose tactical ineptness and lack of strategic insight was chiefly responsible for this disaster, was called home, tried by court martial, pronounced guilty of neglect of duty in battle, and shot, as Voltaire put it, '*pour encourager les autres*'. In reality his execution was not intended by the court, who made urgent representation for a royal reprieve; however, the political mood after the setbacks in the war was such that he was made a scapegoat. Byng was one of the few to come out of this disgraceful episode with honour: he asked God to forgive his judges, as he had himself, and hoped their distress of mind and conscience would subside.[3]

The same angry dissatisfaction with the conduct of the war brought about the downfall of the government and the appointment of William Pitt (the Elder) to head a new ministry. Pitt was the most trenchant advocate of what would later be called a 'blue-water' strategy to concentrate resources on naval rather than Continental war, using sea command to mount overseas expeditions and amphibious descents around the coasts of France to draw off troops from her main armies.

The essence of his system was epitomized in a dispatch to the British ambassador in the Prussian capital, Berlin, from the Earl of Holderness, who, as Secretary of State for the North, was a member of the 'Select Committee' or inner war council at the beginning of Pitt's ministry in 1757:

> you will agree with me in one principle, that we must be merchants while we are soldiers, that our trade depends upon a proper exertion of our maritime strength; that trade and maritime force depend upon each other, and that the riches which are the true resources of this country depend upon its commerce . . .
>
> . . . his Majesty is determined that the fleet intended for the Channel service shall at once be made subservient to the views of defending the British dominions and of protecting trade, and yet at the same time to cover a

number of land forces considerable enough to alarm the coasts of France, and to oblige that power to withdraw a great part of the troops intended to annoy the King [of Prussia] and his allies in Germany, in order to protect their own coasts from invasion.[4]

Finally, Holderness pointed out that Britain's distant operations in America were of 'at least as much consequence' as European operations for 'the ultimate object of the war, the forcing of the enemy to do our will'. It is evident that Pitt's grand strategy for a war dominated by the maritime elements was fully formed from the start.

As First Lord of the Admiralty, Pitt appointed Anson, who had served in that capacity or as senior naval member of the Admiralty board through most of the 1740s and 1750s. The austere dedication, professional expertise and continuity he had brought to the post – in contrast to French Ministers of Marine, who had been changed almost with the seasons – had transformed naval administration and supply, gunnery and tactical training, and had imprinted his own personal code of selfless duty on the service.[5]

The hinge of his strategy, as in the preceding war, was the western squadron; as he expressed it in one of the very few documents he left:

> Our Colonies are so numerous and so extensive that to keep a naval force at each equal to the united force of France would be impracticable with double our navy . . . The best defence [against invasion], therefore, for our colonies as well as our coasts, is to have such a squadron always to the westward as may in all probability either keep the French in Port, or give them battle with Advantage if they come out.[6]

As with all previous attempts at blockade by sea, the squadron could maintain its vigil only so long as the water and beer aboard remained drinkable and the ships' companies remained healthy. This was still little more than six weeks. Hawke, the squadron's first commander in 1755, had found his men going down with fever – probably typhus – within six weeks and had been forced to put back inside two months. 'Had I stayed out a week longer', he had reported, 'there would not have been men enough to have worked the large ships, they fell down so fast.'[7] Anson attempted to rotate ships on station by sending out relief detachments, but the problem remained, and during the first year of Pitt's administration French squadrons were able to take advantage of periods of British absence to carry reinforcements out to Canada, the West Indies and India.

Understandably, a doctrine of accomplishing the mission rather than seeking out and destroying the enemy main fleet had taken root in the French navy, which seemed inevitably to be in inferior numbers. For the British the opposite was the case. The tactical bias of each mirrored the difference. Late in the previous war, Anson had set out articles additional to the printed Admiralty fighting instructions that had come down virtually unchanged from Russell and Rooke; the most important were designed to loosen the formal line of battle in order to press the advantage over an inferior, beaten or fleeing enemy. Thus Article VIII enjoined ships which overlapped the enemy's line either ahead or astern to leave the line without signal to rake the enemy van or rear; Articles IX and X, for use when chasing, instructed the five or seven ships nearest the enemy to draw into line ahead of the main body irrespective of order or seniority to engage the enemy rear and attempt to work up to their van until the rest of the squadron came up – as indeed Hawke's leading ships had done at the second Battle of Finisterre.[8]

Hawke was another embodiment of British naval aggression, and a thinking admiral who had long been dissatisfied with defensive aspects of the printed fighting instructions. In October 1757 he made a small, handwritten alteration to Article XIII of the instructions issued to his captains. This prescribed the signal, a red flag at the fore-topmast head, upon which all ships were 'to use their utmost endeavour in order to engage the enemy in the Order the Admiral has prescribed unto them'. Hawke crossed out 'in the Order the Admiral has prescribed' and inserted in its place 'as close as possible, and therefore on no account to fire until they shall be within pistol shot'.[9] It was a small amendment, but it allowed captains to use their initiative to take advantage of changing situations, obliged them to close to a decisive range, and conveyed Hawke's own offensive spirit.

The following year Anson, briefly hoisting his flag in command of the western squadron, issued an additional instruction in the same vein: if during an action he should haul down the signal for the line of battle, every ship was to engage the ship opposing her 'as close as possible, and pursuing them if they are driven out of the line'. This was particularly significant in view of the previous prohibition on the pursuit of small numbers of enemy ships. It is evident the service was moving towards more aggressive and flexible concepts of the line. The next year Hawke, again in command of the squadron, issued a more emphatic version of Anson's new instruction.[10]

In early 1758 a major British expeditionary force with twenty ships of the line under Vice Admiral Edward Boscawen sailed from Spithead for the French base of Louisbourg, Cape Breton Island, guarding the approaches to the St Lawrence. Shortly afterwards two French expeditions to reinforce Louisbourg were neutralized: the first, from Toulon, was forced back to base by a British Mediterranean squadron which captured the 80-gun flagship and a smaller liner; the second, gathering in the Basque Roads off La Rochelle, was surprised by Hawke and fled shorewards, escorts and transports alike running themselves aground and casting guns and stores overboard to escape in the shallows as the tide rose. Without substantial succour, Louisbourg fell in July. It was too late in the season for the British to enter the St Lawrence, but it was evident that French Canada would be in peril in the coming year.

Meanwhile, after only two years of formal war, the British naval presence around the coasts of France was producing the usual effects. Rocketing insurance rates for French merchantmen – on the London market – had hit trade as much as had British captures, and much of French West Indian commerce was maintained by Dutch ships. Even then cargoes were subject to seizure and forfeit on the basis of a British prize rule of 1756 whereby it was deemed unlawful for a neutral to trade in war with a belligerent's colonies which had been closed to them in peace, as of course the French colonies had been. The Admiralty had reports that the French merchants were already complaining of 'the entire destruction of their trade'.[11] For the same reasons, the main naval bases of Brest and Toulon were suffering shortages of timber and naval stores, while the drain of financial resources to the armies fighting in Germany and dispersed to guard against British amphibious descents around the coasts had caused the usual cut in the naval budget. The military were again denouncing the service as useless.

Such was the desperate situation when Louis's ministers concluded that the only way to save Canada in the coming campaigning season, 1759, was to mount an invasion of Great Britain. In 1756 it had been a threat of invasion forcing the Admiralty to keep its main forces in home waters that had allowed the Toulon squadron to seize Port Mahón. It was thought that the same effect would prevent a major British expedition sailing for America. The plan required the Toulon squadron to join the main force in Brest; when easterly winds blew the blockading British into the Atlantic, the combined squadron would break out, sail approximately 100 miles south-easterly down the coast to Quiberon Bay, where 20,000 troops would be embarked in transports, then escort these troops north to the Clyde, whence they would march on Edinburgh. This was only a feint, however. The main assault was to come from the army in Flanders. For the combined fleet would leave the Clyde to sail northabout around Scotland and down the North Sea to Ostend, to cover the passage of this army to the Essex coast. From there the army would march on London.

The overcomplex plan, with its echoes of the mistakes of the first Spanish armada, is an indication of the military cast of the French court; only soldiers could have produced such a precise design and expected it to succeed over such distances at sea. Apart from this, the aims were confused. If the visible preparations at Brest and Quiberon were to achieve the aim of holding British forces in home waters, the chance of the invasion succeeding would be reduced virtually to zero. Yet it was intended that the landing of the Flanders army within two marches of London would create such panic in the City that Britain's financial credit, and hence her ability to continue the war, would be destroyed.

In the event, Pitt, confident of the Royal Navy's strength and aware of the poor condition of the French service, made no changes to plans for two major assaults in America: the advance up the St Lawrence to take the stronghold of Quebec, and a separate expedition to seize the West Indian sugar island of Martinique.

Responsibility for protecting the British Isles lay with the western squadron under Hawke, and to a lesser extent with the Mediterranean squadron watching Toulon under Boscawen. Hawke's orders when he sailed towards the end of May 1759 were first to observe the state of French preparations at Brest, then 'to continue cruising with the Squadron near Ushant or Brest (taking all possible care not to be drove to the westward)', returning after fourteen days to Torbay to water and reprovision from supply ships.[12] Instead Hawke, finding eleven large warships lying in Brest Road with topmasts up and yards crossed, decided it would be imprudent to put back to Torbay,[13] and began to evolve a system of permanent and close blockade, the strategic equivalent of his offensive tactics.

The chief problem to be surmounted was health. With Anson's agreement, he arranged for the supply ships to come out from Plymouth to the fleet on station and transfer provisions at sea. This did not prove as difficult as feared, but the quality, especially of the beer, was so poor that Anson sent a victualling commissioner to Plymouth to oversee the operation. He was eventually successful in finding better sources, and also began sending fresh vegetables and fruit and live cattle to the fleet off Brest, as a result of which scurvy did not break out; and, since Hawke was an enthusiast for cleanliness, the ships remained remarkably free from epidemic diseases. In early September, after practically three months continuously at sea, Hawke could report that 'Except one or two ships, the squadron is very healthy, and for the sake of our Country at this critical juncture, I hope will continue.'[14]

By this date he had thirty ships of the line. Seven were in Plymouth having bottom timbers cleaned and, quite as important in his eyes, allowing the ships' companies rest and recreation; two were detached to watch the troop transports inside Quiberon and the ports further south, leaving twenty-one off Brest against an equal number of French now ready for sea inside. In fair weather Hawke kept his main body some fifty miles west of the tip of the Brest peninsula, Pointe de Saint-Mathieu,[15] in contact through a chain of signalling ships with an inshore squadron of two of the line and frigates off the point. Other frigates were stationed to the south across Douarnenez Bay to watch for vessels approaching from that direction. Whenever the wind was easterly, allowing the French to emerge, Hawke worked up with the main fleet close off Pointe de Saint-Mathieu, practically into the stretch of water called the Goulet leading to the French base. These dispositions were evolved as captains became more familiar with the potentially dangerous, hitherto uncharted inshore waters. But as early as 10 July Hawke had been satisfied that Brest was 'actually blocked up' and had instructed the commander of the inshore squadron not to let 'any neutral vessel, of whatever nation soever, enter it'.[16] The effect on the fleet inside was severe, in both practical and morale terms: virtually the only supplies reaching the port had to be carried overland after being unloaded further down the coast.

This relentless grip on the enemy fleet base formed the cornerstone of a series of victories that year which established Great Britain as the final winner at sea and across the seas; as such it ranks among the most decisive naval campaigns in world history.

The first French colony to succumb was Guadeloupe, taken by the expedition sent to seize Martinique, whose fortress proved too strong.

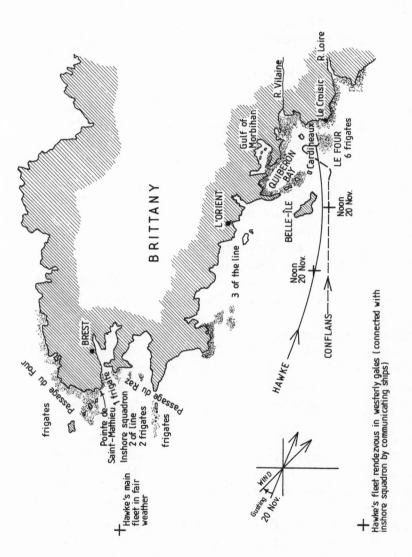

Map 5   Hawke's blockade of Brest, and courses to the Battle of Quiberon Bay, 20 November 1759

Quebec, the key to French North America, fell in September to an amphibious assault up the St Lawrence. Meanwhile the Toulon squadron escaped from the Mediterranean only to be caught by Boscawen off Cape St Vincent, where the greater part was driven ashore near Lagos and destroyed. Finally, in November, Hawke himself reaped the reward for his long watch in one of the most spectacular of all British naval victories.

Early that month a westerly gale had forced him off station into the Channel, and eventually into Torbay for shelter. After the ceaseless motion in the Atlantic, his three-decker flagship was found to be dangerously strained and he shifted his flag to another first rate, the 100-gun *Royal George*, putting out to sea again with twenty-three of the line at the first opportunity, on the 14th, as the wind went round to the north and east. The same wind allowed the French fleet out of Brest.

The French commander-in-chief, Vice Admiral Maréchal Comte de Conflans-Brienne, had little expectation of success. His twenty-one of the line were undermanned and untrained as a body; of the few prime seamen aboard, most had been transferred from a squadron from the West Indies which had entered the port when Hawke was blown into the Channel. Officers and men alike suffered from the demoralization of interminable beleaguerment by an enemy who had flaunted his colours close offshore.

The invasion plans, which had been at best a gamble in the face of British naval superiority, should have been called off after the loss of the Toulon ships, but by then France's position had deteriorated to an extent that made the gamble more necessary than ever. Now Conflans had to face potentially tumultuous winter storms as well as the British fleet. He hoped, but hardly expected, to evade Hawke; if he failed, he wrote, '*je combattrai avec toute la gloire possible*'.[17]

Hawke suspected Conflans had probably seized the opportunity to come out as the wind shifted and sail southward to collect the troop transports. This was confirmed by the master of a homeward-bound supply ship from the small squadron blockading the transports in Quiberon Bay while the British fleet was still pressing down-Channel to resume its station; he had sighted the French fleet the previous day well to the west of Belle-Île off the Quiberon Peninsula. Consequently Hawke, rounding Ushant on the 17th, beat southward under a press of sail against a strong head wind without looking in at Brest. Next day the wind backed into the north-west, allowing him to steer directly for Belle-

Île, but forcing Conflans further out into the Atlantic. So it was that by the early hours of the 20th, when the wind swung round into the west, Hawke was not far behind the French as both fleets stood easterly for the entrance to Quiberon Bay south of Belle-Île.

To the west of the island and working seaward was the small British squadron which had been watching the transports inside the bay. Their sails were sighted from the French fleet as dawn broke, and Conflans made the signals to clear for action, followed by 'general chase'. The few British ships scattered. Conflans split his own fleet, leading the centre division against those fleeing northward, ordering his van to pursue those making south and the rear to lie to, to observe sails that had appeared over the horizon to windward, astern. The chase continued over two and a half hours before suspicions about the sails astern hardened into the awful certainty that they were the British fleet approaching in line abreast. Hawke had ordered this formation at eight on the first report of strange sails ahead, and, despite a fierce and squalling wind, he was bearing down under unreefed topsails.

Conflans was faced with a momentous decision: whether to gather his scattered divisions and form line to give battle in the open sea or to run into the bay where, in the wild conditions, he could not expect the enemy to follow. Almost inevitably he chose the latter course. His mission was to join the transports inside the bay to his fleet. Once inside, he could form a defensive line and wait for gales to blow the enemy from the coast; he could then emerge again with the expedition complete. In his subsequent report he stated, 'The wind was then very violent at west-northwest, the sea very high, with every indication of very heavy weather . . . I had no ground for thinking that if I got in first with twenty-one of the line the enemy would dare follow me.'[18] He therefore hoisted the signal for sailing in line ahead, which required the fleet flagship to lead, and bore away for the seven-mile-wide entrance to the bay between the Cardineaux rocks off the Île de Hœdic to larboard and the Le Four shoal off Pointe du Croisic to starboard.

With his unpractised men and the importance of his assignment, the decision cannot be faulted. Faced with an average adversary, he would no doubt have been justified by events. As it was, Hawke was a man of extraordinary resolution and had complete confidence in his captains and crews born from their months of close blockade work. Over the previous years the enemy had evaded him narrowly on a number of occasions; with their sails in sight downwind, he was determined they should not escape again. Directly he saw Conflans bear away, therefore, he hoisted the flag for general chase, following it with the red cross of St George at the maintopmast head and three guns. This was the signal, contained in Article IX of the recent additional instructions, for the seven ships 'nearest the enemy [to] draw into a line of battle ahead of me, in order to engage till the rest of the ships of the squadron can come up with them'.[19] He also had the flagship's t'gallant sails set, which in that tempestuous weather was as clear an indication of intent. Later he set stunsails as well. Other captains followed his example. As he put it in his dispatch, 'we had very fresh gales at north-west and west-north-west, with heavy squalls. M. Conflans kept going off under such sail as all his squadron could carry and at the same time keep together; while we crowded after him with every sail our ships could bear.'[20]

The scene was the grandest in the long history of Anglo-French wars: under low skies darkened with lines of squalls, the two fleets drove down the spume-lathered swell from the Atlantic, ships heeling wildly as the wind gusted up and shifted a degree or so, tiers of canvas whipped taut, topmasts, t'gallants and slender stunsail booms quivering with the strain, weather rigging stretched bar-tight, timber groaning, water torn through the head gratings as the bows plunged, pressing out wide patterns of foam, the sea surging swiftly down the sides. To larboard, the cliffs of Belle-Île were shrouded in rain and spray; ahead, explosions of foam burst high from the Cardineaux rocks.

For Hawke, exhilaration must surely have been tempered by doubts; he was surging towards a hostile lee shore of which neither he nor his captains or sailing masters had any navigational knowledge, except for the few from the small blockading squadron who were joining him; there were no charts. The November afternoon would be short. Yet, reasoning that where a French ship could go a British could follow, he held his nerve.

Leading the British pursuit was the *Magnanime*, a French-built 74 captured in the previous war. Hawke had sent her ahead earlier to make the land. Through the morning, she and some eight others who stretched ahead in response to Hawke's signal shortened the distance to the French rear, which had been left some miles astern of the other two divisions in the earlier manoeuvres. By noon they had caught up to within three miles; by 2.30, as Conflans, in the *Soleil Royal* passed the Cardineaux, the leaders came up with the last French ships.

The *Magnanime*'s captain, Richard Howe, later to become an outstanding fighting admiral and a legend for not opening his broadside until practically aboard the enemy, pressed on past; he had enjoined his men to be very cool and attentive, and to hold their fire until they could put their hands to the muzzles of the enemy's guns. Two of the leading group with him, the new 74 *Torbay* and the 60-gun *Dorsetshire*, opened fire on the rearmost enemy, the 74-gun *Magnifique*. Hawke, some two miles astern, immediately had the red flag 'to engage the enemy as close as possible' broken out at the *Royal George*'s fore-topmast head.

The leaders bunched as they strove to work along the French formation, itself in no sort of order, and, soon after fire was opened, a violent squall caused the *Magnanime, Montagu* and *Warspite* to collide. The *Montagu* let go an anchor and brought up, losing her jib-boom as she swung; the other two cleared each other without serious damage and continued the pursuit. Coming up with the flagship of the rear division, the 80-gun *Formidable,* Howe closed and engaged at such short range that, despite the heaving decks, few shot missed the hull. In return the *Magnanime*'s foreyard was shot away. Fresh ships took her place, continuing the cannonade.

Conflans, meanwhile, after rounding the Cardineaux, had hauled up for the north-westerly corner of the bay, sheltered by the Quiberon Peninsula, where the troop transports were gathered; but the wind veered suddenly, forcing him off to starboard towards foam-shrouded rocks off the northern shore. He had expected all his ships to get inside the bay before the enemy could reach them, but, seeing his rear division heavily engaged while still outside, the British mixed up with them and evidently intent on entering too, he had the signal made for the fleet to go about in succession, and wore round to lead to their relief.

In the scramble to get in, his line had lost cohesion. The signal only added to the disorder. Several captains failed to see it, many had no room to act on it, some fell aboard consorts as they attempted to go about, and a few who had lost confidence in the admiral simply made for the open sea. 'The confusion was awful', one French officer wrote, 'when the van, in which I was, tried to go about. Part could not do it. We were in a funnel, as it were, all on top of each other, with rocks on one side of us and ships on the other.'[21]

The French rear in action with the advanced British ships – of which four were 74s – passed the Cardineaux shortly before three o'clock and headed towards their consorts in the van and centre, manoeuvring to avoid one another. The other British ships surged in after them, the *Royal*

George under full sail only ten minutes behind the leaders.[22] In the confined space between rocks and shoals, with the light fading, tactical control was impossible; the battle dissolved into wild mêlées during which group and individual encounters were decided by seamanship and gunnery. The British, after months of sea-keeping and drill off Brest, were inevitably superior in both.

The first French ship to strike her colours was the rear-division flagship, *Formidable*, which had been battered by the leading British ships in succession as they worked up the line; shortly before four o'clock, with her *chef d'escadre* and flag captain killed, her starboard timbers riddled, and gun-decks slippery with blood and human remains, the survivors hauled down the ensign to her latest attacker, the 74-gun *Resolution*. Shortly afterwards another of the rear division, the 74-gun *Héros*, which had also sustained a succession of fresh ships, suffering almost 400 killed or wounded, including every one of her officers, struck to the *Magnanime*. In the turbulent seas, Howe was unable to send a boat across, so the *Héros* dropped anchor. Nearby another of the leading British, the *Torbay* under Augustus Keppel, had engaged the 74-gun *Thésée* of the French centre, both ships using their lower batteries of heavy guns. A sudden squall laid them over, and the seas poured green through the gun ports. Keppel instantly had the *Torbay* swung up into the wind to right her, but the *Thésée*'s hands were too inexperienced and she filled and sank within minutes with her sails set. Despite the conditions, Keppel had his boats hoisted out and lowered to the rescue; yet, of her total complement of 650, only twenty-two were saved – nine by one of the *Torbay*'s boats, the rest by boats from the *Royal George* the following morning.[23]

Hawke, meanwhile, had discerned through the gun smoke and the throng of masts and piled canvas the straining white ensign at the main-topmast head of Conflans's *Soleil Royal* as she approached on an opposite course making towards the entrance, and he instructed his flag captain to lay the *Royal George* alongside her. As he closed at about half past four, Conflans bore away to prevent being boarded. Hawke attempted to steer across his stern to rake him, but one of a group seconding the French flagship interposed. Conflans then tried to come up into the wind again, but collided with two other close consorts and fell further to leeward. Fearing he was now in danger of driving on the Le Four shoal at the lee side of the entrance passage, he bore away down-wind towards the eastern part of the bay. Hawke had the helm put up to pursue him, but found himself challenged by another of the group, the 70-gun *Superbe*. The *Royal George* gave her two broadsides, after which, like the *Thésée*, the French ship drove her lee gun ports under, filled, and sank in short time with sails set. A British witness to the astonishing sight attributed it entirely to the French crew's 'want of dexterity in hauling in the guns and letting down the [gun] ports of the lower deck'.[24] A great part of her Breton company, like that of the *Thésée*, was made up of conscripted peasants who had never been to sea.

By this time, with the wind still rising, piling up the seas against the tide, the misty outline of shore, islands and ships dissolving in dusk, Hawke decided no more could be done: 'being on a part of the coast among islands and shoals of which we were totally ignorant, without a pilot, as was the greatest part of our squadron; and blowing hard on a lee shore, I made the signal to anchor'.[25] Desultory fighting continued for a while as darkness closed in and ships dropped anchor where they found themselves.

Conflans, like several of his captains, attempted to feel his way out past the Le Four shoal in the dark, but after two further collisions with consorts he too dropped anchor. At first light the following morning he found himself close by his adversaries and cut his cable to run for the little harbour of Le Croisic at the eastern end of the bay, as did the *Héros*, which had struck to Howe the previous day; both ran aground in shoal water off the headland. Conflans abandoned the flagship and had her burned by the crew; later the *Héros* was burned by a British boarding party.

Eight of the French fleet had succeeded in working out of the bay during the night; they sailed south and made Rochefort. Another badly damaged in the engagement tried to enter the Loire just below the bay, but ran aground and became a total loss. Seven of the line and all the frigates found themselves trapped in the north-eastern corner, where the river Vilaine flows into the bay. Hawke weighed to work up towards them, but was defeated by a fierce northerly wind, while the French ships, jettisoning guns and stores, succeeded in escaping over the bar into the river, except for one which was wrecked on rocks at the entrance.

In all, Conflans lost two 80-gun flagships and five other ships of the line. Hawke lost only two ships: one had run on the Le Four shoal during the night; the other had done likewise that morning, after he had signalled her to follow the French flagship. British casualties were also remarkably light: probably not more then 300 officers and men against some 2,500 French, over half of whom had been left in the wild seas after the *Thésée* and the *Superbe* had rolled and plunged to the bottom.

Although Hawke felt his fleet had accomplished as much as humanly possible, his ardent spirit was not entirely appeased. He reported:

> When I consider the season of the year, the hard gales on the day of action, a flying enemy, the shortness of the day, and the coast they were on, I can boldly affirm that all that could possibly be done has been done. As to the loss we have sustained, let it be placed to the account of the necessity I was under of running all risks to break the strong force of the enemy. Had we but two more hours' daylight, the whole had been totally destroyed or taken; for we were almost up with their van when night overtook us.[26]

Quiberon Bay – or, as it is known in France, Les Cardineaux – put an end to Louis XV's invasion plans and to his battle fleet, which ceased to exist as an effective force. The victory was a natural outcome of the close blockade which had preceded it; this in turn had been made possible by a great increase in battle-fleet strength[27] – due both to new construction and to captures from the enemy – and by the remarkable improvements in supply which had kept the men in fresh meat, green vegetables and fruit. James Lind, the naval doctor who was to contribute most to the elemination of scurvy at sea, found it notable 'that fourteen thousand persons, pent up in ships, should continue, for six or seven months, to enjoy a better state of health upon the watery element, than it can well be imagined so great a number of people would enjoy, on the most healthful spot of ground in the world'.[28]

Notwithstanding the essential contribution of Anson's Admiralty and Pitt and the Parliaments who had voted the large sums necessary for the navy, it was Hawke who initiated the close blockade and persevered in face of the navigational dangers and all that the Atlantic could hurl against him; it was his lonely decision, when Conflans ran for Quiberon Bay, to follow towards a hostile lee shore in a gale and give battle on a short November afternoon in unknown waters beset by rocks and shoals. The potential for disaster was terrifying, as he admitted in a subsequent letter to a family friend: 'it was next akin to a Miracle that half our ships was not ashore in the pursuite of the Enemy, upon their own coast, which wee were unacquainted with'.[29] It has been observed, with justice, that 'no more courageous decision in the handling of a navy's main battle fleet has ever been taken'.[30] In the pantheon of British admirals who have helped to shape history, Hawke stands close by Nelson, whose tactical principles and supreme moral courage he foreshadowed.

The next year the British navy established a tight blockade of the French coast from Dunkirk to Marseilles and Toulon, preventing a junction of the remaining fragments of the French fleet and paralysing French foreign trade and coastal convoys alike. Hawke, in command of the Atlantic section, based his fleet in Quiberon Bay and took the small island of Dumet overlooking the anchorage, using it afterwards to grow vegetables and obtain fresh water for the ships, so saving many supply voyages.

Pitt used the sovereignty of the oceans beyond this ring of naval gunpower to mount great overseas expeditions which Louis had no means of matching. The conquest of Canada was completed, and over the next two years most of France's West Indian islands, her slaving stations in West Africa and her trading posts in India were taken; meanwhile, amphibious assaults on the French coast, the capture of Belle-Île close off Quiberon Bay and the threat of other descents forced Louis to withdraw troops from his armies fighting Britain's allies and mercenaries in Germany.

Ferdinand of Spain had died in 1759. His successor, Charles III, fearing that Great Britain, when she had seized all France's colonies, would turn again on the Spanish empire, prepared to enter the war on Louis's side. At the same time, in Britain the enormous cost of the war and Pitt's evident ambition to break France completely as a naval and colonial power had raised a powerful peace faction within the government. Its leaders considered Pitt's system, 'viz. that of a monopoly of all naval power . . . at least as dangerous to the liberties of Europe as that of Louis XIV'.[31]

Failing to persuade the Cabinet to accept a pre-emptive strike against the Spanish treasure fleet, Pitt resigned in October 1761. His successors nonetheless continued preparations for seizing the last pockets of French power in the West Indies, and when Spain entered the war in early 1762 – after the safe arrival of her treasure fleet – they mounted an even greater expedition to take the key base of Havana in the Spanish–American system. Both assaults succeeded: first Martinique and its dependent small islands, then the supposedly impregnable fortress of Havana, together with a squadron of twelve of the line, a fleet of merchantmen and booty worth nearly $2 million were taken in superbly co-ordinated naval and military operations. Spain was virtually knocked out of the war before she had time to act. Later in the year her Pacific base, Manila in the Philippines, was seized by an expedition from Madras.

The war was ended in 1763 by the Treaty of Paris. Britain's chief negotiator, a leading member of the peace party, acted in the spirit of the objections to Pitt's uncompromising policy: France's main West Indian islands were returned to her, as well as Gorée on the slaving coast of Africa and Belle-Île; Havana and Manila were returned to Spain. Nevertheless, Britain retained the whole of Canada and acquired Florida from Spain. Since France transferred Louisiana to Spain, France was now excluded from North America. Her position in India was also so weakened as to leave the British East India Company dominant.

If Great Britain had given away many of the fruits of the most triumphant war she had ever fought –as Pitt complained – she nevertheless emerged as undisputed mistress of North America and the widest trading empire. Moreover, the value of her exports and re-exports had risen by over 30 per cent during the war, to almost £15 million; her imports had risen by 27 per cent, to £11 million.[32] Over 100 British slaving ships – 65 from Liverpool, now undisputed slaving capital of the country – sailed each year for Africa, carrying on average over 20,000 Negroes to the Americas.[33] The metal and textile industries, agriculture and the entire internal market had been stimulated. Judged by these results and the temporary devastation of French trade and industry, the war had proved a highly successful commercial aggression.

It had also been hugely expensive. Subsidies to Frederick II and the other Continental allies had amounted to some £10 million.[34] Average annual expenditure had been over £18 million, against tax revenue of £8.6 million. The resulting deficits had almost doubled the national debt, from £74 million up to £132 million,[35] which now required over 50 per cent of tax revenue to service. This was the investment in the bid for North America. But, as a contemporary financier wrote, it was not prodigal if what it achieved could not have been done with less.[36] The unprecedented scale of the effort was made possible only by the maturity of the fiscal and financial system; it was this which had enabled Britain to mobilize the savings of her people and foreigners alike – some £15 million, or 14 per cent of the national debt was held abroad, chiefly in the United Provinces.[37]

By contrast, the French financial system was once again in crisis. The national debt was a third lower than Britain's, since Louis had been forced to finance his extraordinary expenses by the old expedients of sales of offices and forced levies, yet he was unable to service it. Most writers who investigated the problem concluded that effective fiscal and financial reform demanded the complete reorganization of society itself.[38] The model held up by many French intellectuals owed most to the ideas of John Locke.

The American Revolution

BRITAIN HAD LITTLE joy of the undisputed sway she had won in North America: the colonists quarrelled with her almost immediately and succeeded in breaking away. In retrospect their achievement seems to have been as unpredictable and unlikely as the outcome of the two great liberation movements preceding theirs, the emergence of the Dutch Republic from Habsburg dominion and William of Orange's 'Glorious Revolution' in England. Yet from the maritime and demotic perspectives it can be seen, like those earlier transformations, to have been a natural development.

The population of the North American colonies had been growing at an extraordinary rate since their beginnings in the previous century, more than doubling every twenty-five years, and by the early 1770s the combined total had passed 2 million.[1] The steep rise, due both to a healthy birth rate and to immigration, was a sure indication of prosperity. Adam Smith pointed this out in his seminal work on political economy, *The Wealth of Nations* (1776), and stated 'Though North America is not yet so rich as England, it is much more thriving, and advancing with much greater rapidity to the further acquisition of riches.'[2] Wages were everywhere far higher than they were in England for the same occupations, the cost of provisions lower, hence the material standard of living was considerably above that in the mother country – or anywhere else in the world.[3]

The colonies were, however, essentially rural. Whereas the Netherlands at the time of their revolt against Spain had been the most industrially advanced, highly urbanized area of Europe, with at least twenty-three towns and cities of over 10,000 inhabitants, in North America in 1770 there were only five of such a size: the seaport cities of Philadelphia, New York, Boston, Charleston and Newport, Rhode Island.[4] Over 90 per cent of the population lived on the land or in small communities less than 2,500 strong.[5]

In the south, plantations worked by slave labour produced tobacco, rice and indigo for export to the mother country. In the middle colonies and New England, some grain was grown for export, but most farmers still produced for their own and neighbourhood consumption; they were of the rugged, self-sufficient sort portrayed by the French nobleman Alexis de Tocqueville after his travels through America half a century later: 'it sometimes happens that the same individual tills his fields, builds his dwelling, contrives his tools, makes his shoes, and weaves the coarse stuff of which his dress is composed'.[6]

Along the coast of New England, communities of fishermen exploited the abundant cod and other fish in the icy waters of the Labrador current from the Grand Banks of Newfoundland to Cape Cod. Almost £300,000 worth of dried and salted fish was sold abroad each year, making it the fourth most valuable colonial export after tobacco (over £750,000), bread/flour and indigo.[7]

Shipbuilding also contributed to export earnings. There were ample timber and ample skills. Like the farmers of the interior, the American shipwright did not confine himself to a single trade, but was master of all crafts required to construct, caulk, paint and rig a ship, and could equally well build a house, make furniture or repair a wagon.[8] As Tocqueville observed with wonder, Americans were 'never fettered by the axioms of their profession', nor rooted in old habits or prejudice, but 'suit their occupation to the exigencies of the moment in the manner most profitable to themselves'. They seemed to him to live in conditions of perpetual change which kept them 'in a state of excitement above the ordinary level of mankind'.[9] From the early days they had specialized in small, fast craft, even for fishing, to outrun their international competitors and pirates and evade the British Navigation Acts – especially in their commerce with the West Indies, where they provided the planting communities with beef, pork, dried fish, flour, bread, Indian corn, timber and timber products, taking home rum, sugar and molasses (the waste product of sugar production, which was used to make rum). They did not restrict themselves, as they were supposed to under the laws, to trade

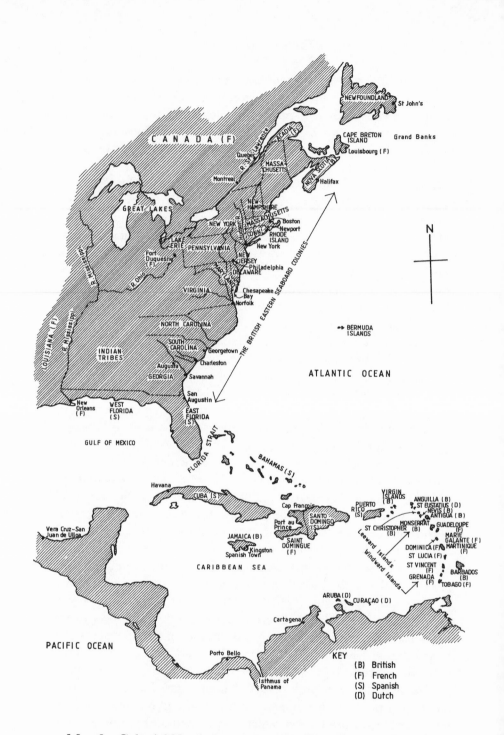

Map 6   Colonial North America and the West Indies in the 1770s

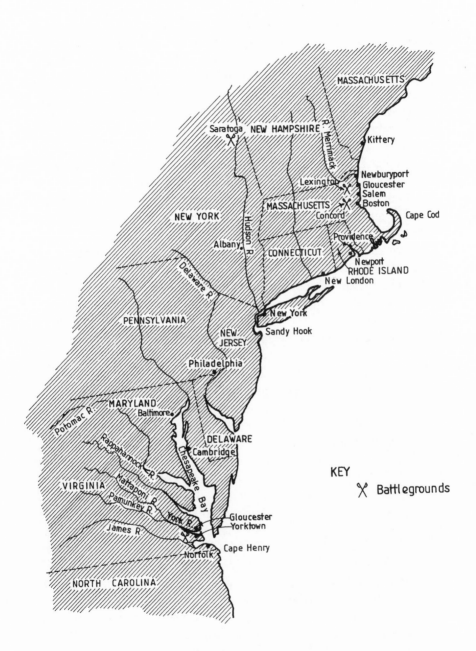

Map 7   Slaving ports and battlegrounds of the American War of Independence

with British colonies, but smuggled promiscuously with foreign islands – the French in particular – even during the war. They did not invent the schooner – contrary to Gloucester, Massachusetts, tradition – but developed it for seagoing traders, and by the 1750s they were practically the only exponents of this fast and rakish type.[10] They also built conventional merchantman for sale to British owners, and small warships to order for the Royal Navy.[11]

Apart from shipbuilding and some ironworking, both concentrated in New England and the middle provinces, the colonies had developed little industry. They remained dependent for most manufactures and practically all luxuries on the mother country. The value of imports of English – and re-exported Irish – linens, woollens, iron and brass wares, cutlery, fashionable furniture, East India Company tea, drugs, spices, millinery and all the accessories of civilized living rose rapidly in the years before the revolution to over £4 million a year.[12] This was considerably more than the colonies earned from exports; a large part of the deficit was made up by shipping and insurance services provided in the major port cities.

Of these, Philadelphia was the greatest. With a population by 1770 of over 30,000 – reminiscent of Amsterdam's before the Dutch Revolution – it was the second largest city in the British empire, surpassed only by London. Its trade had been stimulated by provisioning British forces in the Seven Years War, and its merchants (who owned three-quarters of the tonnage clearing on translatlantic voyages) had opened new lines of commerce permitted them by the Navigation Acts with Spain and the Mediterranean, and also sent a few ships each year directly to Africa to bring back slaves – not withstanding an open declaration of hostility by the Quakers, the founding fathers of the city and the colony of Pennsylvania, against all who invested in or supplied cargoes for the trade.[13] They had also increased their share of the vessels engaged in the colonial commerce with Great Britain. They formed a confident elite who lived in grand style, and, like their counterparts in the second largest American city, New York, and the other thriving northern seaports, Boston and Newport, Rhode Island, had attained a degree of power within their own community and control over their own commerce which disposed them to want greater autonomy.

Meanwhile the British government's attitude to the colonies had developed from a simple 'mercantilist' desire to control colonial trade and shipping for the benefit of the mother country into a belief that the colonists should contribute to the costs of their own defence. This was a response to the huge expenses of the war during which the French had been expelled from the continent, and part of the usual post-war attempt to reduce the vastly increased national debt. It also appeared fully justified by the need to maintain British forces in North America in peacetime: some 8,000 troops were stationed to defend frontier colonists against Indian attack and also to prevent settlers moving westward into the territory of Indians who had so recently been allies against the French;[14] while the North American squadron comprised twenty-six warships – the largest naval detachment outside the home fleet – to deter a French descent, protect imperial trade and fishing, and enforce the Navigation Acts. Policing the laws was indeed a major part of the navy's duty.[15] American trade with the enemy in the West Indies during the late war and the impossibility of dealing with smugglers in American vice-admiralty courts – since American juries would never convict on this charge – were issues that rankled.

The government revealed its intentions in an Act of Parliament within months of the Treaty of Paris in 1763. The most significant provision empowered Royal Navy ships to seize smugglers, allotting officers and crews half the proceeds – in line with wartime captures of contraband – and granting the squadron commander half of the other half or Crown share. It was a powerful incentive. It was followed in April 1764 by the Revenue or 'Sugar' Act, designed both to raise revenue and to render smuggling less profitable. A duty of threepence a gallon was to be levied on the import into the British colonies of foreign molasses, and, to inhibit smuggling, traders were required to give bonds, to present detailed cargo lists, or 'cockets', to the customs before starting loading, and, when loading in British colonies, to obtain certificates from a Justice of the Peace detailing the origin, quality and quantity of all rum, sugar and molasses taken aboard. These requirements – particularly the need to take out bonds and 'cockets' before loading – made things difficult and more costly for legitimate traders as well, and were in many cases simply impracticable, as when the loading quay was miles from the nearest customs house.

In Boston and New England ports the Act was seen as an alarming threat. The timber and so-called 'damaged fish' – fit only for consumption by slaves – they supplied to the West Indian planters were staple exports. The rum they made from molasses brought home on the return voyage was not simply a popular liquor but a currency used for trading in furs and skins and by those merchants, principally from Newport, Rhode Island, taking part in the West African slave trade. Moreover, the Act accompanied a proposal for a 'Stamp Act' to tax all kinds of transactions – although the colonists were allowed a year to suggest a more acceptable means of raising the revenue necessary to meet the costs of their defence. It seemed evident to New England merchants, traders and a radical Boston group already exercised over British-imposed search warrants to assist enforcement of the Navigation Acts that the British government was seeking not only to remove the trading irregularities which had become traditional and even vital to their economy, but to assert the principle of taxation by Parliament. Boston's representatives to the Massachusetts legislature were instructed to expand on this issue to draw in the interior communities: 'If our trade may be taxed, why not our lands? Why not the produce of our lands and everything we possess and make use of? This we apprehend annihilates our [British Crown] Charter rights to govern and tax ourselves.'[16]

Here was the nub. The colonists were and felt themselves to be thoroughly British; their political institutions were modelled on the British pattern: each colony had a governor, representing the King, an elected Assembly or legislature on the lines of the House of Commons, and an appointed upper chamber known as the Council. As in Britain, the elected legislature had come to wield the real power in all colonies and vote the necessary taxes. The colonists claimed that the British parliament, to which they sent no representatives, had no right to tax them. A frequently quoted phrase, coined earlier by the Harvard-educated Boston lawyer and radical leader James Otis, was 'Taxation without representation is tyranny.' Such was the rhetoric: no doubt it was believed. Nonetheless, it is surely significant that it was in Massachusetts, whose merchants, together with those of Rhode Island and Connecticut, had most to lose from the Sugar Act and the Royal Navy's powers of seizure,[17] that the anti-parliamentary agitation began. Subsequently it was the Massachusetts legislature that established a Committee of Correspondence to liaise and exchange views with the assemblies of the other colonies; and it was a Massachusetts initiative that was to lead to delegations from nine colonial assemblies meeting in New York the following autumn, 1765, to adopt a common stance and present petitions for the repeal of the recent Acts to King George III and both houses of the British parliament.

By this time the Stamp Act had been passed – failing an alternative suggestion from the colonists. In Boston, riots had ensued. Mobs of rowdies organized and fired up by the oratory of radical leaders, in particular a failed businessman and customs collector named Samuel Adams, first terrorized the appointed stamp distributor, who resigned his post, then wrecked the residences of the lieutenant governor and high vice-admiralty and customs officials. Rhode Island followed Boston's lead, then New York and other cities and towns throughout the colonies, making it impossible to impose the stamp duty.

These preliminary skirmishes with the mother country were crucial triggers for revolution, since they brought elected representatives of the widely separated and very different colonies together in concerted action for the first time. They also provided young, discontented or unenfranchised elements within the electorates with a common cause to champion and a common rhetoric. Groups of artisans, mechanics, skilled craftsmen, small traders and others seeking a fairer representation within the colonial legislatures became champions of colonial rights, pushing the merchant elites who held power to adopt ever tougher attitudes towards Britain. So the grand issue between the British parliament and the colonies became driven on the American side by the internal power play of the seaport elites.[18]

The British government might have put down the incipient rebellion at this or practically any later stage by sending sufficient troops to ensure compliance and make examples of the ringleaders. Had the ministers been driven by the compulsions of a Continental court they would no doubt have done so. But they answered to the representatives of merchant power in Parliament, and, while they were determined that the will of Parliament should prevail over the King's unruly colonial subjects, their impulses were more fiscal than military. They attempted to meet the American objections by avoiding internal taxation, instead imposing duties on British manufactured goods imported into the colonies. And an American Board of Customs Commissioners was established on the lines of the British board to enforce collection.

It has been suggested that these duties were designed as a machiavellian provocation to Boston, the boilerhouse of rebellion, since that city was by far the largest importer of the listed goods. Once Boston had been brought into line, the argument runs, the other colonies were expected to comply.[19] If so the operation was badly mishandled, as there were no effective preparations to deal with the riots that should have been anticipated. These broke out in response to the seizure by the customs of a sloop appropriately named *Liberty*, owned by John Hancock, well known to the British as a smuggler and leader of rebellion. The customs commissioners' houses were wrecked, and they and their officers, in terror for their lives, fled aboard the flagship of the North American squadron anchored in Boston harbour. The commander of the squadron wrote home to a senior politician in Opposition: 'What has been so often foretold is now come to pass. The good people of Boston seem ready and ripe for open revolt, and nothing, it is to be imagined, can prevent it but immediate armed force.'[20]

Two regiments were dispatched to Boston directly news of the riots reached England. These enabled the customs commissioners to resume their duties, but did nothing to quell the spirit of rebellion. And if the original intention had been to divide the colonies, it failed. They came closer together and organized boycotts of British imports; coming at a time when British claims to possession of the Falkland Islands threatened war with Spain, this led to a repeal of the duties and a more conciliatory attitude from a new British administration led by Lord North. More significantly, the radical groupings in all the major seaport cities built up their organizations, strengthened inter-colony links, and exploited every opportunity for anti-British agitation, conjuring fears of a conspiracy to subvert colonial liberties and utilize American resources exclusively for the benefit of British monopoly merchants and corrupt politicians, driving the argument ever further towards revolt.

Their moment came in 1773. Parliament passed an innocuous Act designed to help the East India Company out of financial trouble by allowing its ships to unload tea in America without first landing it in England for auction. Influential American merchants had secured agency rights and stood to profit from the direct sales; American colonists stood to gain from lower prices. But the radical groups in the seaports seized on the issue of duty payable on the tea and represented the Act as another sinister design to introduce the principle of taxation without representation.

By chance, the first East Indiamen arrived in Boston. Samuel Adams, John Hancock and their confederates and followers were equal to their historic opportunity. Groups of rowdies in Mohawk Indian dress, brandishing hatchets, boarded the ships, entered the holds, stove in the chests, and consigned £10,000 worth of tea to the harbour waters, watched by approving crowds.[21] When news reached England, Parliament reacted by instituting a naval blockade of Boston harbour – until the tea was paid for – and legislating for a new form of government for Massachusetts which would be compliant to British direction, so apparently confirming the radical thesis of a conspiracy to subvert American liberties.

The resulting furore brought the separate colonies together again. Delegations from twelve of the thirteen – missing only Georgia, which needed British support against the local Indian tribes – met in Philadelphia the following September, 1774, in what was termed the first Continental Congress. Widely differing views were expressed. Those valuing the British connection, or simply resigned to the impossibility of standing up to Britain militarily, supported a proposal for a colonial legislature, the members to be selected by the individual colonies, whose assent would be needed for parliamentary legislation affecting America. Radicals fought hard against this eminently reasonable plan and eventually won approval for a Suffolk County, Massachusetts, proposal to institute another boycott of British goods and disobey the recent 'Intolerable Acts' to impose a new form of government on Massachusetts. Militants in that colony, styling themselves Patriots, meanwhile overturned the government imposed by the new laws.

The final steps to open war came the following April, 1775, when British troops clashed at Lexington and Concord – some twenty miles from Boston – with Massachusetts volunteer militias raised to defend the colony's liberties. Guerrilla attacks by the Patriot militiamen from behind cover on both sides of the British route back to Boston left 273 dead or wounded against American casualties of under 100. These were the opening shots of the American Revolution, for a second Continental Congress convening in May voted to raise a continental army to defend American rights: a Virginian, George Washington, who had led his colony's militia during the Seven Years War, was appointed commander-in-chief.

Ostensibly the revolution was caused by the incompatibility of the British parliament's jealously guarded right to legislate on tax and expenditure throughout the empire and the colonists' equally jealously held rights to tax and govern themselves. It is evident, however, that it was Parliament's use of the Royal Navy to enforce the Navigation Acts, especially with regard to the smuggling trades with the foreign West Indian islands, that provoked the New England merchants to active defiance.[22] Had their vital interests not been threatened by effective enforcement, it is probable that the constitutional arguments deployed by James Otis and his fellows would have remained the stuff of academic debate. But, with their trades endangered, seaport merchants, great and small, adopted Otis's themes to justify confrontation, and in Boston the more militant organized and animated fearsome mobs to terrorize revenue officials, bait British soldiers, and coerce anyone involved in or sympathetic to the legislation of the mother country.

By simplifying the dispute into the issues of taxation and infringement of rights, the seaboard gathered the support of the interior and whipped up a 'patriotic' fervour that raised political consciousness through all classes, increasing the pressure on the merchant and planting elites to adopt a radical stance. This was by no means against their inner feelings. Reason may have told them they gained much from the imperial system and altogether lacked the armed strength to break free, but frustration with the constraints it imposed, combined with a vision of the limitless growth to be expected on the continent and self-confidence born of the recent surge in population and prosperity, had produced profound, if unformed, aspirations for sovereignty.[23]

In the later stages two renegade Britons who brought personal discontents to the colonies helped turn aspiration to commitment. The first was Charles Lee, an intellectually brilliant soldier who hated George III and his entourage for failing to advance him. Declaring America 'the last and only asylum of liberty', he bought land in Virginia in 1773, attached himself to the extreme wing of the revolutionary cause, and published a pamphlet which did much to dispel American apprehensions that colonial militias would not be able to stand against trained troops.[24]

After him, in November 1774, an equally rancorous intellectual, 'Tom' Paine, arrived in Philadelphia. He was one of a great number of self-educated men from humble origins in both Britain and France who lacked formal qualifications for a professional career but drank deep of new political and scientific ideas from books, pamphlets and political clubs. Having passed through a number of jobs, two marriages and dismissal from the excise service for publishing a pamphlet arguing for higher wages, Paine met Pennyslvania's representative in London, Benjamin Franklin, like him a self-taught man of large ideas. Franklin inspired him to seek his fortune in America and gave him letters of introduction. With these he secured a post as editorial assistant on the *Pennsylvania Magazine*. The city was then a seat of artisan radicalism and revolutionary excitement which complemented his own demons, and Paine was able to realize a genius for polemic in numerous articles, among them a powerful indictment of the institution of slavery. And, discerning beneath the colonists' quarrel with Britain about taxation that what they really wanted was independence, he argued the case for this in a fifty-page pamphlet titled *Common Sense*. This so captured the American mood that within four months of publication in January 1776 it had sold 120,000 copies. It is regarded as the single most influential publication on America's path to independence.

That a majority of Americans – by no means all – finally viewed independence as their goal was ultimately due to the failures of successive British governments over a decade. They had done enough to provoke revolt but not enough to demonstrate the will and power to command respect. They had given way on matters of principle, allowed Boston to simmer for years despite alarming reports from the North American squadron on the state of rebellion in the city, and finally reacted with arbitrary interference and insufficient force.

On 2 July 1776 delegates to a third Continental Congress in Philadelphia approved a motion for independence and assigned the task of drafting the declaration to a committee of three leading figures of the radical movement: John Adams from Boston, the Philadelphian Benjamin Franklin and a Virginian, Thomas Jefferson. Adams and Franklin, although both powerful political writers, left the work of composition to Jefferson, a lawyer of towering erudition and culture with a formidable intellect, who two years before had published an essay demonstrating that the British parliament had no authority to legislate for the colonies.[25] To justify separation from the mother country, he proceeded from propositions derived from John Locke and embracing the latest thinking of the French political philosophers inspired by Locke:

We hold these truths to be self-evident, that all men are created equal, that they are endowed by their Creator with certain unalienable Rights, that among these are Life, Liberty and the pursuit of Happiness – That to secure these rights, Governments are instituted among Men, deriving their just powers from the consent of the governed, – That whenever any Form of Government becomes destructive of these ends, it is the Right of the People to alter or abolish it, and to institute new Government . . .[26]

With these phrases 'the People' was enthroned. It was a historic precedent. No doubt it owed as much to the special energy of democratic politics as evolved in colonial America, and the colonists' indifference to distinctions of rank, as to the declared interpretation of the 'social contract' of Hobbes, Locke and most recently Jean-Jacques Rousseau. In the same way, the undefined notion of 'the pursuit of Happiness'[27] was a perfect reflection of the individualism, activity and optimism of colonial society. There was of course a dichotomy between the assertion that all men were created equal and the practice of slavery. This, too, arose from the nature of colonial society. The Virginian Jefferson owned slaves since he had inherited a great estate, but he abhorred the institution – as did his colleagues – and the Quakers of Pennsylvania had already freed their own slaves; nevertheless, a denunciation of slavery written into the first draft of the Declaration was excised to prevent the southern colonies breaking from the united front.[28]

From propositions, the Declaration proceeded to list the 'abuses and usurpations' visited on the colonies by a British king seeking to establish 'an absolute tyranny' over them, so arriving at the final statement that 'these United Colonies are, and of Right ought to be Free and Independent States . . . Absolved from all Allegiance to the British Crown'.[29] Unlike the United Provinces' break from Spain or the English break from the threat of absolute monarchy by the Stuarts, there was no resort to religion; the arguments reflected the new age of reason. It will be recalled that David Hume had by this date characterized reason as 'the slave of the passions'. More remarkable was the confidence implicit in the rolling phrases; for this there was no military justification. Soon after the document was signed on 4 July (1776) by the delegates of all thirteen colonies below the St Lawrence, Benjamin Franklin took ship for France to press for the financial and military aid without which the rebellious colonies could not possibly survive.

A few weeks before the Declaration of Independence, Adam Smith published his masterwork, *An Inquiry into the Nature and Causes of the Wealth of Nations*. The conjunction was not chance. The gestation of the book had coincided with that of the American Revolution. Discontent in the colonies had sharpened Smith's focus on the stifling effects of the control of trade and industry in the mercantilist system of national monopolies. His work was the theoretical complement to the American plunge for independence.

He had long sought answers to the question of how so often self-interested individuals were 'led by an invisible hand . . . [to] advance the interest of the society'. In *The Wealth of Nations* he showed the invisible hand to be the effect of competition in free markets. Conversely, he showed how regulation, excessive duties on foreign imports, and monopoly rights drove prices up – no doubt to the advantage of the merchants concerned, but to the detriment of 'the great body of the people' as consumers, and thereby of the wealth of the nation as a whole. He inveighed against 'the mean rapacity, the monopolizing spirit of merchants and manufacturers', and identified their monstrous effects:

> Commerce, which ought naturally to be, among nations, as among individuals, a bond of union and friendship, has become the most fertile source of discord and animosity. The capricious ambition of kings and ministers has not, during the present and preceding century, been more fatal to the repose of Europe than the impertinent jealousy of merchants and manufacturers.[30]

He argued for 'natural liberty' for men and nations to pursue their own interests unfettered by artificial restraints on labour or trade, and an end to the beggar-my-neighbour policies of the great powers in which a rival's gain was counted as the nation's loss. On the contrary, he asserted, 'A nation which would enrich itself by foreign trade is certainly most likely to do so when its neighbours are all rich, industrious and commercial nations.'[31]

The doctrine of natural liberty and self-interest as the motors of wealth creation led him to the conclusion that slaves, while appearing to cost no more than their maintenance, were in reality more expensive to employ than free men: 'A person who can acquire no property, can have no other interest but to eat as much, and to labour as little as possible. Whatever work he does beyond what is sufficient to purchase his own maintenance can be squeezed out of him by violence only.'[32] He noted that sugar and tobacco planters could apparently afford the expense of slave labour, whereas grain farmers could not.

The Scotsman Adam Smith and the British-American leaders of the American revolution were prophets with a similar vision, but the natural inertia of the international system was such that much discord, animosity and bloodshed were to ensue before their message was heeded.

To THE ADMIRALTY in London the American rebellion was a peripheral irritant. Since the end of the Seven Years War the attention of successive First Lords – the Earl of Egmont, Edward Hawke and from 1771 the fourth Earl of Sandwich – had been fixed on France and Spain. The two

Bourbon powers, joined in a 'Family Compact' and determined to avenge the humiliations of the late war, had yet again built up formidable fleets. Louis XV's first post-war Minister of Marine, the Duc de Choiseul, burning for revenge, had exhorted the French people to contribute to the navy on which, he claimed, the nation's existence depended. The funds that had flowed in were reflected in the names of provinces and cities borne by the ships. The greatest, like the 110-gun *Ville de Paris*, displaced some 4,600 tons – over 1,000 tons more than the largest British first rates; the most numerous third-rate 74s of almost 3,000 tons displaced 500 tons more than British 74s, and all first, second and third rates mounted main batteries of 36-pounders – equivalent to 40 British pounds – against 32-pounders in the equivalent British rates.[33]

The Spanish fleet had been rebuilt under Charles III with equal sense of purpose; by 1770, as Louis dismissed the militant Choiseul for international political effect, the two Bourbon battle fleets combined equalled the British fleet. Since at least forty British ships of the line had been built of unseasoned timber in an emergency programme during the Seven Years War and were quietly rotting, it is likely the Bourbon powers were effectively superior.[34] By 1775 they were superior on paper as well; moreover, the larger size of their vessels, class for class, gave them a combined displacement perhaps 25 per cent greater than the British battle line.[35]

For Sandwich the situation was more alarming than the bare figures indicated. In the first place the French had an advantage in early mobilization; by conscripting from lists of seamen, they could man their ships more quickly at the start of a campaign than the British, who relied for the most part on impressing men from incoming merchant ships. Second, France no longer appeared a threat to her mainland neighbours, and Choiseul, heeding the naval failures and humiliations of the late war, had framed a principle that the country should not be drawn into Continental hostilities. Consequently there was little scope for Britain to form the kind of European coalition against Louis which had in the past invariably drawn off resources and caused French naval collapse.

The British administration took a complacent view of the situation. Lord North's main concern was to sustain financial credit by relieving the burden of national debt. His goal was to pay off at least £1.5 million each year. This meant trimming the naval budget, particularly cutting the numbers employed in the dockyards, whereas what the navy needed was additional building and refitting capacity, especially in the southwest to support the home fleet off the western approaches to the English

Channel; four of the six major yards were in the Thames and Medway, facing east.

In justification of his policy of retrenchment, North told Sandwich he did not recall having ever seen 'a more pacific appearance of affairs' in Europe; France seemed unlikely to go to war for some years. He admitted Britain had 'suffered a little' from unpreparedness at the start of the last two wars, but then her credit and the length of her purse, 'carefully managed during the preceeding times of peace', had carried her through to glory. And, he added, 'Great peace establishments will, if we do not take care, prove our ruin: we shall fail, at the long run, by exhausting in times of tranquillity those resources upon which we are to depend in time of war.'[36]

The argument appeared sound; all great powers had invariably retrenched in peace to prepare their finances for the strain of the next great war. However, the triumphant precedents of the last two wars were not necessarily valid: should Louis and Charles III of Spain enter the war together and co-ordinate their strategy – as they had not done in either of the last two encounters – and should Britain lack a powerful ally on the Continent, as seemed inevitable, the dangers were clear.

Meanwhile there were other significant maritime developments. The hitherto barely charted wastes of the Pacific, still regarded by Spain as her private ocean, were being probed for commercial potential by Britain and France. The first of the recent British expeditions under Commodore John Byron in 1764 also had all the old anti-Spanish aims. This is clear from the First Lord's report to the Cabinet after Byron had reached the Falkland Islands en route for the Strait of Magellan: the Falklands, Egmont stated, were the key to the whole Pacific, commanding 'the Ports and Trade of Chili [,] Peru, Panama, Acapulco, & in one word all the Spanish territory upon that sea. It will render all our Expeditions more lucrative to ourselves, most fatal to Spain.'[37]

Byron made few discoveries on his Pacific crossing but reported on his return that, while sailing through the Tuamotu group (140° west), he had been convinced of land to the southward and had it not been for unfavourable winds he would probably have found the great unknown southern continent, *Terra Australis Incognita*, reputed to exist thereabouts. A second expedition was dispatched in 1766 specifically to seek this continent 'between Cape Horn and New Zealand, in Latitudes convenient for Navigation, and in Climates adapted to the product of commodities usefull in Commerce'.[38]

The same year Choiseul, spurred by the British efforts, dispatched a much grander expedition to the Pacific with ostensibly scientific aims, carrying astronomers and naturalists under the soldier-scholar Louis Antoine de Bougainville. Both British and French found to the south of the Tuamotus the ravishing island of Tahiti. Both were entranced by the spectacular beauty of its peaks and forests, sparkling beaches, and abundant fruits and flowers, and not least by the inhabitants – the men tall and well-proportioned; the young women and girls with hibiscus or jasmine in their dark hair comely beyond imagining and, as it soon emerged, happy for sexual relations without shame. For sailors from the colder society of Europe it was paradise found.

To Bougainville himself the island seemed a Garden of Eden, the life of the populace an idyll of 'ease, innocent joy, and every appearance of happiness'.[39] He revised these first impressions on the basis of talks with a native from a chief's family he carried back to France, who described a rigidly stratified, even tyrannical, society practising human sacrifice and large-scale infanticide. But by then his original reports had sparked French intellectuals to rhapsody. Here was natural man as Rousseau had imagined him – basically good, uncontaminated by the artifice, prejudice and social constraints of civilization. Rousseau's friend the encyclopedist Denis Diderot wrote a *Supplément au Voyage de Bougainville* which circulated in manuscript, proposing a free and tolerant society modelled on the supposed virtues of the Tahitians and most memorably advocating free love. It was an implied critique of his own country, and was not published until after the French Revolution. More perceptive were pleas he made for the Pacific to be left unexploited and uncorrupted by Europeans, although in the real world of commercial and national rivalries these were as fantastical as his Utopia.

Meanwhile the two ships comprising the British expedition arrived home separately. Neither had sighted the great southern continent, but the *Swallow* under Philip Carteret had made a more southerly passage of the Pacific than any previous European ship and so cut into the area the continent was supposed to occupy. It was left to James Cook, in command of the next British expeditions, to establish that it did not exist and in doing so to fix the outlines of Pacific geography.

Cook, surely the greatest of all maritime explorers and cartographers, was the son of a labourer from Scotland who had found work on a Yorkshire farm. His early education was paid for by his father's employer. At eighteen he had gone to sea as an apprentice in east-coast collier barks, teaching himself mathematics at night when his vessel was laid up for winter refit; within six years he had been appointed mate. He was offered command soon after, but chose instead to widen his horizons by entering the Royal Navy as an able seaman. His evident qualities secured his rapid promotion in the non-commissioned ranks, and in the Seven Years War he particularly distinguished himself in sounding and marking the channel up the St Lawrence for the fleet carrying Wolfe's troops to Quebec. It was as a skilled navigator and cartographer that he was chosen in 1768 to command the third British Pacific venture.

This differed from its predecessors in being promoted by the Royal Society, chiefly to participate in an international project to measure the transit of Venus across the sun from widely separated locations across the globe. It was also the first British attempt to study the environment and peoples of Oceania scientifically: a small band of naturalists and artists accompanied the astronomers, and Cook was instructed to report on all aspects of the lands he found and to bring back specimens, drawings and surveys. Beyond intellectual inquiry, however, the voyage was viewed from the Cabinet and the Admiralty, who provided the ships and crews, as another attempt to find the southern continent and so expand British trade and manufacture into a new hemisphere.[40] The newly discovered island of Tahiti was chosen as the location for observing the transit of Venus, after which Cook was instructed to head south, where 'there is reason to imagine that a Continent or Land of great extent may be found'.[41]

Instead he arrived at New Zealand, which had been discovered a century earlier by the great Dutch explorer Abel Tasman and was believed to be one extremity of the great southern continent. He spent six months disproving this by charting the coasts of the two islands, and thence sailed westward, reaching the south-eastern corner of New Holland – later to be renamed Australia – whose eastern extent was entirely unknown and unexplored. He raised the Union flag in a capacious inlet just south of a bay which was to become Sydney harbour, named the place Botany Bay after the numerous new plants discovered there, then coasted northward, surveying and charting, writing descriptions of the aboriginal inhabitants and the extraordinary animal species encountered, marvelling at the superabundance of butterflies, and exploring the great barrier reef by boat. Departing finally from the northernmost cape, which he named after the Duke of York, he claimed the whole eastern seaboard for the King, naming it New South Wales.

Soon after returning to England, he proposed another expedition to clear up the question of the southern continent for good. Sandwich at the Admiralty and his Cabinet colleagues agreed, and in July 1772 Cook set out on his second Pacific exploration. Again he carried astronomers, naturalists and an artist, although this time the primary scientific purposes were laid down by the Board of Longitude, a body established by Parliament in 1714 to evaluate methods of establishing longitude at sea and to adjudicate on the award of prize money to anyone who could solve the problem. The very substantial sum of £20,000 had been offered by the government for a method accurate to within half a degree, or thirty nautical miles at the equator. To date no one had won the prize. Remarkably, the shipping supporting the wealth, power and prestige of western Europe was still navigated across the oceans by de'd reckoning based on estimates of courses, speeds and drift since the last landfall, combined with the last latitude obtained from observing the angle of the sun above the horizon at noon.

Although no one had been awarded the full prize money, a clock-maker, John Harrison, had earned it. He was a self-taught natural genius of whose early life little is known beyond the fact that his father was a carpenter from Yorkshire and the movements of his own first clocks were made from oak. Since first hearing of the prize in about 1725 he had worked single-mindedly to construct a timepiece whose accuracy would be unaffected by violent motion or changes in temperature, so allowing navigators to preserve throughout their voyage an accurate reference time corresponding to the time used in nautical almanacs to record the co-ordinates of heavenly bodies; this would enable them to calculate their position by astronomical observations. The theory was not new, but in practice no clocks were sufficiently accurate or robust.

Harrison's first 'sea clock' had been submitted to the Board of Longitude in 1735, but after sea trials the following year he expressed dissatisfaction with it and was granted funds to make an improved version.[42] The improvements occupied him for over two decades and involved the construction of three entirely new types. The final version, referred to now as H-4 – Harrison's fourth – was a compact watch only 5¼ inches in diameter with jewelled pivot holes to eliminate friction in the movement, and, to adjust for climate change, a bimetallic strip of brass and steel riveted together which flexed according to temperature; in so doing it altered the tension of the balance spring. During two sea trials to the West Indies in 1761–2 and 1764 the watch performed with astonishing accuracy, allowing the longitude of Barbados to be calculated after a seven-week voyage to within 9.8 miles,[43] thus with three times more accuracy than required for the £20,000 prize. However the Board now added new conditions – to Harrison's fury – obliging him to explain the secrets of his mechanism so that others could copy the watch, and withholding the full prize money until it was satisfied the system represented 'a method of common and general utility for finding the longitude at sea'.[44] It was not until Harrison approached King George III, and won his support, that he was granted a bounty by Parliament which brought the receipts for his invention to £18,750 – or some £23,000 if earlier grants from the Board are taken into account.

Meanwhile a professional watchmaker named Larcum Kendall had been commissioned to copy Harrison's watch. The replica he made – known now as K-1 – was entrusted to Cook for sea trials on his second voyage to the Pacific, together with three other marine timekeepers, or chronometers, by another maker. He had carried no chronometers on his first expedition. Besides testing the accuracy of the timepieces, he was instructed to compute his position every day using a rival method of determining longitude by 'lunar distances', measuring the angle between the moon and the sun or particular stars. He found both methods allowed him to calculate his longitude to within a degree and a half, and generally to within half a degree.[45] The problem of longitude was solved, although it was to be over a decade before other clockmakers, inspired by Harrison's success but using mass-production methods, brought the price of chronometers down to a level navigators could afford; then the far more complex system of lunar distances fell into disuse. While Harrison's inventive brain and obsessive determination led to the breakthrough to scientific navigation, the contribution of precision instrument makers, mathematicians and astronomers who compiled the tables for the nautical almanacs – the first British edition was in 1767 – were crucial, as Cook acknowledged in his journal.[46]

One of the human triumphs of Cook's first voyage had been to bring the ships home without losing a man to scurvy. He accomplished the same remarkable feat on his second voyage. He ascribed it to his insistence, against vigorous complaints, that the men eat sauerkraut – pickled cabbage – on meat days and 'portable' (dried) soup on the alternate 'banyan days', and to treating them with 'wort', an infusion of malt which the Navy Board had instructed him to test, directly they showed signs of scurvy.[47] However, he also took great care to procure fresh meat and greenstuffs whenever he touched land, which he did frequently, and there is little doubt that it was the wide range of his measures rather than any particular one that accounted for his success.[48] He seemed to recognize this in his report to the Admiralty, stating that the wort was 'without doubt one of the best antiscorbutic medicines yet discovered', but adding, 'I am not altogether of opinion that it will cure it [scurvy] at sea.'[49] His surgeons, who failed to make controlled experiments, implied much the same, reporting on the wort as the best remedy for the cure of scurvy if aided by sago, currants and sauerkraut. In fact malt has only the faintest trace of ascorbic acid, and these reports, combined with Cook's practical record of keeping his men healthy, had the effect of holding back recognition of a real cure for scurvy, the juice of citrus fruit, for another two decades.

On this second expedition, which has been described as 'arguably the greatest, most perfect of all seaborne voyages of discovery',[50] Cook reached the Pacific via the Cape of Good Hope and the Indian Ocean, then circled the empty waters between New Zealand and Cape Horn from deep into the Antarctic Circle up to the Tropics, finding and charting islands and island groups but finally disproving the myth of *Terra Australis*. Promoted captain on his return, made a fellow of the Royal Society, and lionized by a country in the grip of Pacific fever, he sailed on yet another expedition the following year, 1776, with instructions to solve the last large mystery of that ocean: whether there was an entrance from the north around either America or Siberia. It was his final voyage. Again reaching the Pacific by way of the Indian Ocean, he discovered the Hawaiian islands on his way northward, and after surveying the north-west American coastline up to 70°, where his passage was barred by impenetrable ice, he returned to Hawaii to refit and provision. There, in Kealakekua Bay on 14 February 1779, he was killed by natives in a dispute over thefts from the ship. By then this plain, steady Englishman of infinite resource and the cartographic skills of an artist had surpassed all his contemporaries in Pacific exploration and, in Charles Darwin's phrase, had added a hemisphere to the civilized world. But it is apparent from his journal entries that, like Diderot and other French intellectuals who deplored the European impact on the native peoples of America, he had also seen the other side of the coin and recognized his responsibility for waking the inhabitants of Oceania from a Stone Age slumber to which they could never return.

The settlement of New South Wales, Australia and New Zealand as

British colonies would follow. Before then the British navy made an important advance unconnected with Pacific discovery: the sheathing of ships' hulls with copper as protection against Teredo boring worms in tropical waters. Copper had first come into wide use for this purpose in the early years of the century as new methods of smelting metals, stimulated in England by the wars of Louis XIV, had allowed the production of copper sheet in commercial quantities. By the late 1720s copper sheathing was required by London insurers for merchant vessels trading to West Africa and the Indies.[51] Unfortunately the copper induced severe corrosion of iron hull and rudder fastenings – due to electrolytic action, which was not then understood – and the practice was abandoned.

As the West Indies rose to strategic prominence during the Seven Years War the Admiralty looked at the problem anew, first having the keel of a frigate sheathed with copper, then sheathing three vessels completely. The results were astonishing: not only were the coppered craft impervious to the boring worm, their underwater hulls remained clean and bright and free from marine growth – they not only sailed faster than their non-coppered and encrusted sisters but did not need such frequent docking for cleaning. Nevertheless the corrosion of the hull ironwork was alarming. As a consequence, in 1768 Hawke's Board ordered an experimental sloop built with all underwater fastenings of forged copper instead of iron. This was to prove a satisfactory but expensive solution to the problem. In the meantime the succeeding Board under Sandwich began experimenting with waterproofed brown paper laid over the underwater hull timbers before the copper was applied. The Navy Board controller, the executive head of the dockyards, quickly convinced himself the method was sound, as a result of which in 1778 Sandwich took the extraordinarily bold decision to copper the entire fleet in this way. In terms of ship maintenance it was a huge and costly mistake, as the brown paper did not provide a sufficient seal and after a while ships began literally to fall apart. In strategic terms it was the wrong decision at precisely the right time: in the short term, before the hulls disintegrated, it provided a superiority in speed, ship for ship, that allowed the Royal Navy to survive a period of dangerous numerical inferiority to the combined Bourbon battle fleet.

The War of American Independence
and Chesapeake Bay, 1781

AFTER CHOISEUL'S DISMISSAL in 1770, the splendid navy he had created was mishandled by his successor. Money was saved by running down essential stocks of timber and stores; the officer corps was alienated by administrative 'reforms' on army lines which bore no relation to naval necessities or tradition and proved unworkable.[1] By 1774, when Louis XV died, the service had been crippled. It was rescued by a new Minister of Marine and the Colonies, Antoine de Sartine, appointed in August that year by Louis XVI. At first Sartine was restricted by lack of funds, but as British problems in America worsened, appearing to offer France opportunities of revenge for the last war, the balance of opinion in Louis's innermost council of ministers moved from budgetary and diplomatic restraint towards adventure; the navy budget grew accordingly.

The new policy was signified by the defeat of the Comptroller-General of Finance, Baron Anne Robert Jacques Turgot. He was attempting to reduce Crown debt by strict economy, but his ultimate aim, like that of all his predecessors since the great Colbert, was a complete rationalization of the tax system in order to tap the wealth presently protected by privilege and provincial exemption; it was clearer than ever that without such radical reform France could never exert her full potential nor avoid the financial disasters that crippled her in every war. When a proposal to aid the American rebels in secret was raised in the King's inner circle in March 1776, Turgot argued strongly against: intervention would probably lead to war, which he represented as 'the greatest of evils since it would render impossible for a long time and perhaps for ever a reform [of French finances] absolutely necessary to the prosperity of the state and the relief of its people'. And he warned that a premature use of force risked making French weakness permanent. Perceptively, he suggested that a British victory in America would be the best result for France, since the colonists would have to be held down by force and this would be a constant drain on British resources.[2]

Hitherto Turgot had received powerful support from the foreign minister, the Comte de Vergennes, a career diplomat of long experience who was dedicated to maintaining the peace of Europe by the balance of power. He believed this could best be accomplished through co-operation between Britain and France, the two principal powers with sufficient wealth from colonial trade to subsidize coalitions against Continental rulers attempting to upset the balance. However, he saw no sign of British willingness to co-operate. On the contrary, the old enemy appeared 'a restless and greedy nation . . . powerfully armed and ready to strike at the moment she shall find it expedient', which regarded 'with envious cupidity the prodigious treasure of our plantations in America [the West Indies] and our industry in Europe'.[3]

The analysis was entirely consistent with the history of recent Anglo-French wars and of course with the mercantilist system. Moreover, French trade had grown enormously since the end of the last war and once again rivalled and possibly exceeded that of Great Britain[4] – just the situation in which the last two wars had erupted. The port of Bordeaux, which re-exported colonial produce to the Baltic markets, importing in return Baltic grain, timber, naval stores and textiles, had enjoyed the most spectacular growth; it was now overwhelmingly the largest French port, handling over twice the freight of Marseilles, practically three times that of Nantes or Le Havre/Rouen,[5] its traditional commerce in wines, brandies and manufactured goods overshadowed by West Indian sugar and coffee and commerce in slaves from West Africa. Nantes remained the slaving capital of France, but Bordeaux was second, followed by Le Havre, La Rochelle, Saint-Malo and Honfleur; in all, France's ships carried some 10,000 slaves annually to her West Indian islands.[6] This was considerably fewer than the British carried: in 1771 Liverpool alone had been responsible for transporting 28,000 slaves across the Atlantic, Bristol 9,000 and London 8,000.[7] Nonetheless, French planters in the West Indies, who had to resort to buying slaves illegally from the British or Dutch, had overtaken their British rivals in sugar production inside five years of the end of the Seven Years War.[8]

The whole of this trade on which French commercial growth depended was vulnerable in the Caribbean, the Channel and the North Sea to British naval power. Although the British were preoccupied with the American colonies, and the French ambassador in London reported the government in no political or military condition to fight the Bourbons,[9] Vergennes was no doubt justified in harbouring apprehensions about the designs of British merchants and admirals once the colonists had been brought back to obedience.

His immediate response to the proposal to aid the Americans in secret was positive, principally because of the opportunity offered for weakening Great Britain. His argument was based on the proposition that Britain's trade with North America was basic to her wealth; if France could assist the colonies to break free, it would deprive her of this vital trade and the industries it supported, so reducing the funds – and trained manpower – available for her navy, curtailing her subsidies to Continental allies, diminishing her strength, and radically altering the European balance in France's favour.[10] Such were his stated reasons. Benjamin Franklin, in Paris to enlist French support, did his best to encourage them. Yet the French court was essentially military and dedicated to *la gloire*. The humiliations administered by Pitt in the Seven Years War were still felt bitterly; the desire for vengeance was strong. In addition, sympathy with the American rebels was strong among intellectuals, who tended to see the British colonists as attempting to put into practice their own ideals for a freer, juster society; indeed the author of the proposal to aid the Americans was the popular dramatist, creator of the valet-hero Figaro, propagandist and sometime secret agent Pierre-Augustin Caron de Beaumarchais. Vergennes, for all his long experience and cultured mind, must have been affected by the passions agitating French society. His arguments were surely rationalizations of the prevailing enthusiasm.

Whether he foresaw secret aid leading France into war with Britain, whether he expected merely to damage the British cause without direct involvement is not revealed by his papers. He did not bring up the subject of war before the young king, but it is hard to believe he had any doubts about Britain's response when French shipments to the colonists were discovered, as they must be sooner rather than later. Nor could he have expected the colonists to break free on their own without armed French intervention. And since his argument depended on depriving Great Britain of her colonies and the monopoly rights in their trade, it inevitably implied war.

Aligned with Vergennes in support of the proposal were the navy minister, Sartine, and the senior minister on whom the young king relied most, the seventy-five-year old Comte de Maurepas. Turgot was isolated. He had already raised aristocratic and ecclesiastical fury over his proposed reforms of the tax system, and great rage by attempting to abolish the *corvée* which peasants paid their seigneur, whether aristocratic, ecclesiastical or bourgeois, in lieu of the feudal requirement to provide labour. It is not surprising that Louis, who was not yet twenty-two and lacked self-confidence, decided in favour of Maurepas, Vergennes and secret aid to the Americans, and the same month, May 1776, discarded Turgot. The two decisions which appear so inevitable – Turgot's predecessors under Louis XV having all been dropped after attempting tax reforms – were to determine the success of the American Revolution and lead directly to revolution in France and the end of the Bourbon monarchy.[11] This is clear in retrospect; it is clear Turgot was correct to warn that war would damage French finances irreparably. At the time, the young Louis XVI, his advisers and French society saw only the glorious prospect of humbling the old enemy.

As the King released arms to be sent to America through a fictitious company headed by Beaumarchais, he gave orders to ready twenty of the line in case of British reaction. By August, Sartine had considerably overspent his budget and requested a supplementary grant. Meanwhile Sandwich responded to his spies' reports of activity at Brest and Toulon by increasing the number of 'guardships' manned with three-fifths crews – as a nucleus to counter France's ability to mobilize more rapidly – and ordered a press to bring their complements up to full strength.

In America a Naval Committee appointed by the Continental Congress had established the beginnings of a Continental Navy by buying and arming two sizeable merchantmen and several smaller brigs, schooners and sloops, and commissioning merchant captains or army officers to command. The committee had also authorized the construction of thirteen frigates and numerous smaller warships. The designers and shipyards chosen had all the necessary skills; those frigates which were completed were larger, class for class, and generally faster than British frigates of their rate.[12] Yet the difficulties of arming them, finding experienced officers and trained crews, getting them to sea through the British blockade and deploying them without bases or supply organization had scarcely been addressed in the committee's initial enthusiasm. The programme, like a subsequent programme of November 1776 for three 74-gun ships of the line and a further five frigates, was wildly over-optimistic and counter-productive. Many vessels never reached the sea; of those that did, most were destroyed or captured and taken into the Royal Navy. One such, built at Newburyport, Massachusetts, the 32-gun *Hancock* – renamed *Iris* under British colours – made fortunes in prize money for her British officers, who described her as 'the finest and fastest frigate in the world'.[13]

The smaller vessels acquired by purchase were a sounder investment. Their commanders, instructed to intercept enemy supply vessels and avoid engaging warships, were rewarded with a third of the prize money from captures, to be divided among officers and crews in specific shares.[14] They and numerous privateers operating from creeks and rivers brought in scores of British storeships and victuallers to provide valuable supplies for Washington's army.[15] However the main source of arms in this period were Dutch merchants, via their West Indian depots, principally St Eustatius. Apart from desire for profit, feeling in the United Provinces was running as strongly in favour of the Americans as in France, and for largely similar reasons. In February 1777 the British ambassador at The Hague demanded from the States General immediate action to stop the flow of munitions, failing which the British navy would adopt an unrestricted policy of boarding and seizure. The ultimatum further inflamed opinion against Britain's 'arrogance and tyranny',[16] and the young stadtholder, William V, despite pro-British sympathies, authorized a naval programme for the defence of Dutch shipping.

In March the first four of Beaumarchais's munitions ships sailed for America. It was now clear that war between Britain and France could not long be delayed and might be sparked by any incident. The British government was particularly incensed that American privateers were using French ports as bases from which to prey on trade around the British Isles and French vessels with French crews were being prepared to join the war under American commanders. Intelligence from spies indicated other French ships loading in Biscay ports with muskets, swords, ammunition and uniforms for America and other manufactured goods and commodities the rebels could no longer obtain from Britain.[17] British cruisers haunted the French coast on the lookout for these munitions ships and privateers, and seized suspect vessels; French ships of the line patrolled in pairs to protect their merchantmen.

In January that year, 1777, Vergennes had asked the Spanish government to submit plans for combined operations in case of war with Great Britain. In July he sent a similar, more detailed, request.[18] The Spanish, anxious as ever about the safe return of their Mexican treasure fleet, refused to commit themselves. Whether Louis's inner council had already made a definite decision for war, as seems most probable, events had acquired an irresistible momentum. Vergennes could scarcely turn back. Apart from the imminent likelihood of incidents at sea leading to conflict, Sartine had spent more than 100 million *livres* (£4 million) above normal expenditure readying the fleet and laying in stocks of timber and naval stores.[19] And it was more than ever apparent that the Americans could not win independence without direct assistance; this remained true even after news arrived in early December of an American victory over a British force of some 7,000 men at Saratoga on the upper Hudson river. On the other hand, Sartine's efforts had opened the prospect that a battle fleet almost equal in numbers to the British fleet in commission could be got to sea in the following spring, 1778. Britain had greater reserves and more ships under construction, but these would take months to bring forward and man. In the meantime France could take the initiative at sea.

Franklin and the American commissioners in Paris had been offering trade in return for a military alliance that would bring France into the war. After news of Saratoga, they tried to force the issue by suggesting that Congress might patch up a compromise peace with the British. Vergennes was not deceived; yet he was committed to his policy and, despite another rebuff from Spain, on 6 February 1778 France signed a Treaty of Amity and Commerce and entered into a defensive alliance with the Americans. Vergennes was so focused on the naval war this must provoke, and like Choiseul earlier so mindful of France's repeated failures against Great Britain, that he ignored a dispute that had broken out between Austria and Prussia over the control of Bavaria, whose Elector had died that January without heir. The outcome could alter the balance of power within Germany, yet he averted his eyes, concentrating on his goal, the removal of Britain's grip on North America, so much had the explosive growth in Atlantic trade and Great Britain's rise to maritime dominance affected France's fundamental drives as a Continental power.

In London the response to the Bourbon threat had been as muddled as the attempts to subdue the rebel colonists. This was due in large measure to the system of government. Each minister was responsible to the king – the executive – and ran his own departmental policy with little regard to other departments, often in conflict with them. The First Lord of the Treasury, who headed the government and managed the House of Commons, acted in Cabinet discussions as chairman rather than prime minister and had no power to enforce collective policy. If he lacked the qualities of decision and ruthlessness necessary above all in war, the results were inevitably muddle and drift. North recognized this and his own temperamental inadequacy, and suggested the King replace him with 'one directing minister, who should plan the whole of the operation of government, & controul all the other departments of administration so far as to make them co-operate zealously & actively'.[20] His advice was not heeded. 'Government by departments', as North described it, continued.

The minister with responsibility for the war in America was the Secretary of State for the Colonies, Lord George Germain. His dealings with Sandwich at the Admiralty were crucial, since the warships of the North American squadron were playing a vital role in support of army operations in addition to (and detracting from) their basic duties of blockading the coast and protecting essential supply shipping from the American navy gun vessels and privateers. Relations between the two were difficult, not least because Sandwich was more concerned with the Bourbon naval build-up than with events in the colonies; he had long concluded that France and Spain were 'at bottom our inveterate enemies . . . only waiting for the favourite moment to strike the blow'.[21] Misunderstanding was compounded by Germain's ambitious and devious nature; his warped handling of his officials and officers had led to a chain of military blunders in America, most recently the disaster at Saratoga.[22]

Directly news of the French–American treaty reached London, in March 1778, the entire complexion of affairs altered: imminent war with France – perhaps joined by Spain – became the overriding concern; America was reduced to a 'secondary consideration'.[23] For the Admiralty the situation was highly alarming. The strategy of containing the Brest fleet with a western squadron off Ushant, as perfected by Hawke in the Seven Years War, could not prevent ships from Toulon sailing to America, where they might overwhelm the British squadron there and land sufficient forces to decide the colonial war. Yet Sandwich could not send a squadron into the Mediterranean to contain the Toulon force without exposing it to a possible Franco-Spanish combination; nor did he have the ships to do so without fatally weakening the home fleet; as yet there were barely twenty of the line in commission, with a further twenty preparing for sea, while his intelligence suggested that France and Spain between them would soon have 'upwards of 70 sail' ready for sea.[24]

In April a squadron of eleven of the line sailed from Toulon. It was assumed in the British Cabinet that the ships were bound for America, and Sandwich came under pressure from Germain to dispatch a powerful force after them. He resisted until early June, when reports from two shadowing frigates indicated the French were far across the Atlantic; then he detached thirteen of the line to follow them. It was too late. Nevertheless the British squadron on the North American station baffled the heavier French force by taking a defensive position in shoal water inside Sandy Hook off New York. The French left to blockade the British garrison at Rhode Island.

By this time the Brest fleet had sailed under the Comte d'Orvilliers, a noted tactician, and Louis XVI had formally declared war. Spain remained neutral, but her fleet of twenty-eight of the line in commission could not be excluded from calculation.[25] The British home fleet under Admiral Augustus Keppel put to sea soon after d'Orvilliers in inferior numbers, twenty-four against thirty-two of the line. In the following days six more British liners joined and two French ships parted from d'Orvilliers, so that when on 23 July the fleets came in sight of one another seventy miles west of Ushant they were in equal strength. D'Orvilliers's mission was to capture British trade, not to seek battle, and, as he had the advantage of the wind, Keppel was unable to bring him to action until the 27th, when the fleets exchanged broadsides while sailing past each other on opposite tacks. In the night after this damaging but indecisive encounter d'Orvilliers succeeded in withdrawing and returning to Brest. Keppel, exasperated by his failure to hold the French to action, put back to Plymouth.

He sailed again on 23 August, after learning that d'Orvilliers had put out with twenty-seven of the line, but, despite searching off Ushant, into Biscay and across the Channel approaches on the track of homeward trade, he could find no sign of the French fleet. It is an indication of the still unsolved problem of scurvy that by 8 September Keppel was reporting sickness in his ships and recommending to Sandwich that 'if the health of the people is considered an object . . . no fleet of large numbers should ever be above six or seven weeks at sea'.[26] D'Orvilliers avoided him and entered Brest on the 18th. Keppel somehow kept the sea until the end of October.

The campaign ended with Vergennes and Sartine denied the success they might have expected from their strategic initiative at the start. Keppel had covered all important homecoming convoys, and in American waters the British had regained superiority directly the reinforcing squadron arrived. In November the French squadron in America sailed for the West Indies, followed by the British, who then captured the small island of St Lucia as a watching station off the main French naval base at Martinique. It could be argued that Vergennes had been fortunate: Sandwich, who was keenly aware that Brest was the hinge of strategy for both sides and had written to Keppel that 'defeating the Brest fleet . . . would have most amazing consequences to this country',[27] might have retained all ships at home instead of sending the powerful detachment to America; in which case Keppel would have had an overwhelming superiority off Ushant.[28] However it would have been a bold decision to abandon America for the chance of a decisive fleet action, and it is certain d'Orvilliers would not have been sent out against such odds.[29] Nor would a closer blockage of Brest have achieved much more than Keppel did achieve.

Now that France had lost the advantage of surprise and early mobilization, Sartine could not hope to keep pace with the ships Britain would bring forward. Vergennes advised Louis he could not struggle long on equal terms with the English 'and that a prolonged war . . . could entertain the ruin of his [Majesty's] navy and even his finances'; he urged him, therefore, to pay any price to bring in Spain.[30] Louis agreed, and after intense negotiations a convention was signed between the two Bourbon powers on 12 April 1779, formally activating the terms of the Family Compact. Spain's chief objectives were the recovery of Gibraltar, Minorca and Florida; the price Vergennes had to pay was a strategy centred on the English Channel instead of America. The agreed war plans provided for a combined fleet of thirty French and twenty Spanish ships of the line – with additional Spanish ships if necessary to bring the allied superiority up to four to three – to cover an expeditionary force to seize the Isle of Wight and bombard Portsmouth and ships inside the harbour and in Spithead.

The Brest fleet left for the rendezvous at Corunna in early June, almost a fortnight before the British home fleet, now under Admiral Sir Charles Hardy, put to sea. The Spanish at Cadiz were delayed by adverse winds, and it was not until the end of July that the combined Bourbon fleet steered north for the Channel. By this time the Spanish had insisted on increasing the size of the expeditionary force and changing the objective to Falmouth, from where the major base of Plymouth could be taken and held as hostage for the return of Gibraltar. Since the troops were camped at Le Havre and Saint-Malo, the plans were impractical. Nevertheless, the combined fleet was sixty-six strong against thirty-nine under Hardy, and Sandwich was extremely apprehensive about both the threatened invasion and political dangers at home. He constantly urged Hardy to keep the sea and seek out the enemy: 'I dread the thoughts of your coming into port; for believe me . . . your enemies and mine are watching to take every advantage of us.'[31] In the event the fleets did not sight one another until 31 August, off the western tip of Cornwall. Hardy was to leeward and made away easterly, as he explained to Sandwich 'to draw them up-Channel',[32] coming to anchor in Spithead on 3 September. By this time the French crews were depleted by the usual sickness, which had spread to the Spanish ships, and the following week the combined fleet put back to Brest.

Sandwich had had an enormous scare – unlike George III, who expressed complete confidence in the outcome of a fleet action whatever the odds – but again Vergennes had been denied the success he should have expected for such numerical superiority, and again no important British convoys had been taken. The chances of wind and weather, the difficulties of forcing action on an enemy at sea, the restricted time ships could keep the sea before their companies started falling down with scurvy had, as so many times in the past, saved the island nation; although, even if the fleets had engaged, it is unlikely that the French and Spanish could have co-ordinated their efforts sufficiently to crush Hardy's powerful fleet headed by nine three-deckers mounting from 90 to 100 guns, and even more doubtful if they could have emerged from the encounter in a condition to escort troop transports across the Channel.

Towards the end of September the American navy acquired its first legend. John Paul Jones, one of the American commanders preying on British shipping from French ports, intercepted a Baltic convoy in the North Sea. He was leading a small Franco-American squadron including a new American 36-gun frigate, *Alliance*, built on the Merrimack river, Massachusetts. His own pendant flew from an Indiaman purchased for him by the French Ministry of Marine and renamed *Bon*

Homme Richard as a compliment to his patron, Benjamin Franklin, who used the pseudonym Richard Saunders; he had converted her with much difficulty and armed her with forty-two guns. Two Royal Navy warships escorting the convoy covered the escape of their charges, then turned on Jones's squadron, the senior officer's ship, the frigate *Serapis*, taking on the *Bon Homme Richard*, raking her, then grappling. Jones's men repelled the British boarding party, after which the ships fought a gun duel, muzzle to muzzle. The *Alliance*, commanded by a French naval officer who had sailed to America to volunteer for the new navy two years earlier, joined in, but her shot did more damage to the *Bon Homme Richard* than to the *Serapis*. After some two hours, by which time Jones's ship was riddled, all but two of his guns knocked out and 150 of his crew killed or wounded, a fire broke out aboard the *Serapis*, forcing her commander to haul down her flag. The other British escort also struck her colours.

The action had no strategic significance, and Jones and his surviving men were forced to transfer to his prize two days later, leaving the shattered *Bon Homme Richard* to sink, but the exceptional ferocity of the contest, his refusal to submit and his capture of two Royal Navy escorts raised him to international fame. Louis XVI made him a Chevalier of France, and he was later awarded a congressional gold medal. The son of a gardener on a Scottish estate, one-time master of a slave ship, who had fled to Virginia to escape trial after killing a mutinous sailor, John Paul Jones was much more than an inspirational fighter with an unerring seaman's eye: he was a thinking officer and an ardent champion of sea power for the emerging nation he had adopted, a fitting hero for the new navy.

ALTHOUGH VERGENNES HAD been disappointed in the Channel in 1779, he could be satisfied with results in the West Indies. Stung by the loss of St Lucia, Louis's war council, in which he played the leading role, had ordered a great supply and troop convoy to Martinique; with these reinforcements the French had taken the British island of St Vincent, then Grenada, second only to Jamaica in sugar production. When news reached London that autumn, George III wrote to Sandwich, 'If we lose our sugar islands, it will be impossible to raise money to continue the war', and insisted, 'the islands must be defended, even at the risk of an invasion of this island'.[33]

Sandwich needed no reminder. He admitted to the Cabinet that when it came to Jamaica he spoke 'with trembling'. Spain had ships of the line at Havana, Cuba, 'and as to land forces, what the French have at St Domingo [Saint-Domingue] will . . . be more than sufficient to take Jamaica . . . Indeed I am in constant apprehension of hearing that the blow is already struck.'[34] The problem was that Jamaica lay close downwind of Cuba and Saint-Domingue, at the west, French, end of Hispaniola, but nearly 1,000 miles – ten days' sailing[35] – from the Leeward Islands station where the British squadron of twenty-two of the line watched the French squadron of approximately equal force based on Martinique. Meanwhile in Europe the home fleet could not prevent reinforcements sailing across the Atlantic for the West Indies or America – or indeed India – and Gibraltar and Port Mahón, Minorca, were under siege and naval blockade. Detachments made to relieve the situation in the Mediterranean, West Indies or North America, where it was feared the French West Indies squadron would head, could not leave the home fleet so reduced as to be 'unable to resist the united efforts of the House of Bourbon in these seas'.

Sandwich itemized for the Cabinet the number of ships of the line he hoped to have available by the following spring, 1780; the total came to between eighty-five and ninety. He went on:

> It will be asked why, when we have as great if not a greater force than ever we had, the enemy are superior to us. To this it is to be answered that England till this time was never engaged in a sea war with the House of Bourbon thoroughly united, their naval force unbroken, and having no other war or object to draw off their attention and resources. We unfortunately have an additional war on our hands, which essentially drains our finances and employs a very considerable part of the our army and navy; we have no one friend or ally to assist us; on the contrary all those who ought to be our allies except Portugal act against us in supplying our enemies with the means of equipping their fleets.[36]

This was the nub of the problem for the British government and the measure of Vergennes's genius, that he had drawn the lesson from history and succeeded in isolating Great Britain. The position was worse even than Sandwich represented: British efforts to prevent the Bourbon powers receiving supplies – especially timber and naval stores – by stopping, searching and often seizing ships on the high seas were driving the

Dutch towards open hostility and the Baltic nations into an 'Armed Neutrality' to protect their interests. Britain was utterly alone.

Sandwich ended his exposition to the Cabinet by saying he was 'not yet inclined to despair; if we manage the force we have with prudence, our case does not appear to me yet to be desperate'.[37] One factor behind his cautious optimism was the advantage expected from coppering the bottoms of the entire fleet. A recent memo from the Navy Board controller had suggested that 'When the whole of the Western Squadron is coppered it may defy the power of France and Spain',[38] by which he meant the extra speed gained would allow the squadron to shadow the combined fleet without fear of being brought to action if the odds were too great, or on the other hand to force action if desired. To the controller, coppering appeared to be 'at this critical period the means which Providence has put into our power to extricate us from present danger . . . It is actually more than doubling our number of ships.'[39] The Royal Navy was ahead in coppering – and likely to remain so, since the country had taken an early lead in coke-fired smelting at the beginning of the century and was far ahead in the use of steam-powered machinery. Rolled copper plates could be produced in sufficient quantity only in Britain; France and Spain could acquire them only through Dutch agents, and already shipments to the United Provinces had been seized.

Another invention stemming from Britain's industrial lead was the carronade, a very short, light but large-bored gun manufactured by the Carron Ironworks of Falkirk, Scotland. The secret of the piece was more accurate engineering, which allowed the ball to fit more snugly in the bore without jamming; since less of the explosion gases could escape around the ball, a smaller charge was used, hence the containing metalwork was lighter. A carronade throwing a 32-pound ball, as thrown from the main battery of a first rate, was only four feet in length and weighed 17 hundredweight against some 65 hundredweight for a 32-pounder cannon. Consequently the pieces could be mounted on the upper decks in place of small-bore cannon, increasing the weight of shot fourfold. They were ineffective at long range, but in the close actions the British strove to achieve they were to prove murderously efficient, especially when firing grapeshot or the jagged pieces of metal to cut rigging and kill men known as langridge. The controller wrote to Sandwich that September, 1779, suggesting that 40-gun ships could be brought into the line of battle by equipping them with 32-pounder carronades. He continued, 'The supplying all the ships now fitting with their proper number of these guns, and the whole during the winter with langridge is likewise increasing our power.'[40]

Despite the great fleet and the high proportion of coppered ships Sandwich expected by the following spring, he does not seem to have considered applying his whole effort off the enemy bases to prevent their fleets combining, so strangling and finally crushing their power by decisive fleet action off their own coasts, as in past wars. No doubt the danger to Jamaica and the other British West Indian islands and the need to maintain supply lines over 3,000 miles to the forces in North America seemed to preclude such a strategy; probably he believed there was a shorter way. His final words to the September 1779 Cabinet suggest this: 'we ought in my opinion to husband our strength, and to employ it only on those services which are of the most importance and that have a probability of being attended with success'.[41]

One such was the relief of Gibraltar and Minorca, but the main thrust he proposed, as Pitt had, was the capture of Martinique, the main French naval base and sugar island, whose loss would affect France's entire position in the West Indies and, as he judged, 'probably put an end to the war'. The plan was approved, although in the event Puerto Rico was substituted for Martinique.

For command of the dual expedition he selected Admiral Sir George Rodney, an aggressive fighter and superlative fleet handler, although tarred with a reputation for more blatant greed and dishonesty over prize and other money matters than officers usually betrayed. To control him on this score, Sandwich sent out a commissioner to handle all purchases. Rodney sailed towards the end of December with twenty-two of the line and an armada of supply ships and troop transports. Those destined for the West Indies parted after the fleet cleared the danger zone for French cruisers; Rodney continued southward well to seaward of coastal traffic with the ships for Gibraltar and Minorca. On 8 January 1780 he captured a Spanish convoy loaded with naval stores for Cadiz and the 64-gun escort, and eight days later, rounding Cape St Vincent, he surprised a Spanish blockading squadron of nine of the line, which bore away from him under all sail.

On hoisting his flag, Rodney had made his own additions and amendments to the fighting instructions; the last one modified Anson's and Hawke's signal for 'general chase' by directing each ship to engage from the lee side and not to quit her opponent until she struck.[42] The French doctrine of accomplishing the mission rather than defeating the enemy fleet, the French commanders' tendency to lask away to leeward, firing high to damage masts and rigging, had led Rodney to the conclusion that, especially when chasing, the only way to hold the French from escape downwind was to seek the lee berth himself. Regarding the Spanish in the same light, he now made this new signal. The wind was high, the day closing in as his fastest copper-bottomed ships stretched towards the uncoppered enemy and the Spanish shore beyond, but he was appalled that the captains scrambled into action pell-mell, paying no heed to the signal. Had they done so, he believed they could have taken the whole squadron. As it was, four ships of the line, including the enemy flagship, were captured that night, and one blew up. What became known as the Moonlight Battle was the first great success of the war, achieved with splendid seamanship in wild conditions off a lee shore, and in his public dispatches Rodney praised his officers, revealing his disappointment only to his wife;[43] to Sandwich he wrote, 'as I told your Lordship, when the British fleet take the lee gage, the enemy cannot escape. This event has proved it, and I am fully convinced that every ship of the enemy struck and would have been taken possession of had the weather permitted.'[44]

He supplied Gibraltar and Minorca with two years' provisions without interference from the Spanish fleet in Cadiz, then, leaving the main body to sail for home, in mid-February he parted with four of the line to take up his command in the West Indies. To the north of him, Lieutenant General the Comte de Guichen with seventeen of the line and a great convoy of supply and troop transports from Brest was heading in the same direction. De Guichen arrived at Martinique on 22 March, Rodney at St Lucia just to the south on 1 April. With the ships already on station, each commander had twenty-three of the line, and during the next two months they engaged in a series of manoeuvres and engagements off Martinique during which Rodney attempted to force a decisive battle and de Guichen, who had troops aboard for an invasion of the British island of Barbados, attempted to avoid one.

During the first action, on 17 April, the French line was so loosely formed that Rodney, who had the weather gage, aimed to bring his entire force against the French centre and rear to crush them before the van could come to their aid. However, his signals were easily capable of mis-interpretation, and the commanders of his van squadron and his own van division, supposing he intended a traditional line battle with each ship engaging her opposite number, stretched ahead to get up with the enemy van. To Rodney this was 'barefaced disobedience to orders and signals'.[45] To make matters worse, when his own centre was heavily engaged the admiral commanding his rear wore round without orders after a part of the enemy rear. Rodney's intentions and the skilful approach he had made were entirely frustrated, and what could have been a crucial victory turned into an indecisive line encounter. Thereafter he drilled the fleet with increased rigour and in action shifted his flag to a frigate on the unengaged side of the centre, the better to see precisely what every captain was doing. He warned them that those who failed to obey his instructions to the letter would be instantly superseded.[46]

The contests ended in a draw nonetheless, de Guichen unable to take Barbados, Rodney unable to defeat him, recapture the lost British islands or attack Puerto Rico. Rodney attributed his frustrations to disobedience and ill discipline, and even suggested to Sandwich that certain officers deliberately thwarted him and threw away the chance of victory because of their political attachment to his enemies.[47] Certainly the officer corps was riven by party faction, and several senior officers were so opposed to fighting the Americans that they refused to take up seagoing commands. Nonetheless, the root cause of Rodney's difficulties lay in the signalling system, which had scarcely changed from the previous century. Numerous striped, quartered and multicoloured flags and pendants, many almost impossible to distinguish from a distance, were used to indicate articles in the printed Admiralty fighting instructions. As in the earliest days, the meaning of the signals depended not on the flags alone but on the position from which they were flown; consequently signals could not always be shown from the most visible part of the flagship's rigging.[48] There were no official signal books, and the significance of the hoist, once made out, had to be unravelled from the often wordy article referred to. Had officers not compiled their own manuscript signal books, fleets could hardly have been manoeuvred.

The chances of mistakes and misinterpretations were increased by the different additional instructions, signals and flags used by different commanders-in-chief. On the North American station at the start of the war, Lord Howe, the most able tactician of the day, had produced the first true signal book, in which the flag hoists referred not to the Admiralty instructions but to his own often new instructions contained in an accompanying book. Another tactical innovator, Richard Kempenfelt, served as Captain of the Fleet or Chief of Staff to successive admirals commanding the home fleet from 1779. In his first season he issued scores of new signals and instructions and new designs of flags, but in 1780 he adopted Howe's concept of a signal book and accompanying instructions, and radically reduced the number of flags used to twenty-seven, with seven pendants.

The French service had undergone a similar period of tactical and signalling experimentation during Choiseul's time. Most emphasis had been placed on tight control of the line in battle. In the semi-official manual of evolutions and signals, written by the Comte de Morogues, who had experienced the devastating effects of British close-range fire while commanding the rear French ship, *Magnifique*, at Quiberon Bay, all captains were enjoined to direct their chief care and attention to 'keeping close in line in proper position, where all are mutually to support one another; and by their firm, impenetrable union be the better able to resist the efforts of the enemy'.[49] A special Escadre d'Evolutions had been formed to drill commanders in formal line manoeuvres. These were deprecated by a later French naval historian as more akin to quadrilles than to naval engagements, but they were effective in subsequent engagements.[50]

The French signalling system, hitherto employing thirty-four flags and six pendants flown from seven possible positions,[51] had also been reformed. A senior admiral, the Chevalier du Pavillon, had devised a scheme whereby numbers, each denoting a fighting instruction, were set out together with a few words summarizing the instruction referred to in a table with ten columns and ten lines, thus 100 squares. Each column had a different signal flag painted above, each line had a flag denoted at the left side; consequently with two-flag hoists – the upper flag denoting the column, the lower the line – 100 different instructions could be signalled. A pure numerical system using ten flags denoting the numerals nought to nine, thus capable with three-flag hoists of sending hundreds of instructions in the simplest, most accessible form, had already been invented and published by a French East India Company officer.[52] Had this been adopted it would have anticipated the kind of system to which all navies would eventually turn. As it was, even Pavillon's complex numerical–tabular system marked a distinct advance on previous methods.

A young British officer on the North American station developed a scheme like Pavillon's in 1777 and, although Howe did not adopt it then, Kempenfelt included a similar tabular system as an alternative to the conventional signals used by the home fleet in 1780.[53] However, without an authorized method, British signalling and tactics were in flux.[54] The most aggressive, thinking commanders like Howe and Rodney were attempting to devise means of tying the French in to close action, very conscious, like Morogues, of the prime importance of maintaining their own line, yet producing very different solutions. It was a confusing time, especially for the majority of officers, characterized by Admiral Vernon as despising theory and trusting rather to their own splendid instincts,[55] and it was about to lead to the most significant tactical misunderstanding of the war.

IN NORTH AMERICA the British had taken three of the great seaport cities at the outset of the struggle. French entry into the war, specifically the approach of the Toulon squadron in 1778, had led to the abandonment of Philadelphia; and in 1779, when the French squadron returned to the American coast from the West Indies, the British abandoned Newport, Rhode Island, to concentrate the army on New York. By this time the British Cabinet had altered the focus of land strategy from New England to the south, where there was much loyalist sentiment, and towards the end of that year, after the French squadron had sailed for home, a great expedition had been launched by sea from New York to lay siege to Charleston, South Carolina. On 12 May 1780, as Rodney sparred with de Guichen off Martinique, Charleston surrendered, and with it some 5,000 American troops, 400 cannon, three of the newly constructed frigates, and numerous lesser warships and privateers.

For Sandwich, the American campaign with its long ocean supply line remained a dangerous diversion of resources from home waters and the West Indies, where the struggle with the Bourbons would be decided. Nevertheless the enemy's ability to transfer squadrons and troops with comparative ease between the West Indies and North America meant that the American station could not simply be abandoned. Nor would Germain allow it. Success at Charleston and the sorry financial state to which the Americans had been reduced by four years' interruption to trade and heavy armaments expenditure allowed him to talk up the prospect of imminent success over the rebels – and with it his own importance in Cabinet.[56] Had Sandwich been able to isolate America, the colonists' position would have been hopeless. But there were still too few ships to divide between Brest and Cadiz/Toulon and match enemy strength in the West Indies. Moreover, in spring 1780 the home fleet was refitting after the expedition to relieve Gibraltar and Minorca. With no means of controlling the waters around enemy fleet bases, Sandwich could only attempt to maintain the local balances overseas by sending out detachments to match the squadrons France and Spain dispatched. He managed this successfully through 1780, but at the cost of continued inferiority in home waters and the loss of an important homeward-bound convoy to the combined fleet. The fighting efficiency of the Franco-Spanish force was not, however, tested in a general action.

Towards the end of that year the Dutch applied to join the Armed Neutrality formed by the Baltic powers to protect neutral trade from British interference. At much the same time, further details emerged in London of the extent to which the American rebellion had been assisted by the financiers and merchants of Amsterdam, and in December Great Britain declared war on the United Provinces. While this added another power and another battle squadron of nominally twenty-five of the line[57] – chiefly smaller rates – to Britain's enemies, and required a further detachment of warships from the home fleet to provide a sufficiently powerful North Sea squadron to protect the vital Baltic trade, it offered immediate gains. Rodney in the West Indies was directed to seize the Dutch islands from which the Americans received a large proportion of their supplies, and at home cruisers and privateers snapped up Dutch shipping. In January 1781 some 200 vessels were captured and Dutch trade was brought to a standstill.[58]

In early February Rodney surprised the principal Dutch trading island, St Eustatius, with 150 sail in the roadstead and also captured a convoy of some thirty large vessels which had recently sailed thence for Amsterdam. The coup promised a fortune beyond avarice, but, viewing the stone-built warehouses stretching a mile along the shore and the goods stacked high on the beach before them, he reported the seizure as 'a blow in its consequences that cannot but be most sensibly felt by the Enemy as it has hitherto been the source of most essential succour to them'.[59] He was bitter about British merchants and factors living on the island as Dutchmen, who facilitated this trade with the enemy. Meanwhile, on the West African coast all but one of the Dutch WIC slave-trading forts fell into British hands, and Dutch factories in India and Ceylon and numerous VOC ships were seized in the East. For the former leading naval and commercial power, the war with its long-time maritime ally was an unqualified disaster which was to lead quite soon to revolution.

While Great Britain reaped short-term rewards, her situation in 1781 was the most critical she had ever faced; it even seemed possible Russia might join her enemies, and in Cabinet that January Sandwich painted a stark picture of the consequences should that happen and the country stood 'in actual war with the whole world. I speak here only of those Powers that have any naval force, but among those on the Continent I fear we have no friend that is able or willing to step forth in support of our cause, and it is well known that we have among them some very powerful and eager enemies.'[60] He suggested that the country's finances were exhausted – certainly the national debt had climbed high above the peak reached in the previous war[61] – and that the only way out of their difficulties was to placate Russia by ceding her Minorca; failing this, he foresaw the complete dismemberment of the British empire and over-seas bases and the end of Great Britain's role as a leading power.

Vergennes had recently weathered an equally critical period. The Spanish government, burdened with debt and famine, had announced it was capable of only one more campaign and demanded a gigantic expedition against Jamaica as the sole means of cutting through the deadlock in the western hemisphere and bringing the war to a success-ful conclusion; otherwise Spain would have to seek a separate peace. France's finances were hardly in better shape, and the expedition pro-posed was beyond her resources. Vergennes had, however, managed to secure a compromise: France would send twenty of the line to the West Indies to attack St Lucia, so providing a diversion for whatever Spain wished to attempt at the other end of the Caribbean.[62]

The crisis with Spain, together with debts run up by the navy since the start of the American rebellion, led to the dismissal of Sartine, one of Vergennes's principal allies in the inner council. Once again the extraordinary costs of setting out a great fleet and overseas squadrons – now running at 160 million *livres*, or some £7 million, a year against British naval expenditure of about £9 million a year[63] – had been meas-ured against failure to achieve victory in battle. Sartine was succeeded by the Marquis de Castries, an army general.

To lead the squadron for the West Indies Castries chose Lieutenant General the Comte de Grasse, despite his having just returned in poor health from two campaigning seasons in that theatre, latterly under de Guichen. It was a fateful choice: de Grasse would virtually decide the outcome of the war in America.

He was fifty-one years old, over six feet tall, and considered one of the handsomest men of his time; he was also a thoroughly schooled and battle-hardened professional, who had begun his career at the age of eleven in the naval seminary for noblemen at Toulon. As an ensign, or midshipman, he had been seriously wounded in the bloody action in defence of a convoy against Anson's western squadron in 1747. The captain of his 40-gun ship had been decapitated by a ball and seventy-five men had been killed before the colours had been struck. In the peace before the present war he had commanded a vessel in d'Orvilliers's Escadre d'Evolutions and earned d'Orvilliers's commendation as the most skilled captain in the squadron. That he had collided frequently with other vessels was cited as a mark of confidence: 'I shall always choose the captains who prefer to risk a collision rather than abandon their position with the certainty of failing to execute a movement,' d'Orvilliers had written.[64] Despite his experience in the training squadron, de Grasse did not adopt Pavillon's numerical–tabular signalling system when he took command of the squadron for the West Indies.

He sailed from Brest on 22 March 1781 with twenty of the line, twelve of them coppered, a convoy of merchantmen and smaller detachments of warships in company who would part for the Cape of Good Hope to protect the Dutch colony there, and for India. Fortunately for this great concourse of shipping there were no watching British cruisers and the British home fleet of twenty-eight of the line, which had put to sea for another winter mission to resupply Gibraltar and Minorca, was waiting off the Irish coast for supply ships from Cork. De Grasse cleared the soundings without challenge. Subsequently, after the British home fleet had passed southward, a commerce-raiding squadron of six of the line together with frigates and smaller craft put out from Brest to cruise in the Channel approaches. They surprised the convoy of Dutch prizes Rodney had sent home from St Eustatius, captured over half of them, and put back to Brest just before the British fleet returned from supplying the beleaguered garrisons. Meanwhile, towards the end of April de Grasse had reached Martinique and shepherded his convoy into Fort Royal harbour. Again he enjoyed good fortune, since Rodney had remained at St Eustatius with four of the line refitting after storm damage, and Rear Admiral Sir Samuel Hood, who was awaiting the arrival of the French with a reduced British squadron, was prevented by fluky winds from forcing a close action.

De Grasse embarked troops and sailed again on 8 May, dividing his force to attack both St Lucia and Tobago. The garrison at St Lucia held out, so, expecting Hood's appearance, he concentrated all his force on Tobago, which surrendered on 2 June. From there he put back for Martinique, on the way sighting Rodney, now back with his squadron. Again he was fortunate: evening was approaching, and Rodney decided against attack for fear of being drawn to leeward into a position from which he would be unable to defend Barbados. He therefore passed on to that island, leaving de Grasse to continue to Martinique, where he collected the homeward-bound merchantmen and sailed for Cap-François (Cap-Haïtien), Saint-Domingue, arriving on 16 July.

The orders he had received from Castries before leaving Brest directed him, after his diversionary campaign in the West Indies, to liaise with the Spanish and leave a detachment of ships of the line with them – no more than twelve to fourteen – before taking the rest of his squadron to North America to relieve a French squadron which had arrived the previous year and was blockaded at Newport, Rhode Island. On passage across the Atlantic he had dispatched a message to the Comte de Rochambeau, commanding 6,000 troops who had arrived in America with the French squadron, notifying him he would be at Saint-Domingue at the end of June and requesting pilots for the American coast.

The pilots now arrived in the frigate *Concorde* from Newport, together with dispatches on the situation in America from Rochambeau, the Comte de Barras, who commanded the French squadron, and the French ambassador, La Luzerne. Although Rochambeau had earlier agreed with Washington that they would probe the defences of New York and de Grasse should bring his squadron there in support, the dispatches were most concerned with the desperate situation of the Americans in the south. After the capture of Charleston the previous year, a part of the British force had marched inland under Lord Cornwallis, defeated the southern American army in August, and subsequently fought its way north against guerrilla attacks into Virginia and established a base at Yorktown, where the river York broadened into Chesapeake Bay. There Cornwallis was faced by a colonial corps under the Marquis de Lafayette, the most celebrated of the French volunteers to join the American cause before France entered the war. Lafayette was camped higher up the York river, at the fork of the Pamunkey and Mattaponi rivers. The crucial factor, as indeed throughout the war, was naval force: that side would triumph which could reinforce and supply its own army while denying the same to the enemy. La Luzerne was especially anxious, suggesting to de Grasse, 'It is you alone who can deliver the invaded provinces from that crisis which is so alarming it appears to me there is no time to lose.'[65]

After reading the dispatches, de Grasse made the momentous decision not simply to sail to the Chesapeake rather than New York, but to take his entire squadron, leaving no part for the Spanish and only one ship of the line to escort the homeward trade he had brought to Cap-François. He was aided by the Spanish authorities. Without the active encouragement of the Spanish military commander, who agreed to release all French ships and French troops which had been placed at his disposal, and of the Spanish admiral, who agreed to move a covering force to Cap-François, he could scarcely have interpreted his orders so flexibly.[66] For his part de Grasse promised to return to the West Indies in November and send all the forces he could to aid the Spanish in attacking Jamaica the following spring.

On 28 July he wrote to Barras, commanding the squadron in Newport, to inform him of his decision to make for the Chesapeake, and eight days later he weighed with twenty-eight of the line carrying 3,300 troops. On 11 August, while he was still on his way, the *Concorde* frigate with his letter to Barras reached Newport. Washington learned the contents on the 14th, and immediately made preparations to move south on Yorktown with a part of his army and the whole of Rochambeau's corps – the siege guns to follow in Barras's ships – leaving the rest of his force to hold the main British army under Lieutenant General Sir Henry Clinton in New York with feint manoeuvres. The whole combined operation was a consummate example of inter-allied understanding, trust and flexibility, perfect communications over great distances, and an intuitive grasp by all parties of the principles of the concentration of maximum force, surprise and, its accomplice, deception. De Grasse, on whose decision the campaign turned, and Vergennes, who had insisted Castries allow him latitude and pressed for decisive results in America, were thus able to achieve what has been called in a recent study 'the most important and most perfectly executed naval campaign of the age of sail' – with the possible exception of the later Trafalgar campaign.[67] It is not necessary to accept this large claim to marvel at the flawless strategic decisions made by the French and Americans – in marked contrast to the loose surveillance and conventional responses of the British.

However, Rodney was by this date a sick man and had decided he must return home to recuperate. He had intelligence of the French squadron at Cap-François with the homeward shipping, and anticipated de Grasse providing it with the usual strong escort across the Atlantic, leaving perhaps fourteen of the line to take north – since the West Indian hurricane season was approaching – to join Barras in Newport.[68] He had accordingly prepared a squadron of this strength to sail north under Hood, transferred his flag to the 80-gun *Gibraltar*, which was in need of refit, and on 1 August sailed with two other ships of the line with the homeward trade. The day before they parted, both he and Hood had received intelligence that thirty American pilots for the Chesapeake and Delaware rivers had arrived at Cap-François. It has been suggested this might have alerted them to de Grasse's intention of taking his entire squadron north.[69] Neither was expecting such an unusual move, though – nor indeed was Barras, who had sent the pilots – and if there was an implication, which is doubtful, it was not drawn. Thus the British battle ships in the West Indies were dispersed, three from the Leeward Islands going home with Rodney and the trade, another two convoying merchantmen to Jamaica, three from Jamaica escorting the trade from that island home, leaving after earlier departures on convoy duty only fourteen to sail north with Hood.[70]

The commander-in-chief on the North American station, Vice Admiral Marriot Arbuthnot, had also sailed for home. His successor had been appointed but had not arrived, and before departing in early July Arbuthnot had handed over the small squadron to Rear Admiral Thomas Graves. Through no fault of his own, Graves had wasted several weeks hunting a 'most important' but actually non-existent French supply convoy reported by London; he had then returned to New York in mid-August, where he and General Clinton learned that Rochambeau's troops had left Rhode Island and moved south across the Hudson to join Washington in New Jersey. They began preparing an expedition to destroy Barras's squadron in Newport, but on 29 August Hood arrived with his squadron and the news, gleaned from merchantmen on his way north, that de Grasse had sailed from Cap-François. The same evening it was learned that Barras had left Newport three days earlier with his entire squadron and several transports. Concluding that the French commanders had arranged a rendezvous in the south, Graves, who was senior to Hood, decided to take the combined British squadrons south 'in hopes to intercept one or both if possible'.[71] There was insufficient wind to carry his ships over the dangerously shallow bar at Sandy Hook, and it was not until the late evening of 31 August that he could begin the move south.

He left two ships refitting after an earlier, indecisive encounter with the French squadron off the Chesapeake, and had only five of the line and one 50-gun ship to add to the fourteen Hood had brought from the West Indies. On taking over in July, he had reissued Arbuthnot's individual signals and instructions to his captains over his own signature, no doubt because he regarded himself as merely an interim commander-in-chief. Presumably he issued Hood's captains with the same instructions in the brief time before sailing, although the total lack of comment on the point afterwards suggests he made no particular explanations of the many differences between these and the conventional Admiralty instructions and additional instructions which the captains from the West Indies had used under Rodney.[72] The situation seems to have been made for misunderstandings.

De Grasse had reached the Chesapeake the day before Graves started south. He had disembarked the troops, who had marched to join Lafayette, detached four of the line and a frigate to blockade the York and James rivers where they entered Chesapeake Bay, and anchored with his main body just inside the southern promontory of the bay, Cape Henry, to await the arrival of Barras. He was still there on the morning of 5 September when at about ten o'clock the frigate on lookout to seaward of the cape signalled six sails. They were thought at first to be Barras, but as more sails appeared it was realized they were British. De Grasse, knowing that to remain inside the cape would condemn Barras's squadron when it appeared to an unequal fight and probable total destruction, decided to weigh and stand out to meet the enemy at sea. Shore parties were recalled and signals were made to prepare for action and be ready to make sail. However, both the wind at north-north-east and the flood tide setting into the bay prevented an immediate move.

Graves in his flagship, the 98-gun *London*, was some eighteen miles east of the bay, steering towards the entrance under reefed topsails, making four knots with the fresh breeze on his quarter, when at 9.30 a frigate he had sent to look into the bay signalled a fleet in the south-west.[73] He shook out the reefs and soon after ten made the signal to prepare for action. At eleven, with the *London* now making five knots, he made out the forest of masts inside Cape Henry and recognized he had more than the Newport squadron to deal with: this was either de Grasse or de Grasse and Barras together. He ordered line ahead with two cables (400 yards) between ships. Hood, commanding the van division in the 90-gun *Barfleur*, set studding-sails, and by noon his leading ships had reached within ten miles of the cape.

Soon afterwards the French were seen to be setting sail; the tide had slackened, allowing the northernmost to weather the shoal water off Cape Henry, although those anchored further south would need one or more tacks before they could claw out. At 12.30 de Grasse signalled for line of battle to be formed rapidly on the port tack without regard to order, each ship getting into line where she could. Graves ordered the distance between his ships closed to one cable, then at one o'clock, as the leading French sailed out past Cape Henry, he had the flags hauled down and the signal made for a line of bearing east–west. His intention, as he afterwards reported to Sandwich, was 'to form parallel with them' as they steered eastward towards him, 'extend with them and attack all together'.[74]

Twenty minutes later, as the foremost enemy approached his own van on the opposite tack and somewhat downwind, he signalled his leading ship to alter to starboard, or upwind. Whether he wished to increase the distance between the two fleets as they passed, in order to prevent an action starting before he had extended along their full length and was ready to 'attack them all together', or whether he made the signal because his rear was trailing upwind and he wished to dress the line in the east–west direction he had ordered is entirely unclear. In the *Barfleur's* signal log the order was noted as alter course to *port*. The leading French perhaps bore off the wind a point or so at the same time; at all events, fifteen minutes later, at 1.35 Graves ordered his leading ship to 'lead more large', or off the wind, thus to port. In the *Barfleur* this was entered as starboard.

The headmost ships passed each other in opposite directions, the French some three miles to leeward, and by 2.00 the *Pluton*, leading the French line, was opposite the *London*, lying tenth in the British line at the centre of the centre division. By this time all de Grasse's fleet was in view and Graves was able to count twenty-four of the line and two frigates. He then made the signal for the fleet to wear together. The reason recorded in the *London's* log and Graves's subsequent report was that Hood's van division was approaching too close to the shoal known as the Middle Ground, which lay across the entrance to the bay three miles north of Cape Henry. Yet the *Barfleur*, fourth in the British line, was then, according to her log, still six miles east of Cape Henry. Ten minutes later,

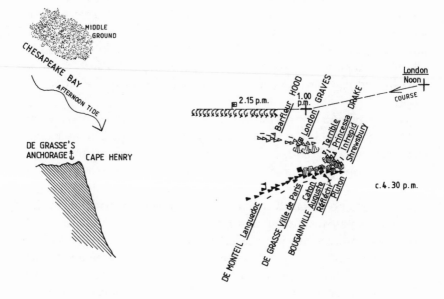

WIND
NNE

MIDDLE
GROUND

CHESAPEAKE BAY

AFTERNOON TIDE

DE GRASSE'S
ANCHORAGE ⚓ CAPE HENRY

2.15 p.m.

Barfleur HOOD

1.00 p.m.

London GRAVES

DRAKE

London
Noon

COURSE

Terrible
Princessa
Intrepid
Shrewsbury

c.4.30 p.m.

DE MONTEIL Languedoc

DE GRASSE Ville de Paris

Caton
Auguste
BOUGAINVILLE
Réfléchi
Pluton

KEY
▼ FRENCH SHIPS
▽ BRITISH SHIPS
| Frigates
◼▼ ◼▽ Commander-in-chief
▲▼ ▲▽ Squadronal admiral
🔥▽ Gunfire
+ Log-book positions

Battle diagram 6   Battle of Chesapeake Bay (Virginia Capes),
5 September 1781

at 2.15, Graves made the signal executive by firing a gun and putting his helm up; the ships wore round together on to the same tack as the French, whereupon he backed his main topsail and lay to in order to allow the French centre, where de Grasse had positioned his great 104-gun *Ville de Paris*, to draw abeam. At 2.30 he signalled the new leading ship, the 74-gun *Shrewsbury* – formerly last in the line – to lead more to starboard. It is not clear how many points he meant her to alter towards the enemy, since this was signified by the number of guns fired, which was not recorded in the logs.

So far Graves had achieved his aims. His intention now was to bring his whole line down together on the enemy, but the signal he had made, number 10 of Arbuthnot's additional instructions, read, 'If at any time I would have the leading ship in the line alter course to starboard I will hoist a flag half red, half white at the main topmast head.'[75] The flag officer commanding what was now the van division, Rear Admiral Samuel Drake in the 70-gun *Princessa*, and the captains from the West Indies naturally interpreted this as an order to alter course in succession as they reached the spot at which the *Shrewsbury* altered, rather than to alter all together with the *Shrewsbury* as Graves intended. Thus the British van was soon closing the enemy at an angle in line ahead instead of lasking down together in a line parallel to the enemy. Graves attempted to correct this by signalling three of the six van ships individually to alter course to starboard and at 3.29 for Hood's division, now in the rear, to make more sail; five minutes later he made Arbuthnot's additional signal number 5 for the fleet in line of battle to alter course to starboard, but nothing he did could correct the original misinterpretation and the elbow which had formed in consequence at the head of his line.

Finally at 3.46 he made the signal for line of battle with one cable's distance between ships and followed this immediately, and without hauling it down, with the signal – again from Arbuthnot's signal book – for 'each ship to steer for and engage his opponent in the enemy's line'; this was made with a white pendant at the fore-topmast head over a red flag – the historic 'bloody flag' that had been the signal for close action since the first Anglo-Dutch wars. At the same time he had the *London*'s helm put up and her main topsail filled to bear down towards de Grasse.

In the *Barfleur* Graves's signal was recorded without the usual meaning assigned, merely as 'a Blue and White chequered flag with a white pendant over it'. From subsequent entries – '4.17 We repeated the signal to engage the Enemy' and '4.20 Hauled down the white pendant

and kept the Blue and Yellow chequered Flag flying under the Red flag'
– it is apparent that the red flag was seen and recognized as the signal
for close action. However, Hood and the captains who had been drilled
by Rodney to unquestioning obedience and allowed no latitude whatever for initiative were unable to resolve the apparent contradiction of
the signal for close action flying at the same time as the signal for the line
of battle, for the French formation was almost a mirror image of the
British, their van close-hauled to windward of the centre and the centre
to windward of the rear, as Hood phrased it.[76] Thus, while the opposing vans were close and closing, the centres and rears were at long range.

Graves recognized the dilemma and at 4.11 ordered the signal for the
line hauled down 'that it might not interfere with the signal to engage
close'.[77] Eleven minutes later he ordered the line signal hoisted again,
'the ships not being sufficiently extended' – *London*'s journal – or 'to push
the ships ahead of me forward, and who were some of them upon my
off beam' as Graves stated in his subsequent report.[78]

By this time firing had begun in the van, and at 4.27 Graves again
ordered the signal for the line hauled down and the red flag for close
action hoisted. It appears from other signal logs that, although the red
flag was hoisted, the signal for the line was not hauled down; in the
Barfleur the exchange of signals was not recorded as taking place for
another hour. Thus, far from Graves's intended close engagement all
along the line, the action was begun under the most unfavourable
circumstances, with Drake's van division bearing down obliquely in line
ahead on the four leading French. The *Shrewsbury* at the head of the line
suffered particularly. A lieutenant of Marines in her next astern, *Intrepid*,
described afterwards in a letter home how, despite the British inferiority
in numbers of nineteen to twenty-four of the line, they had 'boldly run
down' upon the enemy:

> we, the second ship in our Van, engaged two hours and ten minutes, during
> which time we had three ships firing at us, and we blazed away at them above
> 80 barrels of powder . . . The Van ship, the *Shrewsbury* was disabled a good
> deal and we took the fire of her ship from her and obliged her to bear out of
> the line, for which the little *Intrepid* had the thanks of the Admiral for saving
> a 74-gun ship.[79]

Graves himself could not bear down with similar panache because as
firing spread from the van to the ships of his own centre division the 74-

gun *Montagu*, two ahead of the *London*, luffed up into the wind and opened fire at too great a range. To avoid sailing through or masking her broadsides, Graves also had to luff up and back his main topsail. The ships astern of him had to do the same. Hood, following with the rear division and obliged, as he believed, by the signal for the line still flying in the *London* to follow in their wake, could only fulminate about Graves's mismanagement; as he put it afterwards:

> Our centre, then upon a wind under their topsails, began to engage at the same time [as the van], but at a most improper distance scarcely I believe within point blank shot (though the *London* had the signal for close action and the signal for the line ahead at half a cable [*sic*] flying, and lay with her main topsail to the mast the whole time, notwithstanding the French ships pushed on to their van); and our rear, being barely within random shot, did not fire at all until the signal for the line was hauled down.[80]

It was hauled down, according to the *Barfleur*'s signal log, at 5.25, at which time Hood at last felt able to bear down towards the enemy until by his own account he was three-quarters of a mile downwind of Graves's division; however, the French rear bore away to leeward and he scarcely came within range before the sun set. Not wishing to separate from the rest of the British fleet in the dark, he hauled up into the wind again. Soon afterwards, at 6.23, Graves again made the signal for line ahead at a cable's distance and hauled down the red flag. By this time Drake's van division had suffered severe damage, but had forced the leading French ships to bear away to leeward. By 6.30 all firing ceased.

Graves sent frigates to the van and rear instructing them to keep parallel with the enemy during darkness and made the night signal for line ahead at two cables between ships. No doubt he intended renewing battle next day, but damage reports reaching him that evening were discouraging. The *Montagu*, two ships ahead, hailed to say she could not keep the line; despite the comparatively long range at which she had opened fire, she had thirty killed and wounded and four cannon dismounted besides serious mast and rigging damage. Soon after 8.00 the *Shrewsbury* made the distress signal. The frigate that went to her discovered her captain had lost a leg, the first lieutenant and thirteen men were dead, over fifty were wounded; three guns were dismounted, the foremast was shot through in three places, all masts and yards were so badly wounded she was unable to keep her place in the line, and when on the larboard tack she took in water from shot holes. The *Intrepid* was equally incapacitated, with sixty-five shot holes through her starboard side, nineteen on the waterline. These were the most seriously damaged and had by far the heaviest casualties, but all six ships in Drake's van had suffered heavily aloft, and the last, the *Terrible*, which had been making water before the action, almost certainly because her iron fastenings had been eaten away by electrolytic action with the hull copper sheathing, was making over two feet of water every fifteen minutes.[81] De Grasse's leading four ships had also suffered severely, although total French casualties seem to have been rather less – 230 killed and wounded against 336 in the British fleet.[82] In both cases injuries and damage were confined to the leading dozen ships: neither Hood's squadron nor the French rear had sustained anything more than the most minor damage.

The wind veered into the east-north-east and dropped during the night; next morning both fleets formed early in sight of each other, the French some five miles to leeward, and headed south-easterly at barely two knots, the more damaged ships still getting up new masts and yards and splicing rigging, the hands in the *Terrible* manning the pumps but not gaining on the water. The light breeze fell away during the afternoon, and by night there was a flat calm. The following day the wind went round to the south, giving de Grasse the advantage, but he made no attempt to renew the battle, instead, on 9 September, pressing on sail and heading back for the Chesapeake. Entering on the 11th, he found Barras and the transports with the siege-train had just arrived, so he anchored with his fleet to command the York river. For Graves, who had been forced on the 10th to order the *Terrible* abandoned and burned, the news that the Newport squadron had joined de Grasse was confirmation of his impotence; the French advantage was now thirty-six to eighteen of the line. After a council of war, he put back to New York.

There he was joined by reinforcements from England and Jamaica, which brought his force up to twenty-five of the line. After replenishing urgently, preparing fireships to send down on the enemy anchorage and embarking 7,000 troops, he sailed again for the Chesapeake on 19 October. It was too late. Washington had encircled Cornwallis's position with batteries and opened a heavy bombardment on the 6th. By the 15th, parts of the British earthworks were in ruins and Cornwallis had sent a message to New York declaring the situation so precarious he could not recommend the fleet and army running great risks to save him.[83] Two days later he opened negotiations with Washington, and on the 19th – the day Graves sailed to his relief – he surrendered.

'Oh, God!' Lord North exclaimed when he heard of the loss of this second British army in America, 'It is all over!' It was the end of any prospect of regaining the colonies, and it heralded the end of his own administration and Sandwich's career at the Admiralty.

The issue had been decided off Cape Henry on 5 September. De Grasse had created the strategic opportunity and made the right tactical decisions. Whether Graves could have seized the initiative has been debated ever since. Hood had no doubts. He penned his first reactions on the day after the battle: 'Yesterday the British fleet had a rich and most delightful harvest of glory presented to it, but omitted to gather it in more instances than one.'[84]

He argued, first, that Graves had had the opportunity to attack the French van as it scrambled out in very loose order past Cape Henry; second, that Graves, having allowed the French ships out, had failed to bring his whole fleet into action against them, in which case 'several of the enemy's ships must have been inevitably demolished in half an hour's action, and there was a full hour and a half to have done it before any of the rear could have come up'; third, that when Graves attacked he had flown the signal for the line of battle at the same time as the signal for close action and had backed his main topsail, so preventing his centre from pressing on to the relief of his van and preventing Hood from getting into action at all.

Hood was invariably vitriolic about colleagues. Between 12.30 and 1.00, when the leading French began coming out, the *London* was over ten miles east of them – since her log had Cape Henry bearing 'W ½ S 4–5 leagues' (12–15 miles) at noon, her course west by south, speed four knots. The rear was evidently trailing somewhat, as at 1.08 Graves signalled it to make more sail. Moreover, Graves was quite unsure how large a fleet was coming out. To have signalled 'general chase' and run precipitately on the enemy in these circumstances would have been an act of exceptional boldness, flouting all current principles. The most aggressive tactical innovator of the day, Lord Howe, regarded the line as sacrosanct and would no doubt have formed and dressed his ships precisely as Graves did. To have attacked at once must have led to the leading French bearing away, drawing the British downwind after them, allowing de Grasse to gain the wind with his centre and rear. As for Hood's other charges, Graves was attempting – again according to all current principles – to extend his line the full length of the enemy's, to prevent his rear being doubled and taken between two fires, then attempting to bring his whole fleet down on the enemy together. He was defeated only by confusion about his signals and a mistake in the flagship which left the signal for the line flying after he had ordered it hauled down.

Yet Hood's confusion about the line signal flying at the same time as that for close action need not have inhibited him. Article XVII of the Admiralty instructions he had used under Rodney directed each ship to steer for her opponent in the enemy line 'notwithstanding the signal for the line will be kept flying'.[85] No doubt service under Rodney had caused him to suppress any thought of acting outside what he supposed the precise meaning of a signal; the results of recent courts martial had also contributed to a climate of absolute conformity.

Graves's report to Sandwich suggests that Hood's second and third points were valid, but his tone was of extreme disappointment rather than censure: 'I think that had our efforts been made together, some of their van, four or five sail, must have been cut to pieces. The signal was not understood. I do not blame anyone, my Lord. I hope we all did our best.'[86]

The day after the battle he issued a memorandum to the fleet explaining, 'When the signal for the line of Battle ahead is out at the same time with the signal for Battle, it is not to be understood that the latter signal shall be rendered ineffectual by the strict adherence to the former',[87] which was merely to convey the extension, or distances between ships. It was too late then. It might be said that America was lost to Britain because of a signalling misunderstanding, but that is too simple an explanation. De Grasse's fleet was too powerful to be utterly routed, and directly it was joined by Barras's squadron Cornwallis's fate was sealed. Graves was made the scapegoat at the time, and has been by too many historians since.

If anyone is to be censured, surely Rodney and Hood should share the blame for having failed to bring de Grasse to decisive action in the West Indies beforehand, and for assuming, when the French admiral reached Cap-François, that he would do the conventional thing. It was a reasonable assumption; Rodney was a sick man. Nonetheless de Grasse was not watched closely, but was instead allowed to bring off the stroke that ensured the British would lose America.[88]

14

The Saints, 1782, and the Founding of the United States of America

DE GRASSE RETURNED to the West Indies in the winter of 1781 with every French ship of the line in American waters, recovered St Eustatius and other Dutch possessions seized by Rodney, and early in 1782 took the British islands St Christopher, Nevis and Montserrat against bold but vain attempts at intervention by a smaller British squadron under Hood.

Meanwhile in European waters in 1781 the Brest fleet had joined the Spanish in Cadiz, after which the combined Bourbon fleet of forty-nine ships of the line had covered an expedition through the Strait to lay siege to the British garrison on Minorca; subsequently the great fleet steered north for the English Channel. The British home fleet numbered only twenty-seven of the line; nevertheless Lord North's Cabinet, encouraged by Sandwich's professional advisers that 'An inferior fleet of coppered ships under a judicious commander will keep a superior one that is not so in awe',[1] had ordered the fleet out to seek the enemy. The able commander-in-chief, Vice Admiral George Darby, queried over-reliance on copper, suggesting that those enemy ships which were coppered might succeed in bringing him to action 'and thereby give opportunity for the[ir] heavier ships to come up'.[2] The question was not tested, since the combined fleet, struck by the usual sickness, divided without accomplishing anything and returned to its separate home bases.

Subsequently Sandwich's intelligence revealed preparations in Brest for a major convoy to reinforce and supply de Grasse. A plan for the relief of Minorca was put aside, and in early December Kempenfelt was sent out with twelve of the line from the home fleet to intercept the convoy. He sighted it 150 miles off Ushant, but the covering force was nineteen strong and he was unable to do more than cut out a dozen merchantmen and transports. A few days later a severe gale drove the French back to Brest; the convoy was not to reach de Grasse until the following March, 1782. Yet, once again, a British squadron had been baulked by superior numbers of the enemy.

The small core of professional officers on whom Sandwich relied for advice now devised a radical strategy to bring the war to a conclusion in the next campaigning season. It rested again on the so-far untested theory that a small but coppered fleet in home waters could avoid being brought to action by a numerically superior but largely uncoppered enemy, thereby remaining 'in being' and making invasion too hazardous to attempt. The plan was to reduce the home fleet to just twenty of the line, in order to concentrate overwhelming superiority in the West Indies to decide the issue there. To prevent trade falling to the combined fleet in the Channel, convoys would be re-routed northabout around Scotland. It was a desperate strategy, contrary to all precedent and risking much to the chances of wind and weather. That it was conceived at all indicates the extraordinary pressure to which the navy had been subjected by Vergennes's success in maintaining the Bourbon alliance and keeping clear of Continental distractions. It was not to be tested, however, for in March reports reaching London of de Grasse's capture of St Christopher coincided with the news that the garrison on Minorca had surrendered; Lord North's administration fell and Sandwich was replaced at the Admiralty by Admiral Keppel.

Sandwich suffered savage criticism for his conduct of the naval war; yet his failures – most notably, for its consequences, the loss of Cornwallis's army at Yorktown – seem minor compared with the disasters that might have been expected with such a weight of powers ranged against Britain on her own. As he put it in his own defence, 'notwithstanding our inferiority of force, we have not been brought to disgrace';[3] on the other hand, the vital Baltic trade had been secured, practically all important East and West Indies convoys had got through, Dutch shipping had been blockaded in port and Dutch fisheries eliminated, the British position in India had been strengthened and the French East Indies squadron under the redoubtable Pierre André de Suffren, one of the most brilliant, and certainly the most aggressive, of French admirals, had been held to a draw in a succession of dour encounters; Gibraltar had been reinforced and supplied; and the navy had been steadily expanded. When Sandwich left office there were over 100 of the line in commission,[4] and for the first time in the war Britain had a small numerical advantage over the combined battle fleets of France and Spain. Above all, the British fleet was superior in quality, with every ship coppered – against about half the French fleet and just one Spanish liner – and most equipped with carronades which could discharge a terrifying weight of shot at close quarters.

This was Sandwich's legacy. He was a man of charm, sound sense and integrity, with a talent for selecting the right men for important posts. Outside politics and the navy he had wide interests embracing all the liberal arts, particularly music and especially Handel, on the centenary of whose birth in 1784 he promoted and organized a series of grand commemoration concerts in Westminster Abbey on a scale never before seen in the country; they have been described by a modern scholar as 'in some ways the most important single event in the history of English music during the eighteenth century'.[5] Sandwich himself was perhaps the single most important figure in maintaining the English Handel tradition. He was also by any measure an outstanding First Lord of the Admiralty; his good stewardship was to be demonstrated in the first great sea battle under the new administration.

It took place among the Leeward Islands on 12 April 1782, off the Îles des Saintes – 'the Saints' – a small group just south of Guadeloupe. De Grasse, covering a great convoy including the recently arrived supply ships and troop transports that had been driven back to Brest by a gale in December, was on his way from Martinique to Saint-Domingue to join the Spanish contingent of the expedition against Jamaica, as he had promised. Rodney, who had returned to the station and resumed command in February, was pursuing with a small advantage in numbers – thirty-six to thirty of the line – largely the result of collisions in the French fleet. The latest victim, the 74-gun *Zélé*, which had run aboard the *Ville de Paris*, during the night, was under tow by a frigate and trailing somewhat to leeward of the French main body. Rodney ordered ships detached to cut her out, whereupon de Grasse reversed the course of his fleet to protect her – a decision which has been much criticized. The criticism is valid only if he knew just how devastating British close-range gunnery had become, which is doubtful.

The fleets closed on opposite tacks to a south-easterly breeze, the French heading southerly and somewhat to windward so that their van crossed the bows of the leading British ships, which bore up to avoid being raked and steered northerly, paralleling the French on the opposite course to leeward of their line. Fire was opened at about the same time, spreading gradually from ship to ship as each came up, and Rodney signalled his leaders to alter to starboard. Since they had the wind abaft the beam, they did so without difficulty and closed the range. De Grasse, anxious his rear would be doubled as the British van reached the tail of his line, ordered his fleet to wear together on to the same tack as the enemy, but his captains were by then so closely engaged with each passing ship they dared not risk exposing their bows by turning. Half an hour later de Grasse repeated the signal. Still none of his divisional flag officers or captains obeyed. It was shortly after this that the good fortune that had attended all his operations so far deserted him. The wind shifted suddenly into the south, heading his ships, forcing them to alter to starboard and exposing gaps in their line through which ships of Rodney's division passed without at first realizing what they were doing.

In this situation, which arose without plan or signal in the smoke and confusion of battle, the tactical cohesion achieved by the captains drilled under Rodney and Hood and the rapidity and accuracy of fire of British guns' crews and the weight of shot of the upper-deck carronades proved decisive. Rodney's flagship, *Formidable*, passing through the line so close to the *Glorieux* that the French guns' crews could be seen dropping their sponges and handspikes and running below, reduced that ship to a mastless hulk.[6] 'Oh, my Lord,' Rodney wrote to Sandwich after the action, 'the three-decked ships are what must maintain the sovereignty of the sea; nothing can withstand them . . . we gave at least three broadsides to their two during the whole action.'[7]

Much of the credit for the devastating effectiveness of British fire was due to Rodney's first captain – or Chief of Staff – Sir Charles Douglas, an obsessive gunnery innovator who had introduced or reinstated a host of changes to speed the fire and improve the accuracy and arcs of training of the great guns, among them flintlocks instead of linstocks and slow matches to fire the pieces, specially filled goose-quill powder tubes instead of loose powder from powder horns to prime the vents, cartridges with flannel bottoms which left no smouldering debris to be wormed out after each round, and modifications to the hull structure by the gun ports which allowed the great pieces to be pointed, in Douglas's words 'full four points [45 degrees] before or abaft the beam, which I presume is to a degree of obliquity until now unknown in the navy'.[8] He

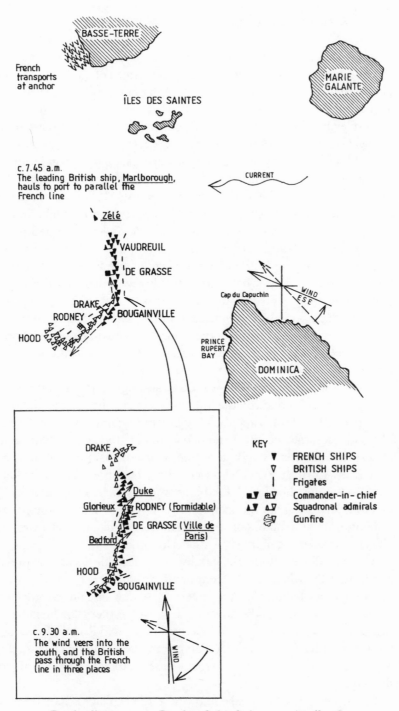

BASSE-TERRE

French transports at anchor

MARIE GALANTE

ÎLES DES SAINTES

c. 7.45 a.m.
The leading British ship, Marlborough, hauls to port to parallel the French line

CURRENT

Zélé

VAUDREUIL

DE GRASSE

Cap du Capuchin

WIND ESE

DRAKE

RODNEY

BOUGAINVILLE

HOOD

PRINCE RUPERT BAY

DOMINICA

DRAKE

KEY
▼ FRENCH SHIPS
▽ BRITISH SHIPS
| Frigates
◗▼ ◖▽ Commander-in-chief
▲▼ ▲▽ Squadronal admirals
🌫 Gunfire

Duke

Glorieux

RODNEY (Formidable)

DE GRASSE (Ville de Paris)

Bedford

HOOD

BOUGAINVILLE

c. 9.30 a.m.
The wind veers into the south, and the British pass through the French line in three places

WIND

Battle diagram 7   Battle of the Saints, 12 April 1782

described after the battle how the *Formidable* 'penetrated the enemy's line of battle between the second and third ship astern of the gallant Grasse, almost totally silencing their fire by pointing her guns . . . as far forward as possible'.[9]

Rodney had had no intention of going through, or as it is celebrated in naval historical literature 'breaking', the French line. His cardinal rule for holding the enemy to close action was to keep downwind, since, as he had told Sandwich after the Moonlight Battle, 'when the British fleet take the lee gage, the enemy cannot escape'.[10] Thus, although de Grasse's fleet was broken by the wind shift into groups caught between tremendous volumes of British fire, most of these separated groups passed downwind and, after sustaining a battle described by Rodney's surgeon as 'one peal of thunder and blaze of fire from one end of the line to the other,[11] for the best part of the day, were able to withdraw and make their escape. Five shattered prizes were left with Rodney, their bloodied decks shambles of smashed timber and tangled rigging, over-turned gun carriages, broken bodies and pieces of what had been bodies, and between decks the mangled carcasses of sheep and cattle among the human remains.

Last to surrender, at sunset, was de Grasse's great flagship, the *Ville de Paris*, although no one could climb aloft to strike her flag as the masts were pierced and tottering, their supporting rigging cut away by shot. She had lost some 400 killed and 600 wounded; the French admiral was almost the only man standing on the quarterdeck amid the dead and wounded. A British officer who went aboard to accept his sword found himself over his shoe buckles in blood at every step. The horror of the battle and its aftermath was increased by swarms of sharks alongside the ships attacking the bodies of the dead as they were cast overboard; one officer estimated the number of sharks at 1,000.[12]

Brought aboard Rodney's flagship next day, de Grasse expressed admiration for what he saw, commenting that his own service was a hundred years behind; he was referring to the discipline, order and cleanliness aboard and the advances in great gunnery, for French warships were as well designed, often better, and he told Rodney he thought his own fleet had been superior, being composed entirely of large ships of seventy-four guns and upwards, whereas Rodney had ten of only sixty-four guns.[13]

The Battle of Chesapeake Bay, or Virginia Capes, had been the turning point of the American war; the Saints marked the turning point in the world war: it re-established the perception of British naval ascendancy lost since the Seven Years War, saved Jamaica, at least for the present campaigning season, threw the French service into an orgy of recrimination and self-doubt, and undermined Vergennes's belief in the possibility of a successful outcome. In August, British peace proposals were brought to Versailles by de Grasse – a subtle touch by the leader of the new administration, Lord Shelburne – and early the following month Vergennes despatched his senior aide across the Channel to conduct serious negotiations.

For both sides financial strain after five years of prodigious naval expenditure lay at the root of the desire for peace. Great Britain fighting alone against practically the entire naval world was spending over £20 million annually. Taxes – particularly land and indirect excise taxes – had been raised and brought in £12 million a year, but the difference had been funded by borrowing, pushing the national debt up to £240 million, almost double its size at the start of the war, over three times the level at mid-century before the Seven Years War; debt charges now consumed 66 per cent of tax revenue.[14]

The Bourbon powers were in worse condition. They had spent less individually but were less able than Great Britain to borrow on sustainable terms. This was clear to Vergennes. On the day his aide left Versailles to negotiate in England, he instructed his ambassador in Spain to exhort the Spanish government, if the occasion arose, not to lose the opportunity to end the war honourably. England was undoubtedly 'very fatigued', he wrote, but so were they themselves, and 'That nation [Great Britain] has in its constitution and the establishments which it has permitted her to form, resources which are lacking to us.'[15] The establishments were first Parliament, which demanded public accounts and reports, thereby giving public finances an orderliness and transparency they entirely lacked in France and Spain, and producing confidence in government stock, and second the efficient, centralized and open system of collecting the taxes on which government loans were secured.

By this date 23 per cent of British income per head was appropriated in taxes – almost twice the French percentage.[16] Moreover, a smaller proportion of what was collected in France found its way to government coffers, as the collectors employed by the private tax farmers each took their cut before passing money up to the next level. Just how much ended in private hands was unknown, since, like government departments, tax farmers published no accounts and were not subject to public scrutiny.

Turgot's successor as Comptroller-General of Finance, the Swiss-born banker Jacques Necker, reputed to be a financial genius, had failed as completely as his predecessors to break the stranglehold of the great financiers who farmed the taxes or to erode the tax privileges enjoyed by the nobility and the clergy. Consequently, although the British paid per head almost three times more tax than the French,[17] it was ordinary French people, not British, who perceived their impositions as peculiarly savage and unjust, as indeed they were, and the system of collection as venal and corrupt, as it was.[18]

Like his predecessors, Necker had had to pay for the concealed and ramshackle system of French finances in high rates of interest on borrowing. He had funded the extraordinary expenses of the war by taking out fixed-term loans and selling annuities at excessively generous rates, between 8 and 10 per cent.[19] Spain, in even more desperate financial straits, had recently been forced up to 20 per cent on loans taken out for the construction of specially designed floating batteries for use against Gibraltar.[20] By contrast, Lord North had been able to borrow throughout the war at the same rates – around 3 per cent – as his predecessors in peace and war since the 1730s: such was the absolute confidence which had been established in the City of London and provincial and foreign capital markets by the open system of parliamentary accounting and the orderly and transparent collection of taxes – accompanied, of course, by faith in the navy's ability to protect the coasts from invasion and trade from serious disruption.[21]

This was perfectly understood in France. The previous year, 1781, Necker had attempted to ape the British system by publishing a French government budget. Like Colbert's earlier attempt to copy the Dutch mercantile system without recognizing its essential core of freedom, Necker failed, no doubt deliberately in this case, to reproduce the openness at the heart of British government finances. By omitting 'exceptional expenditures', as he termed the costs of the war, he produced a surplus of 10 million *livres* when there was a real deficit in the region of 50 million.[22] While this enabled him to take out further large loans to set out the fleet in 1782, it was evident to Vergennes that the scale of borrowing could not be maintained: the navy alone faced an accumulated deficit of 400 million *livres* (over £17 million),[23] while interest payments on the national debt were absorbing an increasingly dangerous proportion of tax revenues. In October, when it appeared that peace negotiations would founder over British intransigence on Gibraltar, he wrote to the French ambassador in Madrid saying he 'trembled' for the next campaigning season:

> The English have to some degree regenerated their navy while ours has been used up . . . the body of good sailors is exhausted and the officers show a lassitude in war which contrasts in a dangerous manner with the energy eagerly manifested not only by the sailors but the entire English nation. Join to that the diminution of our financial means . . . That inconvenience is common, no doubt, also to England, but her constitution gives her in that regard advantages which our monarchical forms do not give us.[24]

The Spanish government, convinced by the utter failure of the floating batteries and its ruined finances that it could not expect to regain Gibraltar – or take Jamaica – finally agreed to be content with Minorca, and peace terms were agreed before the end of the year. To the French negotiator it appeared a miracle; the nature of the miracle was the huge indebtedness of all belligerents. In the treaty signed at Versailles the following year, 1783, France achieved the chief goal for which Vergennes had persuaded Louis to go to war: the independence of the majority of North American colonies, excluding Canada and Newfoundland, which remained loyal to the British Crown. Otherwise France gained little beyond the island of Tobago and the return of St Lucia in the West Indies, greater security for her fishermen on the Newfoundland Banks, the expectation of commerce with the free states of America, and the promise of a trade treaty with Great Britain. In the East she had to accept the dominance the British East India Company had won earlier. For her part, Spain regained Minorca and Florida; the Dutch regained their possessions in the West Indies and Ceylon.

The overall loser, it appeared, was Great Britain; this is how the war is depicted. Yet she was the only belligerent to emerge without serious financial difficulties – merely a much larger debt – and with her economy flourishing.[25] Although she had lost an estimated 3,386 merchant ships during the course of the war,[26] and her overseas trade had fallen by a third, within a year of peace trade was back almost to the pre-war levels and thereafter it expanded at an unprecedented rate of about 6 per cent a year; by 1790 it was over 50 per cent greater than in the best pre-war years.[27] In part this was due to the usual impetus given to the shipbuilding, armament and metal industries by the demands of war – copper sheeting was a notable example – but the main causes lay in proliferating technical invention and enterprise: developments in manufacture noted from earlier in the century had spurred further advances which had begun to coalesce into a veritable revolution in industrial methods.

Between the end of the Seven Years War and the end of the American war, textile production had been boosted by the invention of the 'spinning jenny' (1768), allowing a single operator to work scores of spindles producing yarn; and the 'water frame' (1764) and 'mule' (1779), harnessing water power to weaving machinery, were changing the industry from large-scale domestic production into a factory system. During the same period the Scots instrument maker James Watt had radically improved the efficiency of the primitive steam engines (in use chiefly to pump water from mines) by providing push as well as pull to the piston, and had invented a mechanism to convert back-and-forth to rotary motion, all of which led to demand for steam power in iron, paper and flour mills, iron-making furnaces, waterworks, canal drainage and a host of other applications; by 1790 Watt had become a wealthy man. The metal industries had already been revolutionized by the use of coke instead of charcoal for smelting, and with the wider use of steam engines coal mining had been stimulated; this had led to the construction of canals and improvements to rivers to carry coal, ore and provisions to the industrial towns and manufactured goods out, notably from Manchester to the port of Liverpool. Agriculture had been stimulated to provide for the growing urban population. Altogether Great Britain stood on the threshold of a transformation greater than that wrought by wind power in the United Provinces the previous century; and already an abundance of manufactured goods was winning new markets on cost and quality, stimulating the search for ever wider markets. These were the forces underlying the astonishing growth of trade year by year.

The parallels with the golden age of the United Provinces are evident: constitutional government dominated by a wealthy elite dedicated to the needs of trade, in most cases involved in merchant enterprise, and utterly convinced of the supreme importance of a dominating navy; low interest rates and the availability of credit, enabling the country to fight a war against all her serious rivals combined and at the same time find capital to invest in new forms of manufacture, agriculture and transport; a commercial society served by a free press, relishing the liberty to discuss new ideas and exploit new inventions. The characteristics were all of a piece, both symptoms and causes of merchant trading power. And the

powerful energies released were to be seen even in such a strictly hierarchical service as the navy, epitomized in the rapid adoption of the carronade and the myriad practical advances in great gunnery which had
so impressed de Grasse after his defeat at the Saints.

One manifestation of resurgent trading power was the recapture of
North American markets. In the five years after the war, British exports
to her former colonies averaged 90 per cent of their pre-war value;
thereafter they exceeded it.[28] For Vergennes, who had rationalized his
war as the need to cut Great Britain down to size by depriving her of the
wealth she derived from her American monopolies, this was surely the
bitterest blow. Nor did France gain from a treaty to lower trading tarriffs
which she concluded with Britain in 1786: her industries, which had been
starved of capital and held back by the rigidities of a society in thrall to
officialdom at every level, could not compete. British industry became
the chief beneficiary of the treaty. British textiles even began to dominate markets in the Levant which had been French preserves for a
century.[29]

The resulting economic malaise in France was matched by a deepening financial crisis. While in Britain a new prime minister, William Pitt,
son of the great strategist of the Seven Years War, increased taxes and
introduced a sinking fund to reduce the national debt, Necker's successors presided over a steady increase in the debt inherited from the
American war. The causes lay, as always, in total resistance to fiscal
reform by those benefiting from the system, the high rates of interest
commanded by fixed-term loans – as against low-interest perpetual
loans raised by the British government in the London market[30] – and not
least continued substantial expenditure on the navy. By 1787 French debt
approached the size of British debt, but interest charges were almost
double.[31] In the same year the balance of foreign trade moved sharply
into deficit.[32] This combined financial and economic crisis sparked the
train of events which would lead within two years to the French
Revolution.

Extraordinarily, progress towards this volcanic solution to the
financial problems of the French Crown and the old order of society was
hastened by naval expansion. The navy minister, Castries, believed the
peace signed in 1783 a mere truce before the next outbreak of hostilities,
and planned to increase the battle fleet to a permanent force of eighty
of the line.[33] His successor carried the project forward to such effect that
the revolutionary government inherited seventy-three of the line, mainly

of recent construction, all coppered, equipped with carronades and other British innovations, and including no fewer than seven three-decker first rates of 100 guns and over, fifty-three 74-gun ships – almost twice the number of this staple liner as Sartine had had at the outbreak of the American war – and only four of the smallest 64-gun class. The fleet as a whole was 60 per cent larger in displacement than the pre-war fleet;[34] indeed it was the largest fleet France would have in the sailing era.

The reasons for the build-up defy rational explanation. There was no money to commission such a force if it came to war, nor were there sailors to man it, as demonstrated by extreme difficulties in obtaining men for the smaller fleet of the American war. Meanwhile loans taken out to fund the programme and the huge quantities of timber and naval stores sucked into the country had exacerbated both financial and economic crises. Since Spain, in similar financial straits, increased her navy by some 30 per cent in the same period,[35] it can only be concluded that both Bourbon powers were transfixed by the British navy and British merchant greed, and anticipated the younger Pitt attempting similar colonial expropriations to those achieved by his father. Ultimately, through war and peace, it seems it was British naval and commercial dominance that forced the violent overthrow of Louis XVI and the re-organization of French society.

As THE FRENCH monarchy tottered to ruin, constitutional changes of greater historic significance occurred in North America. The thirteen former British colonies had ended the war as a loose confederation of independent states, economies shattered and levels of personal income sharply reduced,[36] but enjoying constitutions enshrining the rights of their peoples to freedom, equality of opportunity, the possession of property, the pursuit of 'happiness' and government by legislatures elected for limited terms by adult male suffrage with very limited property qualifications. Each state issued its own currency and levied taxes. The Continental Congress had no tax-raising powers, and for the most part the states wished to keep it so: having just rid themselves of the British yoke, they had no desire to raise a powerful continental government in its place.

However, lack of central control carried heavy financial and economic penalties. Robert Morris, a Philadelphia merchant born in England, whose financial operations for Congress funded the war, had attacked the problem in 1781 by establishing a Bank of North America on the lines of the Bank of England. His estimate of the war debt in 1783 was 'above 30 millions of dollars' (some £6.75 million).[37] Much of this was held in congressional promissory notes or certificates, but the inability of Congress either to levy taxes or to enforce requisitions on individual states for their share of the debt caused great uncertainty and the depreciation of the notes, and contributed to lack of credit throughout the confederation. Paper money issued by Congress during the war had lost practically all value, wiped out savings and ruined thousands. On top of this, immediately after the war a buying spree for the British manufactures unavailable for so long led to a balance-of-payments crisis, further inflation and deepening recession. To Morris, subscribers to the Bank, the commercial and moneyed classes (especially those whose businesses and contacts extended between states and overseas), creditors of Congress and those who had entered the revolution with a vision of the limitless opportunities for a unified American future, it was evident that confidence and credit could be restored only by the creation of a central authority with powers to levy taxes, fix duties and regulate the economy.[38] In 1787 a Constitutional Convention met in Philadelphia to address the problem.

The delegates, electing George Washington to the chair, dismissed the idea of amending the articles by which the states had bound themselves to fight the British, and instead set about drafting a new constitution for a federal republic. The outlines were not difficult, since all states had a common British heritage and used similar systems of election to two-tiered legislatures requiring different property qualifications for their members, and all adhered to Locke's principle – accorded the status of divine revelation – of preventing arbitrary or tyrannical government by separating the legislature from the executive and the judiciary.[39] Once a compromise had been agreed between the smaller and the larger states on the number of representatives each would send to the federal chambers, the only substantial problem dividing the delegates was, as earlier with the Declaration of Independence, slavery.

Here no compromise was possible. In the hot southern states, Negro slaves were believed to be a necessity to work the plantations, and they existed in great numbers, constituting a part of the wealth of the plantation owners. In New England and the middle states the land was worked by farmers and free labourers, and not only were there fewer slaves but it was feared the introduction of more could result in a black rebellion; for this reason, Massachusetts, Pennsylvania, New Jersey and Maryland had imposed supposedly prohibitive duties on the import of slaves even before the war.[40] There was also the moral dimension. In the two most important of these states, Massachusetts and Pennsylvania, the God-fearing descendants of the Pilgrim Fathers and the Quakers had come to deplore slavery and the slave trade – indeed this was probably a consensus view among the educated of all states.[41]

Certainly in Europe the leading figures who established the intellectual climate – Voltaire, Montesquieu, Rousseau, Adam Smith, Horace Walpole, Samuel Johnson – had all denounced the institution and traffic of slaves. Dr Johnson's views were so violent he had once proposed a toast 'to the next insurrection of the negroes in the West Indies'.[42] In a volume of his great *Encyclopédie* published in 1665, Diderot had included an essay declaring the traffic in slaves a violation of religion, morality, natural law and human rights.

Religious denunciations, particularly from the Quakers, had made more impression. The Quakers had inspired John Wesley, founder of the Methodist movement taking the gospel to the masses in Britain, to write what proved to be the most influential sustained attack on the trade, *Thoughts upon Slavery* (1774), and Quaker pressure had provoked a House of Commons debate on the subject in the year of the American Declaration of Independence, 1776.[43] No legislation had ensued; the practical merchant and West Indian interest was too strong. It was the same in all countries involved. The vital interests of the French government coincided with those of the Chambers of Commerce of Bordeaux, Nantes and La Rochelle, and Louis's ministers – as deaf to Jesuit and papal condemnations of slavery as to the shafts of the Enlightenment *philosophes* – encouraged the trade by all means and in that year of the American Constitutional Convention, 1787, raised the bounty paid for each slave landed on the further shore to 160 *livres* (over £7).[44]

It was only in North America that religious and moral disgust had provoked action, aided perhaps by apprehension of the consequences of increasing the proportion of blacks in society. Again the Quakers had been at the forefront, persuading the Pennsylvania legislature in 1780 to pass an Act decreeing that Negroes and mulattoes born after that date would be free, thereby ensuring the gradual abolition of slavery in that colony, as it then was. 'We esteem it a peculiar blessing', the preamble ran, 'that we are enabled this day to add one more step to universal civilization by removing as much as possible the sorrows of those who have lived in undeserved bondage.'[45] In 1783 the Supreme Court of Massachusetts had ruled that the Declaration of Rights which affirmed men equal constituted a declaratory abolition of slavery. Other New England and middle colonies had followed suit.[46]

The great southern planters refused to bow to moral concern. They stood as firmly for the enjoyment of their style and retention of their property as the nobles and clergy in France – and in the next century were to meet a similar reckoning. The question thus became whether the new republic would embrace all the former colonies or whether Georgia and South Carolina, divided from the rest by the slave issue, would go their separate ways. Desire for unity overrode the northern conscience. A proposal to ban the import of slaves to the continent was dropped, and, while the word 'slavery' was excluded from the final draft of the constitution, the condition was recognized in a clause on interstate fugitives from justice, including 'persons held to Service or Labour'.[47]

Thus the constitution of the United States was born. The first article vested all legislative power in a Congress consisting of an upper and a lower chamber – the Senate and the House of Representatives – with authority to 'lay and collect Taxes, Duties, Imposts and Excise, to pay Debts and provide for the common Defence and general Welfare of the United States', to borrow money on the credit of the Union, to regulate commerce with foreign nations, among the states and with native tribes, to coin money and regulate its value, to declare war, raise and support armies and provide and maintain a navy, and to dispose of and regulate land and property belonging to the Union.

The second article vested executive power in a president who would hold office for four years. He would be commander-in-chief of the army and navy and the militia of the several states, and could 'with the advice and consent of the Senate . . . make Treaties provided two thirds of the Senators present concur'. While all legislation was to originate in Congress, it had to be passed to the president before becoming law; if he objected, he would return it and make recommendations, whereupon, after consideration, two-thirds majorities would be required in both chambers before it could pass. As in the British model developed since the arrival of 'Dutch William' in 1688, the separation of powers was intended to prevent tyranny but not to lead to deadlock and ineffective government. However, the federal structure of the proposed republic had more in common with the United Provinces of the previous century than with the highly centralized British model, and internal powers left with the individual states provided further checks on the centre.

By the third article, judicial power was vested in a Supreme Court whose judgements on constitutional or interstate disputes would be final. The fourth article provided that new states might be admitted to the Union; the fifth allowed for later amendments to be added to the constitution, and the sixth laid down that all debts contracted by Congress under the original Articles of Confederation would be equally valid against the new United States – a significant indication of where the strongest support for the new constitution lay.

In the subsequent public discussion and pamphlet war over whether the constitution should be ratified by the states, there were striking similarities with the fierce debates in the English parliament at the time of the foundation of the Bank of England soon after William's 'Glorious Revolution'. Then the landed classes feared the merchant/financial interest would take over government and preside over a rising spiral of deficit financing for its own advantage, raising taxes to service the ever-mounting debt and spreading government into ever greater areas of English life.[48] Their fears had not proved exaggerated. It is doubtful if Americans, who had just thrown off the shackles of the resulting mighty fiscal-military machine, recognized the precedents, but it was again the great landowners, joined by small farmers and small businessmen, a great many in debt to their wealthier fellows, who provided the opposition to the proposed federal constitution, discerning behind it the designs of the commercial and moneyed interest and fearing tyranny by an aristocracy of merchant wealth.[49]

No doubt the motives of those in favour of the constitution were not so self-interested as they were painted by the opposition: there was boundless idealism and optimism for a republic created on a clean slate with all history and the latest Enlightenment ideas as guides, granting power not to hereditary nobles, but to the people. For all that, the 'Federalists' were concentrated in the seaport cities and were led by wealthy men of business and finance who attracted to their cause the professional, skilled and unskilled classes dependent on commerce and even those farmers outside whose livelihoods were bound up with city and international markets. Indeed, the dispute over the constitution was characterized by a member of the New York ratifying convention as 'between navigating and non-navigating individuals'.[50] It was the 'navigating individuals' – whose concerns, it will be recalled, had sparked the original rebellion against British rule, and who had influence over the press and in the legislatures – who eventually won the vote in a surprisingly low turnout, and the new constitution was ratified by the majority of states in 1788. The next year ten amendments were passed to give American citizens statutory rights which the British had acquired in common law or by Act of Parliament: freedoms of religion, speech and the press; rights of peaceable assembly; security against unreasonable searches of the person, home or effects; trial by jury; the right not to be a witness against oneself, nor to be oppressed by excessive fines, excessive bail or 'cruel and unusual punishments'.

So the liberalizing inspirations of the great trading cities of the United Provinces, transferred to England under William of Orange and spread under the shelter of British trading and naval supremacy to the North American colonies, were inscribed in the constitution of the infant United States of America.

So too, but without formal adoption, were the commercial and colonizing compulsions. The establishment of land-speculating companies, often subscribed on both sides of the Atlantic, and the westward migration of settlers had preceded the American Revolution; in those colonies where the Crown set limits to westward expansion, it had contributed to the desire for independence. Native tribes such as the Cherokee and the Creek in the south had already ceded vast tracts of territory as payment for trading debts they could never otherwise have met, and with the coming of war these had allied with the British to prevent further encroachment. It might be said that they were the true losers at the Peace of Versailles. Yet in the long run, whatever the outcome in 1783, it is impossible to imagine any native tribes long resisting the expansionary forces and materially powerful system – not to mention the smallpox and syphilis – of the white men and women who had arrived on the commercial tide from Europe. Ruthless exploitation of less materially endowed peoples and their land and every living creature within their power was as much the mark of trading strength and merchant power as were liberal values.

Of these values, freedom was sovereign. All Americans prided themselves on enjoying the greatest freedom to be found anywhere on earth, and none more so than the frontier peoples, described early the following century by an English gentlewoman, Frances Trollope, as the 'I'm-as-good-as-you population' clawing its way through the vast continent, 'by far the greater part of which is still in the state in which nature left it'.[51] This freedom was demonstrated in extreme individuality, informality, indifference to rank or class and, to curious or startled Europeans, often aggressive assertions of the 'liberty' Americans enjoyed.[52] Its effects were equally striking. That acute social observer Alexis de Tocqueville, travelling in America soon after Frances Trollope, wrote in his diary

> Liberty does not carry out each of its undertakings with the same perfection as an intelligent despotism, but in the long run it produces more than the latter. It does not always and in all circumstances give the peoples a more skilful and faultless government; but it infuses throughout the body social an activity, a force and an energy which never exist without it, and which bring forth wonders.[53]

That same activity animated the people of the coast and seaport cities. Freed from British Navigation Acts, merchants developed new markets overseas, and their ships served them with what Tocqueville was to describe as 'a sort of heroism in their manner of trading',[54] undercutting British and European competition and outrunning their vessels with 'clipper' ships; the merchant fleet, spreading its sails in every sea, increased at a rate almost matching the growth of population in the new Union.

The next century would see the twin branches of merchant power in Anglo-Saxon hands carry all before them, the British building a second overseas empire of unparalleled extension, the Americans colonizing their own continent from coast to coast, both under the shelter of British naval supremacy. Accurate prediction is not granted to many, least of all historians, but Alexis de Tocqueville could see the future:

> Nations, as well as men, almost always betray the most prominent features of their future destiny in their earliest years. When I contemplate the ardour with which the Anglo-Americans prosecute commercial enterprise, the advantages which befriend them, and the success of their undertakings, I cannot refrain from believing that they will one day become the first maritime power of the globe. They are born to rule the seas, as the Romans were to conquer the world.[55]

Glossary of Nautical Terms

abaft Towards the *stern*.

abeam At right angles to a vessel's *fore-and-aft* line.

aft The *stern* part of a vessel.

after/aftermost Adjectival forms of *aft*.

astern In a vessel's wake.

back (wind) To change direction anticlockwise.

(sails) To *brace* the *yards* so that the wind catches their *sails* from ahead, checking the vessel's progress.

beam The extreme width of a vessel.

'on the beam': the direction at right angles to a vessel's *fore-and-aft* line.

bear (verb) To lie in a certain direction from an observer, usually expressed in *points* from compass north or the *fore-and-aft* line of the vessel.

bear away To put the *helm* (*tiller*) towards the wind, so steering further off (or away from) the wind.

bear down To put the *helm* (*tiller*) away from the wind, so steering up (or closer) into the wind.

'bear down on': to sail towards.

bear up As *bear away*: to steer further off (or away from) the wind.

bearing The horizontal angle to an object from a reference point, usually compass north or the *fore-and-aft* line of the vessel.

beat   To work a vessel to *windward* by sailing *close-hauled* on alternate *tacks*.

boarding   Laying a vessel against another (when fighting) in order to *enter* men in her.

bore (verb)   The past tense of bear; (of guns) pointed towards.

bow   The foremost part of a vessel.

bowsprit   A short mast projecting forward from the *bow*, to which forward *stays* are led.

brace (verb)   To haul a *yard* around horizontally to trim its sail to the wind.

braces   Ropes from the *yardarms* for hauling the *yards* round when trimming sail.

brail (verb)   To gather a *sail* up to its *yard* so that it loses wind, either temporarily or as a preliminary to securing (furling) the sail.

brails (noun)   The running rigging used to *brail* up the *sails*.

breech   The end of the gun where the *charge* is placed.

breech-loader   An early wrought-iron gun with a detachable '*breech*-piece' or *chamber*, which could be loaded and fired more rapidly than a '*muzzle*-loader'.

breeching   A stout rope made fast to the vessel's side and around the *breech* of a gun to restrain its recoil.

broadside   The main armament guns on one side of a vessel; it was usual to fire them by *quarters*, sections (or platoons) or as they came on target rather than all together.

bulwarks   The raised sides of a vessel above the upper deck to prevent seas washing aboard or men going overboard.

cable   A large-diameter rope, especially for use with an anchor; a distance of a tenth of a nautical mile, thus 200 yards or 100 *fathoms*.

cannon   A heavy cast-bronze or -iron gun with a length-to-diameter-of-bore ratio of 18–22 to 1. Cannon were cast with an integral *breech*, and hence had to be loaded through the *muzzle* (thus muzzle-loaders); this was slower than breech-loading but allowed a larger *charge* to be fired, which gave the shot or shots higher velocity, hence longer *range*. They fired round shot of 30 lb weight (demi-cannon) upward. Sixteenth-century gunnery tables give a demi-cannon (30 lb) at 5° *elevation* a range of 1,600 yards, rather over three-quarters of a nautical mile.

capstan A drum set vertically on a spindle in the deck and turned manually with capstan bars to heave in *cables* and *warps*.

carriage (gun carriage) A box-like timber structure on small wheels (*trucks*) to support a great gun and allow it to recoil when fired.

carronade A very short, light but large-bored cast-iron gun manufactured by the Carron Iron Foundry Co. of Falkirk, Scotland, from 1779. Accurate casting allowed the shot to fit more snugly in the bore than was the case with conventional guns, consequently less of the propellant gases escaped around the ball and a smaller *charge* could be used; hence the extreme lightness of the piece. Devastating at short *range*, carronades were less effective than conventional battery guns at medium to long range. They were further distinguished by a raised foresight for aiming the piece and an iron screw-thread mechanism for adjusting the *elevation*.

cartridge A canvas, cloth, paper or flannel bag containing the propellant *charge* for a *muzzle*-loading gun.

chamber A detachable, jug-shaped *breech*-piece to hold the propellant *charge* for a *breech-loader*, secured for firing with a wedge or a metal pin.

charge The gunpowder whose rapid combustion produced gases which expanded to propel the shot from the gun.

chase-guns Long guns mounted either side of the *stem* or *sternpost* to fire ahead or *astern*.

chef d'escadre A French squadron or division commander, approximately equivalent to a rear admiral in the British navy.

close-hauled Sailing with the *yards braced* forward to the maximum extent in order to steer as close as possible (between six and seven *points*, or 67–79°) to the direction from which the wind is blowing.

convoy A number of ships under escort by warships or armed merchantmen.

course (1) The direction a vessel is steering. (2) The lower sail on fore*masts* and mainmasts.

culverin A long cast-bronze or -iron gun with a length-to-diameter-of-bore ratio of 25–30 (or more) to 1. Like the *cannon*, a *muzzle*-loader, it threw a roundshot of average 18 lb (demi-culverin 9 lb). Sixteenth-century gunnery tables give the culverin an advantage in range over the cannon of almost half a nautical mile (950 yards) at 5° *elevation*.

de'd (deduced) reckoning Calculation of navigational position worked entirely from courses steered and speeds measured since the last known position, with allowance for tide or current.

downwind   To *leeward*, away from the direction from which the wind is blowing.

ebb   A falling tide.

elevation (of gun)   The angle the bore is inclined above the horizontal – achieved by levering the *breech* end with *handspikes* against the stepped sides of the *carriage*, and placing timbers and wedges to hold the breech at the proper height.

enter   To jump aboard an enemy after *boarding* her.

fathom   A nautical measure of six feet, used for *sounding* depths and measuring lengths of *cable*.

fetch   When sailing, to reach a point of land or another vessel, or bring it *abeam*.

flagship   A *ship* carrying (and flying the flag of) the admiral (or commodore) commanding a fleet, squadron or division.

flood   A rising tide.

fore-and-aft   From *stem* to *sternpost*.

forecastle (fo'c'sle)   A raised structure at the forward end of a warship, mounting light guns.

foremast   See *masts*.

foresail   See *sails*.

forward   Towards the *bow*.

frigate   A *ship*-rigged, single-gun-deck warship built for speed, employed as a scout for a fleet, or as a dispatch vessel, commerce raider or *convoy* escort.

galleass   A hybrid oar- and sail-propelled warship.

galleon   A sailing warship with greater length-to-breadth ratio than an average merchantman and a *forecastle* set back from the head of the *stem*.

galley   An oared warship with main-battery guns firing forward over the *stem*.

gunwale (pronounced *gunn'l*)   The uppermost timber of a vessel's side.

halyard   A rope to hoist (or lower) a *yard* or *fore-and-aft sail*.

handspike   A timber lever for moving, *laying* and *training* great guns.

hatch An opening in a deck to permit access for persons, stores, cargo or guns.

haul The seaman's term for pulling.

haul round To turn (a vessel).

haul the wind To point a vessel closer to the direction from which the wind is blowing.

hawser A large-diameter rope for securing a vessel alongside a quay, or towing or *warp*ing her against the wind or tide.

heave to To stop a sailing vessel in open sea by shortening and/or *back*ing some sail and lashing the *helm* down (to *leeward*) so that she alternately comes up into and falls away from the wind, thereby making no progress.

heel (noun) The angle a vessel is leaning to one side.

(verb) To cause a vessel to lean over to one side, usually for repairs or cleaning.

helm A *tiller* by means of which the *rudder* is angled to steer the ship.

hulk A type of rounded, broad-*beam*ed merchant vessel.

hull The main body of a vessel.

hulling (shot) Striking the *hull* as opposed to the *masts* and rigging of an enemy.

impress See *press*.

inshore Towards the land.

jib-boom A spar extending *forward* from the *bowsprit*.

keel The principal centre-line timber lying *fore-and-aft* along the bottom of a ship, on which the *hull* structure is raised.

larboard That side of a vessel to the left when looking *forward*; later called the port side.

lask To sail with the wind on the *quarter*, i.e. well *abaft* the *beam*.

lay To give a gun its proper *elevation* for the *range* to the target.

lead A lead weight on a line marked in *fathoms* used for *sounding* the depth of water beneath a vessel.

lee The side opposite that from which the wind is blowing.

lee shore Land towards which the wind is blowing.

leeward (pronounced *lieuw'd*) The direction away from the wind, or downwind.

leeway A vessel's drift downwind from the *course* she is steering.

letter of marque/reprisal The commission for a *privateer* to attack enemy trade.

lie to As *heave to*: to stop in the open sea to keep a fleet together at night, in poor visibility or to repair damages, or in heavy weather to prevent storm damage.

liner Eighteen-century term for a *ship of the line*.

linstock A staff notched to hold a *match* for firing a gun.

luff The leading edge of a *sail*.

luff up To turn the bow towards the direction from which the wind is coming ('into the wind').

masts The three masts of a *ship* were named, from *forward*, foremast, mainmast and mizzen mast. Above the lower masts were topmasts, and above them topgallants (t'gallants) which took the same name – thus 'fore-topmast' etc. Larger ships of the sixteenth century had a small fourth mast known as the bonaventure mizzen.

match A small-diameter line (rope) impregnated with incendiary composition and kept alight in action to fire great guns.

muzzle The mouth end of a gun.

offing The direction away from land towards the open sea.

pinnace (1) A small two-masted and oared vessel used for taking messages from fleet/squadron commanders to other vessels or to carry dispatches. (2) A ship's boat with eight, later sixteen, oars.

point (1) One of thirty-two divisions of the compass card, each point representing $11^1/_4°$. (2) A measurement of direction with reference to a vessel's *fore-and-aft* line – e.g. four points on the *starboard bow*.

point blank The *range* at which a gun is fired horizontally.

poop The short uppermost deck at the *stern* of a vessel.

port See *larboard*.

press (impress) To require the service of men for the defence of the country, advancing them a sum of money (prest). Naval service being unpopular, force was often needed to recruit men from merchant vessels, seaports and sometimes inland towns.

privateer   A privately owned and armed vessel operating against the merchant ships of the enemy.

prize   (1) An enemy vessel captured by a warship or privateer. (2) Cargo taken from a merchant ship and condemned as contraband by an admiralty court.

prize crew   The small party sent aboard a captured *prize* to sail her into port.

prize money   The proceeds from the sale of captured ships or cargo condemned in an admiralty court.

quarter   That part of a vessel between about mid-length and the *stern*.

'on the quarter': the direction from a vessel midway between *abeam* and *astern*.

quarterdeck   The length of the upper deck *abaft* the main*mast*.

quarters   The different stations for men in action.

race   A strong or confused tide rip caused by a restricted passage for the tide to flow through, an uneven seabed, or two tides crossing.

rake (verb)   To fire *broadside* guns from across an enemy's *bow* or *stern* so that the shot sweeps the length of his deck.

rake/rakish (noun/adjective)   The degree the masts or *bow* of a vessel are angled from the perpendicular.

range (of gun)   The distance between a vessel and her target.

reach   To sail with the sails more or less square to the wind, thus with the wind on or *abaft* the *beam*.

reef   To shorten a sail by gathering a section up to the *yard* and securing it with short lengths of rope sewn into the sail known as reef points.

rove   The past tense of reeve: to thread a rope through something.

rudder   A vertical timber piece hinged on the *sternpost* and angled by the *tiller* to steer the vessel.

sails   Square sails were spread from *yards* secured to *masts* at right angles to a vessel's *fore-and-aft* line but with freedom to move laterally. Sails took their name from their mast, the lowest, largest sails being the foresails and mainsails, or *courses*, above them the fore-topsail, fore-t'gallant sail etc. Triangular fore-and-aft sails were also set from *stays*, or in the case of the mizzen and bonaventure mizzen masts from spars lying generally in a fore-and-aft direction.

schooner   A vessel with two or more *masts*, each rigged with *fore-and-aft sails*; originally with square *topsails* on the foremast.

set (noun)   (1) The angle at which a *sail* is set. (2) The direction in which a tide or current is flowing.

(verb)   (1) To rig a *sail* for sailing. (2) To trim a sail to the proper angle to the wind.

ship   A generic term for seagoing vessels, but strictly a three-*masted* vessel with square *sails* on all masts.

ship of the line   A warship powerful enough to fight in the line of battle: by the eighteenth century, a ship with two or more gun-decks.

shrouds   Standing (fixed) ropes from the mastheads to the vessel's side (or, in the case of the upper *masts*, to the *top*) *abaft* the mast to give the mast support from lateral and astern wind pressure.

sounding   Measuring the depth of sea below a vessel by casting a *lead* over the side attached to a line marked in *fathoms*.

spritsail   The square *sail* set from a *yard* on the *bowsprit*; it was superseded in the sixteenth century by triangular *fore-and-aft* sails set on *stays* from the fore-mast.

square-rigged   Describes a vessel spreading largely square *sails*.

starboard   That side of a vessel to the right when looking *forward*.

stay   A standing (fixed) rope running from the masthead to support a *mast* in a fore and (for backstay) aft line.

stem (noun)   The foremost central timber rising from the *forward* end of the *keel* to form a vessel's *bow*.

(verb)   Indicates a vessel holding her own or making only slight headway against the tide.

stern   The end of a vessel furthest from the *bow*.

sternpost   The *aftermost* central timber rising from the *after* end of the *keel*.

studding-sail   A small *sail* spread from a spar at the *yardarm*, thus extending the normal (plain) sail area for extra speed.

stunsail   The colloquial term for a *studding-sail*.

swivel   A light gun mounted on a vertical pin on the *bulwarks*, and thus free to point in any direction.

tack (noun)   The direction a sailing vessel is moving in in relation to the wind; thus 'on the *starboard* tack' means 'with the wind on the vessel's starboard side'.

(verb)   To turn a sailing vessel through the wind on to the other *tack* (noun) – i.e. to put her about by first turning her *bow* towards the wind.

tiller   A timber attached to the head of the *rudder* by means of which the rudder is angled to steer the vessel.

top   A platform built just below the masthead to spread the *shrouds* of the *mast* above (topmast or t'gallant); from the earliest days, used by sharpshooters to fire down or lob grenades on the enemy decks when in action.

train (verb)   To aim a gun by moving it laterally.

trucks   Small timber wheels for gun *carriages*.

van   The leading squadron or division.

veer (wind)   To change direction clockwise.

warp (noun)   A light *cable* used in moving a vessel by hauling her along.

(verb)   To heave a vessel along by means of *cables* or *warps* led to the *capstan*.

wear   To put a sailing vessel on the opposite *tack* by first turning her *bow* away from the wind.

weather   That side or direction from which the wind is coming.

weather gage   The position to *windward* of the enemy.

weatherly   Describes a ship good at making way towards (into) the wind.

weigh   To raise the anchor from the seabed.

wind direction   The *point* from which the wind is blowing.

windward   That side or direction from which the wind is blowing.

wore   Past tense of *wear*.

yard   The spar to which a square *sail* is bent (secured).

yardarms   The ends of a *yard*.

References and Notes

Sources are referenced by author only, unless more than one book is shown in the Bibliography by the same author, when an abbreviated title is given.

Abbreviations used:
MM   *The Mariner's Mirror*
NMM   The National Maritime Museum, Greenwich, London
PRO   Public Record Office, Kew, London

Introduction

1. Gray, p. ix.
2. First was *The Influence of Sea Power upon History, 1660–1783*, Boston, 1890.
3. Ibid., Methuen, London, 1965 edn, p. 88, cited Kennedy, *British Naval Mastery*, p. 1.
4. Cited Andrews, *Trade, Plunder*, p. 9.
5. Rodger, *Safeguard*, p. 432.
6. See Glete, i, pp. 131, 135–7, 148, 161; and see Kennedy, *Great Powers*, pp. 57–8, 71.

Chapter 1: The Prehistory of Modern Maritime Power

1. See R. S. Lopez, 'Market Expansion – the Case of Genoa', *Journal of Economic History*, vol. 24, no. 4 (Dec. 1964), esp. pp. 459ff.
2. R. Foster, 'Foreword', in Tibbles, p. 26; Thomas, *passim*.

3. Israel, p. 115.
4. Ibid, pp. 106–7; Schama, pp. 39–40.
5. Schama, p. 40.
6. Ibid., pp. 40–1.
7. Israel, pp. 156–7.
8. Letter of 6 May 1573, cited C. Duffy, p. 58.
9. By the 1580s none was even in service: see Glete, i, p. 184; Cederlund, p. 122.
10. Glete, i, p. 124.
11. Ibid., p. 127.
12. Ibid., p. 132; ii, p. 549.
13. Ibid., i, pp. 133–8; ii, pp. 596, 607.
14. Ibid., i, p. 112.
15. Israel, p. 117.

Chapter 2: The Spanish Armada, 1588

1. C. Read, *Mr Secretary Walsingham and the Policy of Queen Elizabeth*, Clarendon Press, Oxford, 3 vols., 1925, iii, pp. 82–3, cited Rowse, *Expansion*, pp. 241–2.
2. See Kennedy, *British Naval Mastery*, pp. 25–6.
3. See Neale, p. 289; Rowse, *Expansion*, p. 380.
4. See Pierson, *Commander*, pp. 63–4.
5. Ibid., p. 78.
6. See N. A. M. Rodger, 'The Development of Broadside Gunnery, 1540–1650', *MM*, vol. 82, no. 3 (Aug. 1996), pp. 301ff.
7. Ibid., pp. 305–6; Landström, pp. 112–13, 337–8.
8. See Padfield, *Guns*, p. 46.
9. See G. Parker, 'The *Dreadnought* Revolution of Tudor England', *MM*, vol. 82, no. 3 (Aug. 1996), pp. 270–1.
10. T. Glasgow Jr, 'Gorgas' Seafight', *MM*, vol. 59, no. 2 (May 1973), pp. 180–1.
11. See R. Pollitt, 'Bureaucracy and the Armada', *MM*, vol. 60, no. 2 (May 1974), pp. 120–1.
12. Ibid., pp. 126–8.
13. Cited Rodgers, p. 253.
14. See I. A. A. Thompson, 'The Appointment of the Duke of Medina-Sidonia to the Command of the Spanish Armada', *Historical Journal*, vol. 12, 1961, p. 202.
15. Ibid., pp. 198–210.
16. Parma to Philip, 31 Jan. 1588, in M. A. S. Hume, p. 201.
17. Medina-Sidonia to Idiáquez, 16 Feb. 1588, in ibid., pp. 207–8; and see Pierson, *Commander*, pp. 80–1.
18. Idiáquez to Medina-Sidonia, 20 Feb. 1588, cited Pierson, *Commander*, p. 82.

19. Philip to Medina-Sidonia, 20 Feb. 1588, in M. A. S. Hume, pp. 12–23.

20. Pierson, *Commander*, p. 100.

21. See I. A. A. Thompson, 'Spanish Armada Guns', *MM*, vol. 61, no. 4 (Nov. 1975), pp. 367–70; and analysis in Padfield, *Armada*, pp. 64–5.

22. Cited Mattingley, pp. 191–2.

23. Medina-Sidonia's General Orders, May 1588, in M. A. S. Hume, p. 290.

24. Medina-Sidonia to Philip, 1 July 1588, cited C. Lloyd & G. Naish, iv, p. 25; Medina-Sidonia to Philip, 21 and 24 June 1588, in M. A. S. Hume, pp. 314, 317–18; Philip to Medina-Sidonia, 5 July 1588, in ibid., pp. 326–8.

25. Israel, p. 286. Zeeland contributed 15.8 per cent, Friesland 13.3 per cent, Utrecht 6.6 per cent.

26. Cited Cerovski, p. 68.

27. Howard to Burghley, 29 Feb. 1588, in Laughton, *Spanish Armada*, i, p. 85.

28. Ibid.

29. Howard to Burghley, 8 April 1588, in ibid., p. 138.

30. Medina-Sidonia to Philip, 30 July 1588, in M. A. S. Hume, pp. 357–8.

31. See I. A. A. Thompson, op. cit. (ref. 21 above), pp. 355–71; Padfield, *Armada*, pp. 62–5; G. Parker, op. cit. (ref. 9 above), p. 281.

32. See, for instance, Padfield, *Armada*, p. 107.

33. See Pierson, *Commander*, pp. 235–43.

34. Cited A. R. Smith, p. xvii.

35. Henry Whyte to Walsingham, 8 Aug. 1588, in Laughton, *Spanish Armada*, ii, p. 63.

36. See N. A. M. Rodger, op. cit. (ref. 6 above), esp. pp. 313–14.

37. Medina-Sidonia to Philip (diary), Aug. 1588, in Laughton, *Spanish Armada*, ii, p. 396.

38. Howard to Walsingham, 21 July 1588, in ibid., i, p. 288.

39. Report of deserters, Holland, 3 Aug. 1588, in ibid., ii, p. 79; and Pedro Calderon's account in M. A. S. Hume, p. 441.

40. Howard to Sussex, 22 July 1588, in Laughton, *Spanish Armada*, i, p. 299.

41. 'A Relation of Proceedings', cited ibid., p. 11.

42. Ibid., p. 12.

43. Medina-Sidonia to Moncada, 2 Aug. 1588, in M. A. S. Hume, p. 359.

44. Medina-Sidonia to Philip (diary), Aug. 1588, in Laughton, *Spanish Armada*, ii, p. 399.

45. Pedro Calderon's account, in M. A. S. Hume, p. 443.

46. Medina-Sidonia to Parma, 4 Aug. 1588, in ibid., p. 360.

47. Medina-Sidonia to Parma, 6 Aug. 1588, in ibid., pp. 362–3.

48. Parma to Philip, 22 June 1588, in ibid., pp. 315–16.

49. Supplementary secret instructions, 1 April 1588, in ibid., p. 250.

50. Seymour to Walsingham, 12 and 20 July 1588, in Laughton, *Spanish Armada*, i, pp. 254–5, 286.

51. See Manrique to Idiáquez, 11 Aug. 1588, in M. A. S. Hume, p. 375.
52. Medina-Sidonia to Philip (diary), Aug. 1588, in Laughton, *Spanish Armada*, ii, p. 401.
53. Estrada, cited Monson, ii, p. 307.
54. Relation of galleass *Zuniga*, in M. A. S. Hume, p. 461.
55. Pedro Calderon's account, in ibid., p. 444.
56. Ibid.
57. Wynter to Walsingham, 11 Aug. 1588, in Laughton, *Spanish Armada*, ii, p. 10.
58. Pedro Calderon's account, in M. A. S. Hume, p. 444.
59. Ibid., p. 445.
60. Fenner to Walsingham, 14 Aug. 1588, in Laughton, *Spanish Armada*, ii, p. 40; and see G. Parker, op. cit. (ref. 9 above), p. 280.
61. Captain Alonso de Vanegas, cited Pierson, *Commander*, p. 164; and see G. Parker, op. cit. (ref. 9 above), p. 274.
62. Ibid., pp. 280–3.
63. Drake to Walsingham, 8 Aug. 1588, in Laughton, *Spanish Armada*, i, p. 341.
64. See Pierson, *Commander*, p. 165.
65. Howard to Walsingham, 8 Aug. 1588, in Laughton, *Spanish Armada*, i, p. 341.
66. De Cuellar.
67. Medina-Sidonia to Philip, 23 Sept. 1588, in M. A. S. Hume, p. 432.
68. See Padfield, *Armada*, pp. 190–1; Pierson, *Commander*, Appendix, Battle Order, pp. 235–43.

Chapter 3: The Downs, 1639

1. 1596 and 1597; Philip III sent another armada north in 1601, which was again scattered by gales.
2. See Israel, pp. 115, 308–9.
3. See Barbour, p. 131.
4. Al-Djarmūzi, *History*, p. 315, cited Sergeant, p. 122.
5. C. Duffy, pp. 80–2.
6. Israel, p. 253.
7. Boxer, *Dutch Seaborne Empire*, p. 21.
8. "The total Habsburg sailing navy in the 1590s may have reached 40–50,000 tons (displacement)': Glete, i. p. 149.
9. Ibid., pp. 156–9.
10. Israel, pp. 321–2.
11. Boxer, *Dutch Seaborne Empire*, p. 49; Barbour, p. 50.
12. Amsterdam from 60,000 to 116,000 between 1600 and 1632, Leiden from 26,000 to 54,000 in the same period: Israel, p. 328.
13. See Padfield, *Tide of Empires*, i, pp. 171–2.

14. See Dom. F. M. de Mello, *Epanaphora Bellica IV, conflito do Canal*, Lisbon, 1676, pp. 502–23, cited Boxer, *Tromp*, p. 35.

15. See Padfield, *Tide of Empires*, i, pp. 49–51.

16. See Schama, pp. 251–2; Israel, pp. 610, 713.

17. See Kennedy, *Great Powers*, p. 89; Schama, pp. 252–3.

18. Kennedy, *Great Powers*, p. 89; Barbour, p. 83; Wilson, *Economic History*, p. 121.

19. Wilson, *Economic History*, p. 120, estimates per capita income as: England £1. 4s. od.; France £1. 5s. od.; Holland £3. 1s. 7d.

20. Ibid., pp. 31, 101, 123; and see Israel, pp. 611–12.

21. Jones, *Britain and the World*, pp. 6off.; Israel, pp. 610–11, 713–14.

Chapter 4: The Dutch Golden Age

1. Cited Israel, p. 3.

2. Temple to Lady Giffard, 10 Oct. 1667, cited Courtenay, i, p. 116.

3. Cited Dickson, p. 4.

4. Israel, p. 1.

5. Ibid.; Schama, pp. 266–71.

6. Israel, p. 677; Schama, pp. 402–3.

7. Schama, p. 412.

8. Ibid., p. 265.

9. Owen Feltham, *A Brief Character of the Low Countries*, London, 1627, cited Schama, p. 265.

10. Israel, p. 678.

11. Ibid., p. 682.

12. See Schama, pp. 472, 579–603.

13. Hugo Grotius, *De Antiquitate Reipublicae Batavicae*, Amsterdam, 1610, cited Israel, pp. 421–2.

14. F. J. L. Krämer, ed., *Lettres de Pierre de Groot a Abraham de Wicquefort, 1664–74*, Utrecht, 1894, p. 95, cited Bromley & Kossman, p. 23.

15. See J. de Witt's thesis, July 1654, cited Israel, p. 725.

16. Cited Pontalis, i, pp. 54–5.

17. See ibid., pp. 300ff.; Israel, p. 719.

18. Quota system for financing the Generality (percentages, 1658): Holland 58.25, Zeeland 9.25, Friesland 11.6, Utrecht 5.75, Groningen 5.75, Gelderland 5.6, Overijssel 3.1, Drente 0.95: Israel, p. 286.

19. Ibid., p. 277.

20. Schama, pp. 65, 283; and see Israel, p. 231.

21. Dutch standing army: 1643 – 60,430; 1651 – 24,395: Israel, p. 602.

22. See Paul Butel, 'France, the Antilles, and Europe in the 17th and 18th Centuries . . .', in Tracy, pp. 157–9.

23. Barbour, p. 24.

24. However, it did extend credits to a Lending Bank, established 1614, and made advances to the VOC in 1619: ibid., p. 43.

25. Andrew Yarranton, *England's Improvement by Land and Sea. To Outdo the Dutch without Fighting*, London, 1677, cited Dickson, p. 5.

26. Joseph de la Vega, *Confusion de Confusiones* [1688] *Portions Descriptive of the Amsterdam Stock Exchange*, ed. H. Kellenbenz, Baker Library, Boston, 1957, p. 21, cited Schama, p. 349.

27. See Barbour, pp. 20–1; Murray, p. 59; Schama, pp. 347–50.

28. Melchior Fokkens, *Beschryving der Widjt-Vermaerde Koop-stadt Amstelredam*, Amsterdam, 3rd edn, 1664, cited Schama, pp. 300ff.

29. See Murray, pp. 76ff.; Barbour, p. 69.

30. Israel, p. 999.

31. M. Fokkens, *Beschryving*, op. cit. (ref. 28 above), p. 396, cited Schama, p. 303.

32. Murray, p. 4.

33. William Aglionby, *The Present State of the United Provinces of the Low Countries*, London, 1669, cited Schama, p. 267.

34. See Schama, pp. 166ff.

35. Both stories cited Murray, p. 16.

36. For instance, J. van Beverwijk, *Van de Wtnementheyt des Vrouweliken Geschlachts*, Dordrecht, 2nd edn, 1643, cited Schama, p. 386.

37. 'The struggle between worldliness and homeliness was but another variation on the classic Dutch counterpoint between materialism and morality': Schama, p. 389.

38. See Israel, p. 686.

39. See Schama, pp. 45–6, 68, 561; Israel, p. 738.

40. See Israel, pp. 899ff.

41. See Boxer, *Dutch Seaborne Empire*, p. 81.

42. See Thomas, pp. 159–62.

43. Boxer, *Dutch Seaborne Empire*, p. 99; and see Landes, pp. 142–7.

44. Cited Wynne-Tyson, pp. 211–12; and see Singer, p. 217.

45. See Wynne-Tyson, pp. 92–3.

46. Nicholas Fontaine, *Memoires pour servir a l'histoire de Port-Royal*, Cologne, 1738, ii, pp. 52–3, cited Singer, p. 220.

47. 'Apology for Raymond de Sebonde', *Essays*, Bordeaux, 1588, cited Singer, p. 199.

Chapter 5: Sole Bay, 1672

1. See Rodger, *Safeguard*, pp. 414–16; J. S. Wheeler, 'Prelude to Power', *MM*, vol. 81, no. 2 (May 1995), p. 152.

2. See Glete, i, pp. 178–82.

3. Wilson, *Profit and Power*, pp. 20ff.

4. Ibid., pp. 41ff.; Andrews, *Trade, Plunder*, pp. 268ff.

5. See Pontalis, i, p. 132.

6. Gardiner, i, p. 81.

7. Jones, *Anglo-Dutch Wars*, p. 113.

8. Glete, i, pp. 181–2; ii, p. 550.

9. Tromp to the States General, 14 Dec. 1652, cited Gardiner, iii, p. 120.

10. Wilson, *Profit and Power*, p. 76; Pontalis, i, p. 168.

11. Diary, 22 Dec. 1664, in Pepys (ed. Wheatley), iv, p. 292.

12. Ibid., 23 Dec. 1664, p. 293.

13. Ibid., 30–31 Dec. 1664, p. 299.

14. Glete, i, pp. 189–90; ii, pp. 550, 639.

15. Diary, 16 June 1665, in Pepys (ed. Wheatley), iv, p. 411.

16. See p. 62.

17. April 1653; see Corbett, *Fighting Instructions*, pp. 95ff.; Padfield, *Tide of Empires*, i, pp. 215–22.

18. Corbett's analysis of the evolution of the line of battle (see *Fighting Instructions*, pp. 95–7, 120f.) is more persuasive than Tunstall's (see *Naval Warfare*, pp. 19–20); the efficacy of English gunnery tactics is conveyed in, for instance, 'A Letter from the Hague', 9 June 1653, cited Gardiner, v, p. 100.

19. See R. E. J. Weber, 'The Introduction of the Single Line Ahead as a Battle Formation by the Dutch, 1665–1666', *MM*, vol. 73, no. 1 (Feb. 1987), pp. 5ff.

20. See Jones, *Anglo-Dutch Wars*, p. 174.

21. See Wilson, *Anglo-Dutch Commerce*, pp. 89–90.

22. Diary, 13 June 1667, in Pepys (ed. Wheatley), vi, p. 341.

23. 31 July 1667.

24. See Pontalis, i, pp. 425–6.

25. See Cole, *Colbert*, i, pp. 344, 437.

26. Cited ibid., p. 334.

27. Glete, i, pp. 190–2; ii, pp. 550, 558, 639.

28. Ibid., i, p. 192.

29. Jones, *Anglo-Dutch Wars*, p. 185; from 1662 the WIC had been a subcontractor in the slaving *asiento*, permitted to re-export slaves from Curaçao in Dutch vessels; ibid., p. 35; and see Thomas, pp. 191–2.

30. Jones, *Anglo-Dutch Wars*, p. 186; Schama, pp. 283–5.

31. See Glete, i, p. 192; ii, pp. 550, 580, 639. Glete's estimates of the three leading navies in 1670 are (ships of over 500 tons displacement): United Provinces, 95 of aggregate 90,000 tons displ.; France, 84 of aggregate 103,000 tons displ.; England, 69 of aggregate 75,000 tons displ.

32. Anderson, *Third Dutch War*, p. 396.

33. Narborough's journal, 15 May 1672, in ibid., p. 86.

34. Tunstall, *Naval Warfare*, p. 32.

35. Art. VI, Additional Instructions for Fighting, 18 April 1665, issued by James, in Corbett, *Fighting Instructions*, p. 126; Tunstall, *Naval Warfare*, p. 23.

36. L. van Aitzema, *Saken van Staet en oorlogh*, 'Gravenhage, 1670, v, p. 457, cited Weber, op. cit. (ref. 19 above), p. 9.

37. Anderson, *Third Dutch War*, pp. 396–7.

38. 'An Account of what passed on board the several ships the Duke was in the day of the engagement', in ibid., p. 178; Narborough's journal is silent on the point.

39. Blok, p. 311.

40. Narborough's journal, 27 May 1672, 8.00 a.m., in Anderson, *Third Dutch War*, p. 96.

41. 'An Account of what passed . . .' op. cit. (ref. 38 above), in ibid., p. 178. Narborough, in his journal, has van Nes on the bow, de Ruyter on the quarter: ibid., p. 96.

42. Narborough's journal, 28 May 1672, in ibid., p. 96.

43. Ibid., p. 97.

44. Haddock's account, in ibid., p. 166.

45. Ibid., p. 167.

46. Anderson, *Third Dutch War*, p. 21.

47. Haddock's account, in ibid., p. 167.

48. Anderson, *Third Dutch War*, p. 97.

49. Cited Pontalis, ii, pp. 298–9.

50. Schama, pp. 244–5.

51. Courtenay, i, p. 393.

52. Grey, ii, p. 213.

53. Ibid., p. 203.

54. Treaty of Westminster, 16 Feb. 1674.

Chapter 6: The 'Glorious Revolution', and Beachy Head, 1690

1. Temple to Arlingon, 3 Feb. 1669, in Courtenay, i, pp. 285–6.

2. Spencer House Journals, p. 218, cited Ehrman, p. 258.

3. Mr Garroway, in Grey, i, p. 324.

4. Lord Shaftesbury, in ibid., p. 329.

5. Israel, pp. 843–5.

6. Glete, i, pp. 189–91; ii, p. 558.

7. See Jones, *The Revolution of 1688*, pp. 225–6.

8. Ibid., pp. 228–9.

9. Ibid., pp. 260–1.

10. See Israel, p. 858.

11. See Schama, pp. 53–4, 295–7, 320.

12. See Davis, *English Shipping Industry*, pp. 15–18.

13. S. B. Baxter, *William III*, Longman, London, 1966, pp. 224–5, 229–33, places William's final decision to invade at the end of April 1688, thus before receiving the 'invitation': cited Jones, *The Revolution of 1688*, p. 250; and see ibid., pp. 239–41.

14. Ibid., p. 261.

15. See Campbell, p. 87 especially.

16. *Encycl. Britannica*, x, pp. 69–70.

17. See Ehrman, pp. 234–5; and E. B. Powley, *The English Navy in the Revolution of 1688*, Cambridge University Press, Cambridge, 1928, pp. 67–8, 116–17, cited Jones, *The Revolution of 1688*, p. 233.

18. 26 Nov. 1688.

19. See Ehrman, pp. 247–8.

20. See Powley, pp. 140, 142; Ehrman, p. 265.

21. Torrington to Nottingham, 26 June 1690, cited Ehrman, p. 345.

22. Ibid.

23. Nottingham to Torrington, 29 June 1690, cited Warnsinck, p. 95.

24. Mary/Nottingham to Torrington, 29 June 1690, cited ibid., p. 94.

25. Peter Le Fevre, '"Meer Laziness" or Incompetence: The Earl of Torrington and the Battle of Beachy Head', *MM*, vol. 80, no. 3 (Aug. 1994), p. 290.

26. Cited in E. Chappell, ed., *The Tangier Papers of Samuel Pepys*, Navy Records Soc., London, 1935, p. 138, cited Ehrman, p. 275.

27. Gilles Schey's evidence; cited Peter Le Fevre, op. cit. (ref. 25 above), pp. 291–2.

28. See Warnsinck, p. 101.

29. Ibid.

30. *An Account Given by Sir John Ashby, Vice Admiral, and Rear Admiral Rooke to the Lords Commissioners*, London, 1691, p. 16, cited C. D. Lee, 'The Battle of Beachy Head: Lord Torrington's Conduct', *MM*, vol. 80, no. 3 (Aug. 1994), p. 274.

31. Rooke's account, NMM H15/3; see also Delavall at Torrington's court martial: 'The French squadron edged off from the start . . .' NMM H15/3.

32. *An Account Given by Sir John Ashby. . .*, op. cit. (ref. 30 above), pp. 15–16, cited C. D. Lee, op. cit. (ref. 30 above), p. 277; and see Le Fevre, op. cit. (ref. 25 above), p. 293.

33. See Nottingham to Mary, 6 July 1690, NMM SOU/12.

34. See J. Campbell, *Lives of the British Admirals*, London, 1812, iii, p. 63, cited C. D. Lee, op. cit. (ref. 30 above), p. 270.

35. Portland Papers, viii, p. 30, cited Warnsinck, p. 137.

36. Depositions at Torrington's court martial, NMM H15/3.

37. Cited C. D. Lee, op. cit. (ref. 30 above), p. 271.

38. Torrington's speech in House of Commons, Nov. 1690, cited Ehrman, p. 350.

39. William Blathwayt to Southwell, 3(?) July 1690, NMM SOU/1.

40. See Aubrey, p. 55.

41. See Nottingham to Mary, 22 July 1690, NMM SOU/12.

42. Ehrman, p. 106; Aubrey, pp. 57–8.

43. See A. N. Ryan, 'William III and the Brest Fleet in the Nine Years' War', in Halton & Bromley, p. 51; Ehrman, p. 85.

Chapter 7: Barfleur/La Hougue, 1692

1. Cited Aubrey, p.80; and see Symcox, p. 80.

2. C. de la Roncière, *Histoire de la Marine Française*, Larousse, Paris, 6 vols., 1932, vi, pp. 99–102, cited Aubrey, p. 80.

3. Aubrey, Appendix, pp. 175–8, has van 26, centre 27, rear 29; NMM PLA/13 has 26, 34, 35, thus a grand total of 95 in the British line.

4. Comte de Tourville, *Memoires du maréchal de Tourville*, Amsterdam, 1753, and Eugène Sué, *Histoire de la Marine Française sous Louis XIV*, Paris, 1858, both cited Aubrey, p. 90.

5. See Aubrey, p. 99.

6. Ibid., p. 101.

7. John Dalrymple, *Memoirs of Great Britain and Ireland*, 2nd edn, 1771–88, i, p. 508, cited ibid., p. 121.

8. Crowhurst, p. 18.

9. Symcox, p. 140.

10. See Scoville, p. 383; Brewer, *Sinews of Power*, p. 70.

11. Symcox, pp. 141–5.

12. Ibid., p. 234.

13. See Brewer, *Sinews of Power*, p. 15.

14. Ibid., pp. 19–20.

15. See ibid., pp. 142–8; Dickson, pp. 46–7.

16. Dickson, pp. 48–50.

17. See ibid., p. 50.

18. Cited Israel, p. 856.

19. Brewer, *Sinews of Power*, p. 161.

20. See J. A. Johnston, 'Parliament and the Protection of Trade, 1689–1694', *MM*, vol. 57, no. 4 (Nov. 1971), pp. 410–13.

21. See Ehrman, p. 569; Symcox, p. 234.

22. J. A. Johnston, op. cit. (ref. 20 above), p. 413.

Chapter 8: Málaga, 1704

1. Israel, p. 969; and see Mark A. Thomson, 'Louis XIV and the Origins of the War of the Spanish Succession', in Halton & Bromley, pp. 147–8.

2. Mark A. Thomson, op. cit. (ref. 1 above), p. 159.

3. Chamillart to de Harley, 26 April 1701; G.–B. Depping, *Correspondence Administrative sous le règne de Louis XIV*, Paris, 1850–5, iii, p. 321, cited Scoville, p. 377.

4. Cited Mark A. Thomson, op. cit. (ref. 1 above), p. 151.

5. Cited Owen, p. 34.

6. Tunstall, *Naval Warfare*, p. 64.

7. To the Admiralty, 19 July 1702, cited Corbett, *England in the Mediterranean*, p. 211.

8. Cited Tunstall, *Naval Warfare*, p. 65.

9. See J. H. Harland, 'The Early Steering Wheel', *MM*, vol. 58, no. 1 (Feb. 1972), pp. 41ff.; G. F. Howard, 'The Early Steering Wheel', *MM*, vol. 64, no. 2 (May 1978), pp. 188–9; D. H. Roberts, 'The Origin of the Steering Wheel', *MM*, vol. 75, no. 3 (Aug. 1989), pp. 272–3.

10. Cited J. F. C. Fuller, 'Marlborough', in B. Parker, p. 40.

11. Owen, pp. 284–5.

12. Ibid., p. 69; Mitchell & Deane, pp. 279, 285, 293; Crowhurst, p. 55.

13. See Marlborough to Heinsius, 19/23 Feb. and 7/18 Mar. 1705, cited Hoff, pp. 161, 169.

14. See, for instance, the petitions from gunmakers, weavers, cutlers, dyers, sail-makers, wrought-iron manufacturers etc. to the House of Commons, which influenced British diplomatic attitudes at the Treaty of Utrecht: cited Thomas, p. 231.

15. The Methuen Treaty, 1703; see Kennedy, *British Naval Mastery*, p. 86; Wilson, *Anglo-Dutch Commerce*, p. 8.

16. Marlborough to Heinsius, 19 Aug. 1705, cited Hoff, p. 203.

17. Owen, p. 277.

18. Scoville, pp. 372ff.

19. 'To maintain that in the past 40 years open war has not been declared on consumption and trade would be the same as maintaining that the Seine does not run through Paris': Pierre de Boisguillebert (economic reformer and precursor of the Physiocrats), 1704, cited Scoville, p. 380. Scoville summarizes, 'The wonder is that the economy did not collapse completely', p. 389.

20. Israel, p. 986.

21. Brewer, *Sinews of Power*, p. 90; Wilson, *Economic History*, p. 120.

22. See Brewer, *Sinews of Power*, pp. 65–9.

23. Battle of Oudenarde, 1708.

24. See Dickson, pp. 62ff.

25. Treaty of Antwerp, 1715.

26. See Israel, p. 978.

27. See Israel, p. 986; Brewer, *Sinews of Power*, p. 131.

28. See Wilson, *Anglo-Dutch Commerce*, pp. 65, 173.

29. Scoville, p. 388.
30. Ibid., p. 411.
31. Revocation of the Edict of Nantes.
32. 25 May 1716, Archives Nationales F 12 693, cited Scoville, p. 376.
33. Glete, i, p. 227.
34. See Mitchell & Deane, pp. 279, 285ff.
35. Dickson, p. 50.
36. See Kennedy, *British Naval Mastery*, pp. 87–8.
37. See Dickson, p. 90; Brewer, *Sinews of Power*, pp. 115, 122.
38. See, for instance, Brewer, *Sinews of Power*, pp. 141–3.

Chapter 9: Rule, Britannia

1. See Dickson, pp. 91, 457, 470.
2. Thomas, p. 243.
3. Ibid., pp. 236–7.
4. See Glete, i, pp. 228, 256; ii, pp. 551, 580, 629, 640.
5. See Brewer, *Sinews of Power*, p. 194.
6. Cited without source in Chancellor, p. 136.
7. 12 Mar. 1711, cited Jefferson, p. 11.
8. 10 Oct. 1667, in Courtenay, i, p. 116.
9. Cited Fisher, p. 697.
10. Cited ibid.
11. 'A Letter from Italy', 1704, in Lonsdale, p. 44.
12. Thomas, p. 452.
13. Collins Library of Classics edn, London and Glasgow, *c.* 1920, p. 55.
14. See, for instance, Williams, pp. 148, 392, 429; and Vickery, esp. pp. 9–11, 166, 259, 277, 287–8.
15. Scholes, p. 68.
16. 29 Sept. 1725, in Landa, pp. 493–4.
17. Cited ibid., p. vii.
18. To his son, 7 Feb. 1749, in Chesterfield, p. 106.
19. Ibid.
20. See Israel, pp. 372–3, 430, 786–91.
21. Cited Israel, p. 787; and see Russell, p. 593.
22. Russell, p. 604.
23. Ibid., and pp. 613–19.
24. Cited Russell, p. 654.
25. See, for instance, Lane; and Haley, *The Dutch*.
26. Russell, p. 624.
27. Cited Williams, p. 7.
28. See ibid., p. 8.

29. D. Hume, p. 44.
30. Ibid., p. 677; and see Russell, pp. 687ff.
31. E. C. Mossner's Introduction to D. Hume, p. 22.
32. Landes, p. 276.
33. See A. H. John, 'War and the English Economy', *Engl. Hist. Review*, 2nd Series, vol. VII (1954–5), p. 330.
34. The urban population increased from 13.5 to 21 per cent of the total population between 1670 and 1750: Brewer, *Sinews of Power*, p. 180.
35. Bernal, pp. 474, 524–5; Williams, pp. 105–9.
36. See Williams, pp. 50–1; Rudé, pp. 150–1.
37. Cited Richmond, *The Navy in the War of 1739–48*, i, p. 274.
38. Rodger, *Wooden World*, p. 150.
39. W. Spavens, *The Narrative of William Spavens . . .* , Louth, 1796, p. 36, cited ibid., pp. 150–1.
40. S. Gradish, *The Manning of the British Navy during the Seven Years' War*, Royal Historical Society, London, 1980, reviewed *MM*, vol. 67, no. 3 (Aug. 1981), pp. 295–6.
41. From 'Reformation of Manners (London)', 1702, in Lonsdale, p. 35.
42. Cited Thomas, p. 453.
43. 'Rule, Britannia', 1740, in F. T. Palgrave, *The Golden Treasury*, various edns.
44. John Atkins, *A Voyage to the Guinea, Brazil and the West Indies . . .* , London, 1737, pp. 53–73, 158–80, cited Sir James Watt, 'James Ramsay, 1733–1789 . . . Morning Star of the Anti-Slavery Movement', *MM*, vol. 81, no. 2 (May 1995), p. 156.
45. Niels Steensgaard, 'The Growth and Composition of the Long Distance Trade of England and the Dutch Republic before 1750', in Tracy, p. 131.
46. Thomas, p. 244; David Richardson, 'Liverpool and the English Slave Trade', in Tibbles, p. 73.
47. Thomas, pp. 254, 256.
48. Niels Steensgaard, op. cit. (ref. 45 above), in Tracy, p. 138.
49. Herbert, S. Klein, 'Economic Aspects of the Eighteenth Century Slave Trade', in Tracy, pp. 293–8.
50. Brewer, *Sinews of Power*, pp. 38–40.
51. See Klein, op. cit. (ref. 49 above), in Tracy, p. 288.

Chapter 10: Finisterre, 1747

1. See Ward Barrett, 'World Bullion Flows, 1450–1800', in Tracy, pp. 228–9, 242–3.
2. See Frederic Mauro, 'Merchant Communities, 1350–1750', in ibid., pp.

283–4; and C. R. Phillips, 'The Growth and Composition of Trade in the Iberian Peninsula, 1450–1750', in ibid., pp. 64–5.

3. See Paul Butel, 'France, the Antilles, and Europe in the Seventeenth and Eighteenth Centuries . . .' in ibid., pp. 153, 162ff.

4. See ibid., p. 163; and Mitchell & Deane, pp. 279–80, 399.

5. Paul Butel, op. cit. (ref. 3 above), in Tracy, p. 169. In the 1730s France shipped over 100,000 slaves across the Atlantic: Thomas, p. 254.

6. Herbert S. Klein, 'Economic Aspects of the Eighteen Century Slaving Trade', in Tracy, pp. 290ff.

7. The merchants of Seville found themselves unable to sell clothing in Spanish America because of British smuggled goods: Thomas, p. 246.

8. Sir T. Saunderson, 6 Mar. 1739, in *A Collection of the Parliamentary Debates in England*, London, 1739, iii, p. 23.

9. Sir Robert Walpole, in ibid., iii, pp. 107–9.

10. Ibid., pp. 113–14.

11. Lord Portland in ibid., pp. 19–20.

12. British shipping clearances were over 20 per cent higher in the three years after the war than in the three years before it: A. H. John, 'War and the English Economy', *Eng. Hist. Review*, 2nd Series vol. VII (1954–5), p. 333. Between 1739 and 1748 British exports rose by 2.3 million: Mitchell & Deane, pp. 279–80.

13. See Israel, p. 1007.

14. Ibid., pp. 1067–78; and see Leeb, p. 55.

15. Dickson, p. 216.

16. Ibid., p. 229; Williams, p. 264.

17. Cited Richmond, *The Navy in the War of 1739–48*, i, p. 169.

18. Cited Ekins, p. 18.

19. Richmond, *The Navy in the War of 1739–48*, iii, p. 72.

20. See Brian Lavery, 'The Origins of the 74-gun Ship', *MM*, vol. 63, no. 4 (Nov. 1977), pp. 335ff.; and see Mackay, pp. 71ff.

21. 74-gun common class, 165 ft 6 inches length on gun-deck; 1,547 tons; twenty-eight 32-pdrs main battery, twenty-eight 18-pdrs upper deck, eighteen 9-pdrs quarterdeck and forecastle: Brian Lavery, op. cit. (ref. 20 above), p. 348.

Chapter 11: Quiberon Bay, 1759

1. Glete, i, pp. 265–6.

2. See Corbett, *Seven Years' War*, ii, p. 72; Mackay, p. 128.

3. See Tunstall, *Admiral Byng*, p. 283.

4. Holderness to Sir Andrew Mitchell, 5 July 1757, cited Corbett, *Seven Years' War*, i, pp. 189–90.

5. See Rodger, *Wooden World*, p. 31.
6. Cited without source in R. Middleton, 'British Naval Strategy, 1755–1762: The Western Squadron', *MM*, vol. 75, no. 4 (Nov. 1989), p. 350.
7. Ibid., without source, p. 351; and see Mackay, pp. 131–3.
8. See Tunstall, *Naval Warfare*, pp. 97–8; these additional instructions are attributed to Anson in 1746 or 1747, and issued by Hawke, 12 Aug. 1747; Corbett, *Seven Years' War*, ii, pp. 63–4n.
9. Mackay, pp. 150, 180–1; Tunstall, *Naval Warfare*, p. 105.
10. Tunstall, *Naval Warfare*, p. 106.
11. Mackay, p. 200.
12. 20 May 1759, PRO ADM/1/92, cited ibid., p. 202.
13. Hawke to Admiralty, 27 May 1759, cited ibid., p. 206.
14. 8 Sept. 1759, Hawke Out-Letters, cited ibid., p. 223; and see R. Middleton, op. cit. (ref. 6 above), p. 364.
15. Corbett, *Seven Years' War*, ii, p.28.
16. 7, 9, 10 July 1759, Hawke Out-Letters, cited Mackay, p. 214.
17. Conflans to Berrier, 5 Nov. 1759, cited Marcus, p. 111.
18. Cited Corbett, *Seven Years' War*, ii, p. 61.
19. Ibid., pp. 63–4n.
20. Ibid., pp. 64–5.
21. Cited ibid., p. 66.
22. Leaders passed the Cardineaux *c.* 2.50 p.m., the *Royal George* at 3.00 p.m.: ibid., p. 247.
23. Ibid., pp. 248, 252; Jenkins, p. 134.
24. Cited Ekins, p. 46.
25. Hawke's dispatch 24 Nov. 1759, Hawke Out-Letters, cited Mackay, p. 254.
26. Ibid.
27. 117 of the line in 1755 to 135 of the line in 1760; a 70 per cent advantage over the French fleet in 1755 had become a 140 per cent advantage by 1760: Glete, i, pp. 268, 266.
28. Cited Lloyd, p. 121.
29. Hawke to Sally Birt, 24 Nov. 1759, Hawke Out-Letters, cited Mackay, pp. 255–6.
30. Cresswell, p. 115.
31. Duke of Bedford to Bute, 13 June 1761, cited Corbett, *Seven Years' War*, ii, pp. 172–3.
32. Mitchell & Deane, p. 280.
33. Thomas, p. 265.
34. See Kennedy, *British Naval Mastery*, p. 105.
35. Brewer, *Sinews of Power*, p. 30.
36. Isaac de Pinto, cited Wilson, *Anglo-Dutch Commerce*, p. 76.

37. See Brewer, *Sinews of Power*, pp. 42, 123; Dickson, p. 322.
38. See Beik, p. 32.

Chapter 12: The American Revolution

1. McCusker & Menard, pp. 54, 218–21; Shepherd & Walton, p. 101.
2. A. Smith, i, p. 62.
3. See Palmer, pp. 156, 158.
4. Israel, pp. 114–15; McCusker & Menard, p. 131.
5. McCusker & Menard, p. 250.
6. Tocqueville, i, p. 510.
7. Shepherd & Walton, p. 98.
8. Chapelle, p. 27.
9. Tocqueville, i, pp. 510–11.
10. Chapelle, p. 27.
11. Ibid.; Shepherd & Walton, pp. 241–4.
12. Shepherd & Walton, pp. 107–8, 113, 163.
13. Declaration in 1763; Thomas, pp. 259, 271–2, 456–8.
14. Palmer, p. 158.
15. Stout, pp. 25–6.
16. Boston town meeting, cited Pole, *American Independence*, p. 41.
17. Massachusetts alone paid over a quarter of all collections made under the Sugar Act: Stout, p. 63.
18. See Pole, *American Independence*, pp. 45, 54; Pole, *Political Representation*, pp. 266–7.
19. Oliver M. Dickerson's thesis, cited Stout, p. 112.
20. Sir Samuel Hood to George Grenville, 11 July 1768, in W. J. Smith, ed., *The Grenville Papers*, London, 4 vols., 1852–3, iv, p. 306, cited Stout, p. 122.
21. See Wright, pp. 10–12.
22. See Stout, pp. 165–70.
23. See McCusker & Menard, pp. 352–3.
24. See Thomas J. Fleming, 'The "Military Crimes" of Charles Lee', *American Heritage*, vol. XIX, no. 3 (April 1968), pp. 13–14.
25. 'A Summary View of the Rights of British America', 1774.
26. *Encycl. Britannica*, vi, p. 283.
27. John Adams, in *Thoughts on Government*, Boston, 1776, held that the purpose of government should be 'the happiness of the people'. Earlier, Francis Hutcheson, professor of moral philosophy at Glasgow University, had raised 'happiness' and the general good in political consciousness, and in *A System of Moral Philosophy*, London, 1755, had introduced the notion of 'the greatest happiness for the greatest number'. For the impact of this school of moral philosophy on the institution of slavery, see Thomas, pp. 467ff.

28. Pole, *American Independence*, p. 71.
29. *Encycl. Britannica*, vi, p. 284.
30. A. Smith, i, p. 436.
31. Ibid., i, p. 438.
32. Ibid., p. 345.
33. See Glete, i, pp. 84, 278–9; ii, pp. 552–3, 578.
34. See Kennedy, *British Naval Mastery*, pp. 106, 109–10. Rodger, *Insatiable Earl*, p. 139, states that of the British fleet of 123 of the line in 1771, only 80 were effective.
35. See Glete, i, pp. 84, 278–9; ii, pp. 552–3, 578, 630.
36. North to Sandwich, 5 Sept. 1772, in Barnes & Owen, i, pp. 20–1.
37. Lord Egmont, cited Glyn Williams, 'To Make Discoveries . . . The Admiralty and Pacific Exploration in the Eighteenth Century', *MM*, vol. 82, no. 1 (Feb. 1996), pp. 17–18.
38. Cited ibid., p. 18.
39. Cited Glyndwr Williams, 'Seamen and Philosophers in the South Seas in the Age of Captain Cook', *MM*, vol. 65, no. 1 (Feb. 1979), p. 8.
40. Glyn Williams, op. cit. (ref. 37 above), pp. 19–20.
41. Cited ibid., p. 20.
42. D. A. Baugh, 'The Sea Trial of John Harrison's Chronometer, 1736', *MM*, vol. 64, no. 3 (Aug. 1978), pp. 237–8.
43. Quill, pp. 14–15.
44. Ibid., p. 16.
45. Cook's journal, 15 Jan. 1773, cited D. Howse, 'The Principal Scientific Instruments Taken on Captain Cook's Voyages of Exploration, 1760–80', *MM*, vol. 65, no. 2 (May 1979), p. 134.
46. Ibid., p. 135.
47. See C. Lloyd, 'Cook and Scurvy', *MM*, vol. 65, no. 1 (Feb. 1979), pp. 24–5.
48. See Cuppage, *passim*.
49. Cited C. Lloyd, op. cit. (ref. 47 above), p. 26.
50. Glyndwr Williams, op. cit. (ref. 39 above), p. 14.
51. See E. H. John, 'War and the English Economy', *Engl. Hist. Review*, 2nd Series, vol. VII (1954–5), p. 331.

Chapter 13: The War of American Independence and Chesapeake Bay, 1781

1. See Dull, pp. 11–14; Cormack, pp. 30ff.
2. G. Schelle (ed.), *Œuvres de Turgot et documents le concernant*, Félix Alcan, Paris, 1923, v, cited Dull, pp. 45–6.
3. Cited C. L. Lewis, p. 55.

4. See Paul Butel, 'France, the Antilles, and Europe in the Seventeenth and Eighteen Centuries . . .' in Tracy, p. 153; and Mitchell & Deane, pp. 310–11. Whereas British exports and imports in 1775 totalled some £27 million, total French trade, excluding overland routes through German territories, appears to have been over 700 million *livres* (£30 million).

5. See Paul Butel, op. cit. (ref. 4 above), p. 154.

6. Thomas, p. 275.

7. Ibid.

8. Ibid.; the French West Indies exported 77,000 tons of sugar in 1767, the British West Indies 72,000 tons.

9. Garnier to Vergennes, 8 Mar. 1776, cited Dull, pp. 33–4.

10. See Vergennes, 'Reflections', April 1776, in response to Beaumarchais's 'Considerations', cited Dull, pp. 36–8; and Jean Meyer, 'Les Difficultés du commerce franco-américan vues de Nantes 1776–1790', *French Hist. Studies*, vol. xi, no. 2 (fall 1979), pp. 159–83.

11. See Dull, p. 49.

12. Chapelle, pp. 65, 72ff.

13. Ibid., pp. 72–3; and see Arbuthnot to Sandwich, 13 Sept. 1777, in Barnes & Owen, i, pp. 296–7.

14. Washington's instructions to S. Martingale, 8 Oct. 1775, in Barnes & Owen, i, pp. 99–101.

15. C.-in-C. North America to Sandwich, 13 Jan. 1776, in ibid., p. 104.

16. Israel, p. 1095.

17. See, for instance, letters to Sandwich from Lord Stormont (British ambassador, Paris) 16 April 1777, Middleton (Navy Board controller) 7 July 1777, and political friend William Eden, 20 July 1777 and 28 Aug. 1777, in Barnes & Owen, i, pp. 221ff., 229ff., 245ff.; and Dull, p. 88.

18. Dull, pp. 83, 86.

19. Against peacetime French naval expenditure of 17.8 million *livres*, the estimates for 1778 were 100 million *livres* on top of a naval debt of 40 million: Dull, pp. 134, 345–50.

20. Sir John Fortescue, ed., *The Correspondence of King George III . . .*, Macmillan, London, 6 vols., 1927–8, iv, pp. 215–16, cited Rodger, *Insatiable Earl*, pp. 219–20.

21. Sandwich to North, 8 Dec. 1777, in Barnes & Owen, i, p. 334.

22. See ibid., i, p. 208; and E. Robson, 'The Expedition to the Southern Colonies, 1775–1776', *Engl. Hist. Review*, vol. LXVI (1951), pp. 535–60, containing numerous examples of Germain's blunders: cited Rodger, *Insatiable Earl*, p. 222.

23. See Lord Amherst memo, Mar. 1778, in Barnes & Owen, i, p. 365; and Admiralty instructions to Lord Howe, 22 Mar. 1778, PRO ADM 2/1334, f. 62, cited Rodger, *Insatiable Earl*, p. 277.

24. See 'Draft of State of Force at Home' endorsed by Sandwich, Mar. 1778, and Sandwich to North, 7 May 1778, in Barnes & Owen, ii, pp. 19, 49.

25. See 'Intelligence from Paris', 2 July 1778, in ibid., ii, p. 117.

26. Keppel to Sandwich, 8 Sept. 1778, in ibid., ii, p. 161.

27. Sandwich to Keppel, 7 Aug. 1778, in ibid., ii, p. 139.

28. See argument to this effect in Rodger, *Insatiable Earl*, pp. 276–8.

29. See Dull, p. 121.

30. Vergennes to Louis XVI, 5 Dec. 1778, cited Dull, p. 133.

31. Sandwich to Hardy, 3 Aug. 1779, in Barnes & Owen, iii, p. 55; and for Sandwich's apprehensions, see memo, Aug. 1779, 'Scheme for the Defence of the Coast', in ibid., iii, p. 52.

32. Hardy to Sandwich, 31 Aug. 1778, in ibid., p. 8.

33. George III to Sandwich, 13 Sept. 1779, in ibid., p. 163.

34. Memo read to the Cabinet by Sandwich, George III's copy dated 14 Sept. 1779, in ibid., p. 168.

35. See Captain Johnstone to Sandwich, 19 Oct. 1779, in ibid., p. 183.

36. Memo read to the Cabinet by Sandwich, op. cit. (ref. 34 above), in ibid., pp. 166–70.

37. Ibid., p. 171.

38. Memo by Captain Sir Charles Middleton, undated, in Barnes & Owen, iii, p. 176.

39. Ibid., p. 175.

40. Middleton to Sandwich, 15 Sept. 1779, in ibid., p. 179.

41. Memo read to the Cabinet by Sandwich, op. cit. (ref. 34 above), in ibid., p. 208.

42. J. D. Spinney, 'Rodney and the Saints: A Reassessment', *MM*, vol. 68, no. 4 (Nov. 1982), pp. 379–80.

43. Ibid., p. 380.

44. Rodney to Sandwich, 27 Jan. 1780, in Barnes & Owen, iii, p. 193.

45. Rodney to Sandwich, 26 April 1780, in ibid., p. 211.

46. See J. D. Spinney, op. cit. (ref. 42 above), pp. 381–2; Tunstall, *Naval Warfare*, p. 167.

47. See Rodney to Sandwich, 26 April 1780, in Barnes & Owen, iii, p. 211.

48. See criticism by anonymous writer, undated, NMM SIG/A/8, cited Tunstall, *Naval Warfare*, p. 131.

49. Morogues, p. xx.

50. G. Lacour-Gayet, *La Marine Militaire de la France sous le règne de Louis XV*, Libraire Ancienne Honoré Champion, Paris, 1907, cited C. L. Lewis, p. 48.

51. See Tunstall, *Naval Warfare*, p. 121.

52. Mahé de la Bourdonnais, 1746: see ibid., p. 123.

53. See ibid., pp. 131–2, 150.

54. 'that we who have been so long a famous maritime power should not yet

have established any regular rules for the orderly and expeditious performance of the several evolutions necessary to be made in a fleet . . .': Kempenfelt to Middleton, Jan. 1780, cited Corbett, *Signals and Instructions*, pp. 2–3.

55. Vernon: 'Our sea-going officers despise theory so much, and by trusting only to their genius at the instant they are to act, have neither time nor foundation whereby to proceed on', cited Ranft, pp. 287–8.

56. See Collier to Sandwich, 15 June 1779, in Barnes & Owen, iii, p. 133; and Rodger, *Insatiable Earl*, pp. 278–9.

57. Barnes & Owen, iv, p. 18; but see also Glete, ii, pp. 640–1, giving the Dutch Republic thirty-one of the line.

58. Israel, p. 1097.

59. PRO CO5/258, f. 294, cited Kenneth Breen, 'Sir George Rodney and St Eustatius in the American War . . .' *MM*, vol. 84, no. 2 (May 1998), p. 197.

60. Speech to the Cabinet, 19 Jan. 1781, in Barnes & Owen, iv, p. 24.

61. The national debt was over £160 million, against £132 million at the end of the Seven Years War; the average annual expenditure was £20 million, against average annual tax revenue of £12 million: Brewer, *Sinews of Power*, pp. 115, 30.

62. See Dull, pp. 194–9.

63. Ibid., pp. 345–50.

64. Cited, C. L. Lewis, pp. 48–9.

65. La Luzerne to de Grasse, 4 June 1781, cited Dull, p. 243.

66. See ibid., pp. 243–4.

67. Ibid., p. 239.

68. See Rodney to Arbuthnot (C.-in-C. North America), 7 July 1781, in Barnes & Owen, iv, pp. 134–5.

69. See Kenneth Breen, 'Graves and Hood at the Chesapeake', *MM*, vol. 66, no. 1 (Feb. 1980), pp. 60–1.

70. See ibid., p. 60; Barnes & Owen, iv, p. 126.

71. Graves to Admiralty, 30 Aug. 1781, in Chadwick, p. 53.

72. See Tunstall, *Naval Warfare*, pp. 172–3.

73. Times, distances, wind directions and signals from *London*'s log, *London*'s journal, or *Barfleur*'s log: cited Chadwick, pp. 165ff.

74. Graves to Sandwich, 21 Aug. 1781, in Barnes & Owen, iv, p. 181.

75. Tunstall, *Naval Warfare*, p. 174.

76. Hood to George Jackson, Assistant Secretary of the Admiralty, 16 Sept. 1781, cited Chadwick, p. 87.

77. *London*'s journal, in Chadwick, p. 166; and 'An Account of the Proceedings of the Fleet . . .' enclosed in Graves to Sandwich, 14 Sept. 1781, in Barnes & Owen, iv, p. 185.

78. Graves to Sandwich, 14 Sept. 1781, in Barnes & Owen, iv. p. 182.

79. William Hope to his father, 22 Sept. 1781, cited Alan G. Jamieson, 'Two Scottish Marines in the American War', *MM*, vol. 70, no. 1 (Feb. 1984), p. 27.
80. Hood to Admiralty, 16 Sept. 1781, in Barnes & Owen, iv, p. 190.
81. Damage list, in Chadwick, p. 69.
82. French casualties from *Magazine of American History*, 1881, vol. VII, p. 291, cited C. L. Lewis, p. 160. British casualties listed by ship: Chadwick, p. 68.
83. Cornwallis to Clinton, 15 Oct. 1781, in Chadwick, p. 138.
84. Enclosure dated 6 Sept. 1781 in Hood to Admiralty, 16 Sept. 1781, in Barnes & Owen, iv, p. 189.
85. See Kenneth Breen, op. cit. (ref. 69 above), p. 62.
86. Graves to Admiralty, 14 Sept. 1781; Barnes & Owen, iv, p. 182.
87. Cited Barnes & Owen, iv, p. 142.
88. See Kenneth Breen, op. cit. (ref. 69 above), pp. 59–61.

Chapter 14: The Saints, 1782, and the founding of the United States of America

1. Middleton to Sandwich, 3 Sept. 1781, in Barnes & Owen, iv, pp. 61–2.
2. Darby to Sandwich, 9 Sept. 1781, in ibid., p. 64.
3. Memo, 31 Dec. 1782, in ibid., p. 300.
4. Abstract of ships in commission, Nov. 1781, in ibid., p. 430.
5. E. D. Mackerness, *A Social History of English Music*, Routledge & Kegan Paul, London, 1964, p. 127, cited Rodger, *Insatiable Earl*, p. 311.
6. Gilbert Blane, Rodney's surgeon, cited C. L. Lewis, pp. 240–1.
7. Rodney to Sandwich, 25 April 1782, in Barnes & Owen, iv, p. 264.
8. Douglas to Middleton, 12 July 1779, cited Tunstall, *Naval Warfare*, p. 182.
9. Douglas to Sandwich, 13 April 1782, in Barnes & Owen, iv, p. 257.
10. Rodney to Sandwich, 27 Jan. 1780, in ibid., iii, p. 193; and see J. D. Spinney, 'Rodney and the Saints: A Reassessment', *MM*, vol. 68, no. 4 (Nov. 1982), pp. 377–8, 385.
11. Dr Gilbert Blane, cited Spinney, op. cit. (ref. 10 above), p. 385.
12. C. L. Lewis, p. 251.
13. Rodney to his wife, cited ibid., p. 254.
14. See Brewer, *Sinews of Power*, pp. 30 (annual expenditure), 97 (tax revenue), 115–16 (national debt).
15. Vergennes to Montmorin, 7 Sept. 1782, cited Dull, p. 304.
16. See Brewer, *Sinews of Power*, p. 91.
17. Ibid., p. 90. Palmer, p. 155, agrees the British per-capita tax burden at 34 shillings, but puts the French figure at 21 shillings, thus a ratio of *c.* 3:2 rather than 3:1.
18. See Kennedy, *Great Powers*, pp. 195–8.

19. Brewer, *Sinews of Power*, p. 133; Godechot, p. 70.
20. Montmorin to Vergennes, 1 Nov. 1782, cited Dull, pp. 315–16.
21. See Kennedy, *Great Powers*, p. 108; Dickson, p. 475.
22. Godechot, p. 70.
23. See Dull, pp. 279–80.
24. Vergennes to Montmorin, 1 Nov. 1782, cited Dull, p. 316.
25. See D. Syrett, 'The Organisation of British Trade Convoys during the American War', *MM*, vol. 62, no. 2 (May 1976), p. 178.
26. Crowhurst, p. 69.
27. See Mitchell & Deane, pp. 310–11; and Kennedy, *British Naval Mastery*, p. 118.
28. See Dull, p. 341.
29. See Godechot, p. 72.
30. See Brewer, *Sinews of Power*, p. 133.
31. Kennedy, *Great Powers*, p. 109.
32. Imports 611 million *livres*, exports 542 million *livres*: Godechot, p. 72.
33. See Cormack, pp. 22–3.
34. Glete, i, p. 276.
35. Ibid.
36. See McCusker & Menard, pp. 386ff.
37. Robert Morris to President of Congress, 29 July 1782, cited Pole, *Revolution in America*, pp. 121–2.
38. See Pole, *American Independence*, p. 110; and see S. Osgood to John Adams, 14 Dec. 1783, cited Pole, *Revolution in America*, pp. 137–8.
39. See Pole, *Political Representation*, pp. 25–6. Palmer, p. 233, cites John Adams on the constitution of Massachusetts, of which he was the principal author: 'It is Locke, Sidney, Rousseau and de Mally reduced to practice.'
40. Thomas, pp. 458–61.
41. See, for instance, comments in the convention of delegates of Ipswich, Essex County, 29 April 1778: 'Would to God, the situation of America and the tempers of its inhabitants were such, that the slave holders could not be found in the land', cited Pole, *Revolution in America*, p. 459.
42. Thomas, p. 476.
43. Ibid.
44. Ibid., p. 277.
45. Pennsylvania Act for the Gradual Abolition of Slavery, 1780, cited Pole, *Revolution in America*, pp. 551–2.
46. Thomas, p. 480; Pole, *American Independence*, p. 176.
47. Art. IV, Section 2, US Constitution: see Pole, *American Independence*, pp. 196–7.
48. See p. 155.
49. See Pole, *American Independence*, pp. 197–9.

50. Thomas Treadwell, cited ibid., p. 199; and see Pole, *Political Representation,* p. 539.
51. Trollope, pp. 297, 260.
52. See Pole, *American Independence,* p. 164.
53. 25 Aug. 1831, cited Schleifer, p. 127.
54. Tocqueville, i, p. 509.
55. Ibid., p. 515.

Select Bibliography

Albion, R. G., *Forests and Seapower: The Timber Problem of the Royal Navy, 1652–1862*, Harvard Univ. Press, Cambridge, Mass., 1926

Anderson, R. C., *Naval Wars in the Baltic during the Sailing-Ship Epoch, 1522–1850*, C. Gilbert-Wood, London, 1910 (reprinted Francis Edwards, London, 1969)

—— ed., *Journal of Edward Mountagu, First Earl of Sandwich, Admiral and General at Sea, 1659–1665*, Navy Records Soc., London, 1929

—— ed., *The Journals of Sir Thomas Allin, 1660–1678*, Navy Records Soc., London, 2 vols., 1939

—— ed., *Journals and Narratives of the Third Dutch War*, Navy Records Soc., London, 1946

Andrews, K. R., *Elizabethan Privateering*, Cambridge Univ. Press, Cambridge, 1964

—— *Drake's Voyages: A Re-assessment of their Place in Elizabethan Maritime Expansion*, Weidenfeld, London, 1967

—— *Trade, Plunder and Settlement: Maritime Enterprise and the Genesis of the British Empire, 1480–1630*, Cambridge Univ. Press, Cambridge, 1984

Anscombe, E., & Geach, P. T., *Descartes: Philosophical Writings*, Nelson, London, 1954

Aubrey, P., *The Defeat of James Stuart's Armada*, Leicester Univ. Press, Leicester, 1979

Ballard, G. A., *Rulers of the Indian Ocean*, Duckworth, London, 1927

Bamford, P. W., *Forests and French Sea Power 1660–1789*, Univ. of Toronto Press, Toronto, 1956

Barbour, V., *Capitalism in Amsterdam in the Seventeenth Century*, Johns Hopkins Univ. Press, Baltimore, 1950

Barnes, G. R., & Owen, J. H., eds., *The Private Papers of John, Earl of Sandwich, 1st Lord of the Admiralty, 1771–1782*, Navy Records Soc., London, 4 vols., 1932–8

Barnett, C., *Marlborough*, Eyre Methuen, London, 1974

Beik, P. H., *A Judgement of the Old Regime*, Columbia Univ. Press, NY, 1944

Beloff, M., *The Age of Absolutism, 1660–1815*, Hutchinson, London, 1954

Bennett, J., *Locke, Berkeley, Hume: Central Themes*, Oxford Univ. Press, Oxford, 1971

Beresford, J., *The Godfather of Downing Street: Sir George Downing, 1623–1684*, R. Cobden-Saunderson, London, 1925

Bernal, J. D., *Science in History: Vol. 2, The Scientific and Industrial Revolutions*, C. A. Watts, London, 1954 (refs. from Penguin, Harmondsworth, 1969 edn)

Binning, T., *A Light to the Art of Gunnery*, London, 1689

Blok, P., *The Life of Admiral de Ruyter*, trans. G. J. Renier, Benn, London, 1933

Boxer, C. R., ed. & trans., *The Journal of Maarten Harpertszoon Tromp Anno 1639*, Cambridge Univ. Press, Cambridge, 1930

—— *The Dutch Seaborne Empire, 1600–1800*, Hutchinson, London, 1965

—— *The Portuguese Seaborne Empire, 1415–1852*, Hutchinson, London, 1969

Braudel, F., *The Mediterranean and the Mediterranean World in the Age of Philip II*, Collins, London, 1972

Brewer, J., *The Sinews of Power: War, Money and the English State, 1688–1783*, Unwin-Hyman, London, 1989

Brewer, J. S., & Buller, W., eds., *Calendar of Carew Manuscripts, 1575–1588*, London, 1868

Bromley, J. S., & Kossman, E. H., *Britain and the Netherlands in Europe and Asia*, Macmillan, London, 1968

Brown, H., *The True Principles of Gunnery*, London, 1778

Bryant, A., ed., *The Letters, Speeches and Declarations of King Charles II*, Cassell, London, 1935

Campbell, K., *Sarah Duchess of Marlborough*, Butterworth, London, 1932

Capp, B., *Cromwell's Navy: The Fleet and the English Revolution, 1648–1660*, Clarendon Press, Oxford, 1989

Carter, A., *The Dutch Republic in the Seven Years War*, Macmillan, London, 1971

Cederlund, C. O., ed., *Postmedieval Boat and Ship Archaeology*, Swedish Nat. Maritime Museum, Stockholm, 1985

Cerovski, J. F., ed., *Fragmenta Regalia or Observations of Queen Elizabeth, Her Times and Favourites (c. 1630)*, Associated University Presses, Washington DC, 1985

Chadwick, F. E., *The Graves Papers: and other Documents relating to the Naval Operations of the Yorktown Campaign*, Naval Historical Soc., NY, 1916

Chancellor, E. B., *The XVIIIth Century in London*, Batsford, London, 1920

Chapelle, H., *The History of the American Sailing Navy: The Ships and their Development*, Bonanza Books, NY, 1949

Chesterfield, Lord, *Letters, Sentences and Maxims*, London, 1870

Cipolla, C. M., *Guns and Sails in the Early Phase of European Expansion, 1400–1700*, Collins, London, 1965

Clark, G. N., *The Dutch Alliance and the War against French Trade*, Manchester Univ. Press, Manchester, 1923

Clark, K., *Civilisation: A Personal View*, John Murray, London, 1969

Clerk, J., *An Essay in Naval Tactics*, Edinburgh, 1804

Cole, C. W., *Colbert and a Century of French Mercantilism*, Cass, London, 2 vols., 1964

—— *French Mercantilism, 1683–1700*, Octagon Books, NY, 1965

Corbett, J. S., ed., *Papers relating to the Spanish War, 1585–1587*, Navy Records Soc., London, 1898

—— *England in the Mediterranean: A Study of the Rise and Influence of British Power within the Straits, 1603–1713*, Longmans, Green, London, 1904

—— ed., *Fighting Instructions, 1530–1816*, Navy Records Soc., London, 1904

—— ed., *Signals and Instructions, 1776–1794*, Navy Records Soc., London, 1908

—— *Some Principles of Maritime Strategy*, Longmans, Green, London, 1911

—— *England in the Seven Years' War: A Study in Combined Strategy*, Longmans, Green, London, 1918

Cormack, W. S., *Revolution and Political Conflict in the French Navy, 1789–1794*, Cambridge Univ. Press, Cambridge, 1995

Courtenay, T. P., *Memoirs of the Life, Works and Correspondence of Sir Wm. Temple, Bt.*, London, 2 vols., 1836

Coxe, W., *Memoirs of the Duke of Marlborough*, London, 1895

Cresswell, J., *British Admirals of the Eighteenth Century*, Allen & Unwin, London, 1972

Crowhurst, P., *The Defence of British Trade, 1689–1815*, William Dawson, Folkstone, 1977

Cruikshank, C. G., *Elizabeth's Army*, Oxford Univ. Press, Oxford, 1966

Cuellar, F. de, *A Letter Written on October 4 1589 to King Philip II*, trans. H. D. Sedgwick, London, 1896

Cuppage, F. E., *James Cook and the Conquest of Scurvy*, Greenwood Press, London and Westport, Conn., 1994

Davis, R., *The Rise of the English Shipping Industry in the Seventeenth and Eighteenth Centuries*, Macmillan, London, 1962

—— *The Rise of the Atlantic Economies*, Weidenfeld, London, 1973

Dickson, P. G. M., *The Financial Revolution in England: A Study in the Development of Public Credit, 1688–1756*, Macmillan, London, 1967

Duffy, C., *Siege Warfare*, Routledge & Kegan Paul, London, 1979

Duffy, M., ed., *Parameters of British Naval Power, 1650–1850*, Univ. of Exeter Press, Exeter, 1992

Dull, J., *The French Navy and American Independence*, Princeton Univ. Press, Princeton, 1975

Ehrman, J., *The Navy in the War of William III*, Cambridge Univ. Press, Cambridge, 1953

Ekins, C., *Naval Battles: 1744 to the Peace in 1814*, London, 1824

Fisher, H. A. L., *A History of Europe*, Edward Arnold, London, 1936

Gardiner, S. R. (vols. 1–2) or Atkinson, C. T. (vols. 4–6), ed., *Letters and Papers relating to the First Dutch War*, Navy Records Soc., London, 6 vols., 1899–1930

Glete, J., *Navies and Nations: Warships, Navies and State Building in Europe and America, 1500–1860*, Almquist & Winsell, Stockholm, 2 vols., 1993

Godechot, J., *France and the Atlantic Revolution of the Eighteenth Century, 1770–1799*, Free Press, NY, 1965

Graham, G. S., *Empire of the North Atlantic*, Univ. of Toronto Press, Toronto, 1950

—— *The Politics of Naval Supremacy*, Cambridge Univ. Press, Cambridge, 1965

Gray, C. S., *The Leverage of Sea Power: The Strategic Advantage of Navies in War*, Free Press (Macmillan Inc.), NY, 1992

Grey, A., *Debates of the House of Commons, Vols. 1–3*, London, 1763–69

Guilmartin, J. F., *Gunpowder and Galleys: Changing Technology and Mediterranean Warfare at Sea in the Sixteenth Century*, Cambridge Univ. Press, Cambridge, 1974

Haley, K. N. D., *William of Orange and the English Opposition, 1672–4*, Oxford Univ. Press, Oxford, 1953

—— *The Dutch in the Seventeenth Century*, Thames and Hudson, London, 1972

Halton, R., & Bromley, J. S., eds., *William III and Louis XIV, Essays, 1680–1720*, Liverpool Univ. Press, Liverpool, 1968

Hamilton, N., ed., *Calendar of State Papers relating to Ireland*, London, 1885

Hartmann, C. H., *Clifford of the Cabal*, Heinemann, London, 1937

Hill, C. P., *British Economic History, 1700–1939*, Edward Arnold, London, 1961

Hoff, B. van 'T., ed., *The Correspondence 1701–1711 of John Churchill First Duke of Marlborough and Anthonie Heinsius Grand Pensionary of Holland*, Martinus Nijhoff, The Hague, 1951

Howarth, D., *The Voyage of the Armada: The Spanish Story*, Collins, London, 1981

Hume, D., *A Treatise of Human Nature*, ed. E. C. Mossner, Penguin, Harmondsworth, 1969

Hume, M. A. S., ed., *Calendar of Letters and State Papers relating to English Affairs Preserved Principally in the Archives of Simancas: Vol. IV, Elizabeth, 1587–1603*, London, 1899

Hutchinson, W., *A Treatise on Practical Seamanship*, London, 1777

Israel, J., *The Dutch Republic: Its Rise, Greatness and Fall, 1477–1806*, Oxford Univ. Press, Oxford, 1995

Jefferson, D. W., ed., *Eighteenth-Century Prose*, Penguin, Harmondsworth, 1956

Jenkins, E. H., *A History of the French Navy*, Macdonald & Janes, London, 1973

Jones, J. R., *The Revolution of 1688 in England*, Weidenfeld, London, 1972

—— *Britain and the World, 1649–1815*, Fontana, London, 1980

—— *The Anglo-Dutch Wars of the Seventeenth Century*, Longman, Harlow, 1996

Kamen, H., *The Spanish Inquisition*, Weidenfeld, London, 1965

—— *Spain 1469–1714*, Longman, Harlow, 1983

Kennedy, P., *The Rise and Fall of British Naval Mastery*, Allen Lane, London, 1976, (3rd edn with postscript, Fontana, London, 1991)

—— *The Rise and Fall of the Great Powers*, Unwin-Hyman, London, 1988 (refs. from Fontana, London, 1989 edn)

Kenny, R. W., *Elizabeth's Admiral: The Political Career of Charles Howard Earl of Nottingham, 1536–1624*, Johns Hopkins Univ. Press, Baltimore, 1970

Landa, L. A., ed., *see* Swift, J.

Landes, D. S., *The Wealth and Poverty of Nations: Why Some are So Rich and Some So Poor*, Little, Brown, London, 1998

Landström, B., *The Ship*, Allen & Unwin, London, 1961

Lane, F. C., *Venice, A Maritime Republic*, Johns Hopkins Univ. Press, Baltimore, 1973

Laughton, J. Knox, ed., *State Papers relating to the Defeat of the Spanish Armada, Anno 1588*, Navy Records Soc., London, 2 vols., 1894

—— ed., *Letters and Papers of Charles, Lord Barham, 1758–1813*, Navy Records Soc., London, 3 vols., 1907–10

Leeb, I. L., *The Ideological Origins of the Batavian Revolution*, Martinus Nijhoff, The Hague, 1973

Lemon, R., ed., *Calendar of State Papers, Domestic, 1581–1590*, London, 1865

Lewis, C. L., *Admiral de Grasse and American Independence*, US Naval Inst. Press, Annapolis, 1945

Lewis, M., *Armada Guns*, Allen & Unwin, London, 1961

L'Hoste, P., *see* O'Bryen

Lisk, J., *The Struggle for Supremacy in the Baltic*, Univ. of London Press, London, 1967

Lister, T. H., *Life and Administration of Edward 1st Earl of Clarendon*, London, 1837

Lloyd, C., ed., *The Health of Seamen*, Navy Records Soc., London, 1965

Lloyd, C., & Naish, G., eds., *The Naval Miscellany*, Navy Records Soc., London, 1952

Lonsdale, R., ed., *The New Oxford Book of Eighteenth-Century Verse*, Oxford Univ. Press, Oxford, 1984

Mackay, R., *Admiral Hawke*, Oxford Univ. Press, Oxford, 1965

McCusker, J., & Menard, R. R., *The Economy of British America, 1607–1789*, Univ. of North Carolina Press, Chapel Hill, 1985

Mahan, A. T., *The Influence of Sea Power upon History, 1660–1783*, Boston, 1890 (refs. from Methuen, London, 1965 edn)

Marcus, G., *Quiberon Bay: The Campaign in Home Waters, 1759*, Hollis & Carter, London, 1960

Martin, C., *Full Fathom Five: Wrecks of the Spanish Armada*, Chatto & Windus, London, 1975

Martin, C., & Parker, G., *The Spanish Armada*, Hamish Hamilton, London, 1988

Mattingley, G., *The Defeat of the Spanish Armada*, Jonathan Cape, London, 1959

Mitchell, B. R., & Deane, P., *Abstract of British Historical Statistics*, Cambridge Univ. Press, Cambridge, 1962

Monson, W., *The Naval Tracts of Sir William Monson*, ed. M. Oppenheim, Navy Records Soc., London, 5 vols., 1902–14.

Moorehead, A., *The Fatal Impact: An Account of the Invasion of the South Pacific, 1767–1840*, Harper & Row, NY, 1966

Morogues, Vicomte de, *Tactique Navale*, trans. by 'A Sea Officer', London, 1767

Murray, J. J., *Amsterdam in the Age of Rembrandt*, Univ. of Oklahoma Press, Norman, 1967

Neale, J. E., *Queen Elizabeth*, Jonathan Cape, London, 1934

Newton, A. P., *The European Nations in the West Indies, 1493–1688*, A. & C. Black, London, 1933

O'Bryen, C., *Naval Evolutions or a System of Sea-discipline extracted from the Celebrated Treatise of P. L'Hoste . . .*, London, 1762

Ollard, R., *Man of War: Sir Robert Holmes and the Restoration Navy*, Hodder & Stoughton, London, 1969

—— *Pepys: A Biography*, Hodder & Stoughton, London, 1974

Owen, J. H., *War at Sea under Queen Anne*, Cambridge Univ. Press, Cambridge, 1938

Padfield, P., *Guns at Sea*, Hugh Evelyn, London, 1974

—— *Tide of Empires. Decisive Naval Campaigns in the Rise of the West: Vol. 1, 1481–1654; Vol. 2, 1654–1763*, Routledge & Kegan Paul, London, 1979, 1982

—— *Armada: A Celebration of the Four Hundredth Anniversary of the Defeat of the Spanish Armada*, Gollancz, London, 1988

Padover, S. K., *The Life and Death of Louis XVI*, Alvin Redman, London, 1965

Palmer, R. R., *The Age of Democratic Revolution*, Princeton Univ. Press, Princeton, 1959

Panichas, G. A., ed., *Promise of Greatness*, Cassell, London, 1968

Pares, R., *War and Trade in the West Indies, 1739–1763*, Oxford Univ. Press, Oxford, 1936

Parker, B., ed., *Famous British Generals*, Nicholson & Watson, London, 1951

Parker, G., *The Dutch Revolt*, Allen Lane, London, 1977

—— *Philip II of Spain*, Little, Brown, London, 1978

Parry, J. H., *The Age of Reconnaisance*, Weidenfeld, London, 1963

—— *The Spanish Seaborne Empire*, Hutchinson, London, 1966

—— *Trade and Dominion: The European Overseas Empires in the Eighteenth Century*, Weidenfeld, London, 1971

—— *The Discovery of the Sea*, Weidenfeld, London, 1974

Pepys, S., *The Diary and Correspondence of Samuel Pepys*, ed. Lord Braybrooke, London, 1871

—— *The Diary of Samuel Pepys*, ed. H. B. Wheatley, G. Bell, London, 8 vols., 1949

Pierson, P., *Philip II of Spain*, Thames and Hudson, London, 1975

—— *Commander of the Armada: The Seventh Duke of Medina Sidonia*, Yale Univ. Press, New Haven, 1989

Pole, J. R., *Political Representation in England and the Origins of the American Republic*, Macmillan, London, 1966

—— *The Revolution in America 1754–1788: Documents and Commentaries*, Macmillan, London, 1970

—— *Foundations of American Independence, 1763–1815*, Fontana/Collins, London, 1973

Pontalis, A. L., *John de Witt, Grand Pensionary of Holland*, trans. S. E. & A. Stephenson, London, 2 vols., 1885

Powley, E. B., *The Naval Side of King William's War, 1688–1690*, John Baker, London, 1972

Quill, H., *John Harrison, Copley Medallist, and the £20,000 Longitude Prize*, Antiquarian Horological Soc., Wadhurst, Sussex, 1976

Quinn, D. B., & Ryan, A. N., *England's Sea Empire, 1550–1642*, Allen & Unwin, London, 1983

Ranft, B. McL., *The Vernon Papers*, Navy Records Soc., London, 1958

Regan, T., *The Case for Animal Rights*, Routledge & Kegan Paul, London, 1983

Richmond, H. W., *The Navy in the War of 1739–48*, Cambridge Univ. Press, Cambridge, 3 vols., 1920

—— *The Navy in India, 1763–83*, Ernest Benn, London, 1931

—— *British Strategy, Military and Economic*, Cambridge Univ. Press, Cambridge, 1941

Robertson, C. G., *England under the Hanoverians*, Methuen, London, 1911

Rodger, N. A. M., *The Wooden World: An Anatomy of the Georgian Navy*, Collins, London, 1986

—— *The Insatiable Earl: A Life of John Montagu, Fourth Earl of Sandwich, 1718–1792*, HarperCollins, London, 1993

—— *The Safeguard of the Sea: A Naval History of Britain, Vol. 1, 660–1649*, HarperCollins, London, 1997

Rodgers, W. L., *Naval Warfare under Oars*, US Naval Inst. Press, Annapolis, 1939

Rogers, P. G., *The Dutch in the Medway*, Oxford Univ. Press, Oxford, 1970

Roskill, S. W., *The Strategy of Sea Power*, Collins, London, 1962

Rowse, A. L., *The England of Elizabeth*, Macmillan, London, 1950

—— *The Expansion of Elizabethan England*, Macmillan, London, 1955

Rudé, G., *Europe in the Eighteenth Century: Aristocracy and the Bourgeois Challenge*, Weidenfeld, London, 1972 (refs. from Cardinal, London, 1974 edn)

Russell, B., *A History of Western Philosophy*, Allen & Unwin, London, 1946

Schama, S., *The Embarrassment of Riches: An Interpretation of Dutch Culture in the Golden Age*, Univ. of California Press, Berkeley, 1987

Schleifer, J. T., *The Making of Tocqueville's Democracy*, Univ. of North Carolina Press, Chapel Hill, 1980

Scholes, P. A., ed., *The Oxford Companion to Music*, Oxford Univ. Press, Oxford, 1942

Scoville, W. C., *The Persecution of the Huguenots and French Economic Development, 1680–1720*, Univ. of California Press, Berkeley, 1960

Sergeant, R. B., *The Portuguese off the South Arabian Coast*, Clarendon Press, Oxford, 1963

Shepherd, J. F., & Walton, G. M., *Shipping, Maritime Trade and the Economic Development of Colonial North America*, Cambridge Univ. Press, Cambridge, 1972

Singer, P., *Animal Liberation: A New Ethics for Our Treatment of Animals*, Jonathan Cape, London, 1976

Smith, A., *The Wealth of Nations*, London, 2 vols., 1776–8 (refs. from J. M. Dent, Everyman's Library edn, London, 2 vols., 1950)

Smith, A. R., *Spanish Armada List, 1588*, London, 1886

Spinney, D., *Rodney*, Allen & Unwin, London, 1969

Starr, C. G., *The Influence of Sea Power on Ancient History*, Oxford Univ. Press, Oxford, 1989

Stout, N., *The Royal Navy in America, 1760–1775: A Study of Enforcement of British Colonial Policy in the Era of the American Revolution*, US Naval Inst. Press, Annapolis, 1973

Swift, J., *Gulliver's Travels and Other Writings*, ed. L. A. Landa, Oxford Univ. Press, Oxford, 1976

Symcox, G., *The Crisis of French Sea Power, 1688–1697*, Martinus Nijhoff, The Hague, 1974

Tanner, J. R., *A Descriptive Catalogue of the Naval Manuscripts in the Pepysian Library . . . Cambridge*, Navy Records Soc., London, 1903

—— ed., *Samuel Pepys Naval Minutes*, Navy Records Soc., London, 1926

Thomas, H., *The Slave Trade: The History of the Atlantic Slave Trade, 1440–1870*, Picador, London, 1997

Thompson, I. A. A., *War and Government in Habsburg Spain, 1560–1620*, Athlone Press, London, 1976

Tibbles, A., ed., *Transatlantic Slavery: Against Human Dignity*, HMSO, London, 1994

Tocqueville, A., de, *Democracy in America* (1835, 1840), trans. H. Reeve, Schocken Books, NY, 2 vols., 1961

Tracy, J. D., ed., *The Rise of Merchant Empires*, Cambridge Univ. Press, Cambridge, 1990

Trollope, F., *Domestic Manners of the Americans*, London, 1839 (refs. from Century, London, 1984 edn)

Tunstall, B., *Admiral Byng*, Philip Allan, London, 1928

—— *Naval Warfare in the Age of Sail: The Evolution of Fighting Tactics, 1650–1815*, ed. N. Tracy, Conway Maritime Press, London, 1990

Vickery, A., *The Gentleman's Daughter: Women's Lives in Georgian England*, Yale Univ. Press, New Haven and London, 1998

Wallenstein, I., *The Modern World System*, Academic Press, London, 1974

Warnsinck, J. C. M., *De Vloot van den Koning-stathouder, 1689–1690*, Amsterdam, 1934

Waters, D. W., *The Art of Navigation in England in Elizabethan and Early Stuart Times*, Hollis & Carter, London, 1958

White, T., *Naval Researches*, London, 1830

Williams, B., *The Whig Supremacy, 1714–1760*, Oxford Univ. Press, Oxford, 2nd edn, 1962 (refs. from 1974 reprint)

Williamson, J. A., *Sir John Hawkins*, Oxford Univ. Press, Oxford, 1927

—— *Hawkins of Plymouth*, A. & C. Black, London, 1949

Wilson, C., *Anglo-Dutch Commerce and Finance in the Eighteenth Century*, Cambridge Univ. Press, Cambridge, 1941 (refs. from 1966 edn)

—— *Profit and Power: A Study of England and the Dutch Wars*, Longmans, Green, London, 1957

—— *Economic History and the Historian*, Weidenfeld, London, 1969

—— *Queen Elizabeth and the Revolt in the Netherlands*, Macmillan, London, 1970

Wright, E., ed., *The Fire of Liberty*, Hamish Hamilton, London, 1984

Wynne-Tyson, J., *The Extended Circle: A Dictionary of Humane Thought*, Centaur Press, Fontwell, Sussex, 1985

Index

Wars and naval battles are listed first, to provide a chronological framework for the book. The general index follows, and includes main themes such as: absolutism, economy, finance, freedom, maritime supremacy, merchant government, religion, strategy, tactics, trade. Peripheral subjects, names and places have been omitted. Ships have been indexed by name irrespective of date of build, hence different ships may appear under one heading if they bear the same name.